Assessing the Economic Impact of Tourism

Samuel Meng • Mahinda Siriwardana

Assessing the Economic Impact of Tourism

A Computable General Equilibrium Modelling Approach

palgrave
macmillan

Samuel Meng
University of New England
Armidale, New South Wales
Australia

Mahinda Siriwardana
University of New England
Armidale, New South Wales
Australia

ISBN 978-3-319-40327-4 ISBN 978-3-319-40328-1 (eBook)
DOI 10.1007/978-3-319-40328-1

Library of Congress Control Number: 2016956078

Printed on acid-free paper

This Palgrave Macmillan imprint is published by Springer Nature
The registered company is Springer International Publishing AG
The registered company address is: Gewerbestrasse 11, 6330 Cham, Switzerland

Contents

Abbreviations

AOR	Average Occupancy Rate
ARR	Average Room Rate
ASEAN	Association of Southeast Asian Nations
BOT	Balance of Trade
CD	Cobb–Douglas
CES	Constant Elasticity of Substitution
CET	Constant Elasticity of Transformation
CGE	Computable General Equilibrium
CNTA	China National Tourism Administration
COE	Certificate of Entitlement
CPF	Central Provident Fund
CPI	Consumer Price Index
CRS	Constant Returns to Scale
DOS	Department of Statistics
DTD	Double Tax Deduction
EV	Equivalent Variation
F&B	Food and Beverage
FMD	Foot-and-Mouth Disease
FTA	Free Trade Agreement
FTE	Full-Time Equivalent
GDP	Gross Domestic Product
GFC	Global Financial Crisis

GST	Goods and Service Tax
GTAP	Global Trade Analysis Project
ICT	Information Communication Technology
I–O	Input–Output
IT	Information Technology
LES	Linear Expenditure System
MICE	Meetings, Incentive travel, Exhibitions and Conventions
MMRF	Monash Multi-Regional Forecast
MOM	Ministry of Manpower
MRT	Mass Rapid Transit
MTI	Ministry of Trade and Industry
NCB	National Computer Board
PMB	Preservation of Monuments Board
RoW	Rest of World
RWC	Rugby World Cup
SARS	Severe Acute Respiratory Syndrome
SPG	South Pacific Games
STB	Singapore Tourism Board
STPB	Singapore Tourism Promotion Board
TDAS	Tourism Development Assistance Scheme
TEV	Total Expenditure of Visitors
TPF	Tourism Policy and Forecasting
TR	Tourism Receipts
TSA	Tourism Satellite Account
UK	United Kingdom
UNCTAD	United Nations Conference on Trade and Development
UNWTO	United Nations World Tourism Organization
USA	United States of America
WTTC	World Travel and Tourism Council

List of Figures

List of Tables

1

An Introduction to CGE Modelling

1.1 What Is a CGE Model?

The name 'computable general equilibrium (CGE) model' indicates the main features of this type of model. Equilibrium is a common economic term which means a system reaches a relatively stable state. For example, fluctuations of demand for and supply of apples will cause a change in apple prices: when demand for apples is greater than the supply of apples, apple price will go up, and vice versa. However, over time, the demand and supply will reach a balance and thus the price of apples will be relatively stable. This can be shown as a basic supply and demand graph below.

In Fig. 1.1, at price P1, demand at point B is greater than supply at point A, so the excess demand will pull the price up. At price P2, the demand at point C is less than the supply at point D, the excess supply will push the price down. Only at point E, are supply and demand balanced, so the price (Pe) and quantity (Qe) of apples are stable. Point E is called the equilibrium in the apples market. However, this graph only concerns the equilibrium of one market (the apple market). In reality, different markets are interconnected with each other. For example, the

S. Meng, M. Siriwardana, *Assessing the Economic Impact of Tourism*,
DOI 10.1007/978-3-319-40328-1_1

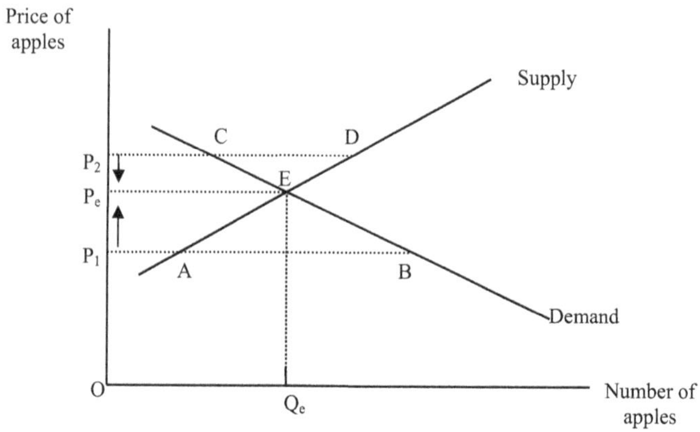

Fig. 1.1 Market equilibrium

apple market and the stone fruit market are closely related. If there is a sudden drop in supply of stone fruits, their price will go up. Facing the increased price of stone fruits, people tend to buy fewer stone fruits but buy more apples. This will cause an increase in apply demand and thus an increase in apple price. In other words, the originally equilibrium in apple market is affected by the condition in the stone fruit market. In this reasoning, equilibrium in the economy can be achieved only when all markets are in equilibrium. This is the concept of general equilibrium. A CGE model can simulate the outcome when the whole economy is in general equilibrium.

A CGE simulation generally starts with a general equilibrium situation (a baseline case or a business-as-usual case). Then a shock (e.g. a tax policy or an event such as the Global Financial Crisis) is introduced and the CGE model can generate the new general equilibrium situation. The term 'computable' in CGE modelling indicates that a CGE model is able to quantify the effect of a shock. Since there are numerous markets in an economy, to model a general equilibrium involves a large amount of data, so it is common that a computer is used in CGE modelling. The term 'computable' also implies that a computer is involved in CGE modelling.

1.2 A Brief Historical Review of CGE Modelling

1.2.1 Walras' Law: The Theoretical Foundation for CGE Modelling

As early as in 1874, Walras (1954) showed that equilibrium conditions in different markets in an economy are not independent and general equilibrium is available at any set of prices. Arrow and Debreu (1954), Debreu (1959), and Arrow and Hahn (1971) turned Walrasian general equilibrium theory into the Arrow–Debreu framework, in which consumers who possess an endowment of factors and commodities are assumed to maximize utility; producers are assumed to maximize profits; market demand for and supply of any commodity are continuous, non-negative, homogeneous of degree zero, and subject to the condition that, at any set of prices, the total value of consumer expenditure equals consumer income. There are four types of equations in this framework: (1) The equations for equilibrium conditions for each market to ensure that supply equals demand for each good and service; (2) the equations for income–expenditure identities to ensure the balance of each account; (3) the equations for behavioural relationships to describe economic agents' reactions to changes in prices and incomes; and (4) the equations for production functions to determine the output for each sector and how the factors of production are allocated. This framework forms the foundation for CGE modelling.

1.2.2 Input–Output Analysis: The Predecessor of CGE Modelling

Input–output (I–O) analysis is based on Walrasian general equilibrium theory and relies on the I–O table. The advantage of this analysis is that it can take into account inter-industry linkages.

Although the idea of inter-industry linkage can be traced back to 1758 when Quesnay published a 'Tableau Economique' and the Leontief model is an approximation of Walrasian general equilibrium theory (Miller and Blair 1985), Leontief was thought to be the father of the I–O model due to the fact that he was the first economist to present a theoretical framework along with the I–O structure of the US economy (Leontief 1936, 1941). The structure of the Leontief I–O model has been reinterpreted again and again by many different researchers. Here we present the fundamental structure of the I–O model as interpreted by Miller and Blair (1985).

In reality, these changes in output, income, and employment may result from direct, indirect, and induced effects. First, an increase in tourist expenditure will cause an immediate impact on the economy. Tourist expenditure increases the sales revenues of firms directly catering to tourist needs. This is called the 'direct effect'. Second, as the sales revenues increase, the firms and organizations in the tourism industry will purchase goods and services from various suppliers who in turn purchase inputs from other firms, and so on. This increased intermediate demand is called the 'indirect effect'. Third, the direct and indirect expenditures increase household income. As the recipients of the direct and indirect expenditures (i.e. the owners of the firms and their employees) spend their increased incomes, the demand for goods and services will increase again, setting off a process of successive rounds of purchases and further consumption. This effect is known as the 'induced effect'. Because of the indirect and induced effects of tourist expenditure, the ultimate increase in total value added, and employment will be much higher than the initial increase in value added and employment in the tourism industry.

The use of I–O analysis was popular in tourism analyses in the 1950s to 1980s because of its ability to estimate the aggregate as well as the sectoral-level economic impacts, and to trace the linkages between industries. However, I–O analysis is subject to some serious shortcomings due to its strict and unrealistic assumptions. These limitations have been widely criticized by CGE modellers (see Briassoulis 1991; Johnson 1999; Blake 2000; Dwyer et al. 2004, 2006).

The obvious drawback of an I–O model is that the I–O ratios are assumed fixed. This is far from the reality and too mechanical. As a result, the model is very rigid and lacks explanatory power. It may be argued that the fixed technical coefficients reflect the fixed technology at a point of time. The immediate response is that technology does change over time and there are many alternative production methods available at any point of time. Since there are different kinds of production functions we can employ to describe production activities, only using the most rigid (and most convenient) one for all industries in the economy is unrealistic.

The other assumption of I–O analysis is that there are no constraints on the capacity of an industry to expand production to meet the additional demands by tourists. This assumption is of course unrealistic as resources are scarce in any economy. This assumption has a number of implications. First, it will exclude any price effects. Since the resources needed for producing additional products are readily available, an expansion of production would not cause any input price change, and thus changes in the demand for the factors of production would not induce any change in the cost. In reality, this is not the case as industrial sectors would have to compete for scarce resources, thus raising the price of factors of production in the face of stronger tourism demand. Second, it rules out the possibility of firms utilizing substitution between factors. As tourism demand pulls up the prices of some inputs, firms will use less of these inputs and use more substitutes in order to minimize cost. However, the fixed I–O ratios in an I–O model fail to reflect firms' behaviour of cost minimization. Third, the I–O analysis based on this assumption cannot take account of any feedback effect—the general equilibrium adjustment due to the relocation of resources among industries. For example, in the case of tourism expansion, an I–O model does not allow for the amount of labour flowing from other industries to the tourism industry and the consequent reduction in production of other industries. It also does not allow for the effects of foreign tourism demand pushing up exchange rates, which discourage other exports and result in increased imports.

Some researchers refined the I–O modelling to overcome some of its limitations. For example, Sadler et al. (1973) incorporated into the model the effects of changes in consumption patterns when income rises; Wanhill (1988), Fletcher and Archer (1991), and West and Gamage (2001) introduced capacity constraints into the basic model. However, these refinements fail to fully capture the general equilibrium adjustment in the model.

1.2.3 Advent of CGE Modelling

The limitations of the I–O model cry out for a more realistic, flexible, and comprehensive general equilibrium model. With the advent and development of computer technology, the CGE model was born and quickly gained popularity.

The early CGE models based on the Arrow–Debreu framework were set up under the conditions of perfect competition (e.g. Dixon et al. 1982). It is criticized that the concept of perfectly competitive market structure is not realistic for the modern economy, so some CGE models incorporating imperfect competition have been developed. Harris (1984) developed a CGE model for a small open economy with scale economies and imperfect competition. Later studies incorporated industrial organization features into multi-country CGE models (e.g. Gasiorek et al. 1992; Harrison et al. 1996, 1997; Adams and Parmenter 1999), and some studies incorporated dynamics into the CGE model to change the static nature of the CGE model (Auerbach et al. 1983; Perroni 1995; Kotlikoff 1998; Dixon and Parmenter 1996; Dixon and Rimmer 2002; Madsen and Sorensen 2002). However, the incorporation of imperfect competition and dynamics into the CGE model increases the complexity of the model. Palstev (2000) claims that dynamic CGE models can provide reasonably accurate predictions if there are no major structural changes in the economy and if the future growth of fundamentals is easy to forecast, but in the case of great uncertainty, the forecasts provided by the models tend to be less accurate.

1.3 Elements of a Standard CGE Model

A standard CGE model mainly includes two components: model structure and database. The CGE model structure is actually a system of equations mimicking the economic interconnection in a real economy. A CGE database includes all data to be fed into the CGE model structure in order to derive simulation results. In this section, we discuss briefly the elements in both components.

1.3.1 Elements in CGE Model Structure

The economic system in reality is very complex and thus involves numerous elements. However, all elements are directly or indirectly related to supply of and demand for goods and services. These are the backbone of a CGE model. An economic system in a CGE model is illustrated in Fig. 1.2.

There are many elements in Fig. 1.2, but the key elements are those in the square textbox with a double line. The three key elements on the very left of the graph, that is, labour, capital, and intermediate inputs, are the resources (or inputs) for producing a good or service (i.e. output). In an equilibrium, this good or service must be purchased by different users (demands), for example, intermediate demand, foreign demand, investor's demand, government demand, and household demand. These different users (demands) are the key elements of the economic system, shown at the bottom of the graph.

All other elements in the graph are linked to the key elements in different ways. First, it is worth noticing the linkage between intermediate inputs and intermediate demand. The intermediate demand for one commodity is also the intermediate inputs for production of other commodities, so the total intermediate demand in the economy should equal

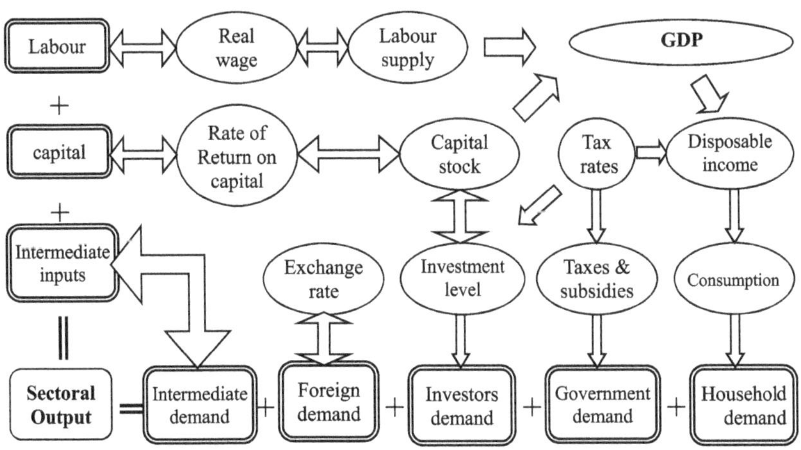

Fig. 1.2 An illustration of economic system in a CGE model

the total supply of intermediate inputs. Second, the production side is influenced by many factors. The real wage rates interact with both labour inputs and labour supply while the rate of return on capital is the centre element on capital inputs and capital stock. All these factors are the determining forces on sectoral output and gross domestic product (GDP) in the economy. Finally, on the demand side, even more variables are involved. Take household demand for example. The household demand for one commodity is greatly affected by total household consumption that in turn is affected by household disposable income. The disposable income is determined by both the income tax rate and gross household income, both of which are a substantial part of GDP. These interactions among the macroeconomic variables make the economic system complicated. A CGE model uses mathematical functions to present the behaviours of economic agents as well as the interactions among the related variables. Through the equation system, the model can evaluate the effect of the change of one or more variables on other variables in the economy.

1.3.2 Elements in CGE Database

The database for a CGE model consists of two parts: parameter values and the flow of income and spending in an economy. Parameters describe the behaviour of economic agents. For example, substitution elasticity for apples and stone fruits can indicate how much a consumer will substitute away from apples (buying fewer apples and more other fruits) when the apple price increases. Parameter values are assigned to the equations in a CGE model and they keep unchanged when modelling is being performed. For a standard CGE model, the income and spending flow data are mainly related to the supply of and demand for goods and services: for example, the types and quantity of goods and services provided by each industry, the commodity flow from the sources to the users, the production taxes paid by each industry, the commodity tax imposed on each type of goods and services, and the wage payment and gross profit of each industry. These data are normally included in a set of I–O tables produced by the national statistical department.

An extended CGE model concerns not only the production and consumption activity but also the interconnection of institutions other than industries, for example, the interconnection between households, between households and the government, between households and financial institutions, and so on. As a result, many more data are required by an extended CGE model. These data can be put into or obtained from a social accounting matrix (SAM).

1.4 Types of CGE Models

There are many types of CGE models. Depending on the criteria of classification, a CGE model can belong to either static or dynamic model, either single-country or global model, either single-region or multi-regional model, either top-down or bottom-up model, either single-household or multi-household model, and either single-occupation group or multi-occupation group model. Based on the research questions being addressed, a CGE model can also be classified as an environmental CGE model, an energy CGE model, an agricultural CGE model, a tourism CGE model, a CGE model on water, a CGE model on land use, a CGE model for trade, and so on. This section will discuss each type of CGE model briefly.

1.4.1 Static Versus Dynamic CGE Models

In reality, investment of an industry is its capital formation, which will increase the capital stock used to produce output, so the industrial investment will cause a change in output over time. This is a dynamic process. In a static CGE model, there is no link between industry investment and industry capital, so the capital dynamic is ignored. However, a static model sometimes is called a comparative static model. This is explained in Fig. 1.3.

Figure 1.3 graphs the GDP against time. A is the level of GDP in the base year 0 and B is the level in year T if no policy change is made. With the policy change (e.g. tariff rate change), the GDP level may

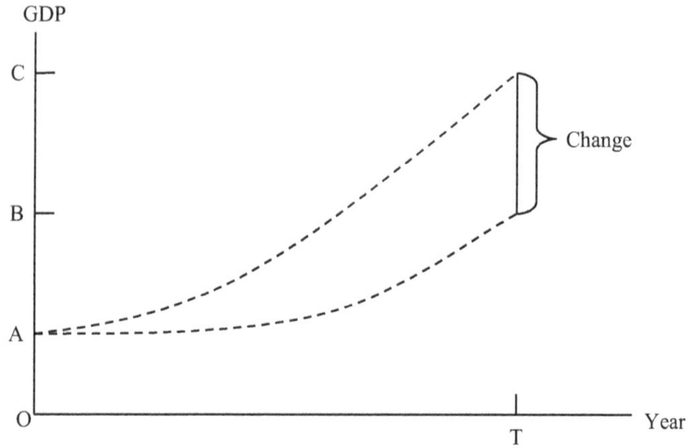

Fig. 1.3 Comparative static interpretation of results in ORANI-G

reach level C, other things being equal. The ORANI-G simulation generates a percentage change of 100(C − B)/A, instead of a static change 100(C − A)/A. The change is comparative static rather than dynamic, because we do not know the dynamic pattern: in the short run, the capital stock in the model is fixed; in the long run, the capital stock is adjusted according to exogenous rates of return; so the model itself tells us nothing about the adjustment paths shown as the dashed line in Fig. 1.3.

Compared with a static model, a dynamic model is generally more advanced. The capital dynamic is one of the key driving forces in the model. Generally, there is another driving force in a dynamic model: the population growth. Currently, dynamic CGE models are also called recursive dynamic CGE models. This is because the dynamic is achieved through period-by-period (usually year-by-year) simulation.

Ideally, a dynamic model should be able to identify the optimal path from the current equilibrium to a new equilibrium. However, due to the complexity of an economic system, it is very difficult to identify the desired new equilibrium (e.g. the output of all commodities in ten years' time) beforehand, and this makes the goal of finding the optimal path unachievable. The way out of this is to let the capital and population dynamic determine the new equilibrium of each year in the future. This is why the current dynamic CGE models are called recursive dynamic.

Moreover, many things besides capital and population can and will change, for example, the technology of production may improve. As a result, a dynamic CGE model cannot rely only on the dynamic of capital and population to project the performance of the economy in the future. Usually, the macroeconomic forecasts (e.g. the GDP in ten years' time) based on macroeconometric models are incorporated into the CGE model to quantify the speed of technological change in each period. This will give a result consistent with economic forecasts but, in the meantime, will inherit any errors embedded in the macroeconometric forecasts.

1.4.2 Single-Country Versus Global CGE Models

The difference between a single-country and a global CGE model is the scope of the model. The advantage of a single-country model is that it can include detailed information about the country and thus can generate detailed results for the country. However, this type of model generally assumes that the rest of world is unchanged and thus cannot include the feedback effect from other countries. This potentially makes the modelling results less realistic.

On the other hand, a global model can take into account the cross-country linkage and provide the whole picture of the world economy. This feature makes a global model a perfect option for studying international trade. Due to limitation of data availability and model size, however, a global model is generally unable to include detailed information for all countries and has limited use in addressing a specific research question for a country.

Currently the solution to utilizing the advantage of both models is to link a single-country model with a global model through multiple simulations, that is, to feed the modelling results of a global model into a single-country model and then to feed the results of single-country model into the global model, and to repeat the procedure until the modelling results from two models converge.

1.4.3 Single-Region Versus Multi-Regional CGE Models

Single-region and multi-regional CGE models are generally two types of single-country models. A multi-regional mode is usually an expanded version of a single-region model. Normally there is only one government in a multi-regional CGE model, so it will give more detailed information on local industries and households, but not much information about the local governments. Depending on the definition of region, a multi-regional CGE model can be at the state (or provincial) level, which includes relatively fewer regions, or at the local government (or electoral area) level, which includes a large number of regions. To reduce the model size, the interregional trade in a CGE model of a large number of regions can be simplified.

1.4.4 Top-Down Versus Bottom-Up CGE Models

These two types of models generally refer to a multi-regional model or a model including detailed micro-level information of an industry. A top-down model simply disaggregates the top-level modelling results to different regions or different firms according to the ratios calculated in advance. Compared with a bottom-up model, fewer data are required by a top-down model, but in the meantime, the modelling results from a top-down model are more likely to be indicative only.

A bottom-up CGE model combines a series of CGE models for each region (or each firm) to form a national model, so the model can simulate and aggregate the regional (or firm level) results to the national level. The model includes detailed information about the regions (firm) and allows different functions to be used for different regions (industries) so as to reflect the features of the region. As a result, the modelling results are more reliable for each region (industry). However, this model requires much more data and computer power.

To utilize the advantage of both models, a modeller can create a hybrid model, where higher-level regions (e.g. state level) are modelled using the bottom-up approach but the results for low-level regions (e.g. local government level) are obtained through the top-down approach.

1.4.5 Multi-Household and/or Multi-Occupation CGE Models

A multi-household CGE model is a further development based on a single-household model. The bottom-up approach is usually used for this purpose and the household income and consumption data can be obtained from household surveys. The important purpose of a multi-household model is to reveal the distributional effect of income and consumption. Compared with a CGE model with only one type of labour input, a multi-occupation CGE model requires more information about wage payment to each occupation group but can assess the impact on each occupation group. Limited substitution effect (e.g. a manager can do the work of a factory worker when it is necessary) is usually assumed for each type of labour. Since multi-occupation exists in reality, a multi-occupation CGE model generally generates more realistic results than a single labour input CGE model.

1.4.6 CGE Models by Research Area

A CGE model can also be named according to a research area, for example, a CGE model studying tourism can be called a tourism CGE model, a CGE model focusing on environment impact can be called an environmental CGE model, a CGE model specialized in energy can be called an energy CGE model, and so on. A CGE model in a specific research area normally involves an area-specific extension based on a standard CGE model.

1.5 Acceptance of CGE Modelling

From 1990 onwards CGE modelling has largely supplanted I–O modelling and become a widely used tool. CGE modelling has become an important tool used by world economic organizations such as the World Trade Organization (WTO), Organisation for Economic Co-operation and Development (OECD), and the World Bank to measure the impact of shocks or policy changes. It is also applied in many areas such as the analysis of trade, the macro-economy, various industries, and the environment and natural resources.

International trade is the area most heavily modelled by CGE researchers. CGE modelling helps to analyse the effects of trade liberalization (e.g. Wang 1999; Scollay and Gilbert 2000; Adams 1998; Anderson 1998; Benjamin and Diao 2000; Brown et al. 2000; Maskus and Konan 1997; Siriwardana 2007), trade protection (e.g. Siriwardana 1996; Kaempfer et al. 1997; Michael and Hatzipanayotou 1998), and international capital linkages (e.g. Merette et al. 2008).

CGE modelling is also widely applied to the macro-economy and various industries. For the macro-economy as a whole, CGE models have been used to investigate the labour market (Graafland and de Mooij 1999; Minford et al. 1997), policy effects (Siriwardana 1998; Swank 1999; Babikerm et al. 2003; Bohringer et al. 2001; Cutler and Strelnikoval 2004), and mega-event effects such as Olympic Games, the 9/11 terrorist attacks, and foot-and-mouth disease (FMD) (McDonald and Roberts 1998; Adelman and Yelddan 2000; Aziz 2000; Doroodian and Boyd 2003; Horridge et al. 2005). Agricultural industry analysis has also been a popular topic (e.g. Beghin et al. 1997; Taylor et al. 1999). CGE modelling has also been applied to other industries such as transportation (Asao and Bo 2005; Bergkvist and Westin 2001; Conrad and Heng 2002) and energy (Galinis and Van Leeuwen 2002; McDonald et al. 2005).

As people pay more attention to the state of the environment, CGE modelling of the environment and natural resources has become very popular in recent years. The practised topics include climate change (Winters et al. 1998; Breuss and Steininger 1998; Berrittella et al. 2004), carbon emissions (Ahammad et al. 2001; Farmer and Steininger 1999; Zhang 1998; Edwards and Hutton 2001; Gottinger 1998), pollution abatement (Dellink et al. 2004; Hyman et al. 2002; Scrimgeoura et al. 2005), and water policy (Seung et al. 2000; Stringer 2001).

CGE modelling can be applied to many other areas. For example, Massey (2001), McGregor et al. (1995), De Santis (2003), and Fidrmuc (2004) used CGE models to analyse the migration phenomenon; Batey and Madden (1999) evaluated the employment impact of demographic change; Acemoglu and Verdier (Acemoglu and Verdier 1998) investigated the relationship among property rights, corruption, and the allocation of talent; Carlstrom and Fuerst (1997) were interested in the relationship between agency costs, net worth, and business fluctuations; Chisari et al. (1999) studied the privatization and regulation of utilities; Diao et al. (1999) considered R&D-driven endogenous growth; Francois and Nelson (1998) explored the relationship between trade, technology, and wages; McGregor (1998) used a CGE model to explain the famine phenomenon; and Rioja (1999) focused on the productiveness and welfare implications of public infrastructure.

1.6 An Evaluation of CGE Modelling

The wide acceptance of CGE modelling largely comes from the advantages of this modelling method. However, CGE modelling also has some drawbacks. This section is devoted to the advantages and disadvantages of CGE modelling.

1.6.1 Advantages of a CGE Model Over Other Simulation Models

There are many kinds of simulation models, for example, the I–O model, the linear programme (LP) model, the real business cycle (RBC) model, and dynamic stochastic general equilibrium (DSGE) model. A CGE model has an advantage over all other simulation models.

Both I–O analysis and CGE modelling take account of the linkages among industries, households, and government; however, the CGE model provides a more flexible, realistic, and comprehensive framework for analysis. As stated earlier, there are a number of limitations for I–O analysis. In I–O analysis, all technical coefficients are assumed fixed. Therefore, the behaviour of economic agents in response to changing economic conditions is not considered. At best it simply assumes their behaviours are mechanically fixed by the Leontief function. By contrast, the CGE model uses various production, consumption, and investment functions to describe economic agents' response to external shocks. Thus, the CGE model is much more comprehensive and realistic, and the results from a CGE model are more reliable.

Both an LP model and a CGE model use the constrained optimization procedure to obtain an equilibrium solution. For example, the producer will maximize profit subject to the constraint of cost (or minimize costs subject to the level of output required by the market); the household will maximize utility subject to the level of income. This will give an optimal consumption or production solution for the economy. However, the LP model only concerns one industry or one firm, so the equilibrium in an LP model is a partial equilibrium. In other words, an LP model cannot take into account the feedback effect in the economy. A CGE model has clear advantage on this front.

An RBC model uses time series data to calibrate the parameter values in the model and then simulates the outcome of a shock. An DSGE model extends a macroeconomic model like the RBC model to a macroeconometric model by introducing a technical random variable. The time series data are also used to calibrate an RBC or DSGE model and to provide a projection based on different policy scenarios. However, due to the limitation of data availability, it is usually difficult to obtain time series data at detailed industry level. As a result, RBC and DSGE models have only a few sectors and are largely regarded as macro models. These types of models are unable to provide simulation results at detailed industry level and thus cannot reveal the sectoral linkage.

1.6.2 Drawbacks of CGE Modelling

One shortcoming is the high cost associated with CGE modelling. CGE models are sometimes criticized as too time-consuming to build and too complicated to use (Mules 1999; Hunn and Mangan 1999). The construction of a CGE model involves the following steps: (1) Deciding the elements (types of industries and other economic agents, commodities, and services) to incorporate into the model based on the I–O tables and the purpose of the CGE modelling. (2) Setting up the assumptions for the model. A CGE model involves four kinds of assumptions: behavioural assumptions, equilibrium conditions, exogenous variables, and detailed scenarios for projections. (3) Using I–O tables and other empirical studies to calibrate the parameters. Building a model takes time as it usually involves numerous sectors and institutions and thus many production functions, utility functions, and market clearance conditions. The complex nature of a CGE model may make the simulation and interpretation of results an enormous task. However, the increasing use of CGE models has seen the development of commercialized CGE models such as ORANI-G, which can save a substantial amount of time. The standardized CGE modelling software like General Equilibrium Model Package (GEMPACK) and training courses decrease the difficulty of using CGE models. It is true that CGE modelling is still more costly than I–O modelling, but the high quality of the simulation results makes CGE models a better option.

Another limitation of CGE modelling is that a considerable number of assumptions are needed in a CGE model. For example, to present the economy, a CGE model has to make assumptions regarding the economic environment, production functions, and utility functions. These assumptions may not precisely describe the behaviour of the economic agents. Even worse, to reduce the complexity of the model and thus minimize the modelling cost, a CGE model may make simplified assumptions (such as perfect competition and constant returns to scale). However, most of the assumptions in CGE models are based on microeconomic theories (e.g. production functions and consumption functions) and empirical studies (e.g. demand elasticities). These reasonable approximations make the measurement problem tractable. Some simplifications in CGE models, as long as they do not contradict reality, should be acceptable. For example, the constant returns to scale assumption for the motor vehicle industry may not be acceptable, but for some industries including tourism, this is a reasonable assumption.

Finally, CGE modelling requires large amounts of data. A CGE model needs a broad range of detailed data at sector and commodity levels to simulate a macro-economy. Although I–O tables or an SAM provides a great deal of data for CGE modelling, other data are also needed. For example, a CGE model needs numerous behavioural parameters like elasticities of substitution, elasticities of expenditure, demand and export elasticities, and various share values. The data collection for a CGE model is a labour-intensive chore which increases the modelling cost. The extensive data requirements of CGE modelling increase both the modelling cost and the possibility of needing to make assumptions.

References

Acemoglu, D., & Verdier, T. (1998). Property Rights, Corruption and the Allocation of Talent: A General Equilibrium Approach. *The Economic Journal, 108*, 1381–1403.

Adams, P. (1998). Long-Run Effects of APEC Trade Liberalisation: An Applied General Equilibrium Analysis. *The World Economy, 21*, 931–952.

Adams, P. D., & Parmenter, B. R. (1999). General Equilibrium Models. In K. Corcoran (Ed.), *Valuing Tourism: Methods and Techniques*. Canberra: Bureau of Tourism Research.

Adelman, I., & Yelddan, E. (2000). The Minimal Conditions for a Financial Crisis: A Multiregional Intertemporal CGE Model of the Asian Crisis. *Economic World Development, 28*(6), 1087–1100.

Ahammad, H., Clements, K., & Ye, Q. (2001). The Regional Economic Impact of Reducing Greenhouse Gas Emissions: Western Australia. *Resources Policy, 27*, 225–233.

Anderson, J. (1998). The Uruguay Round and Welfare in Some Distorted Agricultural Economies. *Journal of Development Economics, 56*(2), 393–410.

Arrow, K., & Debreu, G. (1954). Existence of An Equilibrium for A Competitive Economy. *Econometrica, 22*, 265–290.

Arrow, K., & Hahn, F. (1971). *General Competitive Analysis*. San Francisco: Holden-Day.

Asao, A., & Bo, M. (2005). *Transport Sector and Regional Price Differentials: A Spatial CGE Model for Chinese Provinces*. Japan: School of Information Sciences, Tohoku University.

Auerbach, A., Kotlikoff, L., & Skinner, J. (1983). The Efficiency Gains from Dynamic Tax Reform. *International Economic Review, 24*, 81–100.

Aziz, I. (2000). Simulating Economy-Wide Models to Capture the Transition from Financial Crisis to Social Crises. *Regional Science, 34*, 251–278.

Babikerm, M., Ellerman, A., Reilly, J., & Viguier, L. (2003). Assessing the Impact of Carbon Tax Differentiation in the European Union. *Environmental Modelling and Assessment, 8*, 187–197.

Batey, P., & Madden, M. (1999). The Employment Impact of Demographic Change: A Regional Analysis. *Regional Science, 78*, 69–87.

Beghin, J., Dessus, S., Roland-Holst, D., & Van der Mesbrugge, D. (1997). The Trade and Environment Nexus in Mexican Agriculture. A General Equilibrium Analysis. *Agricultural Economics, 17*, 2–3.

Benjamin, N., & Diao, X. (2000). Liberalizing Services Trade in APEC: A General Equilibrium Analysis with Imperfect Competition. *Pacific Economic Review, 5*(1), 49–75.

Bergkvist, E., & Westin, L. (2001). Regional Valuation of Infrastructure and Transport Attributes for Swedish Road Freight. *Regional Science, 35*, 547–560.

Berrittella, M., Bigano, A., Roson, R., & Tol, R. (2004). *A General Equilibrium Analysis of Climate Change Impacts on Tourism*. http://www.fnu.zmaw.de/fileadmin/fnu-files/publication/working-papers/cgetourismwp.pdf

Blake, A. (2000). *The Economic Effects of Tourism in Spain*. Discussion Paper Series 2000/2, Christel DeHaan Tourism and Travel Research Institute, University of Nottingham. http://www.nottingham.ac.uk/ttri/series.html

Bohringer, C., Welsch, H., & Loschel, A. (2001). *Environmental Taxation and Structural Change in an Open Economy*, ZEW.

Breuss, F., & Steininger, K. (1998). Biomass Energy Use to Reduce Climate Change: A General Equilibrium Analysis for Austria. *Journal of Policy Modelling, 20*, 513–535.

Briassoulis, H. (1991). Methodological Issues: Tourism Input-output Analysis. *Annals of Tourism Research, 18*, 435–449.

Brown, D., Deardorff, A., & Stern, R. (2000). Computational Analysis of the Accession of Chile to the NAFTA and Western Hemisphere Integration. *The World Economy, 23*, 145–174.

Carlstrom, C., & Fuerst, T. (1997). Agency Costs, Net Worth, and Business Fluctuations: A Computable General Equilibrium Analysis. *American Economic Review, 87*(5), 893–910.

Chisari, O., Estache, A., & Romero, C. (1999). Winners and Losers from the Privatization and Regulation of Utilities: Lessons from a General Equilibrium Model of Argentina. *The World Bank Economic Review, 13*(2), 357–378.

Conrad, K., & Heng, S. (2002). Financing Road Infrastructure by Saving in Congestion Costs: A CGE Analysis. *Regional Science, 36*, 107–122.

Cutler, H., & Strelnikoval, I. (2004). The Impact of the US Sales Tax Rate on the City Size and Economic Activity: A CGE Approach. *Urban Studies, 41*(4), 875–885.

De Santis, R. (2003). The Impact of A Customs Union with the European Union on Internal Migration in Turkey. *Journal of Regional Science, 43*(2), 349–372.

Debreu, G. (1959). *Theory of Value*. New York: Wiley.

Dellink, R., Hofkes, M., van Lerlanda, E., & Verbruggen, H. (2004). Dynamic Modelling of Pollution Abatement in A CGE Framework. *Economic Modelling, 21*, 965–989.

Diao, X., Roe, T., & Yelda, E. (1999). Strategic Policies and Growth: An Applied Model of R&D-Driven Endogenous Growth. *Journal of Development Economics, 60*, 343–380.

Dixon, P., & Parmenter, B. (1996). Computable General Equilibrium Modelling for Policy Analysis and Forecasting. In H. Aman, D. Kendrick, & J. Rust (Eds.), *Handbook of Computational Economics* (Vol. 1). Amsterdam: Elsevier Science B.V.

Dixon, P., & Rimmer, M. (2002). *Forecasting and Policy Analysis with a Dynamic CGE Model of Australia*. Preliminary Working Paper, Monash University: Centre of Policy Studies, OP-90.

Dixon, P., Parmenter, B., Sutton, J., & Vincent, D. (1982). *ORANI: A Multisectoral Model of the Australian Economy*. Amsterdam: North Holland Publishing.

Doroodian, K., & Boyd, R. (2003). The Linkage Between Oil Price Shocks and Economic Growth with Inflation in the Presence of Technological Advances: A CGE Model. *Energy Policy, 31*, 989–1006.

Dwyer, L., Forsyth, P., & Spurr, R. (2004). Evaluating Tourism's Economic Effects: New and Old Approaches. *Tourism Management, 25*, 307–317.

Dwyer, L., Forsyth, P., & Spurr, R. (2006). Assessing the Economic Impacts of Events: A Computable General Equilibrium Approach. *Journal of Travel Research, 45*(1), 59–66.

Edwards, T., & Hutton, J. (2001). Allocation of Carbon Permits within a Country: A General Equilibrium Analysis of the United Kingdom. *Energy Economics, 23*, 371–386.

Farmer, K., & Steininger, K. (1999). Reducing CO2-Emissions Under Fiscal Retrenchment: A Multi-Cohort CGE-Model for Austria. *Environmental & Resource Economics, 13*(3), 309–340.

Fidrmuc, J. (2004). Migration and Regional Adjustment to Asymmetric Shocks in Transition Economies. *Journal of Comparative Economics, 32*, 230–247.

Fletcher, J., & Archer, B. (1991). The Development and Application of Multiplier Analysis. In C. Cooper (Ed.), *Progress in Tourism, Recreation and Hospitality Management* (Vol. 1). London: Belhaven.

Francois, J., & Nelson, D. (1998). Trade, Technology and Wages: A General Equilibrium Approach. *The Economic Journal, 108*(450), 1483–1499.

Galinis, A., & Van Leeuwen, M. (2002). A CGE Model for Lithuania: The Future of Nuclear Energy. *Journal of Policy Modelling, 22*(6), 691–718.

Gasiorek, M., Smith, A., & Venables, T. (1992). Trade and Welfare: A General Equilibrium Model. In L. Winters (Ed.), *Trade Flows and Trade Policy After 1992* (pp. 35–61). Cambridge: Cambridge University Press.

Gottinger, H. (1998). Greenhouse Gas Economics and Computable General Equilibrium. *Journal of Policy Modelling, 20*(5), 537–580.

Graafland, J., & de Mooij, R. (1999). Fiscal Policy and the Labour Market: An AGE Analysis. *Economic Modelling, 16*(2), 189–219.

Harris, J. (1984). Applied General Equilibrium Analysis of Small Open Economies with Scale Economies and Imperfect Competition. *American Economic Review, 74*, 1016–1032.

Harrison, G., Rutherford, T., & Tarr, D. (1996). Increased Competition and Completion of the Market in the European Community. *Journal of Economic Integration, 11*(3), 332–365.

Harrison, G., Rutherford, T., & Tarr, D. (1997). Economic Implications for Turkey of a Customs Union with the European Union. *European Economic Review, 41*, 861–870.

Horridge, M., Madden, J., & Wittwer, G. (2005). The Impact of the 2002-2003 Drought on Australia. *Journal of Policy Modelling, 27*, 285–308.

Hunn, C., & Mangan, J. (1999). Estimating the Economic Impact of Tourism at the Local, Regional and State or Territory Level, Including Consideration of the Multiplier Effect. In *Valuing Tourism: Methods and Techniques*. Occasional Paper No. 28. Canberra: Bureau of Tourism Research.

Hyman, R., Reilly, J., Babiker, M., De Masin, A., & Jacoby, H. (2002). Modelling Non-CO2 Greenhouse Gas Abatement. *Environmental and Modelling Assessment, 8*, 175–186.

Johnson, R. (1999). *Input-Output Models With and Without The Multiplier Effect, in Valuing Tourism: Methods and Techniques*. Occasional Paper No. 28. Bureau of Tourism Research Canberra.

Kaempfer, W., Ross, M., & Rutherford, T. (1997). Tariffication of a Distorted Economy: A CGE Analysis. *Review of Development Economics, 1*(2), 207–218.

Kotlikoff, L. (1998). Intergenerational Transfers and Savings. *Journal of Economic Perspectives, 2*, 41–58.

Leontief, W. (1936). Quantitative Input-Output Relations in the Economic System of the United States. *Review of Economics and Statistics, 18*(3), 105–125.

Leontief, W. (1941). *The Structure of American Economy, 1919-1929*. New York: Oxford University press. Reprinted, White Plains: International Arts and Sciences Press, 1976.

Madsen, A., & Sorensen, M. (2002). *Effect of Trade and Market Integration in a Small Open Economy—Dynamic CGE Approach, Danish Rational Economic Agents Model (DREAM)*. Working Papers Series. Denmark: Danish Ministry of Finance.

Maskus, K., & Konan, D. (1997). Trade Liberalization in Egypt. *Review of Development Economics, 1*(3), 275–293.

Massey, D. (2001). Theory of Migration. In *International Encyclopaedia of the Social & Behavioural Sciences* (pp. 9828–9834).

McDonald, S., & Roberts, D. (1998). The Economy-Wide Effects of the BSE Crisis: A CGE Analysis. *Journal of Agricultural Economics, 49*(3), 458–471.

McDonald, S., Sherman, R., & Karen, T. (2005). Impact of Switching Production to Bioenergy Crops: The Switchgrass Example. *Energy Economic, 28*(2), 243–265.

McGregor, P. (1998). Famine: A Simple General Equilibrium Model. *Oxford Economic Papers, 50*(4), 623–643.

McGregor, P., Swales, J., & Yin, Y. (1995). Migration Equilibria/Disequilibria and the Natural Rate of Unemployment in a Regional Context. *International Journal of Man Power, 16*(2), 66–72.

Merette, M., Papadaki, E., Hernandez, J., & Lan, Y. (2008). Foreign Direct Investment Liberalization Between Canada and the USA: A CGE Investigation. *Atlantic Economic Journal, 36*(2), 195–209.

Michael, S., & Hatzipanayotou, P. (1998). General Equilbrium Effects of Import Constraints Under Variable Labour Supply, Public Goods and Income Taxation. *Economica, 66*(263), 389–401.

Miller, R., & Blair, P. (1985). *Input-Output Analysis: Foundation and Extensions*. New Jersey: Prentice-Hall.

Minford, P., Riley, J., & Nowell, E. (1997). Trade, Technology and Labour Markets in the World Economy, 1970-90: A Computable General Equilibrium Analysis. *The Journal of Development Studies, 34*(2), 1–34.

Mules, G. (1999). Estimating the Economic Impact of an Event on a Local Government Area, Region, State or Territory. In *Valuing Tourism: Methods and Techniques*, Occasional Paper No. 28. Canberra: Bureau of Tourism Research.

Palstev, S. (2000). *Moving from Static to Dynamic General Equilibrium Economic Models*. Boulder, CO: Department of Economics, University of Colorado. http://debreu.colorado.edu/papers/move.pdf

Perroni, C. (1995). Assessing the Dynamic Efficiency Gains of Tax Reform when Human Capital is Endogenous. *International Economic Review, 36*, 907–925.

Rioja, F. (1999). Productiveness and Welfare Implications of Public Infrastructure: A Dynamic Two-Sector General Equilibrium Analysis. *Journal of Development Economic, 58*(2), 387–404.

Sadler, P., Archer, B., & Owen, C. (1973). *Regional Income Multipliers, Occasional Papers in Economics*. Bangor: University of Wales Press.

Scollay, R., & Gilbert, J. (2000). Measuring the Gains from APEC Trade Liberalisation: An Overview of CGE Assessments. *The World Economy, 23*, 175–198.

Scrimgeoura, F., Oxley, L., & Fatai, K. (2005). Reducing Carbon Emissions? The Relative Effectiveness of Different Types of Environmental Tax: the Case of New Zealand. *Environmental Modelling & Software, 20*, 1439–1448.

Seung, C., Harris, T., Englin, J., & Notusil, N. (2000). Impacts of Water Reallocation: A Combined Computable General Equilibrium and Recreation Demand Model Approach. *Regional Science, 34*, 473–487.

Siriwardana, M. (1996). The Economic Impact of Tariffs in the 1930s in Australia: The Brigden Report Re-Examined. *Australian Economic Papers, 35* (67), 370–389.

Siriwardana, M. (1998). Can Policy-Makers Learn from History? A General Equilibrium Analysis of the Recovery Policies of the 1930s Great Depression in Australia. *Journal of Policy Modelling, 20*(3), 361–392.

Siriwardana, M. (2007). The Australia-United States Free Trade Agreement: An Economic Evaluation. *The North American Journal of Economics and Finance., 18*(1), 117–133.

Stringer, R. (2001). *Grapes, Wine and Water: Modelling Water Policy Reforms in Australia*, Center for International Economic Studies.

Swank, J. (1999). A General Equilibrium Analysis of Short-Term Interest Rate Policies and the Role of Reserve Requirements. *Journal of Money, Credit and Banking, 23*(3), 205–218.

Taylor, J., Edward, A., & Hampton, S. (1999). Agricultural Policy Reforms and Village Economies: A Computable General-Equilibrium Analysis from Mexico. *Journal of Policy Modelling., 21*(4), 453–480.

Walras, L. (1954). *Elements of Pure Economics or the Theory of Social Wealth* (Trans. W. Jaffé). London: George Allen & Unwin Ltd. [An English translation of Walras' main work Éléments d'économie politique pure, ou théorie de la richesse sociale (1874)].

Wang, Z. (1999). The Impact of China's WTO Entry on the World Labour-Intensive Export Market: A Recursive Dynamic CGE Analysis. *The World Economy, 22*(3), 379–405.

Wanhill, S. (1988). Tourism Multipliers Under Capacity Constraints. *Service Industries Journal, 8*, 136–142.

West, G., & Gamage, A. (2001). Macro Effects of Tourism in Victoria: A Nonlinear Input-output Approach. *Journal of Travel Research, 40*, 101–109.

Winters, P., Murgai, R., Sadoulet, E., De Janvry, A., & Frisvold, G. (1998). Economic and Welfare Impacts of Climate Change on Developing Countries. *Environmental and Resource Economics, 12*(1), 1–24.

Zhang, Z. (1998). Macroeconomic Effects of CO2 Emission Limits: A Computable General Equilibrium Analysis for China. *Journal of Policy Modelling, 20*(2), 213–250.

2

Useful CGE Modelling Packages

2.1 GEMPACK Versus GAMS

The popular software for solving a CGE model include General Equilibrium Model Package (GEMPACK), General Algebraic Modelling System (GAMS), and Mathematical Programming System for General Equilibrium analysis (MPSGE). GAMS was developed in the mid-1970s by Alex Meeraus and Jan Bisschop at the World Bank. It was initially designed to solve large-scale, non-linear optimization problems, but it was adapted to CGE modelling at the World Bank in the mid-1980s. MPSGE was developed by Rutherford in 1987. It is a high-level language, usually used as a subsystem within GAMS. GEMPACK was developed in 1986 specifically for CGE modelling, by Codsi and Pearson at Centre of Policy Studies (CoPs), Australia.

GAMS (General Algebraic Modeling System) is a feature-rich computer language, which provides state-of-the-art capability for optimization and allows control constructs including loops, macro pre-processing, and ability to execute other programs within a GAMS script. It also allows the modeller to define and repeatedly use a function not provided by the GAMS developer. However, the non-linear optimization at levels requires more complicated

S. Meng, M. Siriwardana, *Assessing the Economic Impact of Tourism*,
DOI 10.1007/978-3-319-40328-1_2

equations. This makes a CGE model task-specific. In other words, a slightly change in modelling task may involves significant change in the GAMS codes.

By contrast, GEMPACK gives the modeller less power in creating a function or executing other programs. However, GEMPACK uses the first-order condition (or linear form or percentage change form) to solve the optimization problems. This greatly simplifies the equations in a CGE model. The linear approach was criticized as being inaccurate when the changes are large. This problem is successfully overcome by using a multi-step simulation approach. Hertel et al. (1992) compared the modelling results solved using GAMS and those solved using GEMPACK and showed that the differences were of style rather than of substance. This section discusses the linear modelling approach and the multi-step simulation method.

2.1.1 Advantages of a Linear Model

In the search for the best method to solve general equilibrium models, researchers developed several algorithms which can be classified as either levels or linear systems. There are some positive and some negative aspects for each system, but overall, the linear system has enormous advantages over a levels system.

First, the linear system makes the model size manageable. A model can be large either because of its large number of equations (and variables) or because of the highly non-linearity of its equations. To solve a model with a large number of equations (thousands or even millions), condensation of equations is necessary to satisfy its computing requirements. For a linear system, the condensation is easily achieved by substituting some equations and variables. For a levels system, however, the condensation is much more difficult. Although some methods can limit the size of the constrained maximization problem for a non-linear model, they are often at the expense of reducing the economic detail of the model, which consequently reduces the explanatory power of the model.

Second, model modification is much easier to achieve in the linear system. A model has to be modified over time for various reasons. Since the solution for a linear system only involves the standardized matrix operation, the modification of a linear model most likely involves only changes of some relevant files, for example, making appropriate changes in the input–output data and elasticities files. Even if new variables and equations are required, what needed is to add a few columns and rows to the previous matrix. In short, most times there is no need to rewrite the solution algorithms. For a non-linear system, it is quite the opposite. Since there is no standard application of equation-solving techniques for a non-linear system, the solution algorithm of a non-linear model is based on the specific features of the model. As such, even if a minor modification may require the modeller to rethink and rewrite the algorithms, which is a time-consuming task.

Third, the linear system can provide great flexibility for model applications. In the application of a CGE model, it often involves switching variables between the exogenous and endogenous categories. In a linear model, this switch needs only a reorganization of a matrix (reallocate the columns in a matrix) in the model. However, for a non-linear model, switching variables involves a major model revision and requires extensive rewriting of solution algorithms.

Given these advantages of the linear system, it is little wonder that it is popularly used in many CGE models including ORANI-G.

2.1.2 Percentage Change Linearization Approach

Although a linear system provides much convenience and flexibility for CGE modelling, most of the functions (e.g. production function, demand function, and utility function) in a CGE model are non-linear. To solve this problem, Johansen (1960) developed a method of linearization by taking the percentage change of non-linear equations. This linearization method is further developed by Keller (1980) and Dixon et al. (1982). The Johansen technique (one-step linear solution) is visited here.

The non-linear equation system in a CGE model can be expressed as:

$$F(Z) = 0$$

where Z is a vector of variables of size n, F is a vector of m differentiable functions of Z, and it is assumed that $n > m$. As such, the above equation presents an equation system with m equations and n variables. Differentiating $F(Z)$ will give a linearized equation system in percentage change form, shown as follows:

$$A(Z)z = 0$$

where z is an n * 1 vector interpreted as the percentage changes in Z and $A(Z)$ is an m * n matrix containing the partial derivatives and/or elasticities of F evaluated at Z. $A(Z)$ is unknown because the value of Z depends on the size of z. However, if z stands only for a small percentage change, $A(Z)$ can be approximated as the $A(Z_0)$ where Z_0 is the vector of initial values of Z, which is given. As such, we have, $A(Z_0)z = 0$.

Since $n > m$, to solve the equation system, we need to set $(n - m)$ variables exogenous. Assume z_y is the $(n - m)$ * 1 vector consisting of the exogenous variables and z_x is the m * 1 vector encompassing the other variables (endogenous variables) in vector z. Corresponding to z_x and z_y, we divide matrix $A(Z_0)$ into two: $A_x(Z_0)$ and $A_y(Z_0)$, so the linear system can be rewritten as:

$$A_x(Z_0)z_x + A_y(Z_0)z_y = 0$$

Solving the equation system for z_x, we have,

$$z_x = -A_x^{-1}(Z_0)A_y(Z_0)z_y$$

The m * $(n - m)$ matrix $A_X^{-1}(Z_0)A_y(Z_0)$ is our solution matrix. Its typical element is the elasticity of an endogenous variable with respect to an exogenous variable.

The Johansen technique is preferable because it utilizes standard linear algebra, but the condition for this technique is that the percentage change z cannot be large. Otherwise, it will cause severe linearization error as demonstrated in Fig. 2.1.

The curve in Fig. 2.1 represents the non-linear function and the straight line stands for the estimation of Johansen linearization. If the change of variable X is large (shown as dX in the figure), the Johansen

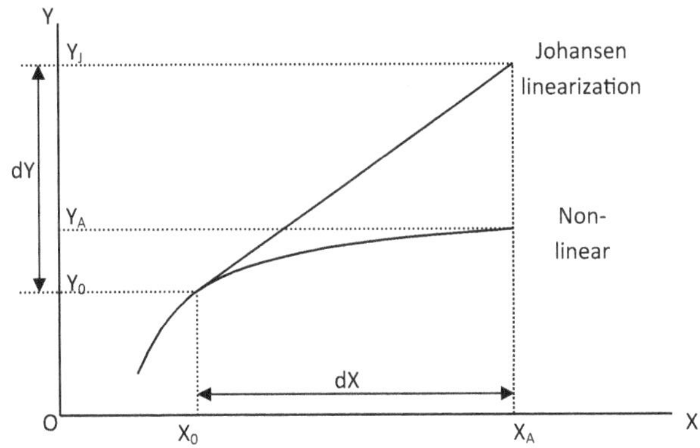

Fig. 2.1 Johansen linearization error

estimation will predict a large change in Y (dY in the figure), while the actual change is fairly small ($Y_A - Y_0$). The estimation error ($Y_J - Y_A$) is obviously not acceptable.

2.1.3 Multi-Step Process to Minimizing the Linearization Errors

To decrease the errors in the Johansen estimation of one-step linearization, the multiple step linearization is used in ORANI-G. The reasoning for this approach is shown in Fig. 2.2.

Figure 2.2 demonstrates a three-step linearization procedure. The procedure divides the total change dX into three parts: first, from X_0 to X_1, then from X_1 to X_2, and finally from X_2 to X_A. The three-step linearization reduces the estimation error remarkably from ($Y_J - Y_A$) to ($Y_3 - Y_A$). If more steps are used, the estimation error will be even less. Theoretically speaking, if infinite steps are used in linearization, the estimation error should disappear. The effectiveness of the multi-step approach has been demonstrated by Hertel et al. (1992).

Hertel et al. (1992) implemented a two-region model to verify whether the levels method and the linearization method had the same solution for the model. The non-linear equation system was solved by using NCPLU program (Preckel 1988), while the linearized model was implemented by

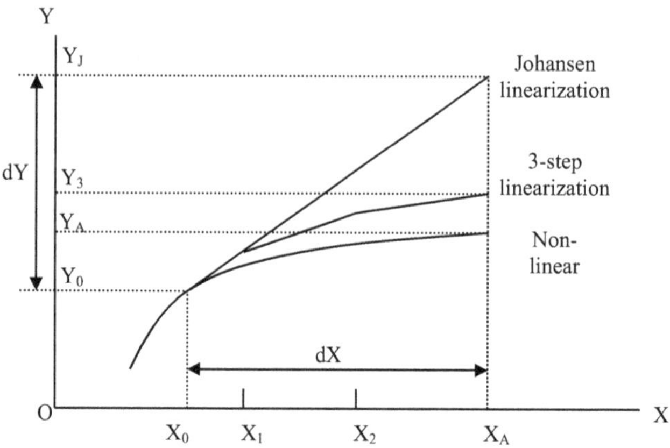

Fig. 2.2 Multi-step process to reduce linearization error

GEMPACK (Codsi and Pearson 1988). The results were remarkable. Both methods obtained exactly the same utility of consumption given the 20 % introduction of a subsidy in food, while the Johansen method overstated the effect. For the predicted price levels, the levels and linearized multi-step solutions only disagreed at the seventh decimal place, while some results of Johansen method differed even in the second digit. This experiment assures us that the multi-step linearization method used in GEMPACK can minimize the linearization error and thus we can be confident with this technique.

However, it is tedious to perform multiple-step linearization because we need to update the matrix $A(Z)$ after each step. Thanks to the development of computer technology, this energy-sapping job can be easily done by a computer.

2.2 How to Use GEMPACK to Do a Simulation

GEMPACK includes a suite of software for model coding, database construction, simulation, and results analysis. For example, TABmate provides the modeller with a convenient environment to create a CGE model which can be recognized by GEMPACK. ViewHAR provides a powerful way for the modeller to create a database which can be used by a CGE model. ViewSOL organizes and displays the modelling results in a convenient way. AnalyseGE can link modelling results to its relevant equations or codes in the CGE model, and GEMPIE can provide graphs for CGE modelling reports.

A CGE model can be implemented in GEMPACK in three ways: RunGEM, WinGEM, and DOS command. For an experienced CGE modeller familiar with DOS commands, tying in DOS commands in the 'shell to DOS' can run a CGE model relatively faster because this approach avoids the usage of computer memory for interface codes. For a novice CGE modeller who is only required to run an existing model, RunGEM or WinGEM is recommended.

2.2.1 Using RunGEM

RunGEM is similar to RunGTAP software provided by Centre for Global trade analysis. Both programs provide a user-friendly interface to run a CGE model. When GEMPACK is installed successfully, there will be either an icon 'RunGEM' on your computer screen or a file named 'RunGEM' in the directory of GEMPACK directory. When you double-click on this icon (or file name), RunGEM will be launched and a 'RunGEM' interface will appear on the screen (see Fig. 2.3).

There are seven tabs on the top of interface, namely, 'Title', 'Model/Data', 'Closure', 'Shocks', 'Output files', 'Solve', and 'Results'. When you click on the 'Model/Data' tab, you can specify the model and the database to be used by RunGEM. Similarly, on clicking on 'Closure' tab, you can type in (or load a closure file to specify) variables to be set exogenous. On clicking on the 'Shocks' tab, you can select from the 'Variable to Shock' list the variables to be shocked and specify the value of shock. For example, for a shock of a 10 % increase in exchange rate, you can select the variable 'phi' and assign a shock value of 10. When you click on 'Add to shock list' button, a line 'phi=10' will appear in the shock-list textbox. This means that the shock is successfully imposed. Likewise, on clicking on the 'output files', you can specify the name of files where the results will be stored. Then, when you click on the tab

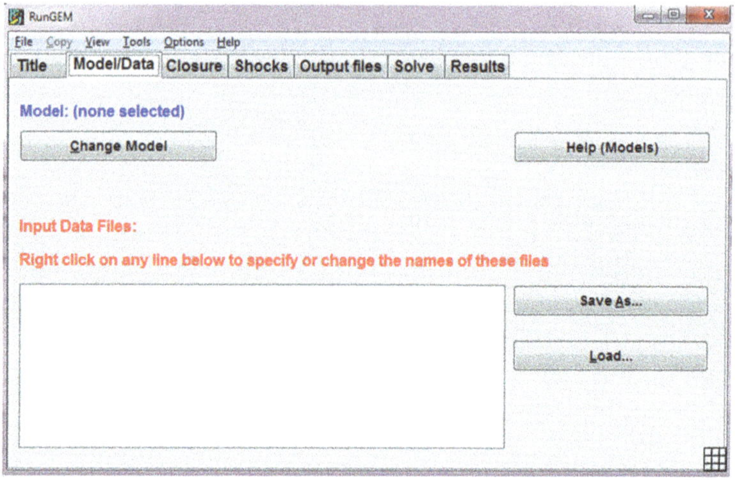

Fig. 2.3 The RunGEM interface

'Solve', the RunGEM will perform simulation and will display the results under the 'Results' tab.

2.2.2 Using WinGEM

RunGEM is very easy to use and requires little knowledge of a CGE model, so it is perfect for a novice CGE modeller. However, for the purpose of learning CGE modelling, winGEM is recommended to implement a CGE model. To run a CGE model in winGEM needs a few files. Most commonly, three files are sufficient to run a CGE model. That is a Tablo file (with an extension .tab) specifying the model structure, a Command file (with an extension .cmf), and a database file (with an extension .har). When you click on the 'winGEM' icon on your computer screen or a file named 'winGEM' in your GEMPACK directory, a row of winGEM menu will appear on the top of the computer screen. When you click on the 'File' menu, a number of options appear in the drop-down panel. On clicking on the 'Change both default directories', you can put as default both the directory for your input file and for GEMPACK working files. Similarly, when you click on the 'Simulation'

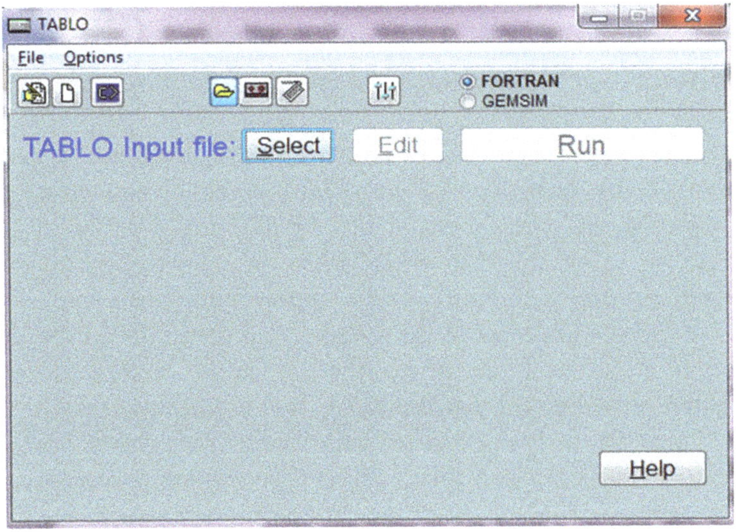

Fig. 2.4 The interface for TABLO implement

menu, a number of options appear on the drop-down panel. By selecting the 'TABLO implement', an interface will appear on the screen (see Fig. 2.4).

Now if you click on the 'Select' button, a new interface will appear, showing the available tab file in the default directory. You can load the Tablo file of interest into winGEM by clicking on the 'Select' next to the words 'TABLO input file'. On the top-right corner are two checkboxes for you to select either 'Fortran' or 'GEMSIM' (different ways of compiling the model). If you select 'Fortran' and click on the 'Run' button, winGEM will perform an initial check and produce an information file (with extension .inf). When you click on 'Go to compile and link' button, a 'compile and link' interface will appear. On clicking on 'Compile and link' button, the winGEM will call a Fortran compile to compile the Tablo file and generate an executable file (with an extension .exe). Likewise, when you click on the 'Go to Run TG program' button, a new interface appears with a 'TG executable' file already selected. When you click on the 'Select' button next to the words 'command file', you can select the command file in the default directory. By clicking on the 'Run' button, winGEM will start to perform the simulation. The simulation results can be viewed by clicking on one of the buttons on the new interface, such as 'View Input/output files', 'Go to View SOL', 'Go to AnalyseGE', and 'Go to GEPMIE'.

If the executable file (with an extension .exe) has already been generated by the modeller, only two files are needed for simulation, that is, the executable file and the command file. In this case, you can click on 'Simulation' menu and then select in the drop-down panel the 'Run TG program' option. An interface will appear. Now when you load the EXE file and the CMF file to the interface and then click on the 'Run' button, winGEM will start to run the simulation. In some cases, the simulation procedure is programmed by the modeller and is stored in a stored input file (with an extension .sti). The STI file can be used with either the 'TABLO implement' or 'Run TG program' options in 'Simulation' menu. In the latter case, you can click on 'Simulation' menu and then select in the drop-down panel the 'Run TG program' option. In the new interface, click on the 'Option' menu and select in the drop-down panel the 'Run from STI file' option. Now load the EXE file and the STI file to the interface and then click on the 'Run' button. GEMPACK will run the simulation according to the commands specified in the STI file.

2.2.3 Viewing Simulation Results

The simulation results can be viewed in different ways. When you click on the 'View input/output files' button, you will be able to view the base input file (the database pre-simulation), the updated input file (the database after simulation), and the output file (the values of interest after simulation). All these data are at levels. When you click on the 'Go to ViewSOL' option, you will be able to view the amount of change or percentage change of variables in the model. All results for variables with only one value (scalars) are listed under the first variable 'macros'. Similarly, when you double-click this row, you can view all results for scalars. All other variables are listed alphabetically with variable arguments listed in the 'Size' column (see Fig. 2.5).

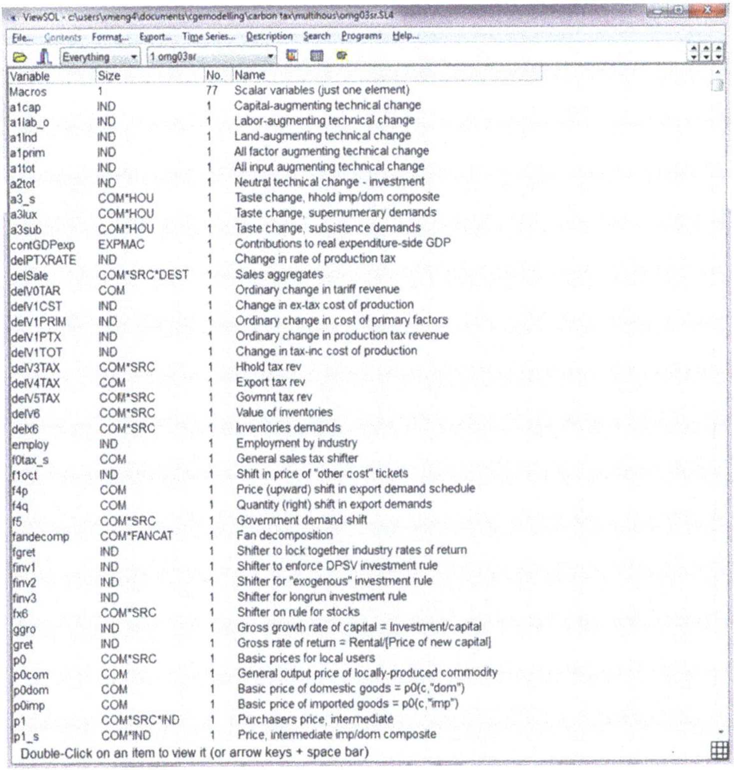

Fig. 2.5 ViewSOL interface

On double-clicking a row, you can view the results for a variable. The results for variables are normally displayed numerically as percentage change or ordinary change, depending on whether the variable is a percentage change variable or an ordinary change variable. On a result interface of ViewSOL, when you right-click on the variable name, a new interface will appear and give you the graph presentation of the results for this variable. As stated earlier, the 'AnalyseGEM' can link the specific results with related Tablo and the 'GEMPIE' can produce comprehensive graphs. Both are very useful in results analysis and reporting.

2.3 How to Use GEMPACK to Construct/ Change a Model

From the previous section, we learnt that mainly three files are necessary for a CGE simulation. A TAB file establishes the model structure, a HAR file provides the database, and a CMF file specifies how the simulation will be done. In some cases, an STI file is also needed for a simulation. This section discusses how to use GEMPACK to create these files.

2.3.1 Creating a TAB File

The operations and equations in a CGE model can be written in a text file. The language in GEMPACK to write the text file is called TABLO and the CGE model structure file created using TABLO language is called a TAB file. In this section, we will learn the basic grammar of TABLO. Since a CGE model is written in a text file (or a TAB file), you can create a TAB file using any word processors like MS Word, Notepad, or Wordpad. However, it is strongly suggested that you use the TABmate program included in GEMPACK. This program has a number of functions allowing you to check the grammar and to create relevant files for modelling. For example, the GEMPACK does not allow a line of TABLO more than certain number of letters (usually 80 letters, space included). The 'Tablo Check' button in the TABmate can check this and other grammar issues.

(1) Specifying in the tab file the files to be used in a CGE model

A CGE model needs to use databases including base year economic data and parameter values. Also, the simulation results need to be written into databases. These databases are files separated from the model structure established in the TAB file, so the database files must be called into the TAB file. The 'file' command is designed for this purpose. For example, the following command tells the computer to use two files: 'basedata' and 'summary'.

```
File BASEDATA # Input data file #;
File (new) SUMMARY ! Output for summary and checking data !;
```

The word 'File' is called a command or a keyword, which is reserved in TABLO language. From the above two lines in a TAB file, we learn a few things. First, each command must finish by a semicolon ';'. Second, any texts between two '#'s or between two '!'s are notes to help the modeller to recall the purpose of this command. These notes are optional and the computer will ignore them, but they are important to let other people understand the model (or help the modeller to recall the meaning of Tablo codes after a long time). Third, when the file does not exist (or you want the computer to create a new file), you need to put an indication '(new)' in front of the file name. Finally, when the same command (or keyword) is used continuously, the repeated command (e.g. the 'File' in second line) can be omitted.

(2) Specifying sets

An economy includes different types of things, such as a number of commodities, industries, regions, and so on. The type of things is called a set. A set can be defined by the 'set' command.

```
Set COM # Commodities# read elements from file BASEDATA header "COM";
SRC # Source of commodities # (dom, imp);
IND # Industries # read elements from file BASEDATA header "IND";
```

The above TABLO declares three sets: COM, SRC, and IND, which represent the commodities, source of commodities (domestically produced or imported), and industries. As shown before, the texts between two '#'s are optional notes. The elements of a set are also given in the above TABLO. For example, two types of sources are indicated by the text '(dom, imp)'. The names for commodities and industries could be a very long list (e.g. an economy has 120 commodity/industry types), so the TABLO tells the computer to read the commodity/industry names from a BASEDATA file (the file has been defined previously) with a header 'com' or 'ind'.

Sometimes, we need to create a set within a set, that is, a subset. For example, while some commodities are tradeable, some are not. A set of 'tradeable commodity' TRADCOM is part of 'commodity' set COM. Subsets TRADCOM and NONTRAD can be declared as follows:

```
Set TRADCOM # Tradeable Commodities# read elements from file BASEDATA
header "TRAD";
Subset TRADCOM is a subset of COM;
NONTRAD=COM-TRADCOM;
```

(3) Specifying variables

Since GEMPACK adopts a linear solution strategy, the variables in TABLO do not indicate the values of each stage; rather, they mean either ordinary or percentage changes. Variables must be declared before being used. The example of declaring variables can be shown as follows:

```
Variable ! Variables used to update above flows !
 (all,c,COM)(all,s,SRC)(all,i,IND) x1(c,s,i) # Intermediate basic
demands #;
(all,c,COM)(all,s,SRC) p0(c,s) # Basic prices for local users #;
(change)(all,c,COM)(all,s,SRC) delV6(c,s) # Value of inventories #;
```

The word 'variable' is a keyword, which can declare one or more variables. In this case, three variables are declared: x1, p0, and delV6, which mean the percentage change in intermediate basic demands, percentage change in basic prices, and ordinary change in value of inventories. Be aware of that, when a variable is for ordinary change, the expression '(change)' must be included. Otherwise, the GEMPACK will treat it as a percentage-change variable. It is a tradition of TABLO to use lower cases for variable names, but the GEMPACK will ignore upper or lower case.

The brackets after each variable contain the arguments of the variable. For example, the expression '(c,s,i)' after x1 indicates that x1 has three arguments: c,s,i. the range of these arguments are given in the expression before x1: (all,c,COM)(all,s,SRC)(all,i,IND), which means argument c refers to all elements in the set 'COM', argument s refers to all elements in the set 'SRC', argument i refers to all elements in the set 'IND'.

(4) Specifying coefficients

Coefficients in TABLO mean values at levels (e.g. the output value or price level in the base year) and parameters. Before using a coefficient, we must declare it and assign a value for it; otherwise, the computer cannot recognize it and will report an error. The example of declaring coefficients is as follows:

```
Coefficient ! Basic flows of commodities (excluding margin demands)!
(all,c,COM)(all,s,SRC)(all,i,IND)  V1BAS(c,s,i)  #  Intermediate
basic flows #;
(all,c,COM)(all,s,SRC)(all,i,IND) V2BAS(c,s,i) # Investment basic
flows #;
(all,c,COM)(all,s,SRC)(all,i,IND)  V1PUR(c,s,i)  #  Intermediate
purch. value #;
(parameter)(all,i,IND) SIGMA1PRIM(i) # CES substitution, primary
factors #;
```

It is noticeable that upper cases are used for coefficients, for example, V1BAS, V2BAS, V1PUR, and SIGMA1PRIM. Again this is the TABLO tradition to aid a human reader. GEMPACK will ignore the upper or lower cases. The brackets show the arguments of a variable and the range of the arguments. When the coefficient is for a parameter, for example, SIGMA1PRIM(i) for the parameter of substitution effect between primary factors (i.e. capital and labour), the expression '(parameter)' must be included.

After the coefficients are declared, they must be assigned values. This can be done through 'read' or 'formula' commands.

```
Read
V1BAS from file BASEDATA header "1BAS";
V2BAS from file BASEDATA header "2BAS";
SIGMA1PRIM from file BASEDATA header "P028";
Formula
(all,c,COM)( all,s,SRC)(all,i,IND) V1PUR(c,s,i) = V1BAS(c,s,i) +
V1TAX(c,s,i);
```

The 'read' command assigns coefficients values from a specified header in a specified file. Some values for a coefficient are calculated from other coefficients. In this case, the 'formula' command is used to assign the value. The above formula shows that the purchaser value of a commodity (from a source for an industry) is the sum of its basic value and the tax on this commodity.

If a coefficient is for a value at levels (i.e. not for a parameter) and the value of coefficient is read into the model, the coefficient needs updating. Updating a coefficient is necessary for two reasons: updating coefficient value is crucial for the multi-step simulation and the updated coefficients in the final step of simulation give the simulation results at levels. The updating of a coefficient is achieved through the 'update' command.

```
Update
(all,c,COM)(all,s,SRC)(all,i,IND) V1BAS(c,s,i) = p0(c,s)*x1(c,s,i);
(all,c,COM)(all,s,SRC)(all,i,IND) V2BAS(c,s,i) = p0(c,s)*x2(c,s,i);
(change)(all,c,COM)(all,s,SRC) V6BAS(c,s) = delV6(c,s);
```

The above 'update' command updates the values for coefficients V1BAS, V2BAS, and V6BAS. It is noticeable that the expression '(change)' is used for V6BAS because the ordinary change variable delV6 is used: the value of V6BAS is equal to its previous value plus the ordinary change (delV6) in V6BAS (the initial value is always omitted in updating formulas). The updating formula for V1BAS and V2BAS looks a bit strange: their values equal to the percentage change in basic price level (p0) times the percentage change in quantity (x1 or x2). This is a convenient shorthand writing provided by GEMPACK. p0(c,s)*x1(c,s,i) stands for P0(c,s)*V1BAS(c,s,i) + a change in P0(c,s)*V1BAS(c,s,i), or P0 (c,s)*V1BAS(c,s,i) + P0(c,s)*V1BAS(c,s,i)*(p0+x1)%. There is no need to update a parameter as it is unchanged during a simulation. For coefficients assigned value through a formula, the updated values can be calculated through the formula so there is no need to update them explicitly.

(5) Writing equations

Equations form an essential part of a CGE model. Equations must be initiated by the keyword (or command) 'equation' so that GEMPACK can recognize the equations. After the keyword 'equation', an unique identifier for the equation must follow, for example,

```
Equation
E_x0dom # Supply of commodities to export market #
(all,c,COM) TAU(c)*[x0dom(c) - x4(c)] = p0dom(c) - pe(c);
E_p0com # Zero pure profits in transformation #
(all,c,COM) p0com(c) = [1.0-EXPSHR(c)]*p0dom(c) + EXPSHR(c)*pe(c);
```

The above two equations share one keyword; the equation identifiers 'E_x0dom' and 'E_p0com' are unique names to identify the corresponding equations. The first equation 'E_x0dom' means that the difference between the percentage change in domestic demand for a commodity and the percentage change in exports of this commodity is proportional to the difference between the percentage change in domestic price of the commodity and the export price of this commodity. The second equation 'E_p0com' means that the percentage change in the basic commodity price 'p0com' is the share weighted average of the percentage change in domestic price and exports price. It is suggested to use an equation identifier starting with 'E_' to aid the human reader.

Since the purpose of an equation is to derive a value for a variable, it is highly suggested to include in the equation identifier the name of variable you intend to solve. For example, the identifier 'E_x0dom' for the first equation includes the name of the variable 'x0dom', while the identifier 'E_p0com' for the second equation includes the name of variable 'p0com'. If you write equations in this fashion, your Tablo file can utilize the TABmate function to pair the equations with variables. This function is very important in generating an automatic closure for simulation.

In TABmate, when your tab file passes the 'tablo check', you can click on the 'Tablo Code' button, which will generate some files for modelling. Then when you click on the 'Tool' menu and select the 'Closure' option in the drop-down panel, the closure file (with an extension CLO) will display on the interface. In this file, you can find the 'directly matching equations and variables' in Sect. 1, 'matching equations and variables (many equations to 1 variable)' in Sect. 2, 'unmatched equations' in Sect. 3, and 'unmatched variables' and 'automatic closure generated by

TABmate Tools' in Sect. 4. This information will help to form correct closures for simulation. We will discuss this further when dealing with the CMF file.

Next, we introduce the equations for three important functions: the Leontief function, the constant elasticity of substitution (CES) function and the constant elasticity of transformation (CET) function. The following sample Tablo are from ORANI-G.

```
Equation E_x1_s # Demands for commodity composites #
(all,c,COM)(all,i,IND) x1_s(c,i) - [a1_s(c,i) + a1tot(i)] = x1tot
(i);
E_x1lab1 # Demand for labour by industry and skill group #
(all,i,IND)(all,o,OCC)x1lab1(i,o)=x1lab_o(i)-SIGMALAB(i)*
[p1lab(i,o)-p1lab_o(i)];
Equation E_q1 # Supplies of commodities by industries #
(all,c,COM)(all,i,IND) q1(c,i) = x1tot(i) + SIGMA1OUT(i)*[p0com
(c) - p1tot(i)];
```

The equation 'E_x1_s' shows that the percentage change in intermediate input demand x1_s(c,i) is the same as the percentage change in output x1tot(i) for each industry (a1_s and a1tot are technological change variables, which are zero in most cases and thus can be ignored). This reflects the requirement of proportional inputs in a Leontief production function. In other words, this is a linear Leontief function.

The equation 'E_x1lab1' indicates that the percentage change in demand for different occupational labour x1lab1(i,o) will follow the percentage change in total industry labour demand x1lab_o(i), but it will also be affected by the difference in the occupational labour price and the aggregate labour price of the industry. In other words, if the price of labour of an occupation increases faster than the aggregate labour price in the industry, that is, p1lab1(i,o)>p1lab_o(i), the labour demand for this occupation will decrease due to the negative sign before the parameter 'SIGMALAB(i)'. This reflects the substitution effect in input demand, so this equation is an expression of linear CES function.

The equation 'E_q1' indicates that the percentage change in production of different commodities q1(c,i) will follow the percentage change in output x1tot(i), but it will also be affected by the difference in the percentage change in commodity price and the percentage change in output price of the industry. This equation is very similar to equation 'E_x1lab1', but here we are concerned with output rather than input demand. The positive sign before the parameter 'SIGMA1OUT(i)' suggests that, if the price of a commodity 'c' increases faster than the average output price of the industry, the industry will produce more commodity 'c' than other goods, that is, q1(c,i)> x1tot(i). This means the industry will transform its output mix according to the relative commodity price change, so this equation is an expression of linear CET function.

(6) Avoiding dividing by zero

There are many zero numbers in a database for CGE modelling. For example, a MAKE matrix (or supply table) is an *n*-by-*n* matrix showing the quantity of *n* types of commodities produced by *n* industries. Theoretically, each industry can produce all *n* types of commodities, but in reality, one industry only produces a few of *n* types of commodities. This will lead to many zero numbers in the MAKE matrix. When the equation is designed to calculate the percentage change of outputs in the MAKE matrix, the dividing by zero will occur to the zero numbers in the MAKE matrix. This will cause an infinity number and, when the model is run by GEMPACK, the model will stop with an error. The GEMPACK provides different ways to solve this problem.

For a level equation or a formula, a 'zerodivide' command can be used to avoid dividing by zero. Before the start of the level equation or formula, you can set a default value for Zerodivide. This command will assign a default value specified when the denominator is of zero value. After the level equation or formula, you need to cancel the default setting by a command 'zerodivide off;', shown in the following example.

```
Zerodivide default 0.5;
Formula
 (all,c,COM)(all,i,IND) V1PUR_S(c,i) = sum{s,SRC, V1PUR(c,s,i)};
 (all,c,COM)(all,s,SRC)(all,i,IND) S1(c,s,i) = V1PUR(c,s,i) /
  V1PUR_S(c,i);
Zerodivide off;
```

In this example, the command 'Zerodivide default 0.5;' will set a value of 0.5 for all S1(c,s,i) when the value for coefficient V1PUR_S(c,i) is zero, so that the dividing-by-zero problem is avoided. The command in the last line cancels out the default setting so that the zerodivide setting will not interfere with other level equations or formulas.

For a linear (or percentage change) equation, the dividing-by-zero problem can be avoided by adding a coefficient or a function. You can introduce a coefficient and assign it with a very small value, for example, 0.00000000001. When you suspect there may be a dividing-by-zero problem in an equation, you can add this coefficient to that equation. The following is an example of this approach.

```
Coefficient
      TINY # Small number to prevent zerodivides or singular matrix #;
Formula
       TINY = 0.000000000001;
Equation
E_p1lab_o # Price to each industry of labour composite #
 (all,i,IND)[TINY+V1LAB_O(i)]*p1lab_o(i) = sum{o,OCC, V1LAB(i,o)
*p1lab(i,o)};
```

In this example, any zero values in V1LAB_O(i) will be replaced by TINY so the dividing-by-zero issue can be avoided. However, this way of avoiding zerodivide can cause inaccuracy because the value of TINY will be added to any values of V1LAB_O(i), no matter the original values are zero or non-zero. To minimize the inaccuracy caused by the introduction of TINY, the value for TINY must be very small. The other way to avoid inaccuracy is to use a function called ID01 or ID0V. Both ID01 and ID0V will not change any non-zero value, but ID01 will replace the zero values with 1 while ID0V will replace zero values with value V as you specified, for example,

```
Equation E_p1mat # Intermediate cost price index #
 (all,i,IND)
  p1mat(i) = sum{c,COM, sum{s,SRC, (V1PUR(c,s,i)/ID01[V1MAT(i)])
*p1(c,s,i)}};
```

In this example, any zero values in V1MAT(i) will be replaced by 1, but any non-zero values in V1MAT(i) will not be altered.

2.3.2 Creating a HAR File

HAR files stand for header array files, which are the format of database file recognized by GEMPACK. Database in other format must be transferred to har files in order to use GEMPACK to conduct a simulation. Header array files are binary files, so they cannot be printed or edited directly in a text editor. GEMPACK provides a number of programs for accessing them; for example, ViewHAR can be used to view and modify a HAR file, SeeHAR can translate HAR files to various text formats, and ModHAR can modify a HAR file in batch or under the Linux system. For a novice modeller, it is sufficient if you know how to transfer data from the spreadsheets to a har file.

After running the WinGEM program, on the top of your computer screen you can find WINGEM menu, in which there is an item called 'HA files'. When you click on this item and select the 'view ViewHAR' in the drop-down panel, the viewHAR interface appears. Likewise, when you click on the 'File' menu in this interface, you can choose 'open a har or SL4 file' or choose 'create new file', and then six items will appear under the main har menu: 'Header', 'Type', 'Dimension', 'Coeff', 'Total', and 'Name' (see Fig. 2.6). These items are the elements of a header, the way the GEMPACK organizes data.

(1) Creating sets

As described in Sect. 2.3.1, 'creating a TAB file', the range that the data encompass is called a 'set' in GEMPACK, for example, the number of commodities, industries, regions, and so on. To create a database in a HAR file, we need to create the sets first.

When you click on the 'sets' in the har file main menu and select 'create new set' item in the drop-down panel, a new interface named 'create new set' appears. On this interface are a few items which require you to put some information in: that is, 'Name' means the set name to

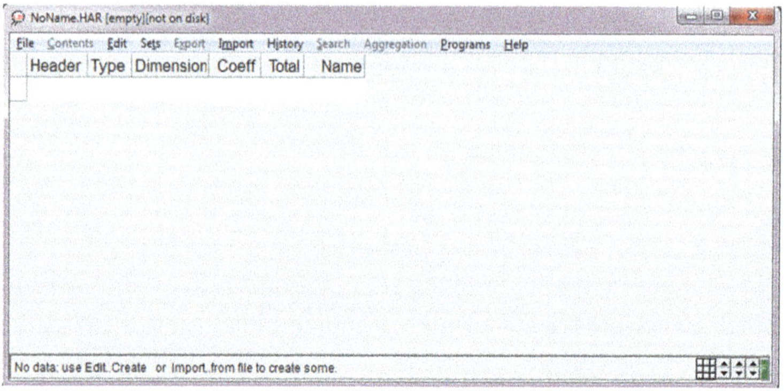

Fig. 2.6 ViewHAR interface

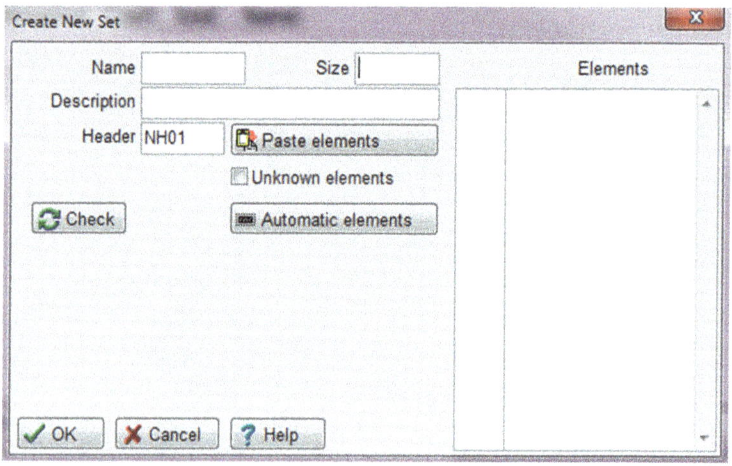

Fig. 2.7 Interface of 'create new set'

specify (e.g. industry); 'Size' means the number of elements in the set (e.g. 35 industries in the industry set); 'Description' gives you a place to describe the set because the set name only allows for maximum 12 characters; and 'Header' means the unique header name for the set (e.g. IND) as only four characters are allowed for the header name (see Fig. 2.7).

The last item is 'Elements', that is, the elements of the set. The 'elements' part can be filled using the 'Automatic elements' button. If you have put '35' for 'size' and then clicked on the 'Automatic elements' button, you will have 35 elements in the 'elements' box. However, these elements are not very meaningful, so it is better to type the names of the industries directly into the 'elements' box, or use the 'Paste elements' button to copy and paste the industry names from a spreadsheet. Set name and elements names are limited to a maximum of 12 characters and must start with a letter. Once you have filled in the required information, you can click on the 'Check' button to find out if the information format is right. Once everything is correct, you can click on the 'OK' button. Then, a new header appears on the har file interface. This means you have successfully created a new set.

(2) Create headers

Once all sets necessary for your database are created, you can create headers which will contain the data for your model. And once you click on 'Edit' button in the har file main menu and select 'create new header' in the drop-down panel, a new interface 'create new header' appears (see Fig. 2.8). There is a choice of header type on the top-left of the interface: Real[RE], Integer[2I], and String[1C]. Usually the default choice Real [RE] is needed for your header.

A number of boxes need filling. A 'four-character header' requires you to fill in a qualified header name. 'Default value' allows you to assign default data for the header. 'Coeff name' asks you to give a coefficient

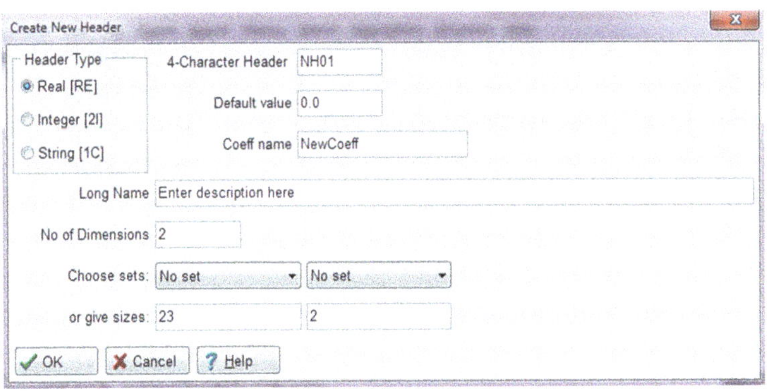

Fig. 2.8 Interface of 'create headers'

name for the header. This name is limited by a maximum of 12 characters. 'Long name' gives you an opportunity to provide a long name to aid memory. 'No of Dimensions' indicates the dimension of the header. By default, there are two dimensions, so there are two selection boxes after the 'Choose sets' beneath the 'No. of dimensions'. If you change the 'No. of dimensions' to three, there will be three selection boxes after the 'Choose sets'. If you click on the drop-down arrows in the selection boxes, the names of sets you have created appear in the drop-down list. Likewise, once you select the correct ones for your header, the size of sets will automatically fill in the box next to the 'or give size'. For example, if your header is going to contain the industry i's input demand for commodity c from source s, you can select sets 'COM', 'SRC', and 'IND' for your header. Once all information is filled in, you can click on the 'OK' button and finish the procedure of creating a new header.

Now you have a new header. By clicking on the header you have created, you can see that a matrix with the default value you specified appears (see Fig. 2.9). There are some selectable boxes beneath the har file main menu. At the very left is a small yellow rectangular area. By clicking on this, you can transpose the matrix (i.e. pivot the table). Next to the yellow area is a small green area. Similarly, when you click on this, then a drop-down panel appears, which allows you to select different display options, for example, 'normal', 'sparse sorted', 'levels with share' and 'hide zero rows and columns'. Next to the green area is a selectable box allowing you to display the shares of rows, columns, or a matrix. The next drop-down box allows you to decide the number of decimal places. There are a few selectable boxes on the right corner. The number of these boxes is equal to the number of dimensions of the header. For example, for a three-dimensional header (commodity*source* industry), there will be three selectable boxes on the top-right corner. On selecting 'all com', 'imp' (i.e. the imported commodities), and 'all ind', the matrix of imported commodities to industries appears on the interface.

The next task is to import the data from the spreadsheet into the header. This is a very simple cut-and-paste procedure, but it needs to be done very carefully. If the commodity type and industry type are 33, the matrix of imports mentioned above will be a 33 * 33 matrix. You can select in the spreadsheet the 33 * 33 matrix and click on the

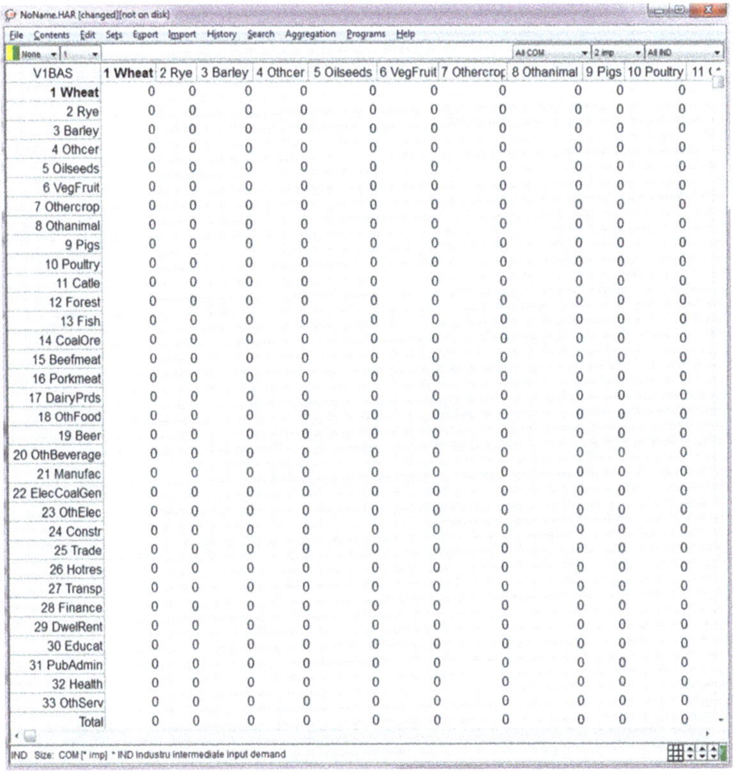

V1BAS	1 Wheat	2 Rye	3 Barley	4 Othcer	5 Oilseeds	6 VegFruit	7 Othercrop	8 Othanimal	9 Pigs	10 Poultry
1 Wheat	0	0	0	0	0	0	0	0	0	0
2 Rye	0	0	0	0	0	0	0	0	0	0
3 Barley	0	0	0	0	0	0	0	0	0	0
4 Othcer	0	0	0	0	0	0	0	0	0	0
5 Oilseeds	0	0	0	0	0	0	0	0	0	0
6 VegFruit	0	0	0	0	0	0	0	0	0	0
7 Othercrop	0	0	0	0	0	0	0	0	0	0
8 Othanimal	0	0	0	0	0	0	0	0	0	0
9 Pigs	0	0	0	0	0	0	0	0	0	0
10 Poultry	0	0	0	0	0	0	0	0	0	0
11 Catle	0	0	0	0	0	0	0	0	0	0
12 Forest	0	0	0	0	0	0	0	0	0	0
13 Fish	0	0	0	0	0	0	0	0	0	0
14 CoalOre	0	0	0	0	0	0	0	0	0	0
15 Beefmeat	0	0	0	0	0	0	0	0	0	0
16 Porkmeat	0	0	0	0	0	0	0	0	0	0
17 DairyPrds	0	0	0	0	0	0	0	0	0	0
18 OthFood	0	0	0	0	0	0	0	0	0	0
19 Beer	0	0	0	0	0	0	0	0	0	0
20 OthBeverage	0	0	0	0	0	0	0	0	0	0
21 Manufac	0	0	0	0	0	0	0	0	0	0
22 ElecCoalGen	0	0	0	0	0	0	0	0	0	0
23 OthElec	0	0	0	0	0	0	0	0	0	0
24 Constr	0	0	0	0	0	0	0	0	0	0
25 Trade	0	0	0	0	0	0	0	0	0	0
26 Hotres	0	0	0	0	0	0	0	0	0	0
27 Transp	0	0	0	0	0	0	0	0	0	0
28 Finance	0	0	0	0	0	0	0	0	0	0
29 DwelRent	0	0	0	0	0	0	0	0	0	0
30 Educat	0	0	0	0	0	0	0	0	0	0
31 PubAdmin	0	0	0	0	0	0	0	0	0	0
32 Health	0	0	0	0	0	0	0	0	0	0
33 OthServ	0	0	0	0	0	0	0	0	0	0
Total	0	0	0	0	0	0	0	0	0	0

Fig. 2.9 Interface of a har file header with default value

'Copy' icon (or press Ctrl+C on your keyboard). Then on the har file interface, click on the 'Import' button and select the third option, 'Paste to screen from Clipboard Ctrl+V'; the data selected in the spreadsheet will be pasted to the har file. Two cautions must be taken to make sure the data are imported correctly. One is that the size of the matrix in the spreadsheet must be exactly the same as that in the har file (e.g. 33 * 33 in the previous example). Second, for a square matrix, the direction of the table in the spreadsheet must be the same as that in the har file. For example, for the imports matrix above, if the table in the har file is com*industry (commodity in each row and industry in each column), the table in the spreadsheet must be the same. Otherwise, the data will be imported incorrectly.

(3) Creating mapping and aggregate data

It is common that the original data are more disaggregated, that is, there are a large number of industries, commodities, regions, and so on. To reduce the computing burden and be focused on the research question, the original data need aggregating. ViewHAR provides a convenient function for this purpose.

Prior to aggregation, you need to create the sets for disaggregate data and for aggregate data. For example, if you want to aggregate 131 industries to 33 industries, you must have a set of size 131 (e.g. a set named IND0) and a set of size 33 (e.g. a set named IND). Then you need to create a mapping. When you click on 'aggregation' in the har file main menu and select 'Create mappings', a new interface appears (see Fig. 2.10).

When you input the name for mapping and for header on the top of the interface and click on the box beneath 'from source set', the names of all set you have created appear in the drop-down box. Now if you select

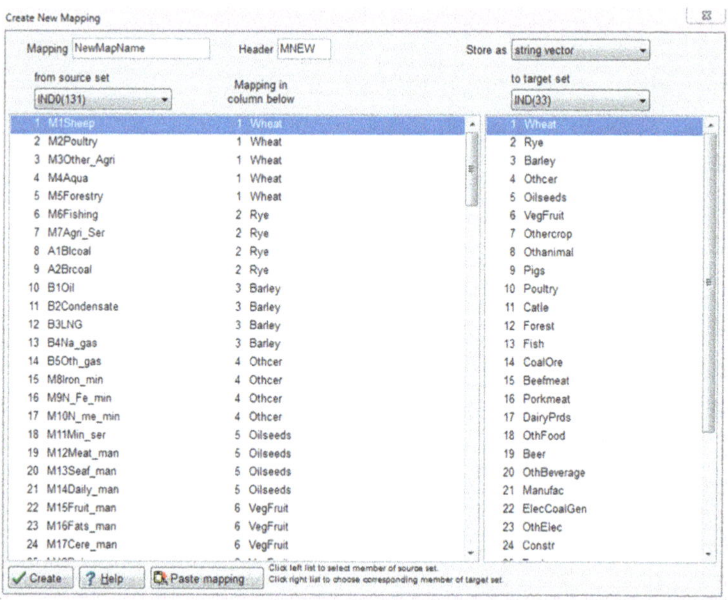

Fig. 2.10 The interface of 'create mappings'

the set 'IND0', the 131 elements of this set will appear in the left column of the textbox below the selectable box under 'from source set'. At the right of the interface, there is a selectable box beneath the words 'to target set'. Once you click on the box and select the set 'IND' in the drop-down panel, the 33 elements of set INDA appear in the textbox below the selectable box. ViewHAR will mechanically provide a mapping, which is shown in the second column in the textbox on the left. In this case, the industry 1, 2, 3, 4, 5 in set IND0 will be mapped to industry 1 in set IND, industries 6, 7, 8, 9 in set IND0 will be mapped to industry 2 in set IND, and so on.

You can change this mechanical mapping by highlighting a row in the left box and then select in the right box an intended element as a targeted mapping element. However, this procedure is time-consuming. Alternatively, you can make a mapping in a spreadsheet, select the mapping and click on the 'Copy' icon in the spreadsheet (or press Ctrl+C on the keyboard), and then click the 'Paste mapping' button on the aggregation interface. In this way, the mapping in the spreadsheet will be copied into the mapping interface. Once you have checked if the mapping is as you have designed, click on the 'Create' button; soon the mapping will be created and there will be a mapping header added to the har file.

Once all mappings are created, for example, mapping of 131 industries to 33 industries, mapping of 131 commodities to 33 commodities, mapping of 11 margins to 4 margins, and so on, you can aggregate your data very easily. When you click on the 'Aggregation' option in the har file main menu and select 'choose mappings', all the mappings you have created will appear on the new interface. Figure 2.11 shows five mappings created in a HAR file.

When the mapping are created, tick the boxes next to mappings suitable for your aggregation and then click on the 'create aggregated file'. The database will be aggregated. There are two checkboxes below the 'Create aggregated file' button. You can check them to include un-aggregated items and/or retain original set names, or uncheck them otherwise. It is strongly suggested that you retain a copy of the original har file prior to aggregation.

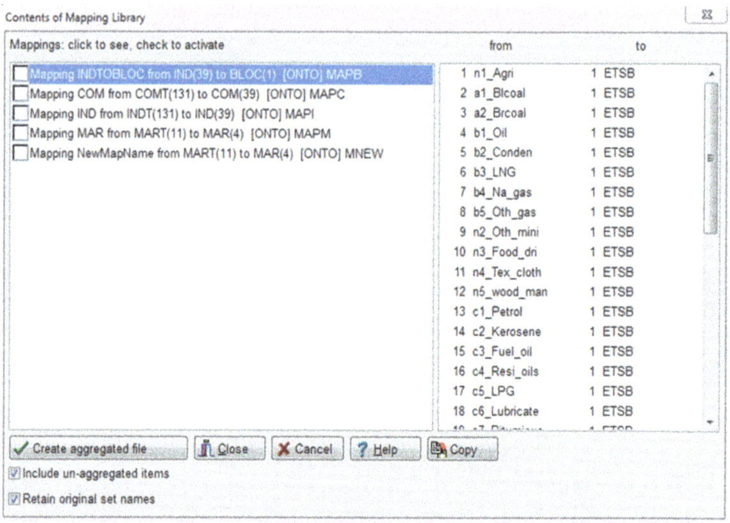

Fig. 2.11 The interface of data aggregation

2.3.3 Creating a CMF File

A CMF file contains information on simulation instruction, simulation environment, and the closure for simulation. We describe the components of a CMF file here.

(1) Assigning useful but optional tasks when performing simulation

Many useful options can be included in a CMF file to provide important information on simulation procedure. The often used commands are:

```
check-on-read elements = warn; ! very often needed
cpu=yes ; ! (Optional) Reports CPU times for various stages
log file = yes; ! Optional
auxiliary files = oz05; ! needed by GEMSIM
```

The first line of command requests that the computer checks the data when the 'read' command in the TABLO file is performed. The computer can provide a warning message if there are issues related to the 'read' command. The second line of command tells the computer to report the CPU time used for various stages of simulation. The third line tells the computer to provide a log file to the simulation. This log file is very useful in identifying problems when the simulation finishes with an error. The last line shows the auxiliary file name if the Tablo is compiled, is necessary for a GEMSIM, but not necessary for Fortran or Tablo-generated (TG) programs. The texts after each '!' of the line are optional notes (or comments) to aid the human reader. The use of '!' here is slightly different from the case of the TABLO file, where a pair of '!'s are needed for a comments. The other difference is that, the codes in a CMF file are not constrained by the rule of a maximum of 80 characters per line.

(2) Specifying the input and output database name

In a TABLO file, the file names for databases are already specified. However, these file names are not necessarily the names of your database used for modelling. The file names in a TAB file are logic names, or aliases. In a CMF file, these logic names are linked to the true database file name. For example, the following commands tell the computer the databases corresponding to the logic names specified in the TABLO file:

```
filc basedata – OZ05.har;
updated file basedata =OZ05.upd;
file summary = OZ05summary.har;
```

It looks an unnecessary burden to use logic names in the TABLO file and then use commands in a CMF file to link the logic names to the true file names. However, this approach allows greater flexibility for a model. Because the logic name in the TABLO file does not necessarily match the true database name, a model (the EXE file generated from a TAB file) can be implemented with different database. In other words, when we change a database or change the name of a database, we only need to change the CMF file—there is no need to change the model.

(3) Specifying the solution method.

There are mainly three types of solution methods in GEMPACK: the Johansen method, the Gragg method, and the Euler method. You can specify the solution method by

```
method = Johansen;
or
method = GRAGG;
steps = 3 5 7;
or
method = EULER;
steps = 2 4 6;
```

Johansen method is a one-step simulation, so it will cause considerable linearization errors when the shocks are large. This method can be used only when the shocks are very small. On the other hand, the Euler method and Gragg method are multi-step solution methods, which can minimize the linearization errors.

(4) Specifying simulation closure

A CGE model is basically a large equation system to solve for a number of variables. Usually the number of variables is greater than the number of equations; this makes the attempt to obtain a solution impossible. To solve the equation system, the number of equations must equal the number of endogenous variables, so some variables must be set as exogenous, that is, be set as given values (usually zeros). Because of the large number of equations and variables in a CGE model, pairing equations and variables involve a significant amount of work. TABmate provides a useful tool to match equations and variables. If you have included a variable name in each equation identifier, all equations will be matched by variables. The rest of the variables will be unmatched and become exogenous in the automatic closure. The following is an automatic closure for ORANI-G.

```
! Automatic closure generated by TABmate Tools...Closure command
!              Variable   Size
Exogenous         a1 ; ! COM*SRC*IND  Intermediate basic tech change
Exogenous       a1cap ; ! IND  Capital-augmenting technical change
Exogenous      a1lab_o ; ! IND  Labor-augmenting technical change
Exogenous       a1lnd ; ! IND  Land-augmenting technical change
Exogenous       a1mar ; ! COM*SRC*IND*MAR  margin tech change
Exogenous      a1oct ; ! IND  "Other cost" ticket augmenting techncal
change
Exogenous      a1prim ; ! IND  All factor augmenting technical change
Exogenous       a1tot ; ! IND  All input augmenting technical change
Exogenous          a1_s ; ! COM*IND   Tech change, intmdiate imp/dom
composite
Exogenous         a2 ; ! COM*SRC*IND  Investment basic tech change
Exogenous         a2mar ; ! COM*SRC*IND*MAR  Investment margin tech
change
Exogenous       a2tot ; ! IND  Neutral technical change - investment
Exogenous          a2_s ; ! COM*IND  Tech change, investment imp/dom
composite
Exogenous         a3 ; ! COM*SRC  Household basic taste change
Exogenous       a3mar ; ! COM*SRC*MAR  Household margin tech change
Exogenous      a3_s ; ! COM*HOU Taste change, hhold imp/dom composite
Exogenous       a4mar ; ! COM*MAR  Export margin tech change
Exogenous       a5mar ; ! COM*SRC*MAR  Governmnt margin tech change
Exogenous     capslack ; ! 1  Slack variable to allow fixing aggregate
capital
Exogenous    delPTXRATE ; ! IND  Change in rate of production tax
Exogenous      f0tax_s ; ! COM  General sales tax shifter
Exogenous       f1lab ; ! IND*OCC  Wage shift variable
Exogenous      f1lab_i ; ! OCC  Occupation-specific wage shifter
Exogenous     f1lab_io ; ! 1  Overall wage shifter
Exogenous      f1lab_o ; ! IND  Industry-specific wage shifter
Exogenous       f1oct ; ! IND  Shift in price of "other cost" tickets
Exogenous     f1tax_csi ; ! 1  % change in powers of taxes on interme-
diate usage
Exogenous    f2tax_csi ; ! 1  % change in powers of taxes on investment
Exogenous     f3tax_cs ; ! 1  % change in powers of taxes on household
usage
Exogenous          f4p ; ! COM  Price (upward) shift in export demand
schedule
```

```
Exogenous    f4p_ntrad ; ! 1  Upward demand shift, collective export
aggregate
Exogenous      f4q ; ! COM  Quantity (right) shift in export demands
Exogenous    f4q_ntrad ; ! 1  Right demand shift, collective export
aggregate
Exogenous     f4tax_ntrad ; ! 1   % change in powers of taxes on
nontradtnl exports
Exogenous    f4tax_trad ; ! 1  % change in powers of taxes on tradtnl
exports
Exogenous      f5 ; ! COM*SRC  Government demand shift
Exogenous    f5tax_cs ; ! 1  % change in powers of taxes on government
usage
Exogenous     f5tot2 ; ! 1  Ratio between f5tot and x3tot
Exogenous      fx6 ; ! COM*SRC  Shifter on rule for stocks
Exogenous    invslack ; ! 1  Investment slack variable
Exogenous     pf0cif ; ! COM  C.I.F. foreign currency import prices
Exogenous      phi ; ! 1  Exchange rate, local currency/$world
Exogenous      qh ; ! HOU  Number of households
Exogenous     t0imp ; ! COM  Power of tariff
Exogenous     w3luxh ; ! HOU  Nominal luxury consumption
Exogenous     x1cap ; ! IND  Current capital stock
Exogenous     x1lnd ; ! IND  Use of land
Exogenous     x2tot ; ! IND  Investment by using industry
Rest endogenous; ! end of TABmate automatic closure
```

Making a workable closure is a challenge for most novice modellers. On this front, the automatic closure will help a lot. However, for various reasons, the automatic closure may be incorrect and the simulation will stop with a message 'E - Error in batch mode' and the log file will report that environment is not ok for using and show how many variables are mismatched. In this case, you need to check the closure file generated by TABmate to find which variables are unmatched and need to be put into the closure.

Even if the automatic closure is working, in many cases, the automatic closure is not exactly what you wanted. For example, in the above closure, the exchange rate is exogenous (it is on the exogenous list) and CPI is endogenous (it is not on the exogenous list). However, you may want to shock consumer price index - CPI (e.g. 10 % increase in CPI). In this case, you need to use a 'swap' command by adding a line in the CMF file:

```
Swap phi=CPI;
```

This command can set phi endogenous and set CPI exogenous; then you can impose a shock on CPI.

(5) Imposing shocks and describing the simulation

Shocks to a model are an amount of change imposed on certain variables. By definition, the values for endogenous variables are determined by the model, so it is impossible to shock an endogenous variable. A shock to a model is imposed by the 'shock' command in the CMF file. To aid the human reader, a description of shocks (or simulation) is provided by 'verbal description' command. A currency appreciation simulation in ORANI-G is prescribed by the following commands:

```
verbal description = ORANIG: currency appreciation, DPSV short run
closure;
shock phi=-5;
```

The first line reminds the reader the purpose of simulation and the second line shows that a 5 % appreciation of home currency (or 5 % depreciation of foreign currency) is imposed for the simulation.

2.3.4 Creating an STI File

STI files or stored input files are text files storing a series of procedures for simulation. These files are normally used by experienced modellers. However, an STI file may include model condensation information and is relevant to model closure specification, so we briefly discuss STI files in relation to model condensation.

If your model passes 'TABLO check' in TABmate, you can run 'TABLO code' toolbox at the top of TABmate interface. Then you can click on the 'Tool' menu and select 'closure' in the drop-down panel.

The closure file is loaded into TABmate. In Sect. 6 'condensation suggestions' of the closure file, backsolving and omitting commands are introduced to reduce the number of variables and equations in the model. You can put the correct format of these commands into the tab file or into an STI file. When condensation is used, the omitted and backsolved variables must be excluded from the exogenous variable list in model closure. If you put the omitted and backsolved variables into the TAB file, you can get the right closure simply by rerunning 'tablo code' to generate a new automatic closure.

When your TAB file is open in TABmate, you can generate an STI file by clicking on the toolbox 'TABLO STI' in the TABmate interface. The STI file is normally stored in the same directory as that of the TAB file. Then, you can click on the 'Simulation' option in the WINGEM main menu and select the 'TABLO implement' option in the drop-down panel, and a new interface appears. When you click on the 'Option' menu in the new interface and select 'run from STI files' in the drop-down panel, the interface asks you to select a stored-input file. Then if you click on the 'Select' button, the STI file will appear on a new interface if you have saved the STI file in the default directory. And when you double-click on the STI file, the new interface disappears and the file is loaded on to the previous interface. When you click on the 'RUN' button, the model will be condensed. Once you follow the instruction 'go to GEMSIM' or 'go to compile and link', you can start the procedure to run a simulation. It is important that you make sure that the closure in the command file has not included any variables in the STI file because these variables are omitted or backsolved.

References

Codsi, G., & Pearson, K. (1988). GEMPACK: A General Purpose Software for Applied General Equilibrium and Other Economic Modellers. *Computer Science in Economics and Management, 1*, 189–207.

Dixon, P., Parmenter, B., Sutton, J., & Vincent, D. (1982). *ORANI: A Multisectoral Model of the Australian Economy*. Amsterdam: North Holland Publishing.

Hertel, T., Horridge, J., & Pearson, K. (1992). Mending the Family Tree: A Reconciliation of the Linearization and Levels School of AGE Modelling. *Economic Modelling, 9*, 385–407.

Johansen, L. (1960). *A Multisectoral Study of Economic Growth*. Amsterdam: North-Holland.

Keller, W. (1980). *Tax Incidence: A General Equilibrium Approach*. Amsterdam: North-Holland.

Preckel, P. (1988). *NCPLU Version 2.2 User's Guide*, Unpublished Paper. West Lafayette, Indiana: Department of Agricultural Economic, Purdue University.

3

Application of CGE Modelling to Tourism

3.1 Suitability of a CGE Model in Tourism Analysis

Due to the features of tourism, CGE modelling is very useful for tourism studies, especially for impact analysis.

It is well known that tourism demand is very volatile, so studies on tourism demand are very important. The tendency and ability of tourists to visit a place are related not only to their tastes, income, and health, but also to the marketing strategy, tourism policies, and sports and cultural events in the destination countries (regions). All these elements can be put into a CGE model to evaluate their influences on tourism demand.

Tourism activities will generate considerable income to destinations. When this income is spent by households it will further increase demand for goods and services and thus will stimulate the economy of the tourism destination. However, the increased demand may also cause a demand-pulled inflation, which will have profound impact on the economy. To analyse this kind of economy-wide impact is the strength of CGE modelling.

Tourism demand for goods and services has large employment effect and strong backward inter-industry linkage. A large part of tourism

S. Meng, M. Siriwardana, *Assessing the Economic Impact of Tourism*,
DOI 10.1007/978-3-319-40328-1_3

demand is catered by services industries such as sightseeing, hotels, restaurants, local transportation, health care, education, and so on. These service industries are largely labour intensive, so the tourism demand can generate considerable employment opportunities in the destination region. The tourism service sectors need to purchase goods and services from manufacturing industries and other service industries. This strong backward linkage means that tourism demand can generate large ripple effects from downstream to upstream industries. Tourism shopping items are generally high value-added and are strongly linked to upstream industries. This further enhances the employment linkage and inter-industry linkage, which can easily be gauged using a CGE model.

3.2 Assessing the Impact of Tourism Demand and Tourism Policy

Partly because it has long been a world leader in developing CGE analyses, Australia seems to be the pioneer in applying CGE analysis to tourism and so far has done significantly more CGE modelling in tourism than any other countries. As early as 1988, the Centre for International Economics (CIE 1988) used a CGE approach to analyse the impact of tourism on the economy. In 1989, the Industries Assistance Commission (IAC 1989) used a CGE model to investigate travel and tourism. In the early 1990s, the Bureau of Tourism Research commissioned a CGE analysis of the economic impact of tourism (Adams and Parmenter 1991, 1992). In 1993, Skene used a CGE model to explore the impacts of tourism on employment (Skene 1993a, b). In 1996, the successor body to the IAC, the Industry Commission, used the ORANI model to explore the economic impact of tourism and events (IC 1996a, b). From the later 1990s onwards, there are a considerable number of studies on tourism using CGE modelling both within and outside Australia.

A majority of the research has focused on the economic impact of tourism demand (or tourism expenditure) and tourism policy. These studies demonstrate that an increase in tourism demand will have a positive effect on the economy as a whole, although it will negatively affect some industries, and also that changes in tourism policy will affect the economic performance and social welfare of the tourism destination.

The early work outside Australia was done by Zhou et al. (1997) in the USA, using both an I–O model and a CGE model to analyse the economic effect of a decline of tourism demand in Hawaii. The assumptions of the CGE model were a competitive economy which included utility maximization in consumption, cost minimization in production, zero pure profit, and market clearance; a small open economy in terms of imports, which was consistent with the fact that the Hawaii's market transactions did not affect the world prices on imported goods; the Armington assumption which implied imperfect substitution between import and domestic goods in demand; sectorally fixed capital in the short run and mobile capital with full employment in the long run. In both models, a 10 % decline in visitor expenditures reduced output in tourism sectors, such as hotels, transportation, and restaurants and bars, with smaller reductions in output for the other sectors. While these output changes were of the same order of magnitude for both models, the CGE results show smaller changes. As a result, Zhou et al. (1997) concluded that the I–O model tended to exaggerate the effect of tourism demand and that the CGE model had advantages over the I–O model because of the ability of the CGE model to account for the resource flows between sectors in the face of changes in prices.

The effect of tourism at Fort Collins—a small city in Colorado, was considered by Burnett et al. (2007). They used a CGE model to examine the impact of a tourism expansion. The model assumed zero investment constraint because the economy could draw resources from 'foreign' savings. It also treated land and capital differently and separated households into six groups. The simulation results showed that the tourism industry contributed the most to the gross city products (counterpart of gross domestic products) per acre and household income per acre. However, crowding out (outflow of labour and capital) occurred in the sectors that employed the highest number of low-wage workers. The positive effects of tourism were offset by the effect of crowding out and thus the conclusions were that tourism expansion could achieve little economic growth.

At the national level in the USA, the economic impacts of tourism were demonstrated by Blake et al. (2001). They used an I–O model and a CGE model to estimate the effects of a 10 % increase in foreign tourist expenditures. At the economy level, they found that while the I–O model estimated a $9.4 billion increase in GDP, the CGE model only suggested a $6.0 billion increase. At the sector level, the CGE model suggested that some tourism and travel sectors such as hotels and accommodation, eating and drinking establishments, air transport, and bus and other local transport had significantly higher increases in output than in the I–O model; and other tourism and travel sectors such as water and rail transport had a lower output increase than the I–O model suggested. Non-tourism industries had a decline in sector output in the CGE model while the I–O model continued to suggest an output increase. Blake et al. (2001) also modelled the effects of replacing indirect taxes with direct taxes, removing taxation in individual sectors and a 10 % increase in air transport productivity. It was found that replacing all indirect taxes with direct taxes led to a GDP increase of $528.4 billion or 2.1 % of GDP in 1997. At the sector level, it was claimed that indirect taxes led to a higher welfare loss than the tax revenue raised in a range of sectors such as recreation and entertainment, auto and truck rental, and retail margin, while in some sectors, such as hotel and lodging establishments, and water and air transport, the welfare loss was much smaller. They also found that a 10 % increase in air transport productivity resulted in a $2.0 billion output increase for the sector and, for the economy as a whole, a $20.6 billion increase in GDP.

Blake (2000) analysed the effects of an increase in tourism and the effects of tourism taxation in Spain. A 49-sector single-country static CGE model was built under the assumption of perfect competition, constant returns to scale, perfectly mobile factors of production, and market clearing in all goods and factor markets. The results showed that a 10 % increase in tourism demand would increase welfare of the destination country by 28 billion Pesetas (0.05 % of GDP) in the long term. They also concluded that raising the tax rates on foreign tourism would increase welfare of destination residents and that the welfare benefits for taxing tourism were more sensitive to tax policy, compared with the tourism demand elasticity.

The small island economies in the European Union (EU) such as Cyprus, Malta, and Mauritius caught the attention of Sinclair et al. (2003). In their paper, a CGE model was employed to quantify the impacts of changes in tourism demand and tourism tax policies on macroeconomic variables and welfare. The model mimicked the real world taxation system by assuming that the government received tax revenue from tax payments and from abroad, spent its revenue on public consumption goods, and transferred the remainder to households, of which a higher proportion of the transfers were directed to the poor than to the rich. The welfare effect was measured by the equivalent variation (EV)—a monetary measure of the change in consumers' real income. With a 10 % increase in tourism demand in the short run, the authors found an increase in GDP—0.6 % for Malta, 0.16 % for Cyprus, and 0.1 % for Mauritius. The increases in GDP in the long run were: 0.5 % for Malta, 0.3 % for Cyprus, and 0.05 % for Mauritius. The reason for the smaller long-run effects for Malta and Mauritius was attributed to the fact that, in the long run, Malta and Mauritius were subject to some crowding-out effects due to labour constraints. They also found that an increase in tourism demand had a positive influence on employment as well as welfare. An increase in the tourism tax (e.g. 15 % value-added tax on restaurants and accommodation) led to a reduction in tourism expenditure, a decrease in GDP, but an increase in destination welfare and in government revenue in all three countries. Under the assumption that a higher proportion of transfer income was directed to poor households, income distribution improved as a result of higher government revenue.

Tourism in Mauritius was also of special interest to Gooroochurn (2004). Gooroochurn used the Ramsey model of optimal commodity taxation and a single-country static CGE model to investigate the efficiency and equity effects of tourism taxation in Mauritius. To evaluate the equity effects, households in the CGE model were classified into eight groups according to income level. Government consumption was treated as a standard demand instead of public goods because of the unavailability of data on the valuation of public goods, and it was assumed fixed to avoid a reduction in welfare of the household sector stemming from the effect of crowding out of private consumption. Foreign savings were also exogenously fixed and the exchange rate brought trade to equilibrium under the small country assumption. Gooroochurn claimed that both analyses confirmed that taxing tourism is more efficient than taxing other sectors and has positive equity effects. The higher efficiency of taxing tourism was attributed to the relatively less elastic demand of tourists and the irrelevance of loss of consumer surplus of international tourists in measuring social welfare. Taxing tourism has positive equity effects because most tourism products are classified as luxury goods and domestic consumption of these goods comes mostly from individuals in the higher income brackets. Gooroochurn and Blake (2004) used a CGE model to further investigate welfare effect of tourism in Mauritius. The simulation results suggested that, with increasing returns to scale in the export-oriented sectors, a tourism boom resulted in lower welfare gains and tended to cause immiserization. On the other hand, when increasing returns to scale was the feature of the tourism-related and non-tradable sectors, a tourism boom resulted in a higher increase in welfare. Under different trade policies, the effects of tourism booms were complicated. With a higher import tariff, a tourism boom led to a higher welfare gain, while import subsidies tended to cause immiserizing growth.

In Africa, Kweka (2004) considered the impact of tourism in Tanzania's economy. A 23-sector static CGE model for the Tanzanian economy was built. The model assumed intersectoral mobility but fixed total supply of primary factors, fixed domestic and foreign savings, a fixed trade balance, and full employment. Tourist expenditure in the model is depicted by a constant elasticity of substitution (CES) function which allows a limited degree of substitution between the goods and services consumed by tourists. Kweka used an SAM for 1992 to calibrate the CGE model and the simulation results showed that, in terms of increases in real GDP, total welfare, and exports, the effect of tourism expansion on the economy was substantial. The study also found that an improvement of infrastructure amplified the effects of tourism expansion and that tourism taxation had a positive effect on tax revenue and welfare.

Mabugu (2002) analysed the effects of tourism policy reform in Zimbabwe. An eight-sector single-country static CGE model was built. The model was an extension of his previous CGE model of the Zimbabwean economy (Mabugu 2001), in that it disaggregated the tourism sector, incorporated tax into the model, and updated the base year. Capital was assumed sector specific but labour mobile across sectors because the focus was on the short-run effects. The conclusions from five simulated policy scenarios were that, because of poorly sequenced macroeconomic policies and a negative political climate, tourism bypassed Zimbabwe.

In Southeast Asia, Narayan (2004) estimated the impact of tourism on the Fijian economy. Based on a 35-sector comparative static CGE model, the simulations suggested that a 10 % increase in demand for tourism in Fiji would increase GDP by 0.5 %, real consumption by 0.72 %, and real national welfare by 0.67 %. Based on the simulation results, Narayan concluded that a tourism expansion would give rise to an appreciation of local currency and increases in domestic prices and wage rates. Consequently, the traditional export sectors would experience a contraction. However, the increase in tourism and non-traditional exports would outweigh the fall in traditional exports, so an increase in tourism demand tended to contribute to an improvement in the balance of payments.

Also in Southeast Asia, Sugiyarto et al. (2003) used a CGE model to study the economic impact of tourism and globalization in Indonesia. The model classified production activities into 18 sectors, labour into 8 groups, capital into 5 categories, and households into 10 groups. Export demand for products was disaggregated into two categories: (1) services, which is consumed by foreign tourists, and (2) agriculture and manufacturing, which are traditional exports. The CGE modelling results showed that tourism expansion had favourable results: it amplified the positive effects of globalization and lessened its adverse effects. Predominantly, production increased and welfare improved even further while the adverse effects of globalization on government deficits and the trade balance were reduced.

In Australia, the economic impacts of tourism have interested many researchers. Adams and Parmenter (1991, 1992, 1993, 1995) used a 19-sector CGE model with a simple dynamic structure to examine the economic impact of changes in tourism demand. Their findings illustrated that an increase in tourism demand resulted in an appreciation of the exchange rate. This in turn led to import substitution and a contraction of the traditional export sector of mining and agriculture which caused the balance of trade to worsen. At the sector level, some sectors (e.g. air transport, restaurants, hotels) experienced direct stimulation from increasing tourism demand, others (e.g. food and clothing) experienced indirect stimulation, while some (e.g. traditional exports) contracted. At the regional level, Queensland experienced an overall negative effect due to a crowding-out effect in the traditional export industry. On the other hand, Victoria experienced the largest expansion because it had one of country's principal airports and had little reliance on traditional exports.

Dwyer et al. (2000) considered tourism impacts under different assumptions about factor supplies, exchange rates, government fiscal policy, and the public sector borrowing requirement. Dwyer et al. (2003) used the Monash Multi-Regional Forecasting (MMRF) CGE model to examine the long-run and short-run effects of tourism demand at intrastate, interstate, and national levels. Their results highlighted the importance of domestic tourism demand for New South Wales (NSW) and of international tourism demand for Australia. The simulations also indicated that, in the short run, the most favourable context for economic impacts was a fixed income real wage, fixed national employment, and a fixed government budget deficit. In the long run, the most favourable context for economic impacts was fixed national employment but variable labour supplies at state level accommodated by interstate migration.

Skene (1993a, b) modelled the impact of tourism in Australia. Based on simulation results, he claimed that, with exogenous government borrowing, an increase in tourism demand reduced unemployment and led to an increase in household consumption. His simulations also revealed that, with a 10 % increase in visitor expenditure, unemployment would fall by over 3 % and that real GDP would grow by around 3.7 %. It was also found that an increase in exports outweighed an increase in imports, which resulted in an improvement in the balance of trade.

Madden and Thapa (2000) used a two-region CGE model of Australia to examine the effects of tourism on NSW and the rest of Australia. They measured the economic contribution of tourism to the NSW economy by comparing the difference between the values of the economic variables actually observed (with tourism) and the values that would have been observed in the complete absence of tourism. This was achieved by hypothetically setting foreign demand for Australia as a tourist destination to zero. For domestic tourism the simulation entailed a change in Australian household preferences away from tourism and towards consumption of other goods and services. The simulations indicated that interstate tourism played a major role in the NSW economy: interstate tourists spent \$4.13 billion in NSW, which would generate over \$8 billion gross state product

(GSP), almost $4.5 billion real household consumption and create around 148,000 jobs in NSW. It was also found that the effect of an Australia-wide tourism expansion was mixed: a slight decrease in real GDP, a small increase in real household consumption, and a negligible impact on employment. These results were explained by the fact that compared with the rest of Australia, the NSW economy was less export-oriented, and thus most industries in NSW were negatively affected by a tourism expansion.

3.3 Assessing the Impact of Mega Events on Tourism and on the Economy

Some studies focused on the impact of mega events such as the Olympics, the 9/11 terrorist attacks, and FMD. The estimation of the event effect generally consisted of two parts. First, various methods were employed to estimate the effect of an event on tourism demand; then a CGE model was used to simulate the economic effect of the change in tourism demand. While CGE estimation was not controversial, the accuracy and reliability of the first step—estimation of the change in tourism demand—incurred considerable criticism. In some cases, different scenarios such as high, central, and low changes in tourism expenditures have been included in a study.

There are different types of mega events. Among them, sport seems to have interested researchers most. For example, the Olympics are the most common topic of mega events analysed. Kasimati (2003) provided a review of related research on economic aspects of the summer Olympics. According to Kasimati, by 2002, there were 13 studies analysing seven cases of the modern Olympic games dated between 1984 and 2002; but only two studies of which adopted a CGE modelling approach.

NSW Treasury (1997) estimated the potential economic impact of the Sydney Olympic Games. The MMRF model was used to gauge the effect of increased tourism expenditure which was based on the increase in tourist arrivals and expenditure due to the Olympics as estimated by KPMG (1993). Because of the uncertainty surrounding future tourism spending, the study modelled a central scenario and formed two other scenarios by allowing for variations in the size of the induced tourism export effect and the macroeconomic setting. The study indicated that the Sydney Olympic Games would boost international and intrastate tourism, thus bringing substantial benefits to the economies of Australia as a whole and NSW in particular. The estimated welfare effects of the Olympics to Australians were estimated to be equivalent to over 1 % of annual private consumption while to NSW it was just under 3 %.

Andersen (1999) also modelled the impact of the Sydney 2000 Olympic Games on the Australian economy. The study also employed the MMRF model. To estimate the economic effects, the study introduced three new industries into the Australian economy—international tourism, interstate tourism, and Olympic operations. The study first estimated the direct impact of the Olympics on tourism, and then used the tourism effects as shocks to simulate the economic impact. The study found that, over the Games period 1994–1995 to 2005–2006, the Sydney 2000 Olympics would generate extra economic activity of $6.5 billion in Australia, of which $5.1 billion would occur in NSW. The model also indicated that the Sydney 2000 Olympic Games would create 5300 jobs in NSW and 2200 jobs in the other states each year in the 12-year Games period.

There have been a number of more recent studies conducted on Olympic modelling. Blake (2005) projected the economic impact of the 2012 Olympics in London. First, visitor spending was estimated based on the following four resources: (1) the London 2012 ticket allocation model to provide an estimate of how many tickets would be purchased by different categories of visitors; (2) studies on the likely numbers of visitors given the ticket sales assumption; (3) London 2012 survey on the number of days that each category of visitors would stay in the UK; and (4) estimates of spending per day per visitor. Second, two CGE models were employed to estimate the economic effect—one for the UK and another for London. Again, three scenarios 'low', 'central', and 'high' were adopted due to the uncertainty of future tourism expenditure. The central scenario simulation indicated that, overall, the London 2012 Olympics would have a positive economic effect: over the 2005–2016 periods, an increase of £1936 million in GDP and of 8164 full-time equivalent (FTE) jobs in the UK. The model also showed that the impact mainly occurred in 2012 and in the post-Games period (2013–2016).

Giesecke and Madden (2007) conducted an ex-post assessment of the Sydney Olympics using the MMRF model. To avoid the risk of over-optimistic estimation of the benefits of the Games, they treated the public services supporting the Games as Games-specific inputs, assumed that the national labour market was in full employment, and undertook a historical simulation to uncover the extent of induced tourism. Under these assumptions, they found the Sydney Olympics generated a net consumption loss of about $2.1 billion.

Li et al. (2007) modelled the economic impact of the Beijing Olympics in China. The paper explored the effect of China's economic reform and that of international tourism induced by the Beijing Olympic Games. Based on relevant data from the China National Tourism Administration (CNTA) and using three scenarios (low, medium, and high tourism receipts per visitor per day), the study estimated the increased tourism receipts due to the Beijing Olympic Games. Utilizing the estimated tourism receipts and a 122-industry CGE model of the Chinese economy, the study investigated the interaction between China's economic reform and inbound tourism and it concluded that an inbound tourism expansion would lead to a shift of production towards tertiary industries, which was desirably in the same direction of economic reforms in China. The results also showed that if the economic reforms in China successfully increased total factor productivity, the economic benefit of hosting the Olympic Games would increase.

Some researchers have estimated the economic effects of other sporting events. For example, Narayan (2003) estimated the long-run economic impact of the 2003 South Pacific Games (SPG) for Fiji. The estimated tourism expenditure in the study was based on the estimated results of Chand (2002)—a total of 10,000 visitors would come to Fiji for the SPG. The findings of the paper were that, with an additional 10,000 visitors, Fiji's real GDP would increase by 0.36 % and the real welfare of Fijians by around 0.51 %. The paper also claimed that, with an expansion in tourism, growth in total exports would be larger than the growth in total imports; and that wage rates, private disposable incomes, and real consumption would rise.

The Industry Commission (1996b) estimated the economic impact of the Grand Prix held by Australia. The MMRF model suggested that the projected impacts were very small compared with the overall size of the economies involved. For example, an Adelaide Grand Prix was slightly good for the size of the South Australian economy and slightly bad for the Victorian economy, with a trivial impact on the economy as a whole.

The economic impact of the 2003 Rugby World Cup (RWC) on the Australian economy commissioned by the Department of Industry, Tourism and Resources (DITR), was estimated by URS Finance and Economics (2004). The MMRF results suggested that the 2003 RWC would have contributed to 5 % of Australian GDP growth in 2003, of which three quarters was generated in NSW and much of the remainder in Victoria and Queensland. The model predicted that the RWC generated an improvement in Australia's overseas trade balance of $14 million in 2003. The industries that were most boosted by the RWC were trade and hotels, and finance and business services while industries such as manufacturing were negatively affected because of a small appreciation of real exchange rate.

Natural or man-made disasters and social instability are also topics of interest to CGE modellers, of which the September 11 terrorist attacks are a typical example. Adams et al. (2002) estimated the impact of the 9/11 events on Australian tourism and the economy. The study used the Monash model to generate the baseline forecasts with the pre-9/11 conditions, and an alternative simulation was undertaken to include the effect of 9/11 events. In comparing the baseline forecast and the alternate simulation, the study concluded that the 9/11 events caused a sharp decrease in international tourism in Australia and that the sizable decrease in tourism demand had a negative effect on aggregate consumption, real GDP aggregate imports, and the terms of trade. The study also indicated serious adverse effects on employment in regions and sub-regions that heavily depended on tourists, but the overall reductions in employment would be just over 10 %.

Using a 98-sector CGE model of the US economy, Blake and Sinclair (2003) estimated the impacts of the 9/11-event on the USA, with and without offsetting policy responses. In the absence of a policy response, the study indicated a severe effect of the terrorist attacks: GDP decreased by $30 billion, the government budget worsened by over $7 billion, and as many as 383,000 FTE jobs were lost. Airport and accommodation sectors were worst affected: among the total 559,000 jobs lost, airlines accounted for 203,000 and accommodation establishments for 174,000. The model also suggested that all crisis management policies proposed were very effective in reducing the adverse effects of the 911 events, but the relative effectiveness varied considerably. In terms of both GDP and the total number of jobs saved, the study suggested that the most efficient policy response was to directly subsidize the sectors that were most severely affected by the crisis.

FMD is another example of catastrophic events analysed through CGE modelling. In Scotland, Blake et al. (2003) modelled the effect of FMD on both tourism and the economy. First, they used a micro-regional tourism model to estimate the reduction in tourism expenditures due to FMD. According to this model, total tourism revenue in 2001 fell by almost £7.5 billion. Next a CGE model was employed to estimate the economic impact of the tourism contraction. The results showed that the economic impact of the tourism contraction was much bigger than that of the reduction in agricultural products affected by FMD: the total fall in GDP was about £2.5 billion pounds, of which £1.93 billion resulted from the tourism expenditure reduction. Moreover, the model suggested that the effects of FMD would last for several years.

Narayan (2003, 2007) applied a CGE model to social instability—estimating the economic impact of the May-2000 Fiji coup. The paper used statistical data after the 2000 coup as the baseline shocks. For example, 39.4 % decrease in visitor arrivals, 33.1 % decrease in investment, F$36.6 million decrease in private transfers abroad, 9.9 % increase in government expenditure, and 3.5 % increase in the real interest rate. Since Narayan (2007) was primarily concerned about the long-run effects, long-run closures were used, for example, capital was mobile across sectors and the capital stock was adjusted to a fixed rate of return to capital. At the macro level, the simulation showed a large contraction of the economy: around 8.2 % fall in real GDP, 14.9 % decline in exports, 4.8 % decrease in government revenue, and F$4.8 million increase in the balance of payment deficit. At the sector level, a sharp fall in visitor arrivals led to a remarkable decrease in the real output for the hotel, transportation, commerce and business services industries.

Pambudi et al. (2009) employed a 'bottom-up' multi-regional static CGE model to estimate the effect of the Bali bombing on the Indonesian economy in the short run. According to the simulation results, Bali itself was worst affected by the Bali bombing: with a 50 % drop in tourism demand, its GDP decreased by 2.33 %, employment by 4.93 %, household consumption by 4.68 %, and imports by 8.95 %. Other popular tourist destinations were also affected, such as Jakarta and Yogyakarta. At sectoral level, the worst affected sectors were the tourism-related and non-tradable sectors. However, export-oriented industries (e.g. textiles, clothing, and footwear) and import-competing industries (e.g. machinery and electronics) expanded.

3.4 Assessing the Impact of Tourism on the Environment and Natural Resources

Studies on the impact of tourism on the environment and natural resources parallel the increasing awareness of environmental problems arising from economic growth and the expansion of tourism. Alavalapati and Adamowicz (1997) investigated the effect of tourism in a tourism-oriented and forest-dependent region. They constructed a two-sector (forest and composite tourism sector) CGE model and conducted simulation experiments under two scenarios: (1) only activity in the forest sector affected the local environment; and (2) environmental damage was caused by activities from both sectors. The results indicated that, under scenario (1), the regional economy benefited from an increase in environmental taxes in the forest sector, but the same policy hurt the economy under scenario (2). When an increase in environmental taxes was imposed on the composite sector, the regional economy suffered under scenario (1) but benefited under scenario (2).

Using a similar two-sector (resource and composite tourism) CGE model, Alavalapati and Adamowicz (2000) estimated the tourism impact on resource extraction under the two scenarios: only activity of the resource sector caused environmental damage results (resource–environment [RE] scenario) and activities of both sectors affected the local environment (integrated tourism–environment [ITE] scenario). The modelling results showed that, in both cases, if a 1 % environment tax was imposed on the resource sector, output in the resource sector fell, the demand for tourism goods increased, and returns to land declined. However, the magnitudes of the changes are larger under the RE scenario. If a 1 % environment tax was imposed on the composite tourism sector, there would be a significant decline in tourism and an expansion in the resource sector under the RE scenario. In the ITE scenario, the tax in the composite sector improved the environment.

Kim and Konan (2004) used both I–O and CGE models to explore the effect of tourism on urban infrastructure in Hawaii. The study aggregated I–O table data so as to obtain the household and visitor demands for infrastructure (such as water, sewer, electricity, propane, etc.), which comprised the baseline estimates. A number of methods, such as an autoregressive integrated moving average (ARIMA) model and the standard cohort component technique, were then used to estimate future visitor spending and population and labour force projections under four scenarios: (1) low visitor spending and low population growth (VLPL); (2) low visitor spending and high population growth (VLPH); (3) high visitor spending and low population growth (VHPL); and (4) high visitor spending and high population growth (VHPH). Based on these estimates, a CGE model was used to simulate the four-scenario demands for infrastructure in 1997, 2010, 2020, and 2030. The simulation results suggested that population growth rather than visitor spending was the key determinant for infrastructure demand.

Wattanakuljarus (2006) used a CGE model to simulate the economic and environmental impacts of tourism in Thailand. In the model, households were assumed to spend disposable income on composite goods, which was divided into subsistence and luxury components. A non-homothetic (Klein–Rubin) utility function was employed to describe the household demand. For tourism demand a Leontief function was employed based on the reasoning that tourists could hardly substitute one good (or service) for another. For simplification the model assumed domestic savings as fixed and that direct income tax rates on households were adjusted to keep government savings constant. The simulations showed that while an inbound tourism expansion could lead to a higher real GDP in Thailand, there was an associated increase in water demand by both the agriculture and non-agriculture sectors, which implied an increase in wastewater discharges or pollution to the environment.

Shrestha (2003) used a CGE model to explore the relationships among tourism, the environment and security in Nepal. After estimating the tourism level, environment level and security level by using a Kalman filter in the State Space Modelling Framework, Shrestha (2003) used a two-sector (agriculture and non-agriculture) CGE model to simulate the interactions between tourism, the environment, and security. The simulation results showed that a decrease in the security level decreased the tourism level, the tourism price, and thus total income; however, the environment level did not decrease. On the other hand, an increase in the security level resulted in an increase in the tourism level, tourism price, and total income of the country, but worsened the environment level.

3.5 Assessing the Distributional Effect of Tourism

More recently, researchers have started to study the distributional effects of tourism. For example, besides the economic and environmental effects of tourism, Wattanakuljarus (2006) also simulated the distributional effect and found that corporations retained the largest portion of tourism revenue (38.87 %). As a result, the richest 20 % of households related to non-agricultural sectors (where the tourism corporations belong) enjoyed 34.02 % of tourism revenue. The richest 20 % in agricultural sectors shared 2.89 %. On the other hand, the poorest 80 % in non-agricultural sectors only gained 16 % but the poorest 80 % in agricultural sectors gained 8.21 %. Based on these results, Wattanakuljarus concluded that promoting inbound tourism is not a pro-poor policy. Wattanakuljarus and Coxhead (2008) used the CGE model to specifically explore the income distribution effects of tourism in Thailand. They found that the growth of inbound tourism demand in Thailand raised aggregate household income, but worsened its distribution. Their explanation of the results was that tourism sectors in Thailand were not especially labour intensive and that an expansion of foreign tourism demand undermined profitability in tradable sectors (such as agriculture) from which the poor would derive a substantial fraction of their income.

Blake et al. (2008) addressed the relationship between tourism and poverty relief by employing a 54-sector CGE model to examine the economic impact and the distributional effects of tourism in Brazil. The model incorporated three channels—price, earnings, and government—by which tourism affected the distribution of income. The model also assumed five types of labour. The supplies of labour and capital were subject to imperfect transformation among sectors. Remuneration was grouped into six categories (five types of labour plus capital earning). A number of conclusions were drawn from the simulation results. First, a large increase in the price of tourism goods, consumed largely by tourists and higher income earners, and a small increase in the price of other goods, consumed by lower income earners, would improve the income distribution. Second, it was believed that the tourism industry employed more unskilled people, who by and large were poor, so an expansion of the tourism industry tended to increase the income of poorer households. Third, tourism expansion would increase government revenue and the government might use this revenue on poverty relief programs. Finally, the simulation results showed that tourism had positive effects on all income groups, but the higher income household group benefited more, so redistributing more government revenue to the poor would improve the distributional inequality.

References

Adams, P. D., & Parmenter, B. R. (1991). *The Medium Term Significance of International Tourism for the Australian Economy*. Report prepared for the Bureau of Tourism Research, Canberra.

Adams, P. D., & Parmenter, B. R. (1992). *The Medium-Term Significance of International Tourism for the State Economies*. Part II. Occasional Paper No. 7. Canberra: Bureau of Tourism Research.

Adams, P. D., & Parmenter, B. R. (1993). *The Medium Term Significance of International Tourism for the State Economies*. Report Prepared for the Bureau of Tourism Research, Canberra.

Adams, P. D., & Parmenter, B. R. (1995). An Applied General Equilibrium Analysis of Tourism in a Quite Small, Quite Open Economy. *Applied Economics, 27*, 985–994.

Adams, P. D., Dixon, P. B., & Rimmer, M. T. (2002). The September 11 Shock to Tourism and the Australian Economy from 2001-02 to 2003-04. *Australian Bulletin of Labour, 27*, 241–257.

Alavalapati, J., & Adamowicz, W. (1997, May 28–31). *Modelling the Economy of a Tourism-oriented, Forest Dependent Region*. Seventh Symposium on Systems Analysis in Forest Resources, Traverse City, MI.

Alavalapati, J., & Adamowicz, W. (2000). Tourism Impact Modelling for Resource Extraction Regions. *Annals of Tourism Research, 27*(1), 188–202.

Andersen, A. (1999). *Economic Impact Study of the Sydney 2000 Olympic Games*. Australia: CREA: Centre for Regional Economic Analysis/University of Tasmania.

Blake, A. (2000). *The Economic Effects of Tourism in Spain*. Discussion Paper Series 2000/2, Christel DeHaan Tourism and Travel Research Institute, University of Nottingham. http://www.nottingham.ac.uk/ttri/series.html

Blake, A. (2005). *The Economic Impact of the London 2012 Olympics*. TTRI Discussion Paper No. 2005/5.

Blake, A., & Sinclair, M. (2003). Tourism Crisis Management: Responding to September 11. *Annals of Tourism Research, 30*(4), 813–832.

Blake, A., Durbarry, R., Sinclair, T., & Sugiyarto, G. (2001). *Modelling Tourism and Travel Using Tourism Satellite Accounts and Tourism Policy and Forecasting Models*. Tourism and Travel Research Institute Discussion Paper 2001/4. http://www.nottingham.ac.uk/ttri/series.html

Blake, A., Sinclair, M., & Sugiyarto, G. (2003). Quantifying the Impact of Foot and Mouth Disease on Tourism and the UK Economy. *Tourism Economics, 9* (4), 449–465.

Blake, A., Arbache, J., Sinclair, M., & Teles, V. (2008). Tourism and Poverty Relief. *Annals of Tourism Research, 35*(1), 107–126.

Burnett, P., Cutler, H., & Thresher, R. (2007). The Impact of Tourism for a Small City: A CGE Approach. *Special Section: Tourism and Regional Science, JRAP, 37*(3), 233–242.

Chand, G. (2002). *Response to the 2003 Budget*. Suva: Fiji Labour Party.

CIE (Centre for International Economics). (1988). *Economic Effects of International Tourism*, Canberra.

Dwyer, L., Forsyth, P., Madden, J., & Spurr, R. (2000). Economic Impacts of Inbound Tourism Under Different Assumptions Regarding the Macroeconomy. *Current Issues in Tourism, 3*(4), 325–363.

Dwyer, L., Forsyth, P., & Spurr, R. (2003). Inter-Industry Effects of Tourism Growth: Implications for Destination Managers. *Tourism Economics, 9*(2), 117–132.

Giesecke, J., & Madden, J. (2007). *The Sydney Olympics, Seven Years On: An Ex-post Dynamic CGE Assessment.* COPS General Paper No. G-168, Monash University.

Gooroochurn, N. (2004). *The Economy-Wide Effects of Tourism Taxation in a Distorted Economy: A General Equilibrium Analysis.* Discussion Paper Series 2004/1, Tourism and Travel Research Institute, University of Nottingham.

Gooroochurn, N., & Blake, A. (2004). *Tourism Immiserisation in Sub-Saharan Countries, Fact or Fiction?* European Trade Study Group, Annual Conference, University of Nottingham, UK.

Industries Assistance Commission. (1989, March). *Some Economic Implications of Tourism Expansion: Inquiry into Travel and Tourism.* Discussion Paper No. 2. Canberra: AGPS.

Industry Commission. (1996a). *Tourism Accommodation and Training Report No. 50.* Canberra: Industry Commission.

Industry Commission. (1996b, October). *State Territory and Local Government Assistance to Industry.* Report No. 55. Canberra: AGPS.

Kasimati, E. (2003). Economic Aspects and the Summer Olympics: A Review of Related Research. *International Journal of Tourism Research, 5*, 434–444.

Kim, K., & Konan, D. (2004, September 2–4). *Using I-O Analysis and CGE Modelling to Estimate Infrastructure Demand in Hawaii.* EcoMod Conference. Input-Output and General Equilibrium Modeling, Brussels.

KPMG (Marwick, P.). (1993). *Sydney Olympics 2000: Economic Impact Study.* Sydney: KPMG.

Kweka, J. (2004, March 21–22). *Tourism and the Economy of Tanzania: A CGE Analysis.* Presented at the Conference on Growth, Poverty and Human Development in Africa, Oxford, UK.

Li, S., Blake, A., & Cooper, C. (2007, October). *China's Economic Reform and the Economic Impact of International Tourism During the Beijing Olympics: A Computable General Equilibrium Modelling Analysis*, at the First Conference of The International Association for Tourism Economics, Palma de Mallorca.

Mabugu, R. (2001). Macroeconomic Effects of a Devaluation in Zimbabwe: A CGE Analysis. *South African Journal of Economics, 69*, 708–733.

Mabugu, R. (2002). Short-Term Effects of Policy Reform on Tourism and the Macroeconomy in Zimbabwe: Applied CGE Analysis. *Development Southern Africa, 19*, 419–430.

Madden, J., & Thapa, P. (2000). *The Contribution of Tourism to the New South Wales Economy*. Report Commissioned by the Sustainable Tourism CRC. Hobart: Centre for Regional Economic Analysis, University of Tasmania.

Narayan, P. (2003). Economic Impact of the 2003 South Pacific Games for Fiji. *Economics Papers, 22*(3), 60–73.

Narayan, P. (2004). Economic Impact of Tourism on Fiji's Economy: Empirical Evidence from the Computable General Equilibrium Model. *Tourism Economics, 10*(4), 419–433.

Narayan, P. (2007). The Long-Run Impact of Coups on Fiji's Economy: Evidence from a Computable General Equilibrium Model. *Journal of International Development, 19*, 149–160.

NSW Treasury. (1997). *The Economic Impact of the Sydney Olympic Games*. New South Wales Treasury and CREA: Centre for Regional Economic Analysis (University of Tasmania).

Pambudi, D., McCaughey, N., & Smyth, R. (2009). Computable General Equilibrium Estimates of the Impact of the Bali Bombing on the Indonesian Economy. *Tourism Management, 30*, 232–239.

Shrestha, N. (2003). *Tourism, Environment and Security: A Computable General Equilibrium Approach: A Case in Nepal*. http://www.igss.ynu.ac.jp/library/collection/thesis/2003/80.pdf

Sinclair, M., Blake, A., & Gooroochurn, N. (2003). *Modelling Tourism Impacts on Small Island Economies: Evidence from Cyprus*, Malta and Mauritius. http://www.irfd.org/events/wfsids/virtual/papers/sids_tsinclairetal.pdf

Skene, J. (1993a, August). *The Economic Impact of Growth in Visitor Expenditure: A Quantitative Assessment*. Bureau of Industry Economics Working Paper No. 92.

Skene, J. (1993b, December). *Some Short-Run Effects of an Increase in International Visitor Expenditure*. Bureau of Industry Economics Working Paper No. 94.

Sugiyarto, G., Blake, A., & Sinclair, T. (2003). Tourism and Globalisation: Economic Impact in Indonesia. *Annals of Tourism Research, 30*(3), 683–701.

URS Finance and Economics. (2004). *Economic Impact of the Rugby World Cup 2003 on the Australian Economy—Post Analysis*. Research Report for Department of Industry, Tourism and Resources.

Wattanakuljarus, A. (2006). *The Nationwide Economic and Environmental Impacts of Tourism: A Computable General Equilibrium Approach for Thailand*. http://www.idrc.org.sg/uploads/user-S/11738541401Anan_FReport.pdf

Wattanakuljarus, A., & Coxhead, I. (2008). Is Tourism-Based Development Good for the Poor?: A General Equilibrium Analysis for Thailand. *Journal of Policy Modelling, 30*(6), 929–955.

Zhou, D., Yanagida, J., Chakravorty, U., & Leung, P. (1997). Estimating Economic Impacts of Tourism. *Annals of Tourism Research., 24*(1), 76–78.

4

Collecting Background Information for a Tourism CGE Model

The chapter is structured as follows. Section 4.1 provides a breakdown analysis of Singapore's economic structure with special interest on the role of tourism in the economy. Section 4.2 analyses the advantages and disadvantages of the tourism industry in Singapore. Section 4.3 demonstrates the performance of tourism in Singapore by international comparison, development over time, and the performance of the hotel and food and beverage sector. Section 4.4 uncovers the characteristics of Singapore tourism. Section 4.5 introduces and analyses Singapore's tourism policies.

4.1 Information on Economic Structure and the Role of Tourism

The Republic of Singapore is an island country to the south of the Malaysian state of Johor and to the north of Indonesia's Riau Islands. After decades of economic development and transformation, Singapore has successfully achieved a diversified and globalized economy. Section 4.1 will

S. Meng, M. Siriwardana, *Assessing the Economic Impact of Tourism*,
DOI 10.1007/978-3-319-40328-1_4

first demonstrate the overall structure of the Singapore economy and then break it down by sector to obtain a more detailed picture of the Singaporean economy and the role of tourism. The 2007 economic survey undertaken by the Ministry of Trade and Industry (MTI) provides the most recent and detailed information. Section 4.1 will draw heavily on the data from that survey.

4.1.1 General Feature of Singaporean Economy and Its Implications

Singapore is characterized by a two-pillar economy. Due to a lack of natural resources, Singapore has hardly any agricultural and mining sectors, so it depends heavily on the manufacturing and service industries shown in Table 4.1.

Table 4.1 shows that the Singapore economy is mainly supported by goods-producing and services-producing industries. The first contributes 29.5% of total value-added of the economy while the latter contributes 65.9%. Given these contributions, one can say that the two pillars of the Singapore economy are not equally sized, as the contribution of the

Table 4.1 Overall economic structure of Singapore

Industries	Value added (% share)	Real growth (%)
Goods producing	29.5	7.2
Manufacturing	24.1	5.8
Construction	3.8	20.3
Utilities	1.6	5.1
Other goods	0.1	0.2
Services producing	65.9	8.1
Wholesale and retail trade	16.2	7.3
Transport and storage	9.4	5.1
Hotel and restaurants	1.9	4.4
Information and communications	3.6	6.3
Financial services	12.4	16.9
Business services	12.5	7.8
Other services industries	9.8	4.2
Ownership of dwellings	4.6	1.3
Total	100	7.7

Source: Ministry of Trade and Industry (2008)

Table 4.2 Sector share of total value-added, 1960–2007

	1960	1970	1980	1990	1994	1997	2004	2007
Goods producing	21.5	32.3	38.9	35.3	34.4	32.5	31.7	29.1
Manufacturing	11.7	20.2	28.1	27.8	25.6	22.5	26.0	23.7
Construction	3.5	6.8	6.2	5.3	7.1	7.9	3.7	3.7
Utilities	2.4	2.6	2.1	1.8	1.5	1.9	1.9	1.5
Other goods	3.9	2.7	1.5	0.4	0.2	0.1	0.1	0.1
Services producing	78.5	67.7	61.1	64.7	65.6	62.4	63.1	64.9

Note: From 1997 the shares of GDP for goods-producing and services-producing industries do not add up to 100 % due to the increased component of ownerships of dwellings

Source: Authors based on data from Department of Statistics (1980–2008), MTI, Singapore year books, various issues

services-producing industries is more than twice that of the goods-producing industries. Table 4.2 demonstrates over time the relative size and growth of the two pillars.

Table 4.2 shows that the importance of the goods-producing industries increased in the 1960s and 1970s but started to drop from 1990. The decreased relative size of the goods-producing industries since 1990 differs remarkably from the small relative size in the 1960s. The relatively small size of goods-producing industries in the 1960s was because the economy was heavily dependent on the 'entrepot' trade, which led to a very small manufacturing base and thus indicated the vulnerability of economy. The decreased relative size of the goods-producing industries since the 1990s is due to the relatively faster rate of growth of the service industries (e.g. 8.1% real growth compared with 7.2% for the goods-producing industries in 2007). A brief check of the composition of the goods-producing industries and the service industries assures us that the Singapore economy has become more diversified.

In the goods-producing industries, it is obvious that the manufacturing industry dominates the others (an 81.7% contribution in 2007). In the services-producing industries, the contribution of trade decreased in 2007 because its growth rate (7.3%) was less than the average growth rate of the service industries. Other service industries such as the financial services and the business services increased significantly (the growth of financial services in 2007 was as high as 16.9%). As a result, although wholesale and retail trade was still the No. 1 contributor (16.2% share of value-added) in the services-producing industries, the contributions of other sectors such as the financial services (12.4% share of value-added), business services (12.5% share of value-added), and transport and storage (9.4% share of value-added) are not far behind the trade sector.

The contribution to GDP of the hotel and restaurant sector, traditionally thought to belong to the tourism industry, was only 1.9% in 2007. However, the contribution of the tourism industry extends far beyond this. First, tourists spend large amounts of money on the transport system, so a significant proportion of revenue in the transport and storage industry should be attributed to tourism. Second, tourism shopping expenditure as the bulk of total tourism expenditure in Singapore contributes directly to the wholesale and retail trade sectors and may indirectly contribute to the manufacturing sector. Third, tourists may make positive contributions to other sectors through their use of services such as information and communications, medical, and financial and business services.

4.1.2 Manufacturing Sector

The manufacturing sector comprises electronics, chemicals, biomedical manufacturing, precision engineering, transport engineering, and general manufacturing industries. Their contribution to value-added is shown in Table 4.3.

Table 4.3 indicates that the Singapore manufacturing sector is dominated by high-technology (high-tech) and high-value-added industries such as electronics, biomedical, and precision engineering. The general

Table 4.3 Structure of manufacturing industry

Industries	Value added (% share)	Real growth (%)
Manufacturing	100.0	5.8
Electronics	29.7	4.0
Chemicals	11.8	3.3
Biomedical manufacturing	24.4	−0.6
Precision engineering	13.0	0.0
Transport engineering	11.9	23.5
General manufacturing	9.2	6.3

Source: Ministry of Trade and Industry (2008)

Table 4.4 Investment commitments in manufacturing industry

Investment commitments	S$ Million	% Share
Electronics	5139	31.9
Chemicals	8632	53.7
Biomedical manufacturing	932	5.8
Precision engineering	412	2.6
Transport engineering	503	3.1
General manufacturing	466	2.9
Foreign	14,279	88.8
Local	1804	11.2
Total	16,084	100.0

Source: Ministry of Trade and Industry (2008)

manufacturing industries only account for 9.2% of value-added to the sector. The contribution of the electronics industries is historically high after the United States and European electronics companies favoured Singapore as their offshore assembly base in the late 1960s, but the contribution of the newly emerged high-tech biomedical manufacturing industry, occupying second place, is only a little less than the electronics industries. Similarly, the contribution of new technological industries, including precision engineering and transport engineering, is larger than that of the chemical industries. Examination of the investment commitments in the manufacturing sector reveals other characteristics (see Table 4.4).

From Table 4.4, it is apparent that the investment commitments of the chemicals and electronics industries are dominant due to the huge fixed costs in these industries. If we check the sources of investment, we find that the bulk of investment comes from foreign countries. This reflects the international influence on the Singapore manufacturing sector—Singapore is a main foreign direct investment (FDI)-receiving country, hosting many multinational factories.

Given the fact that the Singaporean manufacturing industry is mainly concentrated on high-tech export-oriented products, and that investment in the industry is dominated by foreigners, the increase in tourism spending may push up the exchange rate and thus is likely to negatively affect the manufacturing industry. On one hand, the increased exchange rate lets foreign investment in Singapore subject to exchange risk and therefore hinders foreign investment in the industry (people are concerned that the exchange rate will fall in the long run and they will lose money in the future when they take their return on investment back home). On the other hand, it makes Singapore exports more expensive and thus shrinks export demand.

4.1.3 Trade, Hotels, and Restaurants

The wholesale and retail trade is the biggest sector in the services industries contributing 16.8% to total value-added while the hotels and restaurants sector contributes nearly 2 % of total value-added (see Table 4.1). We investigate the trade sector first.

According to MTI (2008), wholesale trade accounts for 88.2 % of the total wholesale and retail trade. It is no wonder that trade is of vital importance to Singapore's economy given its small size, lack of natural resources, strategic geographic position, and legacy from the colonial period. The dominance of wholesale trade over retail trade can be explained by the huge volume of international trade. Singapore's top ten imports and exports by dollars are listed in Table 4.5.

Table 4.5 demonstrates that Singapore's external trade is dominated by intra-industry trade with eight same product types found in the top ten

Table 4.5 Singapore's top ten imports and exports in terms of value

Top 10 exports	%	Top 10 imports	%
Electronic valves	23.5	Electronic valves	19.7
Petroleum products refined	17.1	Petroleum products refined	11.4
Parts for office and data processing machines	6.7	Petroleum Crude	8.5
Telecommunications equipment	5.5	Telecommunications equipment	5.5
Data processing machines	3.4	Parts for office and data processing machines	5.1
Electrical circuit apparatus	2.0	Aircraft	2.3
Electrical machinery	1.7	Data processing machines	2.1
Medicaments	1.6	Electrical circuit apparatus	1.8
Nitrogen-function compounds	1.6	Civil engineering equipment parts	1.8
Civil engineering equipment parts	1.6	Electrical machinery	1.6
Total exports	100.0	*Total imports*	100.0

Source: Ministry of Trade and Industry (2008)

exports list and in the top ten imports list. However, this intra-industry trade is not necessarily the 'entrepot' trade. For example, the top two exports and imports (electronic valves and petroleum products refined) are consistent with the dominant roles of the electronics and chemicals sectors in the manufacturing industry. The third largest imported item, petroleum, spells out the importance of the petroleum refining industry.

With respect to the role of tourism, a tourism expansion is likely to increase retail trade through increased shopping expenditure. For international trade, a rising Singapore dollar induced by a tourism expansion is going to have a negative effect on exports and a positive effect on imports.

In the hotels and restaurants sector, MTI (2008) shows that restaurants contribute almost two-thirds of the value-added in the hospitality industry. Although both hotels and restaurants belong to the core tourism sector, the hotel sector is more dependent on inbound tourism—few Singaporeans need hotels for accommodation but most Singaporeans like to eat out. As a result, both hotels and restaurants will benefit greatly from the direct stimulation of tourism expansion, but hotels will benefit the most.

4.1.4 Financial and Business Services

The growth of financial and business services has been so rapid that their combined contribution (24.9% share of value-added) much outweighs that of the wholesale and retail trade (16.2% share of total value-added). Table 4.6 demonstrates the structure of the financial and business services.

Table 4.6 highlights two imposing characteristics of the financial services sector. One is that banking services accounted for half of the contribution of financial services in 2007. The other is that the growth rates of all financial services were very high in 2007, especially, the growth rate of the financial brokers' services, reaching as high as 24%. The bulky contribution of banking services highlights its leading role in Singapore's financial sector. Singapore is now among the top ten international banking centres. MTI (2008) reveals that, at the end of 2007, there were 112 commercial banks, 50 merchant banks and 3 financial companies in the Singapore domestic financial sector. The total assets/liabilities of

Table 4.6 Structure of financial and business services industry

Industries	Value added (% share)	Real growth (%)
Financial services	100.0	16.9
Banking	50.0	17.6
Stock, Futures and commodity brokers	9.1	24.0
Fund management activities	9.2	17.1
Insurance	12.4	12.6
Others	19.4	16.0
Business services	100.0	7.8
Real estate	46.4	8.0
Legal	4.1	6.6
Accounting	3.4	6.3
Business representative offices	8.8	7.8
Business and management consultancy activities	7.6	6.3
Architectural and engineering activities	9.0	7.0
Others	20.8	8.6

Source: Ministry of Trade and Industry (2008)

commercial banks rose by 14% in 2007 to $581 billion and total nonbank deposits were as high as $315 billion at the end of 2007. Singapore's banking activities are dominated by its services to the Asian Dollar Market. The total assets/liabilities of the Asian Dollar Market increased by US$209 billion, reaching US$907 billion in 2007. Other financial services, although not as important as banking, expanded dramatically. In the stock market, despite the sell-offs in Wall Street and Chinese bourses in February 2007, the benchmark Strait Times Index (STI) recovered one month later and continued its ascent, reaching a peak of 3665 in July 2007. In the securities market, the turnover volume of securities traded on the Singapore Exchange Securities Trading Limited (SGX-ST) rose by 113% to S$682 billion in 2007. In the futures market, the volume of financial futures contracts traded on the Singapore Exchange Derivatives Trading Limited (SGX-DT) increased 21% to 44 million. In the Singapore, foreign exchange market, an average daily turnover of US$262 billion was achieved in 2007, an increase of 38% compared with 2006.

The business services sector tells a similar story. From Table 4.6, it is evident that the real estate segment is the star performer in this sector. The outstanding performance of the real estate segment may reflect real estate booming in recent years and internationalization in this segment. In 2007, the levels of transaction activity in the private residential market reached a record high. Although the price of housing surged by 31% in 2007, many uncompleted units in outside central regions were sold. To make use of higher profit opportunities abroad, some real estate companies invested overseas. According to Leong (2008), the share of overseas revenue of Singapore real estate companies rose significantly during the period from 2000 to 2005. For example, the Keppel Land Company's overseas turnover increased to 64.7% in 2005 from 20.4% in 2000.

Although real estate is still the largest in the business service industry, its share declined from 62% in 1997 to 46% in 2007. Over the same period, non-real estate segments have grown rapidly. Professional services, business representative offices and other business services like R&D and MICE (meetings, incentives, conventions, and exhibitions) activities have increased in relative importance. Their growth reflects the rising demand for these services. For example, in the office market in 2007, occupancy rates were above 93% and rents in the central region rose by 56%.

The relationship between the financial and business industry and the tourism industry is bilateral. On one hand, an expansion of the financial and business industry results in more activities and attracts more visitors from around the world, given the global nature of the financial and business industry in Singapore. On the other hand, a tourism boom may increase the demand for financial and business services instantly and bring more customers in the future if they have a good impression of Singapore's environment and services.

4.1.5 Transportation and ICT Services

The combined contribution of transportation and information and communication technology (ICT) services in 2007 was 13.0% of the total value-added in the Singapore economy, indicating they are significant segments in the services industries. The decomposition of the transport and storage sector is shown in Table 4.7.

It is not surprising to find that water transport is the largest contributor, given Singapore's strategic geographic position and thus the large amount

Table 4.7 Structure of transport and storage sector

Industries	Value added (% share)	Real growth (%)
Transport and storage	100.0	5.1
Land transport and supporting services	18.7	4.6
Water transport and supporting services	44.1	6.8
Air transport and supporting services	23.9	2.6
Storage and services allied to transport	10.5	4.7
Post and courier activities	2.9	7.1

Source: Ministry of Trade and Industry (2008)

of international trade via sea. The importance of Singapore's port was manifest in 2007 records. Vessel arrivals increased by 11% in terms of tonnage and totalled 1.5 billion gross tonnes; container throughput grew by 13% and reached 28 million 20-foot equivalent units; bunker sales rose 11% reaching 32 million tonnes, and sea cargo grew by 7.8%.

Land transport and air transport combined also made significant contributions, matching that of water transport. The growth of land and air transport benefited much from government policies. Land transport included public transport (bus, rail) and private transport (car). Due to the limited space and the high density of population, the public transport system is a priority for Singapore. The Land Transport Authority has developed a convenient integrated public transport system. For air transport, although all Southeast Asian international airports benefit from their strategic location, Singapore has been the most successful by open skies policy, which encourages carriers to break route at its airport. Passenger traffic at Changi airport in Singapore increased 4.8% and reached a record of 36.7 million in 2007, while air cargo registered at Changi Airport was 1.9 million tonnes, a 0.9% decline compared with 2006.

Corresponding with the expansion of transport service, storage and transport allied service increased and accounted for a significant contribution (10.5% of value-added in this sector). The post and courier activities contributed relatively less than the transports, but their growth was the fastest in 2007.

In the ICT service sector, telecommunications accounted for 45.5% of sector value-added contribution, while IT services accounted for 30.9%. Thanks to its popularity and fundamentality, the telecommunications service achieved an 8% growth rate in 2007, while IT services grew at 5.6%. By the end of 2007, more than 900 services had been provided in the telecommunications market, including some innovative products and services such as video telephony and mobile blogging. Mobile penetration reached 123%, one of the highest in the world, while household broadband penetration reached 79%.

The relationship between transport and ICT services industries and the tourism industry are twofold. The tourism boom increases the demand for transport and ICT services and thus promotes the development of these sectors while the high efficiency and quality of transport and ICT services provide convenience to visitors. Together, they are highly likely to attract more visitors to Singapore in the future.

4.1.6 Linkages Among Sectors

Through the sectoral breakdown, we have a clear view of Singapore's economic structure. However, we should bear in mind that the sectors were integrated together through many linkages, therefore the performance of one sector will affect other sectors. The linkages among sectors can be demonstrated by employment spillover and intermediate demand.

The employment spillover effect describes how an increase in final demand in one industry creates employment not only within that industry but also in other industries. Thangavelu and Li (2008) studied the employment linkages and structural changes in Singapore by using I–O tables. They found strong employment linkages between different sectors of the economy, as shown in Table 4.8.

From the second column of the Table 4.8, we can conclude that, in selected industries, there are very strong employment spillovers. First, because the share of intra-industry jobs in the total jobs created by the industry is less than 50% for each industry, we can conclude that more than 50% of jobs are created in other industries. Among these industries, the manufacturing sector (e.g. petrochem, electric, electronic) demonstrate high inter-industry spillover (around 70%), while the service sectors (e.g. commerce, communications, finance) have relatively lower inter-industry spillovers (around 60%). Second, the third and the fourth

Table 4.8 Employment linkages between sectors

Increase in final demand in	Share of total jobs (%) created in 2004 in		
	Intra-industry	Inter-industry	
	Own industry	Manufacturing sector	Service sector
Petrochem	23.5	11.0	51.8
Electric	32.1	10.1	47.6
Electronic	31.3	8.9	50.2
Commerce	44.5	5.1	43.2
Communications	40.6	9.3	42.3
Finance	36.6	4.2	50.5

Source: Thangavelu and Li (2008)

columns show the employment spillover effect between the manufacturing and services industries. The first three rows show that the manufacturing sector has high spillover effect on the service sector (around 50%) but a low spillover effect on industries within the manufacturing sector (only around 10%). By contrast, the last three rows show that the services sector has a high spillover effect on the industries within the sector (42.3–50.5%) but a very low level of effect on the manufacturing sector (only around 5% with the exception of 9.3% for communications industry).

Another way to analyse the linkages among sectors is through intermediate demand. Leong (2008) studied intermediate demand in the business services sector. According to Leong's study, the business services sector derives its demand largely from the intermediate demand by other sectors (intermediate demand accounts for 64% of the total demand). Leong also identified the key drivers of intermediate demand for business services, as shown in Table 4.9.

Table 4.9 shows that intermediate demand for the business services sector largely comes from the wholesale and retail trades as well as manufacturing and financial services. The wholesale and retail trades sector is the largest purchaser of real estate, legal activities, management consultancy, and accounting services, while the construction sector is the main buyer of architectural and engineering activities. Interpretation of Table 4.9 can be demonstrated using the real estate sector as an example. Out of every $1 of intermediate demand in the real estate sector, 29 cents

Table 4.9 Intermediate demand in business sectors in 2000

Producing industry	Main purchasing industry	Share of intermediate output sold to purchasing industry (%)
Real estate	1. Wholesale and retail trades	28.6
	2. Manufacturing	13.1
	3. Food and beverage services	9.4
	4. Other services	8.1
	5. Financial services	7.9
Legal activities	1. Wholesale and retail trades	19.9
	2. Manufacturing	17.9
	3. Financial services	12.6
	4. Real estate	10.3
	5. Government services	9.7
Accounting activities	1. Wholesale and retail trades	22.2
	2. Manufacturing	14.2
	3. Real estate	13.7
	4. Financial services	13.4
	5. Transport and storage	6.2
Architectural and engineering activities	1. Construction	35.6
	2. Architectural and engineering activities	16.7
	3. Real estate	11.1
	4. Manufacturing	14.6
	5. Government services	4.5
Management consultancy activities	1. Wholesale and retail trades	16.3
	2. Manufacturing	11.5
	3. Real estate	8.9
	4. Other services	8.1
	5. Financial services	7.9

Source: Leong (2008)

go to the wholesale and retail trades sector, 13 cents go to manufacturing, 9 cents go to food and beverage services, and 8 cents go to financial services. This linkage can be explained by the fact that real estate supports these sectors by providing the warehousing, retail and office space for shopping malls, and space for banks and financial institutions.

4.2 Information on Tourism Resources

Being small and short in history, Singapore seems unlikely to be a favourite tourism destination. With an area of 707 km^2 (the main island is 682 km^2), Singapore is a city state and the smallest nation in Southeast Asia, with very limited natural resources. In spite of its small size, its population is approximately 4.59 million which makes it the second most densely populated country in the world. The history of Singapore is literally very short—less than 200 years have elapsed since the arrival of the British. This leads to few historical tourism sites in Singapore. Despite these disadvantages, Singapore attracts millions of tourists every year. According to Euromonitor (2007), it is the world's fourth most visited city in terms of visitor arrivals. What attracts so many visitors to Singapore?

4.2.1 Favourable Geographic Position and Tropical Environment

Singapore's strategic position has helped it grow into a major tourism centre. Its geographical location is 136.8 km north of the equator, between latitudes 103°36′ east and 104°25′ east. It connects to Malaysia by two causeway bridges and the Riau Archipelago—the key islands of Indonesia—by a quick ferry trip. Thailand and the Philippines are only a short plane journey away. This central location in Southeast Asia makes Singapore very much the gateway to Southeast Asia. Internationally, Singapore is at the crossroads between Australasia and areas in the northern hemisphere such as Europe, northern America, and northern Asia. The Singapore government utilizes this advantage by encouraging travellers to break their journey at its airport. The unique location and the efficient airport services make Singapore a major transition place. By the end of 2007, the Changi Airport in Singapore was connected by 81 airlines to 189 cities in 60 countries. In 2007, the Changi Airport registered a record of 36.7 million in passenger traffic and 1.9 million tonnes of cargo.

Due to its geographical location, Singapore's weather is warm and humid, and has very limited variation. The maximum temperature is 31 °C while the average minimum is 23 °C. Rain falls throughout the year. During the monsoon season (November to January), there is more consistent rain. Usually showers are heavy and sudden, but they are brief and refreshing. Singapore's climate makes it an ideal place for activities such as swimming, sailing, sunbathing, and other water sports. For people who do not like the tropical weather, Singapore has air-conditioning in almost all of its hotels, restaurants, shops, office buildings, and transport system.

The geographic location and tropical weather grant Singapore limited but valuable natural tourism sites. The Night Safari in Singapore Zoo allows people to explore South American, Asian, and African habitats at night, without any visible barriers between the wild animals and guests. The National Orchid collection in Singapore Botanical Gardens has over 3000 types of orchids. The Jurong Bird Park includes extensive specimens of birds from around the world. The Sungei Buloh Wetlands Reserve, Bukit Timah Reserve, and Pulau Ubin Island provide a quiet retreat from the stress of modern life.

4.2.2 Colonial Historical Legacy

Singapore has been occupied by many nations. Knowledge of Singapore's existence extends back to as early as the third-century AD. By the fourteenth century, Singapore had belonged to the Sri Vijayan Empire. Between the sixteenth and the early nineteenth centuries, Singapore was part of the Malay state of Johor. Control of Singapore was held by the Portuguese in the seventeenth century and by the Dutch in the eighteenth century. As an agent of the British East India Company, Sir Thomas Stamford Raffles arrived in Singapore in 1819 and established Singapore as a trading station. From that point on, Singapore grew dramatically. The free trade policy attracted traders and labour migrants from China, India, and the surrounding Southeast Asian countries. By 1824, only five years after Raffles' arrival, the island grew from a fishing village of 150 people to a city with a population of 10,000.

Due to the influence of British imperialism, Singapore has adopted a Western political and social system. The Republic of Singapore has a unicameral parliamentary system. The government is led by the Prime Minister and the cabinet. The president, who is the chief of state, previously only exercised ceremonial duties, but he can now exercise expanded powers over government budgetary affairs, legislative appointments, and internal security matters. This system has provided much stability.

The colonial history and Asian population provide Singapore with a varied cultural, linguistic, and religious heritage. Although the national language is Malay, official languages also include English, Chinese, and Tamil. English is the most popularly used language: it is used in administration and education and is also widely used in the professions and businesses. Most Singaporeans are bilingual, speaking their mother tongue as well as English. Singapore is also a multi-religious country. According to the Census of Population Office in Singapore (2000), 51% of the population practise Buddhism and Taoism, 14.6% practise Christianity, and 13.9% are Muslims. Malays account for the majority of the Muslims.

Due to the free trade policy initially adopted by Raffles, and the export-oriented and globalization policy adopted later by the Singapore government, Singapore today has a very successful market economy. It is one of the Four Asian Tigers (Hong Kong, Singapore, South Korea, and Taiwan). In terms of tonnage shipped, Singapore is the busiest port in the world. It is the world's fourth largest foreign exchange trading centre (London, New York City, Tokyo, and Singapore). It is also famous for its business-friendly economy.

These historical legacies lend great advantages to Singapore tourism. The rich cultural attraction is embodied in the preserved or reconstructed historical sites and the cultural diversity, reflecting Singapore's colonial history and Chinese, Malay, Indian, and Arab ethnicities. English as one of its numerous official languages makes it easier for visitors in terms of shopping and general living. The stable political and social system provides a safety net for tourists. The highly developed economy and the business-friendly environment attract business activities which bring even more visitors to Singapore. For example, international conferences, exhibitions, and sporting and artistic events draw a large number of tourists to Singapore. A variety of events all year round like Chingay Parade, Singapore Art Festival, and Singapore Garden Festival also deliver exciting times for tourists.

4.2.3 Sound Infrastructure and Efficient Service

Aware of its strategic geographic position and the nature of its being a small city-state, Singapore has put much effort into improving infrastructure. Changi Airport was opened in 1981 with one runway and one terminal. A second runway began operating in 1984 and a second terminal in 1990. A new terminal three commenced operations at the beginning of 2008. Now the overall capacity of Changi Airport is about 70 million passenger movements annually.

Considering the limited space and high density of population, the Singapore government encourages the use of public transportation. On one hand, a quota system is used to regulate the number of new vehicles entering the road system. For example, an intending purchaser of a new vehicle must bid for a Certificate of Entitlement (COE), which gives the right to purchase a new vehicle and to retain its ownership for ten years. On the other hand, the Singapore government devotes effort to developing an integrated public transport system. The mass rapid transit (MRT) came into operation in 1990, which covered a 67-km network of three lines and 42 stations. A 16-km extension to Woodlands opened in 1996. Further extension of MRT is on the way. The target of the Land Transport Authority is to develop a system that will take at least 70% of all morning peak hour trips by 2020 and, in the meantime, offer high service standards in terms of convenience, comfort, and journey times (MTI 2008).

Telecommunications and information infrastructure are at the top of the Singapore government's agenda. Singapore has three satellite earth stations; submarine fiberoptic links to Malaysia, Hong Kong, Taiwan, and Japan; and three international digital gateways. This infrastructure has led outgoing international telephone calls to increase from 3.5 million in 1980 to 146 million in 1994 (Perry et al. 1997). Since the National Computer Board (NCB) was established in the early 1981, information technology infrastructure has been the area of focus. The 1986 National Information Technology Plan encourages electronic data interchange for the distribution of business documents. The second plan introduced by NCB in 1992, IT2000, set out a vision of an 'intelligent island' where information technology and computer networking are available in business and at home. With the effort of NCB, many computer networks have been established. Among them, TradeNet provides access to local and international databases. In 2006, the Information Development Authority of Singapore launched a ten-year master plan, Intelligent Nation 2015, which has endeavoured to put in place a robust information-communication infrastructure (e.g. the implementation of an ultra-high speed and island-wide broadband infrastructure by 2015). As part of this plan, around 6500 free Wi-Fi hot spots were set up around Singapore by the end of 2007. Now visitors in Changi airport can enjoy free internet access and free local phone calls, both of which provide great convenience for visitors.

Apart from the improving infrastructure, efficiency and quality of service are also emphasized in Singapore. Money exchange services are provided in airport and shopping malls. The efficient immigration clearance system has gained an international reputation. Given the sound infrastructure and the high-quality service, one should not be surprised by the visitors' rating of services and facilities. The Singapore Tourism Board (STB) survey (STB 2007) reveals that visitors' overall satisfaction with a trip to Singapore is 82%. Airport facilities/services, immigration clearance, and public transport were given 94%, 90%, and 89% satisfaction ratings, respectively. The degrees of satisfaction for healthcare/medical services, business-related services, tourist information services, and education/enrichment training services were found to be 92%, 87%, 82%, and 88%, respectively. These extraordinarily high levels of overall satisfaction imply a high percentage of repeat visits. According to STB's Annual Report on Tourism Statistics 2006, 61% of 2006 visits were repeat visits.

4.3 Performance of the Tourism Sector

With all of these advantages and very active policies implemented by STB, tourism has become one of Singapore's largest industries. This section will analyse the performance of Singapore tourism from three different angles. First, we put Singaporean tourism in an international context to examine its position in the world; second, we review the development of

Singaporean tourism over time; and finally, we illustrate the performance of hospitality, one of the key sectors in the tourism industry.

4.3.1 International Comparison

Since Singapore is a small city state, it is inappropriate to compare its tourism performance with the performances of other countries such as the USA or China. Rather, Euromonitor International (2007) undertook a city comparison. In its top 150 city destinations ranking, Singapore was ranked the fourth (see the Table 4.10 for the top 15 rankings).

Table 4.10 reveals some interesting features. The No.1 ranking city, London, obtained its position with an impressive 15.6 million international visitors in 2006, well above other world cities. The No. 2 to No. 4 cities are Bangkok, Paris, and Singapore with around ten million tourists each. Their tourist arrivals are so close that any variations may change their ranking. The statistics used by Euromonitor are lower than those published by the STB because of different data sources. If we use the STB data (9,750,919 tourist arrivals in 2006), Singapore would overtake Paris and be ranked No. 3. For rankings No. 5 onwards, tourist arrivals

Table 4.10 World top 15 city destinations 2006

City	Ranking	Tourist arrivals (thousand)
London	1	15,640
Bangkok	2	10,350
Paris	3	9700
Singapore	4	9502
Hong Kong	5	8139
New York City	6	6219
Dubai	7	6120
Rome	8	6033
Seoul	9	4920
Barcelona	10	4695
Dublin	11	4469
Bahrain	12	4418
Shanghai	13	4315
Toronto	14	4160
Kuala Lumpur	15	4125

Source: Euromonitor International (2007)

Table 4.11 Top ten cities by number of meetings 2006

City	Ranking	Number of meetings
Paris	1	363
Vienna	2	316
Singapore	3	298
Brussels	4	179
Geneva	5	169
Helsinki	6	140
Barcelona	7	139
London	8	118
Amsterdam	9	117
New York City	10	93

Source: Euromonitor International (2007)

are much less than those of the top four. So it is fair to say that Singapore's No. 4 position is quite safe and there is potential to achieve a higher ranking.

Taking into account that Singapore is a city state with a short history, the fourth ranking for Singapore is very impressive considering it competes with cities like London and Paris that are abundant in rich tourism resources. Compared with another city in the region, Kuala Lumpur (ranked 15th), a culturally rich and naturally blessed city with the support of the whole country (Malaysia), Singapore's performance is outstanding. Its tourist arrivals are more than double Kuala Lumpur's. Why is there such a large difference? Table 4.11 partly uncovers the mystery.

In terms of numbers of meetings, Singapore was ranked third. In 2006, Singapore held 298 meetings, which is just a little less than the No. 2 ranked city Vienna, but much higher than the fourth city, Brussels. This means Singapore's third position is steady and it has the potential to overtake Vienna to become the No. 2 ranked city regarding meetings. This ranking is essential to Singapore because MICE travel has promotional impacts and MICE travellers have much higher per capita expenditure.

4.3.2 Performance over Time

Besides visitor arrivals, tourism receipts (TR) is another indicator of tourism performance. TRs can be treated as part of services exports, so its contribution to exports is also worth noting. The following table lists the visitor arrivals, TRs, and the contribution of tourism to exports from 1991 to 2005.

Table 4.12 demonstrates the performance of the Singapore tourism industry over time. Generally speaking, the number of visitor arrivals displays an increasing trend. However, in the years 1997, 1998, 2001, and 2003, total visitor arrivals experienced significant declines. The sharp drop in visitor arrivals between 1997 and 1998 can be attributed to the 1997 Asian financial crisis. The negative growth in 2001 is coincident with the 9/11 terrorist attacks in the USA while the large fall in visitor arrivals in 2003 may be the combined effects of the outbreak of disease severe acute respiratory syndrome (SARS) in Asian countries and the prolonged effect of the 9/11 event.

TR seem to display similar movements to visitor arrivals, growing over time and dropping in the face of negative shocks. However, closer examination reveals two interesting features. One is that the drop of TR in periods of negative shocks is not in pace with visitor arrivals. For example, in 1996, before the Asian financial crisis visitor arrivals were growing slightly, while TRs fell by 5.6%. In 1997, when visitor arrivals started to drop, TRs decreased dramatically. Another example is the opposite movements of the two variables in 2002. Visitor arrivals started to rise after the 9/11 event in 2001, but TRs continued to decrease. Another feature is that the change of TR is much more volatile than that of visitor arrivals. For example, in 1992, when visitor arrivals increased by 10.6%, TRs picked up 28.7%. In 2004, when visitor arrivals increased by a massive 35.9% after the 2003 SARS event, TRs increased by even more (41.3%). In negative event years, the volatility of TRs is very apparent. In 1997, visitor arrivals dropped 1.3%, but TR dropped by 9.3%; in 2001, visitor arrivals decreased 2.2% while TR dropped by 9.5%. The asynchronism and different volatilities of the two variables may be explained by the fact that tourists' spending has two components: on shore and off shore. The offshore spending happens before the travel starts, such as airfares and hotel reservations. This spending is lost if tourists cancel their travel plans, so it is likely that tourists will stick to their plan, even in the wake of negative events. However, tourists can choose to spend less in their journeys. So the total tourists' spending is more sensitive than and asynchronous with visitor arrivals.

Table 4.12 Visitor arrivals and tourism receipts in Singapore from 1991 to 2005

Year	Visitor arrivals	% change	Tourism receipts (TR, S$ Million, nominal)	% change	TR as % of services exports	TR as % of total exports of goods and services
1991	5,414,414	NA	7770	NA	32.5	6.0
1992	5,989,837	10.6	10,003	28.7	37.9	7.4
1993	6,425,677	7.3	11,147	12.6	37.1	7.2
1994	6,898,309	7.4	11,264	1.1	32.0	6.1
1995	7,136,538	3.5	11,697	3.8	29.7	5.2
1996	7,292,366	2.2	11,039	−5.6	28.9	4.7
1997	7,197,871	−1.3	10,017	−9.3	26.2	4.0
1998	6,242,152	−13.3	8531	−14.8	22.6	3.6
1999	6,958,201	11.5	9568	12.2	22.6	3.7
2000	7,691,399	10.5	10,081	5.4	20.8	3.2
2001	7,522,163	−2.2	9122	−9.5	18.5	3.1
2002	7,567,110	0.6	8831	−3.3	16.7	2.9
2003	6,127,288	−19.0	6937	−21.4	11.0	2.0
2004	8,328,658	35.9	9800	41.3	12.4	2.3
2005	8,943,029	7.4	10,871	10.9	12.7	2.3

Source: Singapore Tourism Board (2005)

The last two columns reveal three facts about the contribution of TRs to exports. First, TR tends to increase over time. However, its contribution to services exports or to total exports demonstrates a clear decreasing trend, which means that other services exports or exports of goods increase much faster than tourism. Second, the contribution of TR to services is significant despite the decreasing trend. Even in 2003 when the contribution of TR dropped to its lowest level, it still accounted for 11% of services exports. Finally, the bigger the change in TR, the bigger is the change in its contribution to services exports and to total exports. In 1992, a 28.7% increase in TR led to a big jump in its share of exports. Similarly, a big drop of TR in 1998 and 2003 resulted in an unusually low value in its contribution to exports. This implies that TRs are more volatile and more easily subject to external events. This confirms the claim by some economists that tourism is a risky source of earning (e.g. Wilson 1994).

Since TR includes the expenditure from foreign air/sea crew (they are not tourists according to United Nations World Tourism Organization [UNTWO]'s definition), it is arguable that TR is not a good indicator of tourists' spending. Since 1998, STB introduced the total expenditure of visitors (TEV) in its tourism annual report which excluded the expenditure of transit passengers, foreign air/sea crew, and foreign students. The TEV and TR from 1998 to 2006 are listed in Table 4.13.

From the last column in Table 4.13, we see that TEV is the main proportion of TR (around 64%) and its contribution has increased in recent years. So we can say that TR may not be a precise indicator of

Table 4.13 TEV and TR from 1998 to 2006

Year	Total expenditure of visitors (TEV, S$ Million)	% change	Tourism receipts (TR, S$ Million)	% change	TEV/TR
1998	5494	NA	8531	NA	64.4
1999	6033	9.8	9568	12.2	63.1
2000	6293	4.3	10,081	5.4	62.4
2001	5699	−9.4	9122	−9.5	62.5
2002	5426	−4.8	8831	−3.2	61.4
2003	4316	−20.5	6937	−21.4	62.2
2004	6278	45.5	9800	41.3	64.1
2005	7172	14.2	10,871	10.9	66.0
2006	8421	17.4	12,395	14.0	67.9

Source: Singapore Tourism Board (2007)

tourists' spending, but it is a good gross indicator. Another feature the table reveals is that the change of TEV and TR over time has the same pattern, but the growth rate of TEV is higher than that of TR in recent years, but is lower than around 2000. This implies that, contrary to the situation at the turn of the century, the increase in the number of tourists in recent years is faster than the increase in transitional passengers, foreign air/sea crew, and foreign students.

4.3.3 Performance of the Hospitality Industry

Since tourists stay in destination countries only for a short periods of time (less than one year according to UNWTO's definition of tourists), they tend to live in accommodations, such as hotels, and eat in restaurants. According to STB (2005), around 60% of visitors to Singapore choose to stay in a hotel. The hospitality industry is thus very closely related to tourism. The hospitality industry has two components: hotel and food and beverage (F&B). The performance of gazetted hotels can be evaluated by the average room rate (ARR) and room occupancy rate (AOR), as shown in Table 4.14.

Table 4.14 illustrates that the AOR increases over time, with two exceptions. One is in 1998 and another one is in the period from 2001 to 2003. Both can be attributed to negative international events. The ARR shows some fluctuations in the demonstrated period, but it displays an increasing trend in recent years. The increasing AOR and ARR imply that the hospitality industry is doing well. However, the story is not complete without the number of available hotels and hotel rooms (see Table 4.15).

Table 4.14 Standard average occupancy rate (AOR) and average room rate (ARR)

Year	1997	1998	1999	2000	2001	2002	2003	2004	2005	2006
AOR (%)	79.4	71.3	74.9	83.5	76.3	74.4	67.2	80.6	83.8	85.2
ARR (S$)	150.9	137.3	120.0	127.8	133.4	126.0	115.5	121.7	137.0	164.4
% Chg	0.5	−9.0	−12.6	6.5	4.4	−5.6	−8.3	5.4	12.5	20.0

Source: Singapore Tourism Board (2007)

Table 4.15 Supply of hotels and hotel rooms at the end of the year, 1997–2006

	Number of hotels			Rooms available					
				Gazetted		Non-gazetted		Total	
Year	Gazetted	Non-gazetted	Total	No.	% Chg	No.	% Chg	No.	% Chg
1997	94	93	187	29583	2.0	3616	8.0	33199	2.6
1998	101	106	207	30123	1.8	5003	38.4	35126	5.8
1999	99	107	206	29683	−1.5	5203	4.0	34886	−0.7
2000	104	102	206	30469	2.6	5156	−0.9	35625	2.1
2001	103	102	205	30472	0.0	5202	0.9	35674	0.1
2002	101	103	204	30468	0.0	5521	6.1	35989	0.9
2003	99	111	210	29917	−1.8	6013	8.9	35930	−0.2
2004	102	118	220	30300	1.3	6465	7.5	36765	2.3
2005	103	122	225	30445	0.5	6416	−0.8	36861	0.3
2006	103	123	226	30686	0.8	6512	1.5	37198	0.9

Source: Singapore Tourism Board (2007)

Table 4.15 manifests that the number of gazetted hotels increased slightly from 1997 to 2006, while the number of non-gazetted hotels increased significantly over the same period. It is also of interest to note the significant increases during 1997–1998 and 2003–2004. The change in available rooms in gazetted hotels swings slightly over time, but for non-gazetted hotels, there is a significant increase over time, especially during 1997–1998 and during 2001–2003. Despite the fact that an increase in the number of hotels or hotel rooms takes time, the increases during 1997–1998 and 2001–2003 seem unusual considering the Asian financial crisis in 1997, the 9/11 event in 2001 and the SARS in 2003. However, if we combine Table 4.15 with Table 4.14, it is easy to justify the seemingly unusual business decisions and to understand the link between the hotel room supply and the ARR. The record-high ARR in 1997 stimulates hotel supply in 1998, thus both gazetted and non-gazetted hotel rooms increase dramatically. The increased hotel supply dropped the ARR significantly in 1998 and 1999. Again, in 2000 and 2001 increasing ARR led to an increase in hotel supply (mainly non-gazetted this time), which in turn resulted in lower ARR in 2003 and 2004.

The significant increases in AOR, ARR, and available rooms indicate that Singapore's hotel sector is making a good profit. Although data on all hotel revenue is not available, we can use the CESS revenue to evaluate the performance of hotel and F&B. CESS is the imposition of a tax on certain types of hotel, and food and beverage establishments which have been gazetted under the Singapore tourism (Cess Collection) Act Cap. 305C. The total sales turnover of 'Cessable' hotels and F&B establishments calculated from CESS revenue is shown in Table 4.16.

Table 4.16 uncovers the contribution of the hotel and F&B in terms of room revenue, F&B revenue, and total sales turnover. Room revenue displays a rising trend but appears to have fluctuated in the face of negative world events. However, the influence of negative events may be exaggerated since the sharp drops in 1998 and in 2003 may be due, in part, to the slashed ARR as a result of increased non-gazetted hotel rooms. The growth of the F&B industry exhibits a similar pattern to the hotel industry with decreases in 1998 and in 2001–2003. The hotel F&B revenue is less volatile than the hotel room revenue because its price is not subject to changing ARR. From this point of view, it may be a better indicator of the

Table 4.16 Sales turnover of Cessable hotels and other F&B establishments (S$ Million)

Year	1997	1998	1999	2000	2001	2002	2003	2004	2005	2006
Room revenue	1225.5	987.1	923.3	1085.1	1066.6	993.1	752.1	1017.2	1216.0	1503.9
Hotel F&B	813.4	689.0	714.1	781.7	682.1	691.5	616.8	711.7	775.0	794.6
Hotel revenue	2038.9	1676.1	1637.4	1866.8	1748.7	1684.6	1368.9	1728.9	1991.0	2298.5
Other F&B	942.6	890.4	889.1	982.2	1036.2	950.1	884.0	932.6	960.6	1037.2
Total sales turnover	2981.5	2566.5	2526.5	2849.0	2784.9	2,634.7	2252.9	2661.5	2951.6	3335.7

Source: Singapore Tourism Board (2005)

effects of negative world events. The other F&B revenue seems to be even more stable than the hotel F&B revenue. This can be explained by the fact that local residents also contribute to the other F&B revenue. Besides hotels, Singapore has a huge array of restaurants and fast-food chains such as McDonald's, Pizza Hut, KFC, Burger King, Subway, and Mos Burger, which contribute to the revenue of other F&B. Singapore is also famous for the hawker centres. These centres are located near or in shopping centres, which provide numerous versions of traditional food catering for different types of customers. The large number of these centres encourages competition and leads to low prices, which are enjoyed by tourists and local residents alike. Finally, the total sales turnover is more stable than hotel room revenue. The reason is apparent in that F&B revenue is less volatile and the F&B component accounts for more than half of the total sales turnover.

4.4 Characteristics of Tourism Market

Based on recent first-hand data from the tourism survey undertaken by STB, this section identifies the key characteristics of Singapore's tourism, which are important in estimating the economic impact of tourism, designing tourism policy, and improving the performance of the tourism industry.

4.4.1 A Holiday and Business/MICE Destination

Visitor arrivals by visiting purpose are shown in Fig. 4.1.

While holiday making (37% in 2006) is the major component of the Singapore tourism industry, the business/MICE (meetings incentive travel, convention and exhibition) travellers rank second in importance. The general increase in the share of holiday visitor arrivals implies an improved tourism environment in Singapore, and the continuing increase in business/MICE travel reflects the Singapore government's effort to proactively attract business/MICE travellers. With the share of holiday and business/MICE travel increasing, the shares of other components such as visiting friends/relatives have fallen.

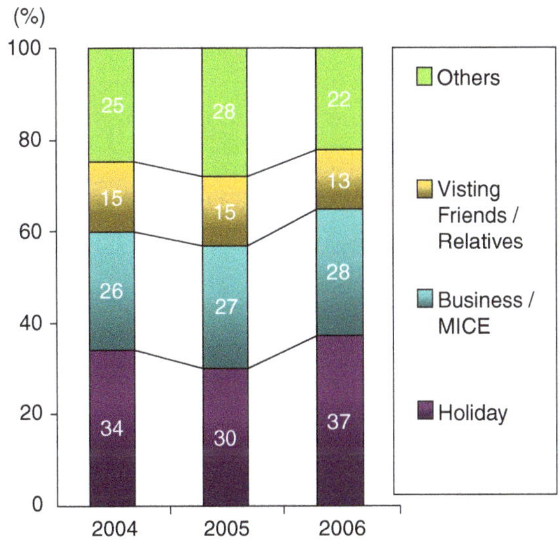

Fig. 4.1 Visitor arrivals by visiting purpose in recent years

The survey results on visiting purposes are confirmed by the results on travelling companions. The survey shows that 58% of visitors have companions: half of them are with a spouse, 20 % are with friends, 10 % are with business associates, and the rest are with siblings, parents, children, partner/ boyfriend/girlfriend, and relatives. Apart from the visitors with business associates, the majority of the visitors with companions are likely to be on holiday. Despite the fact that most of the travellers (58 %) have companions, there are a considerable number of lone travellers to Singapore. It seems reasonable to assume that, due to income and safety reasons, the majority of these single travellers are male and are travelling for holiday or business purposes. As such, the number of total male travellers will outweigh the number of female travellers. This reasoning is consistent with visitor arrivals by gender, shown in Table 4.17.

From Table 4.17, it is obvious that male visitors far outweigh female visitors. When it comes to age group, it is quite interesting to find that from age 15 to 34 the number of visitor arrivals increases but decreases afterwards, which may imply the income effect, the life style attractiveness, and the significance of business travellers: when people are young

Table 4.17 Visitor arrivals by gender and age group

Thousand							
	1997	2002	2003	2004	2005	2006	2007
Total	7197.9	7566.8	6126.9	8328.6	8943.0	9751.0	10284.5
Sex							
Males	4540.6	4205.4	3418.0	4553.5	4810.8	5167.7	5352.9
Females	2657.3	3017.2	2462.5	3479.4	3675.7	4000.0	4207.5
Age (years)							
Under 15	485.1	543.0	425.7	619.7	677.2	719.0	767.7
15–19	202.7	226.7	169.9	254.3	283.2	316.9	362.5
20–24	516.5	512.1	426.8	579.9	630.1	694.7	736.1
25–34	1808.3	1852.2	1505.5	2009.4	2156.1	2309.0	2390.5
35–44	1674.6	1757.0	1463.0	1965.1	2118.7	2278.0	2349.3
45–54	1343.2	1418.8	1150.9	1533.3	1614.3	1770.4	1846.0
55–64	755.6	830.7	664.2	913.8	971.7	1097.0	1182.1
65 & over	364.1	400.9	300.5	427.0	467.0	541.8	611.2
Not stated	47.8	25.6	20.5	26.2	24.6	24.3	39.3

Note: Data for visitor arrivals excludes arrivals of Malaysians by land
Source: Singapore Tourism Board (2005)

(e.g. under 25 years old), they generally do not have enough income to afford their travel and thus, compared with other groups, the visitor arrivals in this age group are relatively low (the significantly higher visitor arrivals for age under 15 years old may be because they are accompanied by adults). When they become older, they have sufficiently high income, and thus the number of visitor arrivals increases sharply in the age group 25–34. High visitor arrivals between the ages of 25 and 54 may also be an indication of business travel and the attractiveness of Singapore city life to young and middle-aged people. As people grow older (55 and above), they have higher disposable income, but are less likely to be on business trips and often prefer a quiet environment to the busy city life and thus visitor arrivals in this age group are fewer compared with age group 25–34. However, visitor arrivals in the 55-and-above age groups have picked up significantly in recent years, which may signal the development of Singapore's relaxing recreational sites or the preference change of the older visitor.

4.4.2 Diverse but Uneven Tourism-Generating Markets

Visitor arrivals by region in 2006 are shown in Fig. 4.2, which highlights the importance of different regions to the Singapore tourism industry.

Southeast Asia is the most important tourism market for Singapore, followed by North Asia and Europe. South Asia and Oceania have similar market shares while the America's share is slightly less. These rankings demonstrate the importance of the geographic and economic position of the region to Singapore's tourism industry. Southeast Asian countries are Singapore's nearest neighbours so they contribute the most to Singapore's visitor arrivals. The geographic importance is made even more explicit by the total contribution of the Asian region (as high as 73%). The importance of the economy in the region is prominent when we compare South

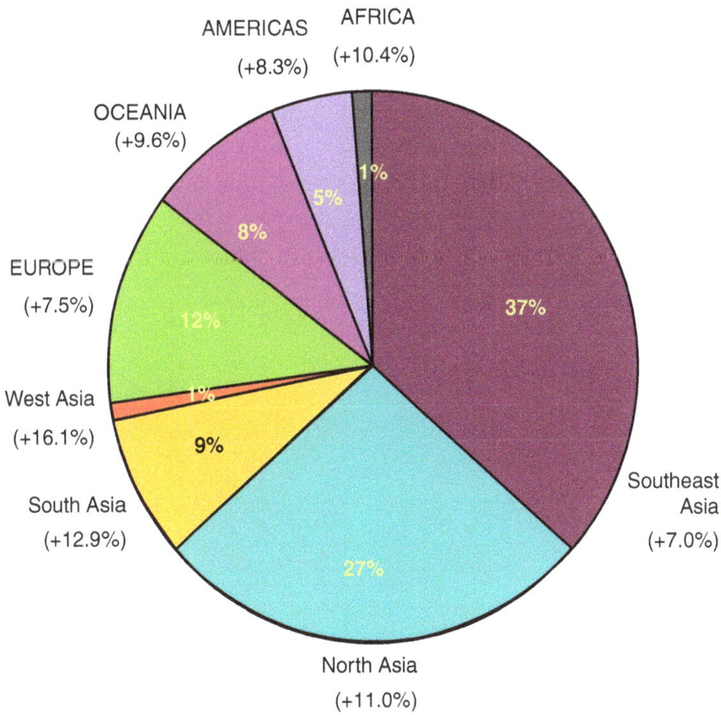

Fig. 4.2 Visitor arrivals by region in 2006

Asia with Europe. The South Asia region is much nearer to Singapore than Europe, but its market share (9%) is significantly less than the latter (12%). A feasible explanation lies in the higher income of European countries than that of developing countries in South Asia. However, these market shares are changing over time. For example, the market shares of North Asia, South Asia, and West Asia increased in 2006 due to outstanding growth in visitor arrivals (11.0%, 12.9%, and 16.1%, respectively).

The visitor arrivals by country also confirm our findings (see Fig. 4.3). The significance of both Indonesia and China to the Singapore tourism industry stands out. Visitors from Indonesia are nearly twice those from China while Chinese visitors are 1.5 times higher than the third largest market, Australia. The second important group of countries consists of Australia, India, Malaysia, and Japan, each of which contributes around 600,000–700,000 visitor arrivals. The rest of the top ten countries have a combined contribution of 1,820,000 visitor arrivals. China, South Korea, and the Philippines are high potential markets in terms of growth in visitor arrivals (more than 20% growth from 2005 to 2006). The different growth rates of visitor arrivals in tourism markets has led to a ranking change in the top ten tourism markets overtime (see Table 4.18).

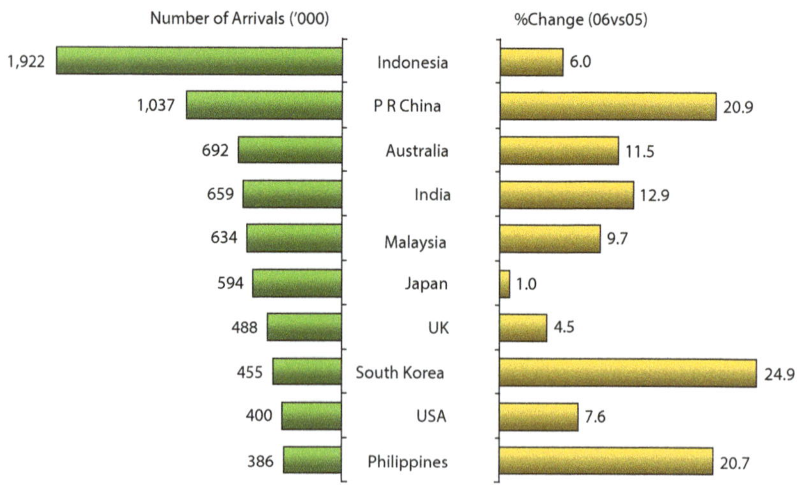

Fig. 4.3 Top ten visitor arrivals by country in 2006

Table 4.18 Top ten tourism-generating markets by visitor arrivals in recent years

Ranking	2002	2003	2004	2005	2006
1	Indonesia	Indonesia	Indonesia	Indonesia	Indonesia
2	Japan	P.R. China	P.R. China	P.R. China	P.R. China
3	P.R. China	Malaysia	Japan	Australia	Australia
4	Malaysia	Japan	Australia	Japan	India
5	Australia	Australia	Malaysia	India	Malaysia
6	UK	UK	India	Malaysia	Japan
7	India	India	UK	UK	UK
8	South Korea	South Korea	South Korea	Thailand	South Korea
9	USA	USA	Thailand	USA	USA
10	Hong Kong	Thailand	USA	South Korea	Philippines

Source: Singapore Tourism Board (2005)

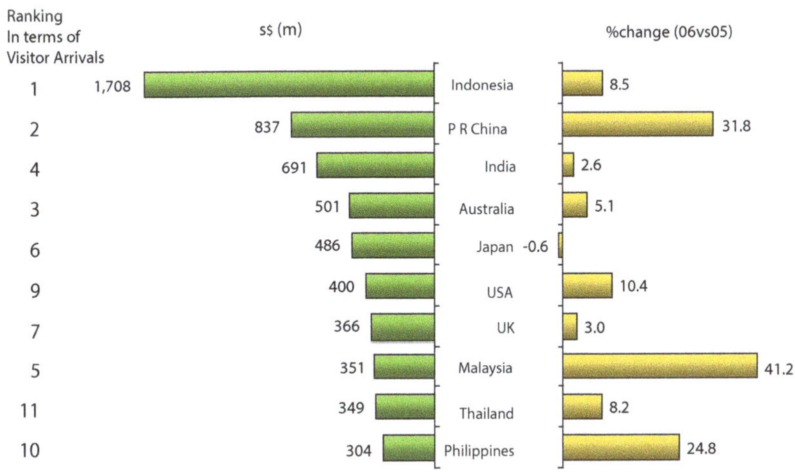

Fig. 4.4 Top ten tourism-generating markets by TEV in 2006

Due to its proximity and relatively large population, Indonesia was the most important contributor in terms of visitor arrivals for the period 2002–2006. Japan dropped from second to sixth place, a reflection of its gloomy economy, while good economic performance has seen China jump from third place to second. Australia has advanced over Malaysia and Japan into third place in recent years.

The economic importance of the tourism markets can be more precisely revealed by TEV. Figure 4.4 shows the amount of TEV in 2006 and

Table 4.19 Average per capita expenditure for top ten tourism-generating countries ($)

	2002	2003	2004	2005	2006
Total	717	705	754	802	864
Indonesia	800	792	838	868	889
China	467	475	652	741	807
India	1482	1323	1069	1154	1048
Australia	646	615	727	768	724
Japan	727	736	747	830	817
United States	875	855	904	976	1001
United Kingdom	716	698	754	761	750
Malaysia	405	397	443	430	553
Thailand	815	778	827	851	979
Philippines	834	760	844	762	788

Source: Singapore Tourism Board (2005)

percentage change of 2006 over 2005 for the top ten tourism-generating markets.

Figure 4.4 shows the importance of Indonesia, China, and India for TEV in Singapore. Indonesia, again, displays its dominant role for the Singapore tourism industry with its impressive TEV, twice as much as that of China. The rest of the top ten countries have also made considerable contributions. When we turn to TEV growth in 2006 over 2005, we find that Malaysia, China, and the Philippines markets have high growth potential. If we compare the ranking by TEV and by visitor arrivals, we find that, for India, Japan, and USA, the TEV ranking is higher than correspondent ranking of visitor arrivals. The reason is depicted in Table 4.19, per capita spending of visitors in these countries is significantly higher.

The average per capita expenditure of visitors shows that Indonesia, China, India, Japan, United States, Thailand, and the Philippines are the more valuable markets for Singapore's tourism industry as their per capita contributions are the highest.

4.4.3 Gateway Tourism

Singapore as a small city state may lack tourism resources but its strategic geographic position implies massive gateway tourism. The importance of

Table 4.20 Visitor arrivals by length of stay in recent years (thousands)

Length of stay (days)	1997	2002	2003	2004	2005	2006	2007
Total	6922.9	7373.7	5976.5	8057.5	8591.5	9348.5	9769.5
Under 1	1303.7	1718.3	1429.7	1793.2	1862.6	2163.0	2327.8
1	1778.7	1951.8	1534.9	2052.6	1984.2	2175.4	2223.7
2	1397.6	1292.9	1031.7	1444.1	1568.6	1634.9	1675.5
3	975.4	906.1	698.8	1028.9	1165.0	1189.4	1232.2
4	428.3	429.3	348.8	499.6	582.5	622.4	648.5
5	237.9	241.0	202.4	279.4	324.7	344.4	362.7
6	157.2	160.8	136.0	183.9	216.8	232.4	236.7
7	125.8	128.0	110.3	142.1	165.7	181.7	176.9
8–10	159.9	163.5	143.0	190.4	213.2	232.7	240.0
11–14	160.6	198.1	178.5	219.3	255.4	297.7	224.8
15–29	130.4	120.7	107.8	151.5	165.7	174.0	280.6
30–59	40.0	40.6	35.7	48.6	59.1	65.1	104.5
60 & over	27.5	22.6	18.9	23.8	28.1	35.3	35.6
Average	3.3	3.1	3.2	3.2	3.4	3.4	3.6

Source: Based on Singapore year book, Department of Statistics, (2008)

Note: Data for visitor arrivals refers to visitors who left Singapore during the period specified and excludes arrivals of Malaysians by land, which are mainly migrant workers

gateway tourism in Singapore is manifest in its visitor arrivals by length of stay, displayed in Table 4.20.

The significantly high visitor arrivals for a length of stay less than one day can be explained by transitional travel since Singapore is a major air hub. The high level of visitor arrivals for a length of stay between one and three days may indicate the limited space and resources in Singapore. Most people may find that three days are long enough for sightseeing in Singapore. High living expenses (e.g. accommodation) also prevents people from staying too long. However, the average length of stay has increased in recent years, which may be an indication of increased tourism activities or tourism sites in Singapore and/or the good performance of the world economy.

Aware of the importance of gateway tourism, the Singapore government has made a great deal of effort to utilize its strategic geographic advantage. One area of focus has been on encouraging travellers to break route at its airport. In order to do so, Singapore has adopted an open skies policy that allows foreign airlines to compete for passengers in Singapore. Consequently,

Table 4.21 Number of air passengers 1980–1994

Year	Arrival	Changes	Departure	Changes	In transit	Changes
1980	3,140,723	NA	3,151,032	NA	1,002,794	NA
1985	4,323,587	1,182,864	4,397,908	1,246,876	1,135,335	132,541
1990	7,237,233	2,913,646	7,166,347	2,768,439	1,217,173	81,838
1994	10,134,000	2,896,767	10,069,000	2,902,653	1,442,040	224,867

Source: Department of Statistics, Singapore year book, various issues

a large number of international airlines use Changi as a transit stop between Europe and the Asia-Pacific. This policy not only increases the number of transitional passengers but also increases the number of visitors, as shown in Table 4.21.

Table 4.21 shows that the numbers of arrival, departure, and in-transit passengers have increased over time, but the increases in passenger arrivals and departures are much greater than transition increases. For example, in 1990, passenger arrivals and departures increased by nearly three million on 1985 numbers, but passengers in transit only increased by approximately 82,000. This suggests an increase of more than two million non-transit visitors to Singapore.

The Singapore government is also devoted to enhancing regional cooperation so as to forge regional tourism and business alliances. The STB maintains a close government-to-government relationship with many regional countries. In Southeast Asia, the STB has developed seven bilateral/trilateral government-to-government agreements and commitments such as Indonesia–Singapore Tourism Co-operation, Malaysia–Singapore Tourism Council, Singapore–Vietnam Tourism Co-operation, and Indonesia–Malaysia–Singapore Growth Triangle (Tourism Working Group). In North Asia, STB has formed different levels of cooperation with China. For example, there exists the high-level CNTA (China National Tourism Administration)-STB bilateral meeting, Singapore-Sichuan Trade and Investment Committee (tourism sub-committee), and the Singapore–Shangdong Business Council (tourism component). In South Asia and Oceania, STB supports the Singapore–India Tourism Cooperation and the new Singapore–Australia partnership.

4.4.4 Tourism Shopping and Health Tourism

If we break down the TEV into different parts, we can determine how tourism can contribute to the growth of Singapore's economy. The breakdown of major visitors' expenditure items is shown in Fig. 4.5.

Figure 4.5 portrays that, of S$8421 million TEV, shopping is the largest part (44%), while the hotel sector enjoys 27%. The third largest share is occupied by the F&B industry (12%), followed by medical/healthcare (9%) and local transport (6%). The direct revenue from tourism, sightseeing/entertainment, comprises less than 1.5% (S$124m out of S$8421m) of TEV.

Comparing the distribution of tourism expenditure over time, we can uncover some interesting features of Singapore tourism spending, shown in Table 4.22.

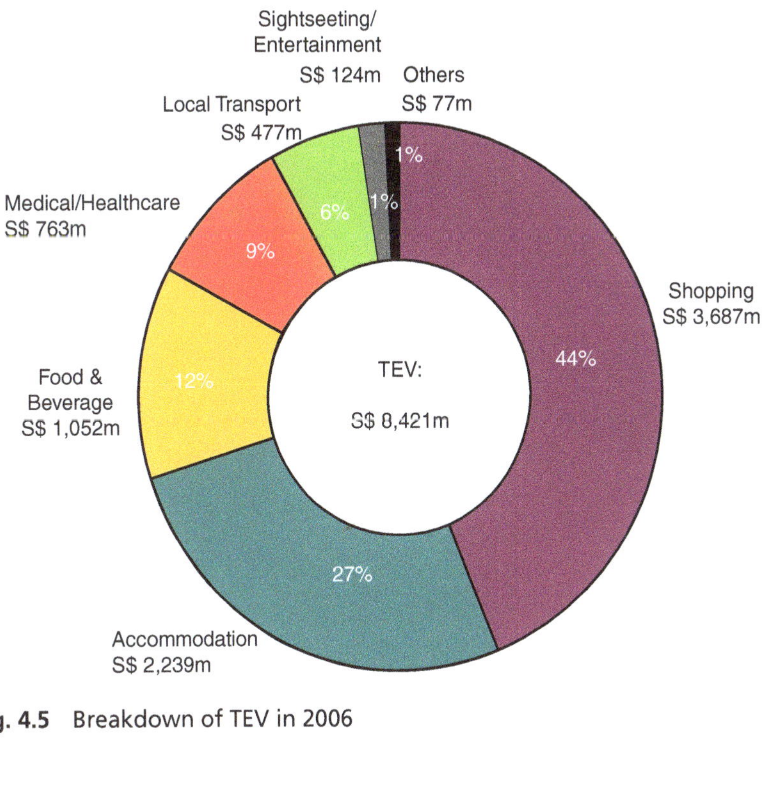

Fig. 4.5 Breakdown of TEV in 2006

Table 4.22 Distribution of tourism expenditure on major items (%), 2001–2006

Year	2001 (%)	2002 (%)	2003 (%)	2004 (%)	2005 (%)	2006 (%)
Shopping	49	53	53	50	46	44
Accommodation	23	22	21	22	25	27
Food and beverage	14	13	13	14	14	12
Medical/Healthcare	4	3	4	6	8	9
Local transport	6	5	5	6	6	6
Sightseeing/Entertainment	4	4	2	2	2	1
Others	0	0	2	1	0	1

Source: Singapore Tourism Board, Annual report on Tourism statistics, various issues

Table 4.22 demonstrates the trends of tourism spending on main items. First, the proportion of spending on healthcare and on accommodation increases over time. The increasing proportional spending on healthcare in recent years illustrates the increasing tourists' demand for Singaporean healthcare. With the efforts of the Singapore government, Singaporean healthcare services are of high standard and of a relatively low cost, which attract large number of people from Southeast Asia, especially Indonesia. By contrast, the increasing proportional spending on accommodation reflects the increasing price of accommodation in Singapore and the rigidity of tourism spending on it. Combining Tables 4.22 and 4.14, we can find that the percentage change in tourism spending on accommodation follows exactly the same pattern as the change of the ARR: when the latter decreased from S$133.4 to S$115.5 per night during 2001–2003, the proportion of tourists' spending on accommodation dropped from 23% to 21%; from 2003 to 2006, as the ARR climbed from S$115.5 to S$164.4 per night, the tourists' spending on accommodation jumped from 21% to 27% of the total spending. The relationship between ARR and the proportional spending on accommodation can be explained by the rigidity of tourists spending on accommodation: tourists have to acquire accommodation even if the prices of accommodation rise.

Second, the percentages of expenditure on both F&B and local transport are quite stable. The steady proportional spending on local transport and F&B may result from two facts. One is that, like accommodation, these two items are necessities for tourists when they are on their journey, so the demand for them cannot vary much, other things being equal. Another fact is that the prices of local transport and F&B are more stable compared with prices of other items. The Singaporean local transport system is largely dominated by the government, which is averse to seeing large price fluctuations. F&B services involve large number of private agents and the fierce competition pushes the prices close to operating cost. Moreover, since the prices of these two items have a large impact on Singaporean residents' daily life, it is beneficial for both the government and private agents to keep the prices stable.

Third, the proportional spending on sightseeing and shopping decreases in the period considered. One reason for this decreasing trend is that these activities pay the price for the increased proportion of spending on other services. As the MICE tourists increase, the sightseeing spending will fall behind. As the accommodation and healthcare bill goes up faster, the increase in spending on shopping must slow down. The relationship between accommodation and shopping spending is very illustrative: as the spending on accommodation decreases from 25% to 22% during 2001–2003, the shopping spending increases from 49% to 53%; after 2003, the spending on accommodation increases dramatically from 22% to 27% and as a result, the shopping spending has to decrease from 53% to 44%. Another reason is that, unlike accommodation and transport, sightseeing and shopping are not indispensable for tourists. The flexible nature of sightseeing and shopping means that the proportion of spending on them is subject to the change of spending on other necessary items.

Since shopping expenditure is a major part of TEV (around 50% in the displayed period), the Singapore tourism surveys also have broken it down to different shopping items. Table 4.23 lists the distribution of shopping items from 2004 to 2006 (the surveys before 2004 use different shopping categories, so they are not comparable).

Table 4.23 illustrates that the proportions of tourism shopping spending on different items are quite stable. The largest proportion of shopping—spending on fashion and accessories—has remained the same for three years. With the one exception of spending on Consumer Tech in 2004 (the reason is unknown), the spending on other items has varied no more than 2% in the period. This almost fixed proportional shopping spending

Table 4.23 Distribution of tourism shopping items (%)

Year	Fashion and accessories (%)	Consumer tech (%)	Jewellery (%)	Cosmetics and wellness products (%)	Edibles (%)	Gifts (%)	Watch and clocks (%)	Tobacco cigarettes and alcohol (%)	Others (%)
2004	32	27	11	8	5	5	3	3	6
2005	32	24	13	9	6	5	4	3	4
2006	32	24	11	10	6	6	3	4	4

Source: Singapore Tourism Board, Annual report on Tourism statistics, 2004–2006

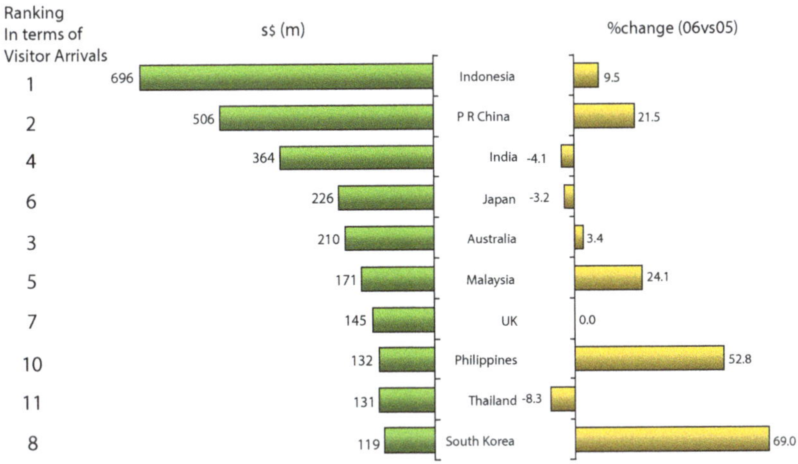

Fig. 4.6 Top ten tourism shoppers in 2006

pattern reflects the luxury nature of tourism shopping—the tourism shopping items are not necessities for daily life so tourists are very flexible in the face of a relative price change. The change in the price of one good may lead to the opposite change in tourists demand, so tourists' total spending on this good does not change much. As a result, the proportion of spending on it may not change.

To find the biggest tourism shoppers, STB has also ranked shopping spending for different tourism-generating markets (see Fig. 4.6).

Figure 4.6 indicates that the biggest shoppers are from Indonesia, China, and India. The average shopping spending of tourists from these three countries is more than twice that of any other countries. If we compare the rank of shopping spending with that of visitor arrivals, we find that people from India and Japan shop more than expected. If we compare the breaking-down TEV rankings (see STB 2005) and the shopping spending rankings, we find that visitors from the USA tend to spend more on services, whereas visitors from Malaysia, for example, tend to spend more on shopping.

4.5 Information on Tourism Policies

The tourism boom and its significant contribution to the Singapore economy are, to some extent, due to the government's emphasis on active tourism policies. The Singapore government recognized the significance of the tourism industry to its economy as early as 1964 when it established the Singapore Tourism Promotion Board (STPB), while Singapore was still in the federation of Malaysia. The newly born STPB, with only 25 staff, welcomed 91,000 visitors in the first year. In later years, STPB (or STB) actively engaged in coordinating the efforts of hotels, airlines, and travel agents, innovating new tourism products, and responding to negative shocks to the tourism industry such as the world economic recession in 1985, the Asian financial crisis in 1997, the 9/11 terrorist attacks in 2001, and the outbreak of SARS in 2003. The tourism policies of STPB were so successful that STPB itself was renamed STB in 1997 reflecting the importance of the tourism industry and tourism policy. The STB has now become an important entity, with its head office in Singapore, 22 regional offices, and 2 marketing representatives spread over the world. Despite the success of STPB (or STB), economic and historical conditions constrained the evolution of its policies. The evolution of Singapore's tourism policies over time can be categorized into the following three stages.

4.5.1 Modernist Aspiration (1965–1985)

After independence in 1965, the new nation was desperate to reconfigure its urban infrastructure and broaden its fledgling economy. Thus, modernization was the mainstream ideology. Correspondingly, the tourism policies were shaped by modernist aspirations. Throughout the 1960s and 1970s, the strategies to promote tourism concentrated on encouraging investment in infrastructure and developing 'garden attractions and modern hotels' (Chang and Yeoh 1999, p. 10). As a result, many new hotels were built, some existing hotels were expanded, and tourist attractions like the Resort Island of Sentosa and the Jurong Birdpark were constructed. In terms of cultural attraction, STPB marketed Singapore as an 'instant

Asia', a place where the various 'Asian cultures' may be found (Chang 1998; Chang and Yeoh 1999). Attractions attempting to encapsulate the 'melting pot' of Asian cultures were created. For example, in 1976, the Singapore Handicraft centre opened as a showcase of Asian arts and craft and the 'instant Asia cultural show' was staged, which featured dances incorporating the different 'races' in Singapore (Chang and Yeoh 1999).

However, the recession in the tourism industry in the early 1980s spurred STPB's rethinking of its tourism policies. In 1982, the visitor arrivals growth rate decreased to 4.5%, the lowest level since the formation of STPB. In the following year, it plummeted even lower into negative territory for the first time (−3.5%). In 1984 and 1985, growth in visitor arrivals once again became positive but the rate of growth was very slow. The slowdown of the tourism industry can most likely be attributed to changes in the world and local economic climates. Following the oil shocks experienced in 1982–1983, the world economy slipped into recession in 1985. The local economy also slowed because of a slowdown of the manufacturing sector and a decrease in Singapore's competitiveness in labour-intensive operations due to a wage correction policy in 1979. However, STPB recognized that the weaknesses of the existing tourist products were also reasons for the slowdown of the tourism industry. The emphasis on modernist urban and economic development meant that the conservation of natural, historical, and cultural attractions was sacrificed. The Tourism Task Force Report of 1984 pointed to the need to look into the loss of Singapore's 'oriental mystique and charm' which had been wrought by the rapid erasure of 'old buildings, traditional activities and bustling road activities' from the urban landscape (MTI 1984, p. 6).

4.5.2 Heritage Tourism (1986–1995)

Heritage preservation efforts were initiated as early as the 1950s under the former colonial powers. However, the efforts more befitted the mood in the 1960s of progress and development rather than preservation, so little was done before 1970. The celebration of the 150th anniversary of Singapore in 1969 provided the catalyst for further consideration of the preservation question.

In 1971, the Preservation of Monuments Board (PMB) was established to take charge of the gazetting and preservation of national monuments. However, since industrialization and urban redevelopment took precedence in the name of providing better employment, environmental improvements, and investment opportunities, the success of PMB in the 1970s was very limited.

The 1980s saw an increased emphasis on urban conservation as a means of preserving heritage. One reason was the emergence of nostalgia and a harking back to the past as a reaction to the relentless drive of economic development and the consequent 'industrialization of everyday life' (Chua 1995). Another reason was the search for new economic direction after the recession in 1985. In 1986, the MTI unveiled the Tourism Product Development plan. The plan devoted US$223 million to the redevelopment of ethnic 'enclaves' and historically significant sites such as Chinatown, Little India, Kampong Glam, the Singapore River, the Raffles Hotel, and Bugis Street. These policies were explicitly aimed at creating 'local cultural consciousness' (Teo 1994, p. 132) among Singaporeans, as well as creating attractions for the enjoyment of tourists.

In 1993, the STPB released a new master plan called the Strategic Plan for Growth. This plan assessed all of the achievements since the Tourism Product Development Plan and claimed that Singapore's tourism infrastructure was generally well developed. Rather than pursue a continued focus on new attractions, it emphasized refinement of tourist landscape in Singapore.

4.5.3 Tourism Capital (1996–Present)

In 1996, STPB published Tourism 21: Vision of a Tourism Capital. The aim of Tourism 21 was that Singapore would become a primary destination with extensions to complementary destinations in Asia-Pacific region. The meaning of Tourism Capital was twofold. On the one hand, Singapore must provide easy and convenient linkage to regional tourism attractions, namely, tourism regionalisation or gateway tourism, and on the other hand, Singapore must provide primary tourism attractions so that tourists stay longer and spend more in Singapore. Tourism 21 largely addressed gateway tourism.

Tourism 21 noticed that Singapore had several distinct advantages and thus could become the gateway to Southeast Asia. It had the potential to harvest 'gateway tourism' via its sophisticated transportation and telecommunications infrastructure, political stability, manpower, social settings, and strategic location. Its strategy was to encourage members of the tourism industry in the region to break their traditional geographical boundaries and package complementary products so as to increase Singapore's attractions with regional tourist destinations. By doing so, Singapore became a 'tourism hub' or a 'primal node' benefiting from tourism flows within Southeast Asia (Yeoh and Chang 2001).

Tourism 21 purported to change the image of Singapore. Singapore's clean, green environment, and world-class infrastructure, in the eyes of tourists, was more impressive than the exotic, multicultural experience being offered by 'instant Asia'. Hence, STPB created a new tagline 'New Asia—Singapore', which suggests, according to STPB (1996, p. 5), 'a Singapore which is progressive and sophisticated, yet still a unique expression of the Asian soul'. In implementing Tourism 21, STB tended to bring concepts from abroad into the Singapore lifestyle by actively seeking to match-make foreign franchises with local ventures. The results were an influx of Western companies such as Planet Hollywood, Starbucks, and Tony Roma's. STB also actively sought to host cultural and entertainment events such as the staging of world renowned musicals like 'Cats' and 'Les Miserables', and performances by the late Luciano Pavarotti and Michael Jackson, so as to establish Singapore as a regional arts and cultural hub.

In January 2005, the Minister for Trade and Industry unveiled the STB's new plan to ensure that tourism remains a key economic pillar: Tourism 2015. If we were to say that Tourism 21's main emphasis was gateway tourism, Tourism 2015 by contrast is more interested in increasing Singapore's tourism attractiveness. In Tourism 2015, the government committed S$2 billion to a Tourism Development Fund to support initiatives in infrastructure development, capability development, and anchoring iconic/major events and product development. Tourism 2015 also identifies the three key tourism areas of focus: '(a) strengthening

Singapore' position as a leading convention & exhibition city in Asia with a strong and dynamic business environment, (b) developing Singapore as a leading Asian leisure destination by providing an enriching experience that is uniquely Singapore, and (c) establishing Singapore as the services centre of Asia—a place where visitors come to enjoy high-end quality services such as healthcare and education services' (STB 2005). By increasing tourism attractions, Tourism 2015 endeavours to achieve the following bold targets: tripling TRs to S$30 billion and doubling visitor arrivals to 17 million.

References

Census of Population Office. (2000). *Singapore Census of Population 2000.* Singapore: Department of Statistics.

Chang, T. (1998). Regionalism and Tourism: Exploring Integral Links in Singapore. *Asia Pacific Viewpoint, 39*(1), 73–94.

Chang, T., & Yeoh, B. (1999). New Asia—Singapore: Communicating Local Cultures through Global Tourism. *Geoforum, 30*, 101–115 (Directions: The Business Magazine).

Chua, B. (1995). *Communitarian Ideology and Democracy in Singapore.* London: Routledge.

DOS (Department of Statistics, Singapore). (1980-2008). Singapore Year Book, Various Issues. Singapore: Ministry of Trade & Industry.

Euromonitor. (2007). *Top 150 City Destinations: London Leads the Way.* http://www.euromonitor.com

Leong, K. (2008). Overview of Singapore's Business Services Sector. In *Economic Survey of Singapore.* Singapore: Ministry of Trade and Industry.

MTI (Ministry of Trade and Industry). (1984). *Ministry of Trade Report of Tourism Task Force*, Singapore.

MTI (Ministry of Trade and Industry). (2008). *Economic Survey of Singapore*, Singapore.

Perry, M., Kong, L., & Yeoh, B. (1997). *Singapore: A Developmental City State.* England: Wiley.

STB (Singapore Tourism Board). (2005). *Singapore Sets Out to Triple Tourism Receipts To S$30 Billion by 2015.* https://app.stb.gov.sg/asp/new/new03a.asp?id=2483

STB (Singapore Tourism Board). (2007). Annual report on tourism statistics.

STPB (1996). *Tourism 21: Vision of Tourism Capital*. Singapore: Singapore Tourist Promotion Board.

Teo, P. (1994). Assessing Socio-Cultural Impacts: The Case of Singapore. *Tourism Management, 15*(2), 126–136.

Thangavelu, S., & Li, T. (2008). Employment Linkages and Structural Changes in Singapore. In *Economic Survey of Singapore*. Singapore: Ministry of Trade and Industry.

Wilson, P. (1994). Tourism Earnings Instability in Singapore. *Journal of Economic Studies, 21*(1), 41–51.

Yeoh, B., & Chang, T. (2001). Globalizing Singapore: Debating Transnational Flows in the City. *Urban Studies, 38*(7), 1025–1044.

5

Constructing a Tourism CGE Model

Based on the review of previous studies and the background information of the economy as well as the tourism industry, it is clear that tourism demand and its inter-industry linkage are very important to a tourism CGE model. This chapter demonstrates how to incorporate tourism demand into a CGE model and how tourism demand is linked to various industries. CGE modelling was already introduced in Chap. 1. This chapter will discuss CGE models in more details, including functions and solutions, the TABLO codes, and the structure of nested functions.

The derivation of mathematical functions in this chapter is for intermediate CGE modellers who wish to go deeper to test the rigour of a CGE model. For a novice CGE modeller, the mathematical derivation of functions can be ignored, but a good understanding of the solutions and TABLO codes for these functions is necessary for building a tourism CGE model. After having studied this chapter, the reader should be able to create a tourism CGE model from scratch or, alternatively, change an existing CGE model like ORANI-G to a tourism CGE model.

The structure of this chapter is arranged as follows. Section 5.1 explains the ways to model tourism demand and briefly describes the general features of the model. Section 5.2 considers the production of goods

S. Meng, M. Siriwardana, *Assessing the Economic Impact of Tourism*,
DOI 10.1007/978-3-319-40328-1_5

and services. The production function (including input demand function and output mix function) for each sector will be discussed and derived. Section 5.3 derives the investors' demand function, while Sects. 5.4 and 5.5 discuss the households and tourist utility functions, respectively. The household utility function is characterized by a linear expenditure system (LES). In order to embody the different tourism spending patterns on shopping and non-shopping goods, the tourist utility function consists of three constant elasticity of substitution (CES) functions, a Leontief function, and a Cobb–Douglas function. Based on these utility functions, the demands of households and tourists for goods and services are derived. In Sect. 5.6, the demand functions for other final demand sectors—foreign and government sectors—are defined. Relevant macroeconomic variables are discussed in the following sections: income, direct taxes, and investment in Sect. 5.7; indirect taxes, zero pure profit condition, and price system in Sect. 5.8; external balance in Sect. 5.9; and price indices, wage indexation, and GDP price deflator in Sect. 5.10. Section 5.11 presents the market clearing equations. The last section demonstrates the complete model, which lists all equations, variables, parameters, and coefficients.

5.1 How to Incorporate Tourism into a CGE Model

The entry point of tourism in a CGE model is tourism expenditure. The data on detailed tourism expenditure on goods and services can be obtained by tourism surveys. Domestic tourism expenditure is part of household consumption, and the inbound tourism expenditure is very similar to exports of the destination country (or region), so the tourism expenditure can be modelled in a way similar to modelling household consumption or exports. However, since tourism is a demand-side concept, to model the tourism industry proved to be difficult. One may think that the tourism industry means the hospitality sector (e.g. hotels and restaurants) and the sightseeing sector. These are traditional or narrowly defined tourism sectors which primarily cater for tourists. Many other industries (e.g. transportation and retailing) also are significant providers of tourism goods and services. How to model all tourism-related industries collectively becomes a challenge to tourism CGE modelling. Three approaches to this challenge are discussed in this section.

5.1.1 Creating a Real Tourism Industry

The direct approach is to create a tourism industry based on tourism survey data. For example, if a tourism survey reveals that tourism expenditure on restaurants accounts for 80% of the output of the restaurant sector, all inputs (including intermediate inputs, labour, and capital) in the restaurant sector are to be split into two parts according to the ratio of 80:20. Namely, 80% of inputs belong to the tourism-related restaurant sector, and 20% of inputs belong to the remaining (or non-tourism) restaurant sector. Then, all split tourism-related sectors are combined together to form a tourism sector.

The benefit of this approach is that we can have a concrete tourism sector which produces one tourism product and sells it to tourists. This tourism sector is real because, just like any other sectors, it uses various intermediate inputs, labour, and capital to produce output. As a result, we can easily calculate the impact on employment, profit, value added, and tax.

However, there are a few drawbacks to this approach. First, this approach requires a significant amount of work on a database in separating sectors into tourism-related or non-tourism components. Second, more computing power is required because of the addition of a tourism sector and tourism products. Finally, the major drawback is that the separation of one sector into a tourism-related sector and a remaining sector does not reflect the reality. This causes an important complication in the modelling results. For example, if the tourism demand for restaurant food increases, the tourism-related restaurant sector will perform well, so it will increase its demand for various inputs and thus bid up the input prices. Bearing in mind that both tourism-related restaurants and non-tourism restaurants use similar inputs, the competition between tourism-related and non-tourism restaurants necessitates that the resources will move from non-tourism restaurants to tourism-related restaurants. This will lead to worse-off non-tourism restaurant sectors. By the same reasoning, all remaining sectors after split will be hit by an increase in tourism demand. This result is not true because there is no split sector in reality.

5.1.2 Creating a Shadow Tourism Industry

This is an indirect approach in order to avoid the undesired consequences of splitting a sector artificially in the direct approach. The indirect approach features a 'shadow' tourism industry that buys the goods and services from other industries according to tourism expenditure patterns and then bundles them and sells them to tourists. Essentially, the shadow tourism industry acts as a middleman. Since there are no capital and labour inputs in the shadow tourism industry, it is impossible to calculate the value-added or employment effect directly for this shadow industry. The calculation of value-added and the employment effect in this approach is a bit complicated.

The impact on employment and value-added is obtained through the ratio of sectoral wage payment to output value and the ratio of sectoral gross operating surplus to output value. For example, if the tourism demand for restaurant food accounts for 80% of the output of the sector in the base year, 80% of wage payment as well as gross operating surplus are attributable to the tourism sector. The value added is the sum of wage payment and gross operating surplus attributable to tourism. After a simulation of a policy shock (e.g. 10% decrease in tourism tax), the sectoral output, wage payment, and gross operating surplus will change, as does the proportion of tourism demand for the sectoral output. Based on the new ratios, we can calculate the wage payment and gross operating surplus after the policy shock. Comparing them with the numbers prior to the policy shock, we can have changes in employment, gross operating surplus, and value added for the tourism sector.

The merit of this approach is that we avoid the untruthful splitting of a sector and can have a graspable tourism sector on the supply side, which is consistent with a traditional definition of industry. However, this approach also has a number of shortcomings. First, the modelling cost will increase because the creation of a shadow tourism sector will cause a modification of the database and requires more computing power. When the tourism demand function is simple, for example, a Leontief function describing choice of a single group of tourists, the increase in modelling costs is small. However, when one wants to study the tourism expenditure pattern in detail, for example, different demand functions for the tourism demand for different commodities and for tourists from different countries and regions, the number of tourism sectors and tourism goods that have to be added to the model is considerable, and so will be the modelling costs. Second, the total output for the economy will be inflated because the tourism products are sold twice: once from the other industries to the tourism industry and then from the tourism industry to the tourists. However, the value-added and GDP will not be affected because the total final demand is unchanged. Finally, the Leontief function normally used for production can capture the characteristics of the tourism demand revealed by a tourism survey, but will be unable to reflect any variation in the tourism expenditure pattern. Changes in the tourism expenditure pattern happen from time to time. For example, during an economic downturn, tourism travel may not reduce significantly and immediately because most tourism travels are booked in advance. However, the tourism shopping expenditure may be affected sharply. A change in the tourism expenditure pattern is hard to be modelled by this approach.

5.1.3 Modelling the Tourism Industry Directly from the Demand Side

This approach discards the attempt to create a tourism industry from the supply side and view the tourism industry directly from the demand side. The tourism industry output is the total amount of the tourism demand. Tourism employment and the value-added are calculated in the same way as in the shadow tourism industry approach. Since there is no need to create an industry from the supply side, the model structure in this approach is much simpler, and the work on the database will be reduced. More importantly, this approach can reflect the characteristics of the tourism expenditure pattern and allow for variations from this pattern, thanks to the flexibility of using different functions for tourism demand. For example, a tourism taste variable can reflect a change in the tourism expenditure pattern directly; the use of a CES function can reflect the flexible choice of tourists when the relative prices of tourism gifts change; and a Leontief function on tourism service demand can reflect the inflexibility of tourism service demand (e.g. a tourist cannot substitute accommodation service for food service even if the accommodation price increases dramatically). Due to the advantage of modelling the tourism industry directly from the demand side, this approach is illustrated in this book.

5.1.4 The Overview of a Tourism CGE Model

Based on the characteristics of the Singaporean economy and tourism, this chapter will develop a CGE model—SINGATOUR. The model basically consists of the production and consumption of goods and services. On the production side, producers purchase inputs and produce commodities. The producers' production procedure will be mimicked by their production functions, in which their demands for various inputs (intermediate inputs and primary factors) will be derived. On the consumption side, the demand of each final user (e.g. households, government, exports, and investment demand) will be derived. For the purpose of this study, we extract the international tourism consumption from exports and household consumption. Besides the demand for inputs by producers and the demand for goods and services by final users, the price system, market clearance conditions, the investment level, and various macroeconomic variables, such as GDP, CPI, BOP, and real wages, will be addressed by the model. Although solutions for most of the production functions and demand functions are readily available from previous studies, to ensure the correctness and soundness of the model, we derive our solutions independently. By doing so, the authors have found some pitfalls or imperfections in the existing derivation, although the final results are the same.

The SINGATOUR model is a static CGE model based on ORANI-G (Horridge 2000), so it belongs to the Johansen class of CGE models. The model uses the neoclassical economic assumptions: perfectly competitive economy with constant returns to scale; the industries are supposed to minimize cost, while the household is expected to maximize utility; labour is perfectly mobile across industries while the capital is treated as industry-specific; and the market keeps clearing continuously. Zero profit conditions are assumed for all industries because of the assumption of perfect competition in the economy. Since Singapore is a small open economy, it is assumed that it is a price taker in the world market and its investment level is generally not constrained by its saving level—foreign investment is readily available; a flexible exchange rate regime is also adopted to reflect the reality in Singapore.

In the model, the Singapore economy is represented by 35 industries which produce 35 goods and services, 35 representative investors, 1 household sector, and 1 government. Twenty-one tourism demands from 21 - tourism-generating countries are added as independent final demands for the purpose of the study. To reflect the fixed technology in production at a certain period of time, a Leontief function is adopted as the top-level production function. Imported and domestic commodities are assumed imperfectly substitutable, so the Armington assumption (imperfect substitution between imported and domestic goods) is applied. The LES is adopted for household utility while a nested Leontief function—Cobb–Douglas—CES function is used for tourism demand.

5.2 Production of Goods and Services

The production function in the model is a four-level nested function with constant returns to scale. The structure of the production function is shown in Fig. 5.1. At the top level, a constant elasticity of transformation (CET) function is used to determine the output mix. At the second level, a Leontief function reflects the fixed technology in production at a certain period of time; at the third level, the CES function reflects the possible substitutions between imported and domestic goods, or between capital

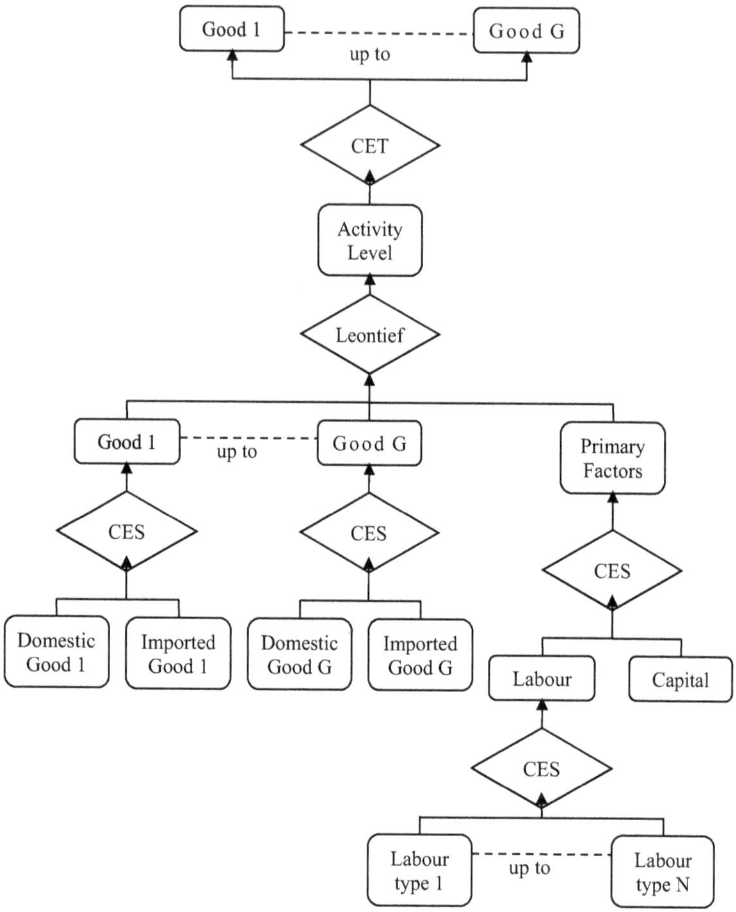

Fig. 5.1 Production of goods and services

and labour; and at the bottom level, a CES function is used to form the composite labour inputs. We start with the Leontief function at the second level and then go down through the third level to the bottom level. Lastly, we address the CET function at the top level.

5.2.1 Demand for Composite Inputs

The demand for composite inputs is characterized by a Leontief function. The Leontief function is a fixed-proportion production function, shown as follows:

$$Z_j = \underset{i=1,\cdots,g,pf}{\text{Leontief}} \left\{ X_{ij}^{\text{ID}} / A_{ij}^{\text{ID}} \right\} = \min \left(\frac{X_{1j}^{\text{ID}}}{A_{1j}^{\text{ID}}}, \frac{X_{2j}^{\text{ID}}}{A_{2j}^{\text{ID}}}, \ldots, \frac{X_{gj}^{\text{ID}}}{A_{gj}^{\text{ID}}}, \frac{X_{(pf)j}^{\text{ID}}}{A_{(pf)j}^{\text{ID}}} \right),$$

$$\text{j} = 1, 2, \ldots h$$

where
i—the number of commodities
j—the number of industries
ID—intermediate demand
Z_j—the activity level of industry j
X_{ij}—composite intermediate input i in industry j
A_{ij}—technical coefficient: the proportion of effective input i in output level
$X_{(pf)j}$—composite primary factor input in industry j

To minimize cost, the firm must use each of the composite inputs in proportion to the activity level, so the optimal demand for composite inputs are as follows:

$$X_{ij}^{\text{ID}} = Z_j A_{ij}^{\text{ID}}$$

and

$$X_{(pf)j}^{\text{ID}} = Z_j A_{(pf)j}^{\text{ID}}$$

or in the percentage-change form:

$$x_{ij}^{\text{ID}} = z_j + a_{ij}^{\text{ID}} \tag{5.1}$$

and

$$x_{(pf)j}^{\text{ID}} = z_j + a_{(pf)j}^{\text{ID}} \tag{5.2}$$

5.2.2 Demand for Intermediate Inputs

The imports and domestic products are imperfect substitutes (Armington, 1969), so a CES production function is appropriate to be used to create composite effective inputs from imported and domestically produced intermediate inputs.

The problem to minimize the cost of every composite intermediate input (domestic-imported) can be expressed as:

Minimize $\left(P^{(\mathrm{ID})}_{(id)j}X^{(\mathrm{ID})}_{(id)j} + P^{(\mathrm{ID})}_{(im)j}X^{(\mathrm{ID})}_{(im)j}\right)$,

subject to $Z_jA_{ij} = \left[B_{(id)j}X^{(\mathrm{ID})-\rho_{ij}}_{(id)j} + B_{(im)j}X^{(\mathrm{ID})-\rho_{ij}}_{(im)j}\right]^{-1/\rho_{ij}}$

where

d—domestically produced commodity

m—imported commodity

B—distributional parameter, $B \geq 0$

ρ—substitution parameter, $\rho > -1$ and $\rho \neq 0$

To simplify the derivation, let $\overline{Z_j} = Z_jA_{ij}$ and subscript $s = d, m$. Since we are dealing with one representative composite good in an industry, the subscripts i and j will not change in our derivation (we only need to distinguish imports from domestic goods), so we omit all subscripts i and j and superscript ID in our derivation. As such, the minimization problem can be expressed as:

Minimize $\sum_{s=1}^{2} P_sX_s$, subject to $\overline{Z} = \mathrm{CES}(X_s)$ or $\overline{Z} = \left(\sum_{s=1}^{2} B_sX_s^{-\rho}\right)^{-1/\rho}$

The Lagrangian expression of the problem is:

$$L = \sum_{s=1}^{2} P_sX_s + \lambda(\overline{Z} - \mathrm{CES}(X_s))$$

The first-order conditions are:

$$\frac{\partial L}{\partial X_s} = P_s - \lambda(\partial \text{CES}(X_s)/\partial X_s) = 0 \text{ and } \frac{\partial L}{\partial \lambda} = \overline{Z} - \text{CES}(X_s) = 0$$

Substituting in the above equations the CES function $\text{CES}(X_s) = \left(\sum_{s=1}^{2} B_s X_s^{-\rho}\right)^{-1/\rho}$, we obtain:

$$P_s - \lambda\partial\left(\sum_{s=1}^{2} B_s X_s^{-\rho}\right)^{-1/\rho} / \partial X_s = P_s - \lambda B_s X_s^{-\rho-1}\left(\sum_{s=1}^{2} B_s X_s^{-\rho}\right)^{(-1-\rho)/\rho} = 0 \tag{5.3}$$

and

$$\overline{Z} = \left(\sum_{s=1}^{2} B_s X_s^{-\rho}\right)^{-1/\rho} \text{ or } \overline{Z}^{(-\rho)} = \left(\sum_{s=1}^{2} B_s X_s^{-\rho}\right) \tag{5.4}$$

Substituting (5.4) into (5.3) and solving for X_s, we obtain:

$$X_s = \overline{Z}\left(P_s \lambda^{-1} B_s^{-1}\right)^{-1/(\rho+1)} \text{ or } X_s^{-\rho} = \overline{Z}^{(-\rho)} \lambda^{-\rho/(\rho+1)} \left(P_s B_s^{-1}\right)^{\rho/(\rho+1)} \tag{5.5}$$

Substituting (5.5) into (5.4), we obtain:

$$\begin{aligned} \overline{Z}^{(-\rho)} &= \sum_{s=1}^{2} B_s \overline{Z}^{(-\rho)} \left(P_s \lambda^{-1} B_s^{-1}\right)^{\rho/(\rho+1)} \\ &= \overline{Z}^{(-\rho)} \lambda^{-\rho/(\rho+1)} \sum_{s=1}^{2} B_s^{1/(\rho+1)} P_s^{\rho/(\rho+1)} \end{aligned}$$

Manipulating the above equation, we have:

$$\lambda^{1/(1+\rho)} = \left(\sum_{s=1}^{2} B_s^{1/(\rho+1)} P_s^{\rho/(\rho+1)}\right)^{1/\rho} \tag{5.6}$$

Substituting (5.6) back into (5.5), we have:

$$X_s = \overline{Z}\lambda^{1/(\rho+1)}\left(P_sB_s^{-1}\right)^{-1/(\rho+1)}$$
$$= \overline{Z}\left(P_sB_s^{-1}\right)^{-1/(\rho+1)}\left(\sum_{s=1}^{2} B_s^{1/(\rho+1)}P_s^{\rho/(\rho+1)}\right)^{1/\rho}$$

Putting the subscripts i and j back on, we have the intermediate demand function:

$$X_{(is)j}^{(\mathrm{ID})} = Z_jA_{ij}\left(P_{(is)j}^{(\mathrm{ID})}B_{(is)j}^{-1}\right)^{-1/\left(\rho_{ij}+1\right)}\left(\sum_{s=1}^{2} B_{(is)j}^{1/\left(\rho_{ij}+1\right)}P_{(is)j}^{(\mathrm{ID})\rho_{ij}/\left(\rho_{ij}+1\right)}\right)^{1/\rho_{ij}} \tag{5.7}$$

Since the linear percentage-change form of function is more convenient and is popularly used in some software packages, we need to derive the linear percentage-change form of the above equation. As we did previously, we omit subscripts i and j and superscript ID in the derivation.

$$\text{let } M = \left(P_sB_s^{-1}\right)^{-1/(\rho+1)}\left(\sum_{s=1}^{2} B_s^{1/(\rho+1)}P_s^{\rho/(\rho+1)}\right)^{1/\rho}$$

so equation (5.7) becomes:

$$X_s = Z \times A \times M \tag{5.8}$$

Applying total differentiation to (5.8), we have:

$$\begin{aligned} dX_s &= M \times d(ZA) + ZA \times d(M) \\ &= MA \times dZ + MZ \times dA + ZA \times dM \end{aligned} \tag{5.9}$$

To obtain percentage-change form, we divide (5.9) by X_s:

$$\frac{dX_s}{X_s} = \frac{MAZ \times dZ}{X_sZ} + \frac{MZA \times dA}{X_sA} + \frac{ZAM \times dM}{X_sM}$$

Using (5.8), we have:

$$\frac{dX_s}{X_s} = \frac{dZ}{Z} + \frac{dA}{A} + \frac{dM}{M} \tag{5.10}$$

in equation (5.10),

$$\begin{aligned}
dM &= \left(\sum_{s=1}^{2} B_s^{1/(\rho+1)} P_s^{\rho/(\rho+1)}\right)^{1/\rho} d\left(P_s B_s^{-1}\right)^{-1/(\rho+1)} \\
&\quad + \left(P_s B_s^{-1}\right)^{-1/(\rho+1)} d\left(\sum_{s=1}^{2} B_s^{1/(\rho+1)} P_s^{\rho/(\rho+1)}\right)^{1/\rho} \\
&= \left(\sum_{s=1}^{2} B_s^{1/(\rho+1)} P_s^{\rho/(\rho+1)}\right)^{1/\rho} (-1)/(\rho+1)\left(P_s B_s^{-1}\right)^{(-1/(\rho+1))-1} B_s^{-1} dP \\
&\quad + \left(P_s B_s^{-1}\right)^{-1/(\rho+1)} \frac{1}{\rho}\left(\sum_{s=1}^{2} B_s^{1/(\rho+1)} P_s^{\rho/(\rho+1)}\right)^{(1/\rho)-1} d\left(\sum_{s=1}^{2} B_s^{1/(\rho+1)} P_s^{\rho/(\rho+1)}\right) \\
&= -\frac{1}{\rho+1} M \left(P_s B_s^{-1}\right)^{-1} B_s^{-1} dP_s \\
&\quad + \frac{1}{\rho} M \left(\sum_{s=1}^{2} B_s^{1/(\rho+1)} P_s^{\rho/(\rho+1)}\right)^{-1} \left(\sum_{s=1}^{2} d\left(B_s^{1/(\rho+1)} P_s^{\rho/(\rho+1)}\right)\right) \\
&= -\frac{1}{\rho+1} M \frac{dP_s}{P} \\
&\quad + \frac{1}{\rho+1} M \left(\sum_{s=1}^{2} B_s^{1/(\rho+1)} P_s^{\rho/(\rho+1)}\right)^{-1} \left(\sum_{s=1}^{2} B_s^{1/(\rho+1)} P_s^{(\rho/(\rho+1))} \frac{dP_s}{P}\right)
\end{aligned}$$

$$\text{let } S_s = B_s^{1/(\rho+1)} P_s^{(\rho/(\rho+1))} \Big/ \left(\sum_{s=1}^{2} B_s^{1/(\rho+1)} P_s^{(\rho/(\rho+1))}\right)$$

$$dM = -\frac{1}{\rho+1} M \left(\frac{dP_s}{P} - \left(\sum_{s=1}^{2} S_s \frac{dP_s}{P}\right)\right)$$

Noticing that $\sigma = 1/(\rho + 1)$ and substituting dM back into (5.10), we have:

$$\frac{dX_s}{X_s} = \frac{dA}{A} + \frac{dZ}{Z} + \frac{dM}{M} = \frac{dA}{A} + \frac{dZ}{Z} - \sigma\left(\frac{dP_s}{P_s} - \sum_{s=1}^{2} S_s \frac{dP_s}{P_s}\right)$$

Using equation (5.7), we can derive:

$$\begin{aligned}
&\frac{P_{(is)j}^{(\mathrm{ID})} X_{(is)j}^{(\mathrm{ID})}}{\sum_{S=1}^{2} P_{(is)j}^{(\mathrm{ID})} X_{(is)j}^{(\mathrm{ID})}} \\
&= \frac{Z_j A_{ij} P_{(is)j}^{(\mathrm{ID})} \left(P_{(is)j}^{(\mathrm{ID})} B_{(is)j}^{-1}\right)^{-1/(\rho_{ij}+1)} \left(\sum_{s=1}^{2} B_{(is)j}^{1/(\rho_{ij}+1)} P_{(is)j}^{(\mathrm{ID})\rho_{ij}/(\rho_{ij}+1)}\right)^{1/\rho_{ij}}}{Z_j A_{ij} \left(\sum_{S=1}^{2} P_{(is)j}^{(\mathrm{ID})} \left(P_{(is)j}^{(\mathrm{ID})} B_{(is)j}^{-1}\right)^{-1/(\rho_{ij}+1)}\right) \left(\sum_{s=1}^{2} B_{(is)j}^{1/(\rho_{ij}+1)} P_{(is)j}^{(\mathrm{ID})\rho_{ij}/(\rho_{ij}+1)}\right)^{1/\rho_{ij}}} \\
&= \frac{P_{(is)j}^{(\mathrm{ID})} \left(P_{(is)j}^{(\mathrm{ID})}\right)^{-1/(\rho_{ij}+1)} \left(B_{(is)j}^{-1}\right)^{-1/(\rho_{ij}+1)}}{\left(\sum_{S=1}^{2} P_{(is)j}^{(\mathrm{ID})} \left(P_{(is)j}^{(\mathrm{ID})}\right)^{-1/(\rho_{ij}+1)} \left(B_{(is)j}^{-1}\right)^{-1/(\rho_{ij}+1)}\right)} \\
&= \frac{\left(P_{(is)j}^{(\mathrm{ID})}\right)^{\rho_{ij}/(\rho_{ij}+1)} \left(B_{(is)j}\right)^{1/(\rho_{ij}+1)}}{\left(\sum_{S=1}^{2} \left(P_{(is)j}^{(\mathrm{ID})}\right)^{\rho_{ij}/(\rho_{ij}+1)} \left(B_{(is)j}\right)^{1/(\rho_{ij}+1)}\right)} = S_s
\end{aligned} \tag{5.11}$$

Thus, S_s is actually the share of imported or domestic goods in producing composite intermediate good *i*.

Putting the subscripts *i* and *j* and superscript ID back on, we obtain the following percentage-change form (we use lowercase letter to represent percentage change):

$$x_{(is)j}^{(\mathrm{ID})} = z_j + a_{ij}^{(\mathrm{ID})} - \sigma_{ij}^{(\mathrm{ID})} \left(p_{(is)j}^{(\mathrm{ID})} - \sum_{s=1}^{2} S_{(is)j}^{(\mathrm{ID})ij} p_{(is)j}^{(\mathrm{ID})}\right) \tag{5.12}$$

where $S_{(is)j}^{(ID)ij}$ stands for the input *i* from source *s* in industry *j* as the share of total intermediate demand for input *i* in industry *j*.

And the percentage change in price for the composite good *i* is:

$$p_{ij}^{(ID)} = \sum_{s=1}^{2} S_{(is)j}^{(ID)ij} p_{(is)j}^{(ID)} \tag{5.13}$$

5.2.3 Demand for Primary Factors

The primary factor demand function is a two-level nested CES function. We think of labour inputs first. Since the labour input is made up of N types of occupation groups, we need to find the demand for each type of labour. The problem of optimal demand for different types of labour can be expressed as:

Minimize $\sum_{o=1}^{N} P_{(pf,L,o)j} X_{(pf,L,o)j}$,

subject to $X_{(pf,L)j} = \left(\sum_{o=1}^{N} B_{(pf,L,o)j} X_{(pf,L,o)j}^{-\rho_{(pf,L)j}} \right)^{-1/\rho_{(pf,L)j}}$

With the similar procedure as we demonstrated in subsection 5.2.2, we can have:

$$X_{(pf,L,o)j} = X_{(pf,L)j} \left(P_{(pf,L,o)j} B_{(pf,L,o)j}^{-1} \right)^{-1/\left(\rho_{(pf,L)j}+1\right)} \times \left(\sum_{o=1}^{N} B_{(pf,L,o)j}^{1/\left(\rho_{(pf,L)j}+1\right)} P_{(pf,L,o)j}^{\rho_{(pf,L)j}/\left(\rho_{(pf,L)j}+1\right)} \right)^{1/\rho_{(pf,L)j}} \tag{5.14}$$

or in the percentage-change form:

$$x_{(pf,L,o)j} = x_{(pf,L)j} - \sigma_{(pf,L)j}\left(p_{(pf,L,o)j} - \sum_{o=1}^{N} S_{(pf,L,o)j}^{(pf,L)j} p_{(pf,L,o)j}\right) \tag{5.15}$$

And the percentage change in prices of composite labour is given by:

$$p_{(pf,L)j} = \sum_{o=1}^{N} S_{(pf,L,o)j}^{(pf,L)j} p_{(pf,L,o)j} \tag{5.16}$$

Next, we derive the demand for capital and composite labour in order to form the composite primary factor. The optimization problem is as follows:

$$\text{Minimize} \sum_{v=1}^{2} \left(P_{(pf,v)j} X_{(pf,v)j}\right),$$

$$\text{subject to } Z_j A_{(pf)j} = \left[\sum_{v=1}^{2} B_{(pf,v)j} X_{(pf,v)j}^{-\rho_{(pf)j}}\right]^{-1/\rho_{(pf)j}}$$

where v = 1 for L and v = 2 for K.

With the same procedure as we derive the demand for intermediate inputs, we can obtain the following demand function for primary factors:

$$X_{(pf,v)j} = Z_j A_{(pf)j} \left(P_{(pf,v)j} B_{(pf,v)j}^{-1}\right)^{-1/\left(\rho_{(pf)j}+1\right)} \times \left(\sum_{v=1}^{2} B_{(pf,v)j}^{1/\left(\rho_{(pf)j}+1\right)} P_{(pf,v)j}^{\rho_{(pf)j}/\left(\rho_{(pf)j}+1\right)}\right)^{1/\rho_{(pf)j}} \tag{5.17}$$

or in the percentage-change form:

$$x_{(pf,v)j} = z_j + a_{(pf)j} - \sigma_{(pf)j}\left(p_{(pf,v)j} - \sum_{v=1}^{2} S_{(pf,v)j}^{(pf)j} p_{(pf,v)j}\right) \tag{5.18}$$

And the percentage change in prices of composite primary factor is:

$$p_{(pf)j} = \sum_{v=1}^{2} S_{(pf,v)j}^{(pf)j} p_{(pf,v)j} \tag{5.19}$$

5.2.4 Output Mix

For some sectors which produce more than one good or service, a CET function is employed to determine the output mix.

The CET function is similar to CES function, However, unlike in CES, there is no restriction on ρ in CET.

$$Z_j = \mathrm{CET}\left(X^{(0)}_{(id)j}\right) = \left(\sum_{i=1}^{g} B_{(id)j} X^{(0)-\rho_{ij}}_{(id)j}\right)^{-1/\rho_{ij}} \quad \mathrm{i} = 1, \ldots g; j = 1, \ldots, h$$

$X^{(0)}_{(id)j}$ stands for one commodity in output mix in industry j.

The problem of maximizing revenue can be expressed as:

$$\text{Maximize} \sum_{i=1}^{g} P^{(0)}_{(id)} X^{(0)}_{(id)j}$$

subject to

$$Z_j = \mathrm{CET}\left(X^{(0)}_{(id)j}\right) = \left(\sum_{i=1}^{g} B_{(id)j} X^{(0)-\rho_j}_{(id)j}\right)^{-1/\rho_j}.$$

Solving this maximization problem, we have the following optimized output mix:

$$x^{(0)}_{(is)j} = z_j - \sigma^{(0)}_j \left(p^{(0)}_{(id)j} - \sum_{i=1}^{g} S^{(0)j}_{(id)j} S_{(id)j} p^{(0)}_{(id)j}\right)$$

However, a little adjustment is applied to this equation due to the convention of GEMPACK. The elasticity of substitution for CET is negative because the PPF curve is concave to the origin, but GEMPACK software conventionally uses the absolute value of elasticity of substitution. So if the absolute value is used for the elasticity of substitution, our equation becomes:

$$x_{(id)j}^{(0)} = z_j + \sigma_j^{(0)} \left(p_{(id)j}^{(0)} - \sum_{i=1}^{g} S_{(id)j}^{(0)j} p_{(id)j}^{(0)} \right) \quad (5.20)$$

And then percentage change in price index for industry j is:

$$p_j^{(0)} = \sum_{i=1}^{g} S_{(id)j}^{(0)j} p_{(id)j}^{(0)} \quad (5.21)$$

5.3 Investors' Demand

Investors in each industry need to buy goods to form the fixed capital. As in the production function, to reflect the fixed technology in the production at a certain period of time, the investors' demand is in the form of Leontief function. However, since it is flexible for investors to choose imported or domestically produced goods, a CES function is employed at the second level, shown in Fig. 5.2.

Mathematically, the investor demand functions are:

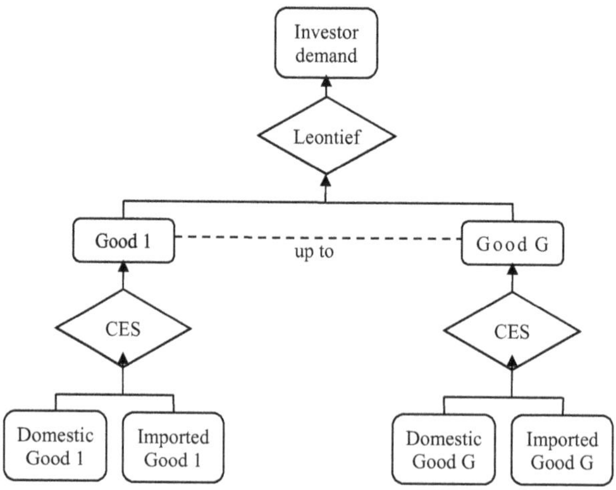

Fig. 5.2 Investors' demand

At the top level:

$$K_j = \underset{i=1,\cdots,g}{\text{Leontief}} \left\{ X_{ij}^{(K)}/A_{ij}^{(K)} \right\} = \min\left(\frac{X_{1j}^{(K)}}{A_{1j}^{(K)}}, \frac{X_{2j}^{(K)}}{A_{2j}^{(K)}}, \ldots, \frac{X_{gj}^{(K)}}{A_{gj}^{(K)}} \right), \quad \mathrm{j} = 1, 2, \ldots h$$

where K_j—investment level for industry j, $X_{ij}^{(K)}$—effective investment in good i for industry j

At the bottom level:

$$\begin{aligned} X_{ij}^{(K)} &= \mathrm{CES}\left(X_{(is)j}^{(K)} \right) \\ &= \left(\sum_{i=1}^{g} B_{(is)j} X_{(is)j}^{(K)-\rho_{ij}} \right)^{-1/\rho_{ij}} \quad (i = 1, \ldots g, j = 1, \ldots h, \mathrm{s} = \mathrm{d}, m). \end{aligned}$$

The demand for composite input X_{ij}^{K} in the linear form is given by:

$$x_{ij}^{(K)} = k_j + a_{ij}^{(K)} \tag{5.22}$$

Since the Leontief function is a fixed proportion function, the task of minimizing the total cost can be disaggregated to minimizing the cost of every composite input—X_{ij}^{K}. So the cost minimization problem is reduced to:

$$\text{Minimize} \sum_{s=1}^{2} P_{(is)}^{(K)} X_{(is)j}^{(K)}, \text{ subject to } X_{ij}^{(K)} = \mathrm{CES}\left(X_{(is)j}^{(K)} \right)$$

The Lagrangian expression is:

$$L = \sum_{s=1}^{2} P_{(is)}^{(K)} X_{(is)j}^{(K)} - \lambda \left(X_{ij}^{(K)} - \mathrm{CES}\left(X_{(is)j}^{(K)} \right) \right)$$

Using the same procedure as we derived for the intermediate demand in production of goods and services, we can obtain the following demand function for capital formation in industry j:

$$X_{(is)j}^{(K)} = K_j A_{ij}^{(K)} \left(P_{(is)j}^{(K)} B_{(is)j}^{(K)-1} \right)^{-1/\left(\rho_{ij}^{(K)}+1\right)} \left(\sum_{s=1}^{2} B_{(is)j}^{(K)1/\left(\rho_{ij}^{(K)}+1\right)} P_{(is)j}^{(K)\rho_{ij}^{(K)}/\left(\rho_{ij}^{(K)}+1\right)} \right)^{1/\rho_{ij}^{(K)}}$$

or in the percentage-change form:

$$x_{(is)j}^{(K)} = k_j + a_{ij}^{(K)} - \sigma_{ij}^{(K)} \left(p_{(is)j}^{(K)} - \sum_{s=1}^{2} S_{(is)j}^{(K)ij} p_{(is)j}^{(K)} \right) \tag{5.23}$$

And percentage change in price for intermediate good i is:

$$p_i^{(K)} = \sum_{s=1}^{2} S_{(is)j}^{(K)ij} p_{(is)}^{(K)} \tag{5.24}$$

5.4 Household Utility

Because households are flexible to substitute one commodity for another in the face of a relative price change, a CES utility function should be considered at the top level. However, following Klein-Rubin (1948), we use the LES because it is difficult to assign the elasticity value in the CES utility function for households. At the second level, the CES function is used as usual. The nested household utility function is shown in Fig. 5.3.

There are two kinds of expression for LES, namely $U\left(X_1^{(H)}, \cdots, X_g^{(H)}\right) = \prod_{i=1}^{g} \left(X_i^{(H)} - \gamma_i\right)^{\beta_i}$ and

$$U\left(X_1^{(H)}, \cdots, X_g^{(H)}\right) = \sum_{i=1}^{g} \beta_i \ln\left(X_i^{(H)} - \gamma_i\right)$$

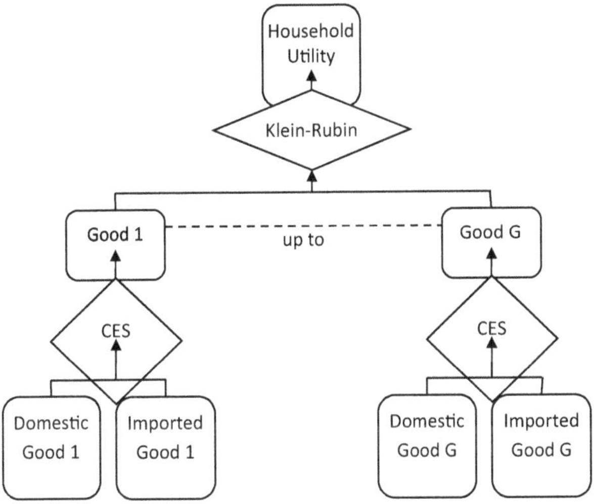

Fig. 5.3 Household utility

where β_i is the marginal budget share and γ_i is the subsistence consumption.

As can be seen, the utility in the second expression is the logarithmic form of utility in the first one. For convenience, this study uses the latter expression.

Originally, the variables and parameters in the expression are for one household. Namely, U is the utility of the household, X_i is the consumption of good i, γ_i is the subsistence consumption (basic consumption) of good i, and β_i is the marginal budget share of good i—the share of supernumerary consumption (luxury consumption) of good i in total supernumerary consumption. However, since this study considers all Singapore households as a whole, U, X_i, and γ_i are aggregates for all households. To derive the results for an average household in an economy with the total number of households of Q, we only need to divide the aggregates by Q.

The utility maximizing problem can be expressed as:

$$\text{Maximize } U\left(X_1^{(H)}, \cdots, X_g^{(H)}\right)$$
subject to
$$X_i^{(H)} = \text{CES}\left(X_{(is)}^{(H)}\right) \text{ and } \sum_{i=1}^{g}\sum_{s=1}^{2} P_{(is)}^{(H)} X_{(is)}^{(H)} = C$$

The Lagrangian expression is:

$$L = U\left(X_1^{(H)}, \cdots, X_g^{(H)}\right) + \lambda_1\left(X_i^{(H)} - \text{CES}\left(X_{(is)}^{(H)}\right)\right) + \lambda_2\left(\sum_{i=1}^{g}\sum_{s=1}^{2} P_{(is)}^{(H)} X_{(is)}^{(H)} - C\right)$$

The first-order conditions are:

$$\partial U / \partial X_i^{(H)} - \lambda_1 = 0 \tag{5.25}$$

$$-\lambda_1\left(\partial \text{CES}\left(X_{(is)}^{(H)}\right) / X_{(is)}^{(H)}\right) + \lambda_2 P_{(is)}^{(H)} = 0 \tag{5.26}$$

$$X_i^{(H)} - \text{CES}\left(X_{(is)}^{(H)}\right) = 0 \tag{5.27}$$

$$\sum_{i=1}^{g}\sum_{s=1}^{2} P_{(is)}^{(H)} X_{(is)}^{(H)} - C = 0 \tag{5.28}$$

Using (5.27) and (5.28) to solve for $X_{(is)}^{(H)}$, we have:

$$X_{(is)}^{(H)} = X_i^{(H)}\left(P_{(is)}^{(H)} B_{(is)}^{(H)-1}\right)^{-1/\left(\rho_i^{(H)}+1\right)}\left(\sum_{s=1}^{2} B_{(is)}^{(H)1/\left(\rho_i^{(H)}+1\right)} P_{(is)}^{(H)\rho_i^{(H)}/\left(\rho_i^{(H)}+1\right)}\right)^{1/\rho_i^{(H)}} \tag{5.29}$$

or in the percentage-change form:

$$x_{(is)}^{(H)} = x_i^{(H)} - \sigma_i^{(H)} \left(p_{(is)}^{(H)} - \sum_{s=1}^{2} S_{(is)}^{(H)i} p_{(is)}^{(H)} \right) \tag{5.30}$$

And the percentage change in price for composite good i is:

$$p_i^{(H)} = \sum_{s=1}^{2} S_{(is)}^{(H)i} p_{(is)}^{(H)} \tag{5.31}$$

Next, we derive the $X_i^{(H)}$. Multiplying (5.26) by $X_{(is)}^{(H)}$ and aggregate over s, we have:

$$\lambda_2 \sum_{s=1}^{2} P_{(is)}^{(H)} X_{(is)}^{(H)} = \lambda_1 \sum_{s=1}^{2} \left(X_{(is)}^{(H)} \partial \mathrm{CES}\left(X_{(is)}^{(H)} \right) / X_{(is)}^{(H)} \right)$$

Since this expression is homogeneous of degree 1, applying Euler's theorem and using equation (5.27), we have:

$$\begin{aligned} &\lambda_2 \sum_{s=1}^{2} P_{(is)}^{(H)} X_{(is)}^{(H)} = \lambda_1 \mathrm{CES}\left(X_{(is)}^{(H)} \right) = \lambda_1 X_i^{(H)} \\ &\text{Let } \lambda_1/\lambda_2 = P_i^{(H)}, \text{ we have} \\ &P_i^{(H)} X_i^{(H)} = \sum_{s=1}^{2} P_{(is)}^{(H)} X_{(is)}^{(H)} \end{aligned} \tag{5.32}$$

Substituting (5.32) into equation (5.28), we have:

$$\sum_{i=1}^{g} P_i^{(H)} X_i^{(H)} - C = 0$$

With the above equation, the maximization problem becomes choosing $X_i^{(H)}$ to maximize:

$$U\left(X_1^{(H)}, \cdots, X_g^{(H)} \right) \text{ subject to } \sum_{i=1}^{g} P_i^{(H)} X_i^{(H)} = C.$$

The Lagrangian expression is:

$$L = U\left(X_1^{(H)}, \cdots, X_g^{(H)}\right) + \lambda\left(\sum_{i=1}^{g} P_i^{(H)} X_i^{(H)} - C\right)$$

The first-order conditions are:

$$\partial U / \partial X_i^{(H)} - \lambda P_i^{(H)} = 0 \qquad (5.33)$$

$$\sum_{i=1}^{g} P_i^{(H)} X_i^{(H)} - C = 0 \qquad (5.34)$$

According to the LES:

$$U\left(X_1^{(H)}, \cdots, X_g^{(H)}\right) = \sum_{i=1}^{g} \beta_i \ln\left(X_i^{(H)} - \gamma_i\right)$$

Then, (5.33) becomes:

$$\beta_i / \left(X_i^{(H)} - \gamma_i\right) - \lambda P_i^{(H)} = 0$$

or

$$X_i^{(H)} = \gamma_i + \beta_i / \lambda P_i^{(H)} \qquad (5.35)$$

Substituting (5.35) into (5.34), we have:

$$C = \sum_{i=1}^{g} P_i^{(H)} \left(\gamma_i + \beta_i / \lambda P_i^{(H)}\right) = \sum_{i=1}^{g} P_i^{(H)} \gamma_i + \frac{1}{\lambda} \sum_{i=1}^{g} \beta_i$$

Since $\sum_{i=1}^{g} \beta_i = 1$, $\qquad (5.36)$

$$\lambda = 1 / \left(C - \sum_{i=1}^{g} P_i^{(H)} \gamma_i\right)$$

Substituting (5.36) back into (5.35), we have:

$$X_i^{(H)} = \gamma_i + \beta_i \left(C - \sum_{r=1}^{g} P_r^{(H)} \gamma_r \right) / P_i^{(H)} \tag{5.37}$$

So far, we have obtained the household demand function in levels form. However, empirically it is hard to estimate β_i and γ_i for each commodity. However, the demand and expenditure elasticities are often estimated by econometricians. So we try to express this function using elasticities.

Applying partial differentiation to the above equation, we can derive the expenditure elasticity ($\varepsilon_{i,e}$), the cross-price elasticity (ε_{ir}), and own-price elasticity (ε_{ii}):

$$\begin{aligned} \varepsilon_{i,e} &= \left(\Delta X_i^{(H)} / X_i^{(H)}\right) / (\Delta C / C) = \left(\partial X_i^{(H)} / \partial C\right)\left(C / X_i^{(H)}\right) \\ &= \left(\beta_i / P_i^{(H)}\right)\left(C / X_i^{(H)}\right) = \beta_i C / \left(P_i^{(H)} X_i^{(H)}\right) \end{aligned} \tag{5.38}$$

$$\begin{aligned} \varepsilon_{ir} &= \left(\Delta X_i^{(H)} / X_i^{(H)}\right) / \left(\Delta P_r^{(H)} / P_r^{(H)}\right) \\ &= \left(\partial X_i^{(H)} / \partial P_r^{(H)}\right)\left(P_r^{(H)} / X_i^{(H)}\right) = \left(-\beta_i \gamma_r / P_i^{(H)}\right)\left(P_r^{(H)} / X_i^{(H)}\right) \\ &= \left(-\beta_i \gamma_r P_r^{(H)}\right) / \left(P_i^{(H)} X_i^{(H)}\right) \end{aligned} \tag{5.39}$$

and

$$\begin{aligned} \varepsilon_{ii} &= -\varepsilon_{i,e} - \sum_{i \neq r} \varepsilon_{ir} = -\beta_i C / \left(P_i^{(H)} X_i^{(H)}\right) - \left(-\beta_i \sum_{i \neq r} \gamma_r P_r^{(H)}\right) / \left(P_i^{(H)} X_i^{(H)}\right) \\ &= -\beta_i \left(C - \sum_{i \neq r} \gamma_r P_r^{(H)}\right) / \left(P_i^{(H)} X_i^{(H)}\right) \end{aligned} \tag{5.40}$$

Fully differentiating (5.37), we have:

$$d\left(X_i^{(H)}\right) = \frac{\beta_i\left(-\sum_{r\neq 1}\gamma_r \times dP_r^{(H)}\right)}{P_i^{(H)}} + \frac{P_i^{(H)}\beta_i d\left(C-\sum_{r=1}^{g}P_r^{(H)}\gamma_r\right)-\beta_i\left(C-\sum_{r=1}^{g}P_r^{(H)}\gamma_r\right)dP_i^{(H)}}{\left(P_i^{(H)}\right)^2}$$

$$= \frac{-\beta_i\left(\sum_{r\neq 1}P_r^{(H)}\gamma_r\frac{dP_r^{(H)}}{P_r^{(H)}}\right)}{P_i^{(H)}} + \frac{\beta_i P_i^{(H)}\gamma_r dP_i^{(H)}-\beta_i\left(C-\sum_{r\neq 1}P_r^{(H)}\gamma_r-P_i^{(H)}\gamma_i\right)dP_i^{(H)}}{\left(P_i^{(H)}\right)^2}$$

$$= \frac{-\beta_i\left(\sum_{r\neq 1}P_r^{(H)}\gamma_r\frac{dP_r^{(H)}}{P_r^{(H)}}\right)}{P_i^{(H)}} + \frac{-\beta_i\left(C-\sum_{r\neq 1}P_r^{(H)}\gamma_r\right)dP_i^{(H)}}{\left(P_i^{(H)}\right)^2}$$

So,

$$\frac{d\left(X_i^{(H)}\right)}{X_i^{(H)}} = \frac{-\beta_i P_r^{(H)}\left(\sum_{r\neq 1}P_r^{(H)}\gamma_r\frac{dP_r^{(H)}}{P_r^{(H)}}\right)}{P_i^{(H)}X_i^{(H)}} - \frac{\beta_i\left(C-\sum_{r\neq 1}P_r^{(H)}\gamma_r\right)}{P_i^{(H)}X_i^{(H)}}\frac{dP_i^{(H)}}{P_i^{(H)}}$$

Substituting (5.38) and (5.40) into the above equation, we have:

$$\frac{d\left(X_i^{(H)}\right)}{X_i^{(H)}} = \sum_{r\neq 1}\left(\varepsilon_{ir}\frac{dP_r^{(H)}}{P_r^{(H)}}\right) + \varepsilon_{i,e}\frac{dP_i^{(H)}}{P_i^{(H)}}$$

So, we have the following linear percentage-change form of the household demand for goods:

$$x_i^{(H)} = \varepsilon_{i,e} p_i^{(H)} + \sum_{r \neq i} \varepsilon_{ir} p_r^{(H)} \tag{5.41}$$

$$p_i^{(H)} = \sum_{s=1}^{2} S_{(is)}^{(H)i} p_{(is)}^{(H)} \tag{5.42}$$

If the own-price elasticities and cross-price elasticities are available, equation (5.41) is a handy linear demand function. In reality, the cross-price elasticities are hard to obtain, but the expenditure elasticities are easily estimated. So, we have to derive the linear demand function based on expenditure elasticity only. First, we derive the formula to calculate the marginal budget share.

Manipulating equation (5.38), we have:

$$\beta_i^{(H)} = \varepsilon_{i,e} \times \left(P_i^{(H)} X_i^{(H)} / C \right) = \varepsilon_{i,e} \times S_i^{(H)} \tag{5.43}$$

This is the formula to calculate the marginal budget share. Next we calculate the subsistence consumption from the expenditure elasticity and the Frisch parameter.

The Frisch parameter is defined as the negative ratio between household's total expenditure and the supernumerary expenditure, namely:

$$\text{Frisch} = -C / \left(C - \sum_{r=1}^{g} P_r \gamma_r \right),$$

or

$$C - \sum_{r=1}^{g} P_r \gamma_r = -\, C/\text{Frisch}$$

Substituting the above equation and (5.43) into (5.37), we have:

$$X_i^{(H)} = \gamma_i + \varepsilon_{i,e}\left(P_i X_i^{(H)}/C\right)(-C/\text{Frisch})/P_i = \gamma_i - \varepsilon_{i,e} \times X_i^{(H)}/\text{Frisch}$$

or

$$\gamma_i = X_i^{(H)} + \varepsilon_{i,e} \times X_i^{(H)}/\text{Frisch} = X_i^{(H)}(1 + \varepsilon_{i,e}/\text{Frisch})$$

or

$$\gamma_i/X_i^{(H)} = 1 + \varepsilon_{i,e}/\text{Frisch} \tag{5.44}$$

We have obtained the solution for subsistence consumption in (5.37) in levels form. Finally, we derive the solution in percentage-change form.

Let θ_i be the supernumerary consumption for each commodity and α_i be the supernumerary consumption shares, and then it follows:

$$X_i^{(H)} = \gamma_i + \theta_i \tag{5.45}$$

and

$$\alpha_i = \theta_i/X_i^{(H)} = \left(X_i^{(H)} - \gamma_i\right)/X_i^{(H)} = 1 - \gamma_i/X_i^{(H)}$$

Substituting (5.44) into above equation to calculate α_i, we have:

$$\alpha_i = -\varepsilon_{i,e}/\text{Frisch} \tag{5.46}$$

Manipulating (5.37) and noticing the definition of the marginal budget share β_i and the supernumerary consumption, we have:

$$\begin{aligned} P_i^{(H)}\left(X_i^{(H)} - \gamma_i\right) &= \beta_i\left(C - \sum_{r=1}^{g} P_r^{(H)}\gamma_r\right) = \beta_i\left(\sum_{r=1}^{g} P_r^{(H)}\left(X_r^{(H)} - \gamma_r\right)\right) \\ &= \beta_i\left(\sum_{r=1}^{g} P_r^{(H)}\theta_r\right) \end{aligned}$$

Let W be the total nominal luxury expenditure, then:

$$P_i^{(H)}\theta_i = \beta_i W \tag{5.47}$$

Differentiating equation (5.45) and (5.47), we have the following demand function in percentage-change form:

$$x_i^{(H)} = (1 - \alpha_i)\dot{\gamma}_i + \alpha_i \dot{\theta}_i \tag{5.48}$$

and

$$x_i^{(H)} + p_i^{(H)} = w \tag{5.49}$$

where $\dot{\gamma}_i$, $\dot{\theta}_i$ is the percentage change in γ_i, θ_i, respectively, $(1-\alpha_i)$ is the subsistence consumption share for each commodity, and α_i is the supernumerary consumption share.

Differentiating the household utility function:

$$\overline{U}Q = U\left(X_1^{(H)}, \cdots, X_g^{(H)}\right) = \sum_{i=1}^{g} \beta_i \ln\left(X_i^{(H)} - \gamma_i\right)$$

we have:

$$d\overline{U}/\overline{U} + dQ/Q = \sum \beta_i \times d\theta_i/\theta$$

or

$$\overline{u} + q = \sum \beta_i \times \dot{\theta}_i \tag{5.50}$$

This is the function for the average utility per household in linear form.

5.5 Tourism Demand

Since we use a single-country model to analyse inbound tourism, the income from tourists is decided outside of the model. Thus, we assume that the total tourism spending is dependent on tourists' sensitivity to the price level of tourism goods. When it comes to the spending on specific tourism goods, the tourism expenditure pattern matters.

In any journey, tourists require certain amounts of different services such as accommodation, food, and transportation, regardless of their relative price, because it is difficult for tourists to substitute one good or service for another. As such, a Leontief function is proper to describe this tourists' spending pattern.

However, tourism shopping expenditure is totally different. Tourism is widely considered as a luxury activity, so tourism shopping is most likely concentrated on luxury goods and is more flexible than general shopping. In the case that some tourists are financially constrained, their shopping spending will be a very small part of the total tourism shopping expenditure because tourism shopping is not an indispensable part of their expenditure. Since the subsistence part of tourism shopping expenditure is negligible, the LES function used in the household sector reduces to the Cobb–Douglas (CD) function. This reasoning is confirmed by the Singapore Tourism Survey data (STB, 2004, 2005, 2006): the proportion of tourism shopping expenditure on different categories of goods has barely changed in recent years. As such, a CD function is suitable to describe the tourism shopping pattern.

With this knowledge, we have the following tourism expenditure pattern: at the top level, the tourism demand is determined by their demand for composite tourism shopping and non-shopping services, described by the CES function; the composite tourism non-shopping services are made up of a fixed proportion of various goods, which in turn is a flexible composition (CES function) of imported and domestic goods; and the composite tourism shopping services are a CD composition of a range of goods that in turn are CES composited imports and domestic goods. The structure of the nested tourism utility function is shown in Fig. 5.4.

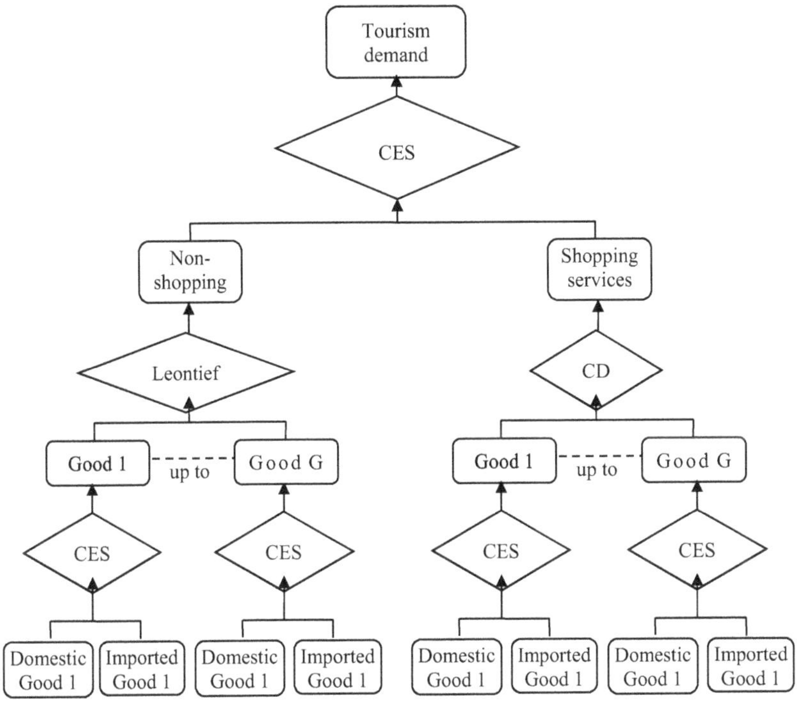

Fig. 5.4 Tourism demand

5.5.1 Demand for Composite Tourism Services

For a normal good, the quantity demanded is inversely proportional to its own price, so a typical demand curve is downward sloping. As such, we use the following equation to depict the demand for the composite tourism services in Singapore:

$$Q_k = F_{qk}\left(P_k^{(T)}/F_{pk}\right)^{\varepsilon_k} \tag{5.51}$$

where

Q_k – demand for composite tourism services by tourism-generating market
F_{qk} – quantity shift variable
P_k – aggregate price for tourism services by tourism-generating market
F_{pk} – price shift variable
ε_k – tourism demand elasticity

or in the percentage-change form:

$$q_k - f_{qk} = -\varepsilon_k \left(p_k^{(T)} - f_{pk} \right) \tag{5.52}$$

We assume that the prices faced by different tourism-generating markets are the same and sum up the tourism demands from all tourism-generating markets in order to obtain the aggregate inbound tourism demand.

5.5.2 Demand for Tourism Shopping and Non-Shopping Services

Since we use the CES function at the top level, the decision on spending on tourism shopping and non-shopping services can be expressed as:

$$\text{Minimize} \sum_{v=1}^{2} \left(P_{v,k}^{(T)} X_{v,k}^{(T)} \right),$$

$$\text{subject to } Q_k = \left[\sum_{v=1}^{2} B_{v,k} X_{v,k}^{(T)-\rho_k} \right]^{-1/\rho_k},$$

where v = 1 for tourism shopping, and v = 2 for tourism services.

With the same procedure used to derive for the solution to the earlier CES demand functions, we can obtain the following demand function for tourism shopping and non-shopping services:

$$X_{v,k}^{(T)} = Q_k \left(P_{v,k}^{(T)} B_{v,k}^{(T)-1} \right)^{-1/(\rho_k+1)} \times \left(\sum_{v=1}^{2} B_{v,k}^{1/(\rho_k+1)} P_{v,k}^{(T)\rho_k/(\rho_k+1)} \right)^{1/\rho_k} \quad (5.53)$$

or in the percentage-change form:

$$x_{v,k}^{(T)} = q_k - \sigma_k^{(T)} \left(p_{v,k}^{(T)} - \sum_{v=1}^{2} S_{v,k}^{(T)(1k)} p_{v,k}^{(T)} \right) \quad (5.54)$$

The percentage changes in prices are:

$$p_k^{(T)} = \sum_{v=1}^{2} S_{v,k}^{(T)(1k)} p_{v,k}^{(T)} \quad (5.55)$$

5.5.3 Tourism Shopping Expenditure Pattern

Mathematically, tourists' shopping decision can be expressed as:

$$X_{1k} = \mathrm{CD}\left(X_{i(1k)}^{(T)} \right) = \prod_{i=1}^{g} X_{i(1k)}^{(T)\beta_{i(1k)}} \quad (i = 1, \cdots, g)$$

and

$$X_{i(1k)}^{(T)} = \mathrm{CES}\left(X_{(is)(1k)}^{(T)} \right)$$

$$= \left(\sum_{s=1}^{2} B_{(is)(1k)} X_{(is)(1k)}^{(T)-\rho_{i(1k)}} \right)^{-1/\rho_{i(1k)}} \quad (s = d, m; i = 1, \cdots, g)$$

The cost minimization problem can be expressed as follows:

Minimize $\sum_{i=1}^{g} \sum_{s=1}^{2} P_{(is)(1k)}^{(T)} X_{(is)(1k)}^{(T)}$, subject to, $X_{1k} = \mathrm{CD}\left(X_{i(1k)}^{(T)} \right)$ and $X_{i(1k)}^{(T)} = \mathrm{CES}\left(X_{(is)(1k)}^{(T)} \right)$.

The Lagrangian expression is:

$$L = \sum_{i=1}^{g}\sum_{s=1}^{2} P_{(is)(1k)}^{(T)} X_{(is)(1k)}^{(T)} + \lambda_1\left(X_{1k} - \mathrm{CD}\left(X_{i(1k)}^{(T)}\right)\right) + \lambda_2\left(X_{i(1k)}^{(T)} - \mathrm{CES}\left(X_{(is)(1k)}^{(T)}\right)\right) \tag{5.56}$$

The first-order conditions are:

$$\partial\left(\sum_{i=1}^{g}\sum_{s=1}^{2} P_{(is)(1k)}^{(T)} X_{(is)(1k)}^{(T)}\right)/\partial X_{i(1k)}^{(T)} - \lambda_1\left(\partial \mathrm{CD}\left(X_{i(1k)}^{(T)}\right)/\partial X_{i(1k)}^{(T)} + \lambda_2 = 0 \tag{5.57}$$

$$\sum_{s=1}^{2} P_{(is)(1k)}^{(T)} - \lambda_2\left(\partial \mathrm{CES}\left(X_{(is)(1k)}^{(T)}\right)/\partial X_{(is)(1k)}^{(T)} = 0 \tag{5.58}$$

$$X_{1k} - \mathrm{CD}\left(X_{i(1k)}^{(T)}\right) = 0 \tag{5.59}$$

$$X_{i(1k)}^{(T)} - \mathrm{CES}\left(X_{(is)(1k)}^{(T)}\right) = 0 \tag{5.60}$$

Solving this minimization problem involves two stages. First, we use (5.58) and (5.60) to solve for $X_{(is)(1k)}$ .With the same procedure as we derive the intermediate input demand, we have the following results:

$$X_{(is)(1k)}^{(T)} = X_{i(1k)}^{(T)}\left(P_{(is)(1k)}^{(T)} B_{(is)(1k)}^{(T)-1}\right)^{-1/\left(\rho_{i(1k)}+1\right)}\left(\sum_{s=1}^{2} B_{(is)(1k)}^{1/(\rho_{ik}+1)} P_{(is)(1k)}^{(T)\rho_{ik}/(\rho_{ik}+1)}\right)^{1/\rho_{i(1k)}} \tag{5.61}$$

or in percentage-change form:

$$x_{(is)(1k)}^{(T)} = x_{i(1k)} - \sigma_{i(1k)}\left(p_{(is)(1k)}^{(T)} - \sum_{s=1}^{2} S_{(is)(1k)}^{(T)} p_{(is)(1k)}^{(T)}\right) \tag{5.62}$$

$$p_{i(1k)}^{(T)} = \sum_{s=1}^{2} S_{(is)(1k)}^{(T)} p_{(is)(1k)}^{(T)} \tag{5.63}$$

In the second stage, we solve for $X_{i(1k)}$. Using the same procedure as we derived equation (5.32), we have:

$$P_{i(1k)}^{(T)} X_{i(1k)}^{(T)} = \sum_{s=1}^{2} P_{(is)(1k)}^{(T)} X_{(is)(1k)}^{(T)}$$

so equation (5.57) becomes:

$$\partial\left(\sum_{i=1}^{g} P_{i(1k)}^{(T)} X_{i(1k)}^{(T)}\right) / \partial X_{i(1k)}^{(T)} - \lambda_1 \partial \mathrm{CD}\left(X_{i(1k)}^{(T)}\right) / \partial X_{i(1k)}^{(T)} = 0 \tag{5.64}$$

replace $\mathrm{CD}\left(X_{i(1k)}^{(T)}\right)$ with $\prod_{i=1}^{g} X_{i(1k)}^{(T)\beta_i}$, we have

$$P_{i(1k)}^{(T)} = \lambda_1 \partial\left(\prod_{i=1}^{g} X_{i(1k)}^{(T)\beta_i}\right) / \partial X_{i(1k)}^{(T)} = \frac{\lambda_1 \beta_i X_{1k}}{X_{i(1k)}^{(T)}} \tag{5.65}$$

or

$$X_{i(1k)}^{(T)} = \lambda_1 \beta_i X_{1k} / P_{i(1k)}^{(T)}$$

Plugging (5.65) and the definition of CD function into (5.59), we have:

$$X_{1k} = \prod_{i=1}^{g} X_{i(1k)}^{(T)\beta_i} = (\lambda_1)^{\sum_{i=1}^{g} \beta_i} \prod_{i=1}^{g} \left(\beta_i / P_{i(1k)}^{(T)}\right)^{\beta_i} \tag{5.66}$$

since β_i is the budget share, so $\sum_{i=1}^{g} \beta_i = 1$.Thus, from (4.66), we have :

$$\lambda_1 = 1 / \prod_{i=1}^{g} \left(\beta_i / P_{i(1k)}^{(T)}\right)^{\beta_i} \tag{5.67}$$

Substituting (5.67) back into (5.65), we have:

$$X_{i(1k)}^{(T)} = \beta_i X_{1k} / P_{i(1k)}^{(T)} \prod_{i=1}^{g} \left(\beta_i / P_{i(1k)}^{(T)} \right)^{\beta_i} \tag{5.68}$$

This is the solution in levels form. Next, we derive the percentage-change form. First, we rearrange equation (5.68) as:

$$X_{i(1k)}^{(T)} = X_{1k} \left(\frac{P_{i(1k)}^{(T)}}{\beta_i} \right)^{-1} \prod_{r=1}^{g} \left(\frac{P_{r(1k)}^{(T)}}{\beta_r} \right)^{\beta_r} = X_{1k} \left(\frac{P_{i(1k)}^{(T)}}{\beta_i} \right)^{\beta_r - 1} \prod_{r \neq i} \left(\frac{P_{r(1k)}^{(T)}}{\beta_r} \right)^{\beta_r} \tag{5.69}$$

Totally differentiating equation (5.69) and using (5.68), we have:

$$\begin{aligned}
dX_{i(1k)}^{(T)} &= X_{1k} \prod_{r=1}^{g} \left(\frac{P_{r(1k)}^{(T)}}{\beta_r} \right)^{\beta_r} (\beta_i - 1) \frac{dP_{i(1k)}^{(T)}}{\beta_i} \left(\frac{P_{i(1k)}^{(T)}}{\beta_i} \right)^{-1} \left(\frac{P_{i(1k)}^{(T)}}{\beta_i} \right)^{\beta_i - 1} \\
&\quad + X_{1k} \left(\frac{P_{i(1k)}^{(T)}}{\beta_i} \right)^{\beta_i - 1} d \left(\prod_{r \neq i} \left(\frac{P_{r(1k)}^{(T)}}{\beta_r} \right)^{\beta_r} \right) + X_{i(1k)}^{(T)} \frac{dX_{1k}}{X_{1k}} \\
&= (\beta_i - 1) X_{1k} \left(\frac{P_{i(1k)}^{(T)}}{\beta_i} \right)^{\beta_i - 1} \prod_{r=1}^{g} \left(\frac{P_{r(1k)}^{(T)}}{\beta_r} \right)^{\beta_r} \frac{dP_{i(1k)}^{(T)}}{P_{i(1k)}^{(T)}} \\
&\quad + X_{1k} \left(\frac{P_{i(1k)}^{(T)}}{\beta_i} \right)^{\beta_i - 1} \prod_{r \neq i} \left(\frac{P_{r(1k)}^{(T)}}{\beta_r} \right)^{\beta_r} \left(\sum_{r \neq i} \left(\frac{P_{r(1k)}^{(T)}}{\beta_r} \right)^{-1} dP_{r(1k)}^{(T)} \right) + X_{i(1k)}^{(T)} \frac{dX_{1k}}{X_{1k}} \\
&= (\beta_i - 1) X_{i(1k)}^{(T)} \frac{dP_{i(1k)}^{(T)}}{P_{i(1k)}^{(T)}} \\
&\quad + X_{1k} \left(\frac{P_{i(1k)}^{(T)}}{\beta_i} \right)^{-1} \prod_{r=1}^{g} \left(\frac{P_{r(1k)}^{(T)}}{\beta_r} \right)^{\beta_r} \left(\sum_{r \neq i} \beta_r \frac{dP_{r(1k)}^{(T)}}{P_{r(1k)}^{(T)}} \right) + X_{i(1k)}^{(T)} \frac{dX_{1k}}{X_{1k}} \\
&= (\beta_i - 1) X_{i(1k)}^{(T)} \frac{dP_{i(1k)}^{(T)}}{P_{i(1k)}^{(T)}} + X_{i(1k)}^{(T)} \left(\sum_{r \neq i} \beta_r \frac{dP_{r(1k)}^{(T)}}{P_{r(1k)}^{(T)}} \right) + X_{i(1k)}^{(T)} \times \frac{dX_{1k}}{X_{1k}}
\end{aligned}$$

so:

$$\frac{dX_{i(1k)}^{(T)}}{X_{i(1k)}^{(T)}} = (\beta_i - 1)\frac{dP_{i(1k)}^{(T)}}{P_{i(1k)}^{(T)}} + \sum_{r \neq i} \beta_r \frac{dP_{r(1k)}^{(T)}}{P_{r(1k)}^{(T)}} + \frac{dX_{1k}}{X_{1k}} \tag{5.70}$$

So we have the following percentage-change form:

$$x_{i(1k)}^{(T)} = x_{1k} + \left(\beta_{i(1k)} - 1\right)p_{i(1k)}^{(T)} + \sum_{r \neq i} \beta_{r(1k)} p_{r(1k)}^{(T)}$$

or

$$x_{i(1k)}^{(T)} = \mathrm{x}_{1k} - p_{i(1k)}^{(T)} + \sum \beta_{r(1k)} p_{r(1k)}^{(T)}$$

Writing the share in standard form, we have:

$$x_{i(1k)}^{(T)} = \mathrm{x}_{1k} - p_{i(1k)}^{(T)} + \sum_{r=1}^{g} S_{r(1k)}^{(T)1k} p_{r(1k)}^{(T)} \tag{5.71}$$

The percentage change in price of composite intermediate input for industry j is given by:

$$p_{1k}^{(T)} = \sum_{i=1}^{g} p_{i(1k)}^{(T)} S_{i(1k)}^{(T)1k} \tag{5.72}$$

5.5.4 Tourism Non-Shopping Services Demand

The demand for composite tourism non-shopping services can be expressed as:

$$X_{2k} = \underset{i=1,\cdots,g}{\mathrm{Leontief}} \left\{ X_{i(2k)}^{(T)} / A_{i(2k)}^{(T)} \right\} = \min\left(\frac{X_{1(2k)}^{(T)}}{A_{1(2k)}^{(T)}}, \frac{X_{2(2k)}^{(T)}}{A_{2(2k)}^{(T)}}, \cdots, \frac{X_{g(2k)}^{(T)}}{A_{g(2k)}^{(T)}} \right)$$

Thus, the solution for this function gives the tourism demand for composite tourism services:

$$X_{i(2k)}^{(T)} = X_{2k} \times A_{i(2k)}^{(T)}, (i = 1, \ldots g) \tag{5.73}$$

Or in percentage-change form:

$$x_{i(2k)}^{(T)} = x_{2k} + a_{i(2k)}^{(T)}, (i = 1, \ldots g) \tag{5.74}$$

At the bottom level, the CES function is employed to reflect the substitutability of imported goods. So the utility maximization problem can be expressed as:

$$\text{Maximize} \quad \text{CES}\left(X_{(is)(2k)}^{(T)}\right) \text{ subject to } \sum_{i=1}^{g}\sum_{s=1}^{2} P_{(is)(2k)}^{(T)} X_{(is)(2k)}^{(T)} = X_{i(2k)}^{(T)}$$

Solving the constraint maximization problem, we have:

$$X_{(is)(2k)}^{(T)} = X_{i(2k)}^{(T)} \left(P_{(is)(2k)}^{(T)} B_{(is)(2k)}^{(T)-1}\right)^{-1/\left(\rho_{i(2k)}^{(T)}+1\right)} \times \left(\sum_{s=1}^{2} B_{(is)(2k)}^{(T)1/\left(\rho_{i(2k)}^{(T)}+1\right)} P_{(is)(2k)}^{(T)\rho_{i(2k)}^{(T)}/\left(\rho_{i(2k)}^{(T)}+1\right)}\right)^{1/\rho_{i(2k)}^{(T)}} \tag{5.75}$$

or in the percentage-change form:

$$x_{(is)(2k)}^{(T)} = x_{i(2k)}^{(T)} - \sigma_{i(2k)}^{(T)} \left(p_{(is)(2k)}^{(T)} - \sum_{s=1}^{2} S_{(is)(2k)}^{(T)(2k)} p_{(is)(2k)}^{(T)}\right) \tag{5.76}$$

And the percentage change in prices is:

$$p_{i(2k)}^{(T)} = \sum_{s=1}^{2} S_{(is)(2k)}^{(T)(2k)} p_{(is)k}^{(T)} \tag{5.77}$$

5.5.5 TABLO Codes for Tourism Demand

This section displays the excerpt of TABLO codes for tourism demand. With the explanation of TABLO commands in Chap. 2, the reader should be able to read and understand these codes. The codes between two '!'s or between two '#'s are not executable (i.e. GEMPACK software will ignore them). These codes are added to aid the reader's understanding.

```
! Excerpt 19A of TABLO input file: !
! tourism shopping demands !

Coefficient (parameter)(all,c,COM)(all,g,MKT)
   SIGMA7(c,g) # Armington elasticities: tourism shopping#;
   Read SIGMA7 from file BASEDATA header "7AMK";
Coefficient ! Source Shares in Flows at Purchaser's prices !
 (all,g,MKT) V7PUR_CS(g) # Total shopping expenditure by tourists #;
 (all,c,COM)(all,g,MKT) V7PUR_S(c,g) # Dom+imp tourism shopping
value #;
 (all,c,COM)(all,s,SRC)(all,g,MKT) S7(c,s,g) # tourism shopping
source shares #;
Zerodivide default 0.5;

Formula
 (all,c,COM)(all,g,MKT) V7PUR_S(c,g) = sum{s,SRC, V7PUR(c,s,g)};
  (all,c,COM)(all,s,SRC)(all,g,MKT)  S7(c,s,g)  =  V7PUR(c,s,g)  /
V7PUR_S(c,g);
 (all,g,MKT)        V7PUR_CS(g) = sum{c,COM, V7PUR_S(c,g)};
Zerodivide off;

Variable
 (all,g,MKT) p7_cs(g) # Tourism shopping price index #;
 (all,g,MKT) x7_cs(g) # Total real tourism shopping expenditure #;
 (all,g,MKT) w7_cs(g) # Total Nominal tourism shopping expenditure #;
```

```
(all,c,COM)(all,g,MKT) x7_s(c,g) # tourism shopping use of imp/dom
composite #;
 (all,c,COM)(all,g,MKT) p7_s(c,g) # purchase price,shopping
imp/dom composite #;
(all,c,COM)(all,g,MKT) a7_s(c,g) # Taste change, shopping imp/dom
composite #;
 (all,c,COM)(all,s,SRC)(all,g,MKT) a7(c,s,g) # Taste change,
shoppins basic #;
Equation
E_x7 # Source-specific commodity demands #
(all,c,COM)(all,s,SRC)(all,g,MKT)
x7(c,s,g)-a7(c,s,g) = x7_s(c,g) - SIGMA7(c,g)*[ p7(c,s,g)+a7(c,s,
g)-p7_s(c,g)];

E_p7_s # Effective price of commodity composite #
(all,c,COM)(all,g,MKT) p7_s(c,g) = sum{s,SRC, S7(c,s,g)*[p7(c,s,
g)+a7(c,s,g)]};

E_x7_s # Tourism shopping demand for composite commodities #
 (all,c,COM)(all,g,MKT) x7_s(c,g) = w7_cs(g) - p7_s(c,g) + a7_s(c,g);

E_p7_cs # tourism shopping price index #
(all,g,MKT) p7_cs(g) =
sum{c,COM, sum{s,SRC, [V7PUR(c,s,g)/(V7PUR_CS(g)+TINY)]*p7(c,s,
g)}};

! Excerpt 19B of TABLO input file: !
! tourism non-shopping demands !

Coefficient
 (parameter)(all,c,COM)(all,g,MKT)
SIGMA8(c,g) # Armington elasticities: tourism general#;
Read SIGMA8 from file BASEDATA header "8AMK";
Coefficient ! Source Shares in Flows at Purchaser's prices !
 (all,g,MKT) V8PUR_CS(g) # Total non-shopping expenditure by tour-
ists #;
  (all,c,COM)(all,g,MKT) V8PUR_S(c,g) # Dom+imp tourism
non-shopping value #;
 (all,c,COM)(all,s,SRC)(all,g,MKT) S8(c,s,g) # non-shopping
source shares #;
```

```
Zerodivide default 0.5;
Formula
 (all,c,COM)(all,g,MKT)  V8PUR_S(c,g) = sum{s,SRC, V8PUR(c,s,g)};
  (all,c,COM)(all,s,SRC)(all,g,MKT)S8(c,s,g)  =  V8PUR(c,s,g)    /
V8PUR_S(c,g);
 (all,g,MKT)        V8PUR_CS(g) = sum{c,COM, V8PUR_S(c,g)};
Zerodivide off;

Variable
 (all,g,MKT) p8_cs(g) # Tourism non-shopping price index #;
 (all,g,MKT) x8_cs(g) # Total real tourism non-shopping expenditure #;
 (all,g,MKT) w8_cs(g)  # Total Nominal tourism non-shopping expendi-
ture #;
  (all,c,COM)(all,g,MKT) x8_s(c,g) # non-shopping use of imp/dom
composite #;
   (all,c,COM)(all,g,MKT)  p8_s(c,g)  #  purchase  price,non-shop
imp/dom composite #;
 (all,c,COM)(all,g,MKT) a8_s(c,g) # Taste change, non-shopimp/dom
composite #;
  (all,c,COM)(all,s,SRC)(all,g,MKT)   a8(c,s,g)  #  Taste  change,
basic #;

Equation
E_x8 # Source-specific commodity demands #
(all,c,COM)(all,s,SRC)(all,g,MKT)
x8(c,s,g)-a8(c,s,g) = x8_s(c,g) - SIGMA8(c,g)*[p8(c,s,g)+a8(c,s,
g)-p8_s(c,g)];

E_p8_s # Effective price of commodity composite #
(all,c,COM)(all,g,MKT) p8_s(c,g) = sum{s,SRC, S8(c,s,g)*[p8(c,s,
g)+a8(c,s,g)]};

E_x8_s # Tourism non-shopping demand for composite commodities #
 (all,c,COM)(all,g,MKT) x8_s(c,g) = x8_cs(g) + a8_s(c,g);

E_p8_cs # tourism non-shopping price index #
 (all,g,MKT)p8_cs(g)=
  sum{c,COM,sum{s,SRC,[V8PUR(c,s,g)/(V8PUR_CS(g)+tiny)]*p8(c,s,
g)}};
```

```
! Excerpt 19C of TABLO input file: !
! Top nest of tourism demand !

Coefficient
 (parameter)(all,g,MKT)SIGMA9(g)  # Armington elasticities: tour-
ism top#;
Read SIGMA9 from file BASEDATA header "TOUR";
Coefficient ! Source Shares in Flows at Purchaser's prices !
 (all,g,MKT)  V9BAS(g) # Total non-shopping expenditure by tourists #;
 (all,g,MKT)  V9PUR(g) # Total non-shopping expenditure by tourists #;
Formula
 (all,g,MKT)  V9BAS(g) =
   sum{c,COM,sum{s,SRC,V7BAS(c,s,g)}}+sum{c,COM,sum{s,SRC,V8BAS
(c,s,g)}};
 (all,g,MKT)  V9PUR(g) = V7PUR_CS(g) + V8PUR_CS(g);
Variable
 (all,g,MKT) p9(g) # Tourism price index #;
 (all,g,MKT) x9(g) # Total real tourism expenditure #;
 (all,g,MKT) w9(g)  # Total Nominal tourism expenditure #;
 (all,g,MKT) f9q(g)  # Quantity shift term for tourism demand #;
 (all,g,MKT) f9p(g)  # Price shift term for tourism demand #;
 (all,g,MKT) f7_cs(g)  # Overall shift term for tourism shopping #;
 (all,g,MKT) f8_cs(g) # Overall shift term for tourism non-shopping #;
Coefficient (parameter)(all,g,MKT)
       ELSD(g) # Tourism demand elasticities#;
       (all,g,MKT)S7PUR_CS(g) # share of tourism shopping#;
       (all,g,MKT)S8PUR_CS(g) # share of tourism services#;
(parameter) EX78 # set to 1 to calculate x9 when both x7 and x8 are
exogenous#;
       Read ELSD from file BASEDATA header "ELSD";
       Read EX78 from file BASEDATA header "EX78";
zerodivide default 0.5;
Formula
(all,g,MKT)S7PUR_CS(g)=V7PUR_CS(g)/[V9PUR(g)];
(all,g,MKT)S8PUR_CS(g)=V8PUR_CS(g)/[V9PUR(g)];
Zerodivide off;
Equation
E_x7_cs # Source-specific commodity demands #
(all,g,MKT)x7_cs(g)+ f7_cs(g)  =  x9(g)  -  SIGMA9(g)*[p7_cs(g)-p9
(g)];
```

```
E_x8_cs # Source-specific commodity demands #
(all,g,MKT)x8_cs(g)+ f8_cs(g) = x9(g) - SIGMA9(g)*[p8_cs(g)-p9
(g)];

E_p9 # effective tourism price for each market #
(all,g,MKT)p9(g) =
 S7PUR_CS(g)*[p7_cs(g)]+S8PUR_CS(g)*[p8_cs(g)];

E_x9 # Total real tourism non-shopping expenditure #
 (all,g,MKT)x9(g) -f9q(g)=
 (1-EX78)*{-ABS[ELSD(g)]*[p9(g) - phi - f9p(g)]}+EX78*
 {S7PUR_CS(g)*x7_cs(g)+S8PUR_CS(g)*x8_cs(g)};

E_w7_cs # Total Nominal tourism shopping expenditure #
 (all,g,MKT) w7_cs(g)= x7_cs(g) + p7_cs(g);

E_w8_cs # Total Nominal tourism non-shopping expenditure #
 (all,g,MKT) w8_cs(g)= x8_cs(g) + p8_cs(g);

E_w9 # Total real tourism shopping expenditure #
 (all,g,MKT) w9(g)= x9(g) + p9(g);

! Excerpt 19D of TABLO input file: !
! Aggregation of tourism markets !

Set
 AMERICA # tourism market # (Canada, USA) ;
 Subset AMERICA is subset of MKT;
Set
  ASIASE # tourism market # (Indonesia, Malaysia, Philippines,
Thailand) ;
 Subset ASIASE is subset of MKT;
Set
  ASIANOR # tourism market # (China, Taiwan, HongKong, Japan,
SouthKorea) ;
 Subset ASIANOR is subset of MKT;
Set
 ASIASOU # tourism market # (India) ;
 Subset ASIASOU is subset of MKT;
Set
 EUROPE # tourism market #
 (France, Germany, Italy, Netherlands, Switzerland, UK) ;
```

```
 Subset EUROPE is subset of MKT;
Set
 OCEANIA # tourism market # (Australia, NewZealand) ;
 Subset OCEANIA is subset of MKT;
Set
 AFRICA # tourism market # (SouthAfrica) ;
 Subset AFRICA is subset of MKT;

Variable
 p9_amarica # Tourism price index #;
 x9_amarica # Total real tourism expenditure #;
 w9_amarica # Total Nominal tourism expenditure #;
 p9_asiase  # Tourism price index #;
 x9_asiase  # Total real tourism expenditure #;
 w9_asiase  # Total Nominal tourism expenditure #;
 p9_asianor # Tourism price index #;
 x9_asianor # Total real tourism expenditure #;
 w9_asianor # Total Nominal tourism expenditure #;
 p9_asiasou # Tourism price index #;
 x9_asiasou # Total real tourism expenditure #;
 w9_asiasou # Total Nominal tourism expenditure #;
 p9_europe  # Tourism price index #;
 x9_europe  # Total real tourism expenditure #;
 w9_europe  # Total Nominal tourism expenditure #;
 p9_oceania # Tourism price index #;
 x9_oceania # Total real tourism expenditure #;
 w9_oceania # Total Nominal tourism expenditure #;
 p9_africa  # Tourism price index #;
 x9_africa  # Total real tourism expenditure #;
 w9_africa  # Total Nominal tourism expenditure #;
 p9_world   # Tourism price index #;
 x9_world   # Total real tourism expenditure #;
 w9_world   # Total Nominal tourism expenditure #;

Equation
E_x9_amarica # tourism demands for the region#
sum{g, AMERICA, V9BAS(g)}*x9_amarica = sum{g, AMERICA, V9BAS(g)*x9
(g)};
```

```
E_p9_amarica # effective tourism price for the region #
sum{g, AMERICA, V9BAS(g)}*p9_amarica = sum{g, AMERICA, V9BAS(g)*p9
(g)};

E_w9_amarica # Total real tourism expenditure #
w9_amarica= x9_amarica + p9_amarica;

E_x9_asiase # tourism demands for the region#
sum{g, ASIASE, V9BAS(g)}*x9_asiase = sum{g, ASIASE, V9BAS(g)*x9
(g)};

E_p9_asiase # effective tourism price for the region #
sum{g, ASIASE, V9BAS(g)}*p9_asiase = sum{g, ASIASE, V9BAS(g)*p9
(g)};

E_w9_asiase # Total real tourism expenditure #
w9_asiase= x9_asiase + p9_asiase;

E_x9_asianor # tourism demands for the region#
sum{g, ASIANOR, V9BAS(g)}*x9_asianor = sum{g, ASIANOR, V9BAS(g)*x9
(g)};

E_p9_asianor # effective tourism price for the region #
sum{g, ASIANOR, V9BAS(g)}*p9_asianor = sum{g, ASIANOR, V9BAS(g)*p9
(g)};

E_w9_asianor # Total real tourism expenditure #
w9_asianor= x9_asianor + p9_asianor;

E_x9_asiasou # tourism demands for the region#
sum{g, ASIASOU, V9BAS(g)}*x9_asiasou = sum{g, ASIASOU, V9BAS(g)*x9
(g)};

E_p9_asiasou # effective tourism price for the region #
sum{g, ASIASOU, V9BAS(g)}*p9_asiasou = sum{g, ASIASOU, V9BAS(g)*p9
(g)};

E_w9_asiasou # Total real tourism expenditure #
w9_asiasou= x9_asiasou + p9_asiasou;
```

```
E_x9_europe # tourism demands for the region#
sum{g, EUROPE, V9BAS(g)}*x9_europe = sum{g, EUROPE, V9BAS(g)*x9
(g)};

E_p9_europe # effective tourism price for the region #
sum{g, EUROPE, V9BAS(g)}*p9_europe = sum{g, EUROPE, V9BAS(g)*p9
(g)};

E_w9_europe # Total real tourism expenditure #
 w9_europe= x9_europe + p9_europe;

E_x9_oceania # tourism demands for the region#
sum{g, OCEANIA, V9BAS(g)}*x9_oceania = sum{g, OCEANIA, V9BAS(g)*x9
(g)};

E_p9_oceania # effective tourism price for the region #
sum{g, OCEANIA, V9BAS(g)}*p9_oceania = sum{g, OCEANIA, V9BAS(g)*p9
(g)};

E_w9_oceania # Total real tourism expenditure #
 w9_oceania= x9_oceania + p9_oceania;

E_x9_africa # tourism demands for the region#
sum{g, AFRICA, V9BAS(g)}*x9_africa = sum{g, AFRICA, V9BAS(g)*x9
(g)};

E_p9_africa # effective tourism price for the region #
sum{g, AFRICA, V9BAS(g)}*p9_africa = sum{g, AFRICA, V9BAS(g)*p9
(g)};

E_w9_africa # Total real tourism expenditure #
 w9_africa= x9_africa + p9_africa;

E_x9_world # tourism demands for the region#
sum{g, MKT, V9BAS(g)}*x9_world = sum{g, MKT, V9BAS(g)*x9(g)};

E_p9_world # effective tourism price for the region #
sum{g, MKT, V9BAS(g)}*p9_world = sum{g, MKT, V9BAS(g)*p9(g)};

E_w9_world # Total real tourism expenditure #
 w9_world= x9_world + p9_world;
```

5.6 Exports and Other Final Demands

Since we assume households own all primary factors and there is no pure profit in production, corporations have no position in final demand. Besides households, investors, and tourists, which we have already addressed, there are two more final demand sectors in our study—foreigners and government sectors. We consider their demand functions in this section.

5.6.1 Foreign Demand for Exports

For a normal good, the quantity demanded is inversely proportional to its own price, so we use the following equation to depict the foreign demand for Singaporean exports:

$$X_{(id)}^{(E)} = F_{(Qi)}^{(E)} \left(P_{(id)}^{(E)} \Phi / F_{(Pi)}^{(E)} \right)^{\varepsilon_{iie}}, \quad i = 1, \cdots, g \tag{5.78}$$

where $X_{(id)}^{(E)}$ – volume of exports of good i
Φ – exchange rate (S\$ per unit foreign currency)
$F_{(Qi)}^{(E)}$ – quantity shift variable
$P_{(id)}^{(E)}$ – foreign currency receipt per unit of export of good i
$F_{(Pi)}^{(E)}$ – price shift variable
ε_{iie} – export demand elasticity

or in percentage-change form:

$$x_{(id)}^{(E)} - f_{(Qi)}^{(E)} = -\varepsilon_{iie} \left(p_{(id)}^{(E)} + \phi - f_{(Pi)}^{(E)} \right), \quad i = 1, \cdots, g \tag{5.79}$$

Since Singapore is a small country and thus a price taker in world markets, the elasticity in the equation is expected to be quite large for most tradables, and thus the demand curve will be fairly flat.

5.6.2 Government Demand

In reality, the government demands not only goods and services, but also labour and other primary factors. However, to simplify the model, we assume the government obtains the needed primary factors from the services provided by the service sectors. As such, the government only demands goods and services. Since the function of the government is to service households, we further assume that the government demand for goods and services is proportional to the total household real consumption in the long run:

$$X_{(is)}^{(G)} = C_R H_{(is)}^{(G)} F_{(is)}^{(G)}, C_R = C/\mathrm{CPI} \quad i = 1, \cdots, g; \quad s = d, m \tag{5.80}$$

where $X_{(is)}^{(G)}$ – government demand for good i from sources
C_R – real aggregate household expenditure
$H_{(is)}^{(G)}$ – ratio of overall shift in government demand to real aggregate household consumption
$F_{(is)}^{(G)}$ – shift variable

or in the percentage-change form:

$$x_{(is)}^{(G)} = c_R + h_{(is)}^{(G)} + f_{(is)}^{(G)} \tag{5.81}$$

$$c_R = c - cpi \tag{5.82}$$

The shift variable is useful when we need to fix the government demand in the short run.

5.7 The Price System

There are mainly two types of prices in an economic system: basic values and purchaser's prices. The difference between basic value and purchaser's prices makes up the margins and indirect taxes. Margins are not a concern for this study since there is no margin sector in Singapore input–output tables (the trade sector is treated as a normal services producer). For taxes, there are many kinds of indirect taxes in Singapore such as import duties, sales taxes, and taxes on production. To simplify the study, we follow the traditional practice of ORANI models to single out sales taxes as the difference between two types of prices and put other indirect taxes in the basic value.

5.7.1 The Basic Values

There are two assumptions for the basic values. One is the zero pure profit assumption: there is no pure profit in any economic activities (e.g. producing, importing, and exporting). This assumption is implied by the assumption of the perfectly competitive economy. The other is the uniform prices assumption: basic values are uniform across users and across producers and importers. Since the basic values involve different types of goods, such as domestic consumption goods, capital goods, imports, and exports, we address them in turn (we use the superscript (0) to stand for basic values).

First, the basic values of domestic consumption goods. For domestic goods, the basic values are prices received by producers, excluding sales taxes; under the zero pure profit and uniform basic value assumption, the basic value of the output of industry j should be equal to the total payments to intermediate inputs primary factors plus tax on production (TP), shown as follows:

$$\sum_{r=1}^{g} P_{(rd)}^{(0)} X_{(rd)j}^{(0)} = \sum_{i=1}^{g} \sum_{s=1}^{2} P_{(is)j}^{(\mathrm{ID})} X_{(is)j}^{(\mathrm{ID})} + P_{(pf,L)j} X_{(pf,L)j} + P_{(pf,K)j} X_{(pf,K)j} + (\mathrm{TP})_j \tag{5.83}$$

or in the percentage-change form:

$$
\begin{aligned}
\sum_{r=1}^{g}\left(p_{(rd)}^{(0)}+x_{(rd)j}^{(0)}\right)S_{(rd)j}^{(0)} = & \sum_{i=1}^{g}\sum_{s=1}^{2}\left(p_{(is)j}^{(\mathrm{ID})}+x_{(is)j}^{(\mathrm{ID})}\right)S_{(is)j}^{(\mathrm{IC})j} \\
& +\left(p_{(pf,L)j}+x_{(pf,L)j}\right)S_{(pf,L)j}^{(\mathrm{IC})j} \\
& +\left(p_{(pf,K)j}+x_{(pf,K)j}\right)S_{(pf,K)j}^{(\mathrm{IC})j}+(tp)_j S_{(tp)j}^{(\mathrm{IC})j}
\end{aligned} \tag{5.84}
$$

The superscripts (IC) represents the total industry cost.

Second, the basic values of the capital goods. According to the conformation of capital goods, no primary factor is involved in its production, so the basic values are given by:

$$
P_{(pf,K)j}^{N}X_{(pf,K)j}^{N}=\sum_{i=1}^{g}\sum_{s=1}^{2}P_{(is)j}^{K}X_{(is)j}^{K} \tag{5.85}
$$

or in the percentage-change form:

$$
p_{(pf,K)j}^{N}+x_{(pf,K)j}^{N}=\sum_{i=1}^{g}\sum_{s=1}^{2}\left(p_{(is)j}^{K}+x_{(is)j}^{K}\right)S_{(is)j}^{(K)j} \tag{5.86}
$$

These basic values are used to calculate the investment expenditure.

Third, the basic values of imports. For imported goods, the basic values are prices received by importers—import duties are included. There are two kinds of prices in international trade practice: the f.o.b. (free on board) price and the c.i.f. (cost, insurance, and freight included) price. Following the traditional trade practice, we use the c.i.f. price for imports. The basic value is given as follows:

$$
P_{(im)}^{(0)}=P_{(im)}^{(M)}\Phi T_{(im)}^{(M)},\quad i=1,\cdots,g;\ \ s=d,m \tag{5.87}
$$

where $P^{(0)}_{(im)}$ – basic value of imported good i
$P^{(M)}_{(im)}$ – foreign currency c.i.f.price of imported good i
Φ – exchange rate (S$ per unit foreign currency)
$T^{(M)}_{im}$ – power of tariff on imported good i (tariff rate plus one)

or in percentage-change form:

$$p^{(0)}_{(im)} = p^{(M)}_{(im)} + \phi + t^{(M)}_{(im)} \tag{5.88}$$

Finally, the basic value for exports. In the same fashion, we can obtain the following basic value for exports, but we accept the traditional practice using f.o.b. price for exports:

$$P^{(E)}_{(id)}\Phi = P^{(0)}_{(id)}T^{(E)}_{(id)}, \quad i = 1, \cdots, g; \tag{5.89}$$

where $P^{(E)}_{(id)}$ – foreign currency f.o.b.price paid by foreigners
Φ – exchange rate (S$ per unit foreign currency)
$P^{(0)}_{(id)}$ – basic value of exported good i
$\mathrm{T}^{(E)}_{(id)}$ – power of tariff on exported good i

or in the percentage-change form:

$$p^{(E)}_{(id)} + \phi = p^{(0)}_{(id)} + t^{(E)}_{(id)} \tag{5.90}$$

5.7.2 The Purchasers' Prices

According to the definition of purchasers' prices, they are the basic values multiplied by the power of sale taxes (tax rate plus one). For the sake of flexibility, we allow the government to impose different sales tax rates according to different user groups. The following equations express the purchaser's price for intermediate demand, investors' demand, household demand, tourists' demand, and government demand, respectively.

$$P^{(\mathrm{ID})}_{(is)j} = P^{(0)}_{(is)} T^{(\mathrm{ID})}_{(is)j}, \quad i = 1, \cdots, g; s = d, m, \quad j = 1, \cdots, h \tag{5.91}$$

$$P^{(\mathrm{K})}_{(is)j} = P^{(0)}_{(is)} T^{(K)}_{(is)j}, \quad i = 1, \cdots, g; s = d, m, \quad j = 1, \cdots, h \tag{5.92}$$

$$P^{(H)}_{(is)} = P^{(0)}_{(is)} T^{(H)}_{(is)}, \quad i = 1, \cdots, g; s = d, m \tag{5.93}$$

$$P^{(T)}_{(is)} = P^{(0)}_{(is)} T^{(T)}_{(is)}, \quad i = 1, \cdots, g; s = d, m \tag{5.94}$$

$$P^{(\mathrm{G})}_{(is)} = P^{(0)}_{(is)} T^{(G)}_{(is)}, \quad i = 1, \cdots, g; s = d, m \tag{5.95}$$

or in percentage-change form:

$$p^{(\mathrm{ID})}_{(is)j} = p^{(0)}_{(is)} + t^{(\mathrm{ID})}_{(is)j}, \quad i = 1, \cdots, g; s = d, m, \quad j = 1, \cdots, h \tag{5.96}$$

$$p^{(\mathrm{K})}_{(is)j} = p^{(0)}_{(is)} + t^{(K)}_{(is)j}, \quad i = 1, \cdots, g; s = d, m, \quad j = 1, \cdots, h \tag{5.97}$$

$$p^{(H)}_{(is)} = p^{(0)}_{(is)} + t^{(H)}_{(is)}, \quad i = 1, \cdots, g; s = d, m \tag{5.98}$$

$$p^{(T)}_{(is)} = p^{(0)}_{(is)} + t^{(T)}_{(is)}, \quad i = 1, \cdots, g; s = d, m \tag{5.99}$$

$$p^{(\mathrm{G})}_{(is)} = p^{(0)}_{(is)} + t^{(G)}_{(is)}, \quad i = 1, \cdots, g; s = d, m \tag{5.100}$$

5.8 Income, Consumption, and Investment

Since the model assumes no pure profit in production, the industries have no income (corporate earnings go to the capital provided by investors). On the other hand, since the household sector owns all primary factors (labour and capital), all primary factor income goes to households. Government income comes from indirect taxes and direct taxes (mainly income tax).

5.8.1 Household Income, Consumption, and Budget Constraint

Household income is made up of returns from capital and labour. Household consumption is determined by household disposable income (household income less income tax and plus social benefit transfer) and its propensity to consume. The social benefit transfer is relatively small, so we omit it from our model. But the contribution to the Central Provident Fund (CPF) is compulsory for Singapore households according to the CPF rules, so it must be excluded from the gross household income when we calculate disposable household income. Since the CPF contribution is only taxed when it is withdrawn on retirement, we will deduct it from the gross household income before applying income tax. Mathematically, the household income and consumption can be expressed as:

$$Y^H = \sum_{j=1}^{h} P_{(pf,L)j} X_{(pf,L)j} + \sum_{j=1}^{h} P_{(pf,K)j} X_{(pf,K)j} \tag{5.101}$$

$$C = F^H \left(Y^H - \mathrm{CPF}\right)\left(1 - T_Y^H\right) \tag{5.102}$$

where F^H is the ratio of household consumption to household disposable income. T_Y^H is the income tax rate.

C is total household consumption.

In percentage-change form, they are:

$$y^H = \sum_{j=1}^{h} \left(p_{(pf,L)j} + x_{(g+1,L)j}\right) S_{(pf,L)j}^{Y} + \sum_{j=1}^{h} \left(p_{(pf,K)j} + x_{(pf,K)j}\right) S_{(pf,K)j}^{Y} \tag{5.103}$$

$$c = f^H + \left(Y^H / \left(Y^H - \mathrm{CPF}\right)\right) y^H - \left(\mathrm{CPF} / \left(Y^H - \mathrm{CPF}\right)\right) cpf - \left(T_Y^H / \left(1 - T_Y^H\right)\right) t_Y^H \tag{5.104}$$

Given this household income and consumption function, we have the following household budget constraint (savings in the household account):

$$\Delta B^H = \left(Y^H - \text{CPF}\right)\left(1 - T_Y^H\right) - C^H \tag{5.105}$$

5.8.2 Government Income

Government income is made up of various taxes. The direct tax is mainly the income tax on households while indirect tax includes taxes on production and commodity taxes on intermediate inputs, investment demand, household and tourists' consumption, government spending, and imports and exports. So the government income can be expressed as follows:

$$\begin{aligned} Y^G = & \sum_{i=1}^{g} P_{(im)}^{M} \Phi X_{(im)}^{M}\left(T_{(im)}^{M} - 1\right) + \sum_{i=1}^{g} P_{(id)}^{(0)} X_{(id)}^{E}\left(T_{(id)}^{E} - 1\right) \\ & + \sum_{i=1}^{g}\sum_{s=1}^{2} P_{(is)}^{(0)} X_{(is)}^{H}\left(T_{(is)}^{H} - 1\right) + \sum_{k=1}^{q}\sum_{i=1}^{g}\sum_{s=1}^{2} P_{(is)}^{(0)} X_{(is)k}^{T}\left(T_{(is)k}^{T} - 1\right) \\ & + \sum_{i=1}^{g}\sum_{s=1}^{2} P_{(is)}^{(0)} X_{(is)}^{G}\left(T_{(is)}^{G} - 1\right) + \sum_{j=1}^{h}\sum_{i=1}^{g}\sum_{s=1}^{2} P_{(is)j}^{(0)} X_{(is)j}^{ID}\left(T_{(is)}^{ID} - 1\right) \\ & + \sum_{j=1}^{h}\sum_{i=1}^{g}\sum_{s=1}^{2} P_{(is)j}^{(0)} X_{(is)j}^{K}\left(T_{(is)}^{K} - 1\right) + T_Y^H\left(Y^H - CPF\right) + \sum_{j=1}^{h}(TP)_j \end{aligned} \tag{5.106}$$

or in percentage-change form:

$$
\begin{aligned}
y^G = {} & \sum_{i=1}^{g} t_{(im)}^{M} S_{(TM,i)}^{G} + \sum_{i=1}^{g} \left(p_{(im)}^{M} + \phi + x_{(im)}^{M} \right) S_{(tM,i)}^{G} \\
& + \sum_{i=1}^{g} t_{(im)}^{E} S_{(TE,i)}^{G} + \sum_{i=1}^{g} \left(p_{(id)}^{(0)} + x_{(im)}^{E} \right) S_{(tE,i)}^{G} \\
& + \sum_{j=1}^{h} \sum_{i=1}^{g} \sum_{s=1}^{2} t_{(is)j}^{\mathrm{ID}} S_{T(\mathrm{ID}),(is)j}^{G} + \sum_{j=1}^{h} \sum_{i=1}^{g} \sum_{s=1}^{2} (p_{(is)}^{(0)} + x_{(is)j}^{\mathrm{ID}}) S_{t(\mathrm{ID}),(is)j}^{G} \\
& + \sum_{j=1}^{h} \sum_{i=1}^{g} \sum_{s=1}^{2} t_{(is)j}^{K} S_{TK,(is)j}^{G} \\
& + \sum_{j=1}^{h} \sum_{i=1}^{g} \sum_{s=1}^{2} (p_{(is)}^{(0)} + x_{(is)j}^{K}) S_{tK,(is)j}^{G} \\
& + \sum_{i=1}^{g} \sum_{s=1}^{2} t_{(is)}^{G} S_{(TG,is)}^{G} + \sum_{i=1}^{g} \sum_{s=1}^{2} \left(p_{(is)}^{(0)} + x_{(is)}^{G} \right) S_{(tG,is)}^{G} \\
& + \sum_{k=1}^{q} \sum_{i=1}^{g} \sum_{s=1}^{2} t_{(is)k}^{T} S_{(TT,is)k}^{G} + \sum_{k=1}^{q} \sum_{i=1}^{g} \sum_{s=1}^{2} \left(p_{(is)k}^{(0)} + x_{(is)k}^{T} \right) S_{(tT,is)k}^{G} \\
& + \sum_{i=1}^{g} \sum_{s=1}^{2} t_{(is)}^{H} S_{(TH,is)}^{G} + \sum_{j=1}^{h} (tp)_j S_{(tp)j}^{G} \\
& + \sum_{i=1}^{g} \sum_{s=1}^{2} \left(p_{(is)}^{(0)} + x_{(is)}^{H} \right) S_{(tH,is)}^{G} + t_Y^H S_{(tH,Ycpf)}^{G} \\
& + y^H S_{(tH,Y)}^{G} - cpf^H S_{(tH,\mathrm{CPF})}^{G}
\end{aligned} \tag{5.107}
$$

where $S_{(TM,i)}^{G}$ means the share of tax-included importation of good i in the total government income; $S_{(tM,i)}^{G}$ stands for the share of imports tax revenue on good i in the total government income; $S_{(tH,Ycpf)}^{G}$ stands for the share of tax revenue on CPF-excluded household income in the total government income; $S_{(tH,Y)}^{G}$ stands for the share of tax revenue on

CPF-included household income in the total government income; $S^{G}_{(tH,CPF)}$ stands for the share of tax revenue on CPF in the total government income; and other shares have a similar meaning.

Considering the government income together with government consumption, we can obtain the internal balance:

$$\Delta B^{G} = Y^{G} - \sum P_i^{G} X_i^{G} \tag{5.108}$$

5.8.3 Investment and Capital Accumulation

Investment comprises investment in both private and public industries. The rate of return theory is used to explain the allocation of investment among private industries while the investment in the public sector is assumed to be determined by the total real investment level.

Equations (5.109)–(5.114) show the investment in private industry. Specifically, equation (5.109) defines that the current net rate of return on fixed capital is the gross rate of return (the rental value divided by cost of capital) minus the rate of capital depreciation (assumed fixed). Equation (5.110) demonstrates that investors are cautious about investment, so the expected rate of return ($R_j(1)$) is positively linked with the current rate of return ($R_j(0)$) but negatively related to the ratio of future capital stock to current capital stock (more investment will drive down the rate of return). Equation (5.111) simply assumes that there is an expected economy-wide rate of return ($R(1)$) and the investment in each industry is to reach this expected rate of return. Equation (5.112) is to define the future capital stock as the current investment plus the current capital stock after depreciation. It is assumed that capital in industry j takes one period to install, but the period can be a number of years. Since the model is static, determining the exact calendar time is not necessary. Equation (5.113) and equation (5.114) are to define the investment expenditure for each private industry and the total investment level for all private industries in the economy.

Equation (5.115) and equation (5.116) depict the investment in the public sector. V_{R} is the real investment level of the economy (including both public and private sectors), which is the total investment (V) divided by the investment goods (or capital goods) price index (KPI). F_j^V is a shift variable.

$$R_j(0) = \frac{P_{(pf,K)j}}{P^P_{(pf,K)j}} - D_j \tag{5.109}$$

$$R_j(1) = R_j(0)\left(\frac{X^{(1)}_{(pf,K)j}}{X_{(pf,K)j}}\right)^{-\delta_j} \tag{5.110}$$

$$R_j(1) = R(1) \tag{5.111}$$

$$X^{(1)}_{(pf,K)j} = X_{(pf,K)j}(1 - D_j) + X^N_{(pf,K)j} \tag{5.112}$$

$$V_j = P^N_{(pf,K)j} X^N_{(pf,K)j} \tag{5.113}$$

$$V = \sum_{j \in J} V_j \tag{5.114}$$

$$V_j = (V_R)^{S_j^V} F_j^V \tag{5.115}$$

where

$$V_{\mathrm{R}} = V/\mathrm{KPI} \tag{5.116}$$

or in percentage-change form:

$$r_j(0) = \left(p_{(pf,K)j} - p^N_{(pf,K)j}\right) \tag{5.117}$$

$$-\delta_j\left(x^{(1)}_{(pf,K)j} - x_{(pf,K)j}\right) + r_j(0) = r_j(1) = r(1) \tag{5.118}$$

$$x^{(1)}_{(pf,K)j} = x_{(pf,K)j}\left(1 - S^{(1)j}_{(N)j}\right) + x^{\mathrm{N}}_{(pf,K)j} S^{(1)j}_{(N)j} \tag{5.119}$$

$$v = \sum_{j \in J} \left(p^N_{(pf,K)j} + x^N_{(pf,K)j}\right) S_j^V \tag{5.120}$$

$$v_j = i_R S_j^V + f_j^V \tag{5.121}$$

$$v_R = v - \text{kpi} \tag{5.122}$$

where $S_{(N)j}^{(1)j}$ is the gross investment (new capital) in industry j as the percentage of future capital stock in industry j, and S_j^V is the investment in industry j as the percentage of total investment in the economy.

The total investment level V is subject to the availability of finance, so it must be met by household savings, government savings, and external balance. Since we do not take into account investment across the nation, the external balance is the same as the trade balance:

$$V = \Delta B^H + \Delta B^G + \Delta B^T \tag{5.123}$$

5.9 Imports, Exports, and Balance of Trade

The aggregate demand for imports is the sum of imports demanded by industries, households, tourists, and government. Total exports are the sum of all exported commodities. The balance of trade equals total exports minus total imports. To avoid using actual units in the balance of trade, we express it as the proportion of GDP. Mathematically, we have:

$$X_{(rm)}^{(M)} = \sum_{j=1}^{h} X_{(rm)}^{(\mathrm{ID})} + \sum_{j=1}^{h} X_{(rm)}^{(K)} + X_{(rm)}^{(H)} + \sum_{k=1}^{q} X_{(rm)k}^{(T)} + X_{(rm)}^{(G)}, \quad r = 1, \cdots, g \tag{5.124}$$

$$M = \sum_{r=1}^{g} P_{(rm)}^{(M)} X_{(rm)}^{(M)} \tag{5.125}$$

$$E = \sum_{r=1}^{g} P_{(rd)}^{(E)} X_{(rd)}^{(E)} \tag{5.126}$$

$$B = (E - M)/\text{GDP} \tag{5.127}$$

or in percentage-change form:

$$\begin{aligned} x_{(rm)}^{(M)} &= \sum_{j=1}^{h} x_{(rm)}^{(\text{ID})} S_{(\text{ID})j}^{M(rm)} + \sum_{j=1}^{h} x_{(rm)}^{(K)} S_{(K)j}^{M(rm)} + x_{(rm)}^{(H)} S_{(H)}^{M(rm)} \\ &+ \sum_{k=1}^{q} x_{(rm)k}^{(T)} S_{(T)k}^{M(rm)} + x_{(rm)}^{(G)} S_{(G)}^{M(rm)} \end{aligned} \tag{5.128}$$

$$m = \sum_{r=1}^{g} (p_{(rm)}^{(M)} + x_{(rm)}^{(M)}) S_{(rm)}^{M} \tag{5.129}$$

$$e = \sum_{r=1}^{g} (p_{(rd)}^{(E)} + x_{(rd)}^{(E)}) S_{(rd)}^{E} \tag{5.130}$$

$$100\Delta B^{T}/\text{GDP} = Ee - Mm - (E - M)\text{gdp} \tag{5.131}$$

We did not use the percentage-change form for the balance of trade because it can be positive or negative.

5.10 Price Indices, Wage Indexation, and GDP Price Deflator

Since we are concerned with the real value in the model, indexation is indispensable. To facilitate simulations in percentage-change form, ORANI uses production indexation for consumer price index, capital price index, and wage indexation. They are shown as follows:

$$\text{CPI} = \prod_{s=1}^{2} \prod_{i=1}^{g} \left(P_{(is)}^{H}\right)^{S_{(is)}^{H}} \tag{5.132}$$

$$\mathrm{KPI} = \prod_{j \in J} \left(P^{N}_{(pf,K)j} \right)^{S^{K}_{j}} \tag{5.133}$$

$$\mathrm{WI} = \prod_{j \in J} \left(P_{(pf,L)j} \right)^{S^{L}_{j}} \tag{5.134}$$

or in the percentage-change form:

$$\mathrm{cpi} = \sum_{i=1}^{g} \sum_{s=1}^{2} S^{(H)}_{(is)} p^{(H)}_{(is)} \tag{5.135}$$

$$\mathrm{kpi} = \sum_{j \in J} S^{(K)}_{j} p^{N}_{(pf,K)j} \tag{5.136}$$

$$\mathrm{wi} = \sum_{j \in J} S^{L}_{j} p_{(pf,L)j} \tag{5.137}$$

The wages can also be indexed to the consumer price index:

$$P_{(pf,L,o)j} = (\mathrm{CPI})^{\varpi} F_{(pf,L,)} F_{(pf,L)j} F_{(pf,L,o)j}, \quad i = 1, \cdots, g \tag{5.138}$$

where ϖ – wage-CPI indexation parameter
$F_{(pf,L)}$ – overall wage shift variable
$F_{(pf,L)j}$ – industry wage shift variables
$F_{(pf,L,o)j}$ – industry and occupation wage shift variables

or in percentage-change form:

$$p_{(pf,L,o)j} = \varpi \times \mathrm{cpi} + f_{(pf,L)} + f_{(pf,L)j} + f_{(pf,L,o)j}, \quad i = 1, \cdots, g \tag{5.139}$$

GDP can be defined from the income side or the expenditure side. From the income side, nominal GDP equals the total payment to labour and capital and aggregate value of indirect taxes, namely:

$$\begin{aligned}
\mathrm{GDPI} = & \sum_{j=1}^{h}\sum_{o=1}^{N} P_{(pf,L,o)} X_{(pf,L,o)} + \sum_{j=1}^{h} P_{(pf,K)} X_{(pf,K)} \\
& + \sum_{i=1}^{g} P^{M}_{(im)} \Phi X^{M}_{(im)} \left(T^{M}_{(im)} - 1\right) + \sum_{i=1}^{g} P^{(0)}_{(id)} X^{E}_{(id)} \left(T^{E}_{(id)} - 1\right) \\
& + \sum_{i=1}^{g}\sum_{s=1}^{2} P^{(0)}_{(is)} X^{H}_{(is)} \left(T^{H}_{(is)} - 1\right) + \sum_{i=1}^{g}\sum_{s=1}^{2} P^{(0)}_{(is)} X^{G}_{(is)} \left(T^{G}_{(is)} - 1\right) \\
& + \sum_{k=1}^{q}\sum_{i=1}^{g}\sum_{s=1}^{2} P^{(0)}_{(is)} X^{T}_{(is)k} \left(T^{T}_{(is)k} - 1\right) + \sum_{j=1}^{h}\sum_{i=1}^{g}\sum_{s=1}^{2} P^{(0)}_{(is)j} X^{ID}_{(is)j} \left(T^{ID}_{(is)} - 1\right) \\
& + \sum_{j=1}^{h}\sum_{i=1}^{g}\sum_{s=1}^{2} P^{(0)}_{(is)j} X^{K}_{(is)j} \left(T^{K}_{(is)} - 1\right) + \sum_{j=1}^{h} (\mathrm{TP})_{j}
\end{aligned} \tag{5.140}$$

or in the percentage-change form:

$$
\begin{aligned}
\text{gdpi} = &\sum_{j=1}^{g}\sum_{o=1}^{N}\left(p_{(pf,L,o)j} + x_{(pf,L,o)j}\right)S^{\text{GDPI}}_{(pf,L,o)j} \\
&+\sum_{j=1}^{g}\left(p_{(pf,K)j} + x_{(pf,K)j}\right)S^{\text{GDPI}}_{(pf,K)j} + \sum_{i=1}^{g} t^{M}_{(im)}S^{\text{GDPI}}_{(TM,i)} \\
&+\sum_{i=1}^{g}\left(p^{M}_{(im)} + \phi + x^{M}_{(im)}\right)S^{\text{GDPI}}_{(tM,i)} + \sum_{i=1}^{g} t^{E}_{(id)}S^{\text{GDPI}}_{(TE,i)} \\
&+\sum_{i=1}^{g}\left(p^{(0)}_{(id)} + x^{E}_{(id)}\right)S^{\text{GDPI}}_{(tE,i)} + \sum_{i=1}^{g}\sum_{s=1}^{2} t^{H}_{(is)}S^{\text{GDPI}}_{(TH,is)} \\
&+\sum_{i=1}^{g}\sum_{s=1}^{2}\left(p^{(0)}_{(is)} + x^{H}_{(is)}\right)S^{\text{GDPI}}_{(tH,is)} + \sum_{k=1}^{q}\sum_{i=1}^{g}\sum_{s=1}^{2} t^{T}_{(is)k}S^{\text{GDPI}}_{(TT,is)k} \\
&+\sum_{k=1}^{q}\sum_{i=1}^{g}\sum_{s=1}^{2}\left(p^{(0)}_{(is)} + x^{T}_{(is)k}\right)S^{\text{GDPI}}_{(tT,is)k} + \sum_{i=1}^{g}\sum_{s=1}^{2} t^{G}_{(is)}S^{\text{GDPI}}_{(TG,is)} \\
&+\sum_{i=1}^{g}\sum_{s=1}^{2}\left(p^{(0)}_{(is)} + x^{G}_{(is)}\right)S^{\text{GDPI}}_{(tG,is)} + \sum_{j=1}^{h}\sum_{i=1}^{g}\sum_{s=1}^{2} t^{\text{ID}}_{(is)j}S^{\text{GDPI}}_{T(\text{ID}),(is)j} \\
&+\sum_{j=1}^{h}\sum_{i=1}^{g}\sum_{s=1}^{2}(p^{(0)}_{(is)} + x^{\text{ID}}_{(is)j})S^{\text{GDPI}}_{T(\text{ID}),(is)j} + \sum_{j=1}^{h}\sum_{i=1}^{g}\sum_{s=1}^{2} t^{K}_{(is)j}S^{\text{GDPI}}_{TK,(is)j} \\
&+\sum_{j=1}^{h}\sum_{i=1}^{g}\sum_{s=1}^{2}(p^{(0)}_{(is)} + x^{K}_{(is)j})S^{\text{GDPI}}_{tK,(is)j} + \sum_{j=1}^{h}(tp)_{j}S^{\text{GDPI}}_{(TP)j}
\end{aligned}
\tag{5.141}
$$

From the expenditure side, nominal GDP equals the total expenditure of final demands (households, tourists, investment, government, and export) minus total imports, shown as follows:

$$\begin{aligned}\mathrm{GDPE} = & \sum_{i=1}^{g}\sum_{s=1}^{2} P^{H}_{(is)} X^{H}_{(is)} + \sum_{k=1}^{q}\sum_{i=1}^{g}\sum_{s=1}^{2} P^{T}_{(is)k} X^{T}_{(is)k} \\ & + \sum_{i=1}^{g}\sum_{s=1}^{2}\sum_{j=1}^{h} P^{K}_{(is)j} X^{K}_{(is)j} + \sum_{i=1}^{g}\sum_{s=1}^{2} P^{G}_{(is)} X^{G}_{(is)} \\ & + \sum_{i=1}^{g} P^{E}_{(id)} X^{E}_{(id)} \Phi - \sum_{i=1}^{g} P^{M}_{(im)} X^{M}_{(im)} \Phi \end{aligned} \tag{5.142}$$

or in percentage-change form:

$$\begin{aligned}\mathrm{gdpe} = & \sum_{i=1}^{g}\sum_{s=1}^{2}\left(p^{H}_{(is)} + x^{H}_{(is)}\right) S^{\mathrm{GDPE}}_{H,is} + \sum_{k=1}^{q}\sum_{i=1}^{g}\sum_{s=1}^{2}\left(p^{T}_{(is)k} + x^{T}_{(is)k}\right) S^{\mathrm{GDPE}}_{Tk,is} \\ & + \sum_{i=1}^{g}\sum_{s=1}^{2}\sum_{j=1}^{h}\left(p^{K}_{(is)j} + x^{K}_{(is)j}\right) S^{\mathrm{GDPE}}_{K,(is)j} + \sum_{i=1}^{g}\sum_{s=1}^{2}\left(p^{G}_{(is)} + x^{G}_{(is)}\right) S^{\mathrm{GDPE}}_{G,is} \\ & + \sum_{i=1}^{g}\left(p^{E}_{(id)} + x^{E}_{(id)} + \phi\right) S^{\mathrm{GDPE}}_{E,id} - \sum_{i=1}^{g}\left(p^{M}_{(im)} + x^{M}_{(im)} + \phi\right) S^{\mathrm{GDPE}}_{M,im} \end{aligned} \tag{5.143}$$

From this expression, we can derive the real GDP (rgdpe) and GDP deflator (pgdpe):

$$\begin{aligned}\mathrm{rgdpe} = & \sum_{i=1}^{g}\sum_{s=1}^{2}\left(x^{H}_{(is)}\right) S^{\mathrm{GDPE}}_{H,is} + \sum_{k=1}^{q}\sum_{i=1}^{g}\sum_{s=1}^{2}\left(x^{T}_{(is)k}\right) S^{\mathrm{GDPE}}_{Tk,is} \\ & + \sum_{i=1}^{g}\sum_{s=1}^{2}\sum_{j=1}^{h}\left(x^{K}_{(is)j}\right) S^{\mathrm{GDPE}}_{K,(is)j} + \sum_{i=1}^{g}\sum_{s=1}^{2}\left(x^{G}_{(is)}\right) S^{\mathrm{GDPE}}_{G,is} \\ & + \sum_{i=1}^{g}(x^{E}_{(id)} S^{\mathrm{GDPE}}_{E,id} - \sum_{i=1}^{g}(x^{M}_{(im)}) S^{\mathrm{GDPE}}_{M,im} \end{aligned} \tag{5.144}$$

$$\text{pgdpe} = \sum_{i=1}^{g}\sum_{s=1}^{2} p_{(is)}^{H} S_{H,is}^{\text{GDPE}} + \sum_{k=1}^{q}\sum_{i=1}^{g}\sum_{s=1}^{2} p_{(is)k}^{T} S_{Tk,is}^{\text{GDPE}} + \sum_{i=1}^{g}\sum_{s=1}^{2}\sum_{j=1}^{h} p_{(is)j}^{K} S_{K,(is)j}^{\text{GDPE}}$$
$$+\sum_{i=1}^{g}\sum_{s=1}^{2} p_{(is)}^{G} S_{G,is}^{\text{GDPE}} + \sum_{i=1}^{g}\left(p_{(id)}^{E} + \phi\right) S_{E,id}^{\text{GDPE}} - \sum_{i=1}^{g}\left(p_{(im)}^{M} + \phi\right) S_{M,im}^{\text{GDPE}} \tag{5.145}$$

5.11 Market Clearing Equations

Market clearing equations ensure demand equals supply for all domestically produced commodities and for all primary factors.

For domestic commodities, the equations are:

$$X_{(rd)}^{(0)} = \sum_{j=1}^{h} X_{(rd)j}^{(\text{ID})} + \sum_{j=1}^{h} X_{(rd)j}^{(K)} + X_{(rd)}^{(H)} + \sum_{k=1}^{q} X_{(rd)k}^{(T)} + X_{(rd)}^{(G)} + X_{(rd)}^{(E)}, \quad r = 1, \cdots, g \tag{5.146}$$

$$X_{(rd)}^{(0)} = \sum_{j=1}^{h} X_{(rd)j}^{(0)} \quad r = 1, \cdots, g \tag{5.147}$$

or in percentage-change form:

$$x_{(rd)}^{(0)} = \sum_{j=1}^{h} x_{(rd)j}^{(\text{ID})} S_{(\text{ID})(rd)j}^{(0)rd} + \sum_{j=1}^{h} x_{(rd)j}^{(K)} S_{(K)(rd)j}^{(0)rd} + x_{(rd)}^{(H)} S_{(H)(rd)}^{(0)rd} + \sum_{k=1}^{q} x_{(rd)k}^{(T)} S_{(T)(rd)k}^{(0)rd}$$
$$+ x_{(rd)}^{(G)} S_{(G)(rd)}^{(0)rd} + x_{(rd)}^{(E)} S_{(E)(rd)}^{(0)rd} \tag{5.148}$$

$$x_{(rd)}^{(0)} = \sum_{j=1}^{h} x_{(rd)j}^{(0)} S_{(0)(rd)j}^{(0)rd} \quad j = 1, \cdots, h \tag{5.149}$$

For primary factors, the equations are:

$$L = \sum_{j=1}^{h} X_{(pf,L)j} \quad j = 1, \cdots, h \tag{5.150}$$

$$K = \sum_{j=1}^{h} X_{(pf,K)j} \quad j = 1, \cdots, h \tag{5.151}$$

or in percentage-change form:

$$l = \sum_{j=1}^{h} x_{(pf,L)j} S^{L}_{(pf,L)j} \quad j = 1, \cdots, h \tag{5.152}$$

$$k = \sum_{j=1}^{h} k_j S^{K}_{(pf,K)j} \quad j = 1, \cdots, h \tag{5.153}$$

5.12 The Complete Model

To conclude this chapter, we list the classified equations in Table 5.1. All the equations are in percentage-change forms. Table 5.2 lists all the variables in the model. Table 5.3 lists all the parameters and shares.

Table 5.1 Equations in the model

Identifier Equation	No. of equations	Subscript range
Input demand	(4g+1)h	j=1,. . .,h i=1,. . .,g s=1,2
(5.1) $x_{ij}^{\mathrm{ID}} = z_j + a_{ij}^{\mathrm{ID}}$		
(5.2) $x_{(pf)j}^{\mathrm{ID}} = z_j + a_{(pf)j}^{\mathrm{ID}}$		
(5.12) $x_{(is)j}^{(\mathrm{ID})} = z_j + a_{ij}^{(\mathrm{ID})} - \sigma_{ij}^{(\mathrm{ID})}\left(p_{(is)j}^{(\mathrm{ID})} - \sum_{s=1}^{2} S_{(is)j}^{(\mathrm{ID})ij} p_{(is)j}^{(\mathrm{ID})}\right)$		
(5.13) $p_{ij}^{(\mathrm{ID})} = \sum_{s=1}^{2} S_{(is)j}^{(\mathrm{ID})ij} p_{(is)j}^{(\mathrm{ID})}$		
(5.15) $x_{(pf,L,o)j} = x_{(pf,L)j} - \sigma_{(pf,L)j}\left(p_{(pf,L,o)j} - \sum_{o=1}^{N} S_{(pf,L,o)j}^{(pf,L)j} p_{(pf,L,o)j}\right)$	(n+4)h	j=1,. . .,h v=1,2 o=1,. . .n
(5.16) $p_{(pf,L)j} = \sum_{o=1}^{N} S_{(pf,L,o)j}^{(pf,L)j} p_{(pf,L,o)j}$		
(5.18) $x_{(pf,v)j} = z_j + a_{(pf)j} - \sigma_{(pf)j}\left(p_{(pf,v)j} - \sum_{v=1}^{2} S_{(pf,v)j}^{(pf)j} p_{(pf,v)j}\right)$		
(5.19) $p_{(pf)j} = \sum_{v=1}^{2} S_{(pf,v)j}^{(pf)j} p_{(pf,v)j}$		
Output mix	(g+1)h	j=1,. . .,h i=1,. . .,g
(5.20) $x_{(id)j}^{(0)} = z_j + \sigma_j^{(0)}\left(p_{(id)j}^{(0)} - \sum_{i=1}^{g} S_{(id)j}^{(0)j} p_{(id)j}^{(0)}\right)$		
(5.21) $p_j^{(0)} = \sum_{i=1}^{g} S_{(id)j}^{(0)j} p_{(id)j}^{(0)}$		

Investors' demand	4gh	$j=1,\ldots,h$ $i=1,\ldots,g$ $s=1,2$
(5.22) $x_{ij}^{(K)} = k_j + a_{ij}^{(K)}$		
(5.23) $x_{(is)j}^{(K)} = k_j + a_{ij}^{(K)} - \sigma_{ij}^{(K)}\left(p_{(is)j}^{(K)} - \sum_{s=1}^{2} S_{(is)j}^{(K)ij} p_{(is)j}^{(K)}\right)$		
(5.24) $p_i^{(K)} = \sum_{s=1}^{2} S_{(is)j}^{(K)ij} p_{(is)}^{(K)}$		
Household utility	7g+1	$i=1,\ldots,g$ $s=1,2$
(5.30) $x_{(is)}^{(H)} = x_i^{(H)} - \sigma_i^{(H)}\left(p_{(is)}^{(H)} - \sum_{s=1}^{2} S_{(is)}^{(H)i} p_{(is)}^{(H)}\right)$:		
(5.31) $p_i^{(H)} = \sum_{s=1}^{2} S_{(is)}^{(H)i} p_{(is)}^{(H)}$		
(5.43) $\beta_i^{(H)} = \varepsilon_{i,e} \times S_i^{(H)}$		
(5.46) $\alpha_i = -\varepsilon_{i,e}$/Frisch		
(5.48) $x_i^{(H)} = (1-\alpha_i)\dot{\gamma}_i + \alpha_i \dot{\theta}_i$		
(5.49) $x_i^{(H)} + p_i^{(H)} = w$		
(5.50) $\overline{u} + q = \sum \beta_i \times \dot{\theta}_i$		
Tourism demand	(8g+5)q	$i=1,\ldots,g$ $s=1,2$ $k=1,\ldots,q$
(5.52) $q_k - f_{qk} = -\varepsilon_k\left(p_k^{(T)} - f_{pk}\right)$		
(5.54) $x_{v,k}^{(T)} = q_k - \sigma_k^{(T)}\left(p_{v,k}^{(T)} - \sum_{v=1}^{2} S_{v,k}^{(T)} p_{v,k}^{(T)}\right)$		
(5.55) $p_k^{(T)} = \sum_{v=1}^{2} S_{v,k}^{(T)} p_{v,k}^{(T)}$		

(continued)

Table 5.1 (continued)

Identifier Equation	No. of equations	Subscript range
(5.62) $x_{(is)(1k)}^{(T)} = x_{i(1k)} - \sigma_{i(1k)}^{(T)} \left(p_{(is)(1k)}^{(T)} - \sum_{s=1}^{2} S_{(is)(1k)}^{(T)(1k)} p_{(is)(1k)}^{(T)} \right)$		
(5.63) $p_{i(1k)}^{(T)} = \sum_{s=1}^{2} S_{(is)(1k)}^{(T)(1k)} p_{(is)(1k)}^{(T)}$		
(5.71) $x_{i(1k)}^{(T)} = x_{1k} - p_{i(1k)}^{(T)} + \sum_{r=1}^{g} S_{r(1k)}^{(T)1k} p_{r(1k)}^{(T)}$		
(5.72) $p_{1k}^{(T)} = \sum_{i=1}^{g} p_{i(1k)}^{(T)} S_{i(1k)}^{(T)1k}$		
(5.74) $x_{i(2k)}^{(T)} = x_{2k} + a_{i(2k)}^{(T)}$		
(5.76) $x_{(is)(2k)}^{(T)} = x_{i(2k)}^{(T)} - \sigma_{i(2k)}^{(T)} \left(p_{(is)(2k)}^{(T)} - \sum_{s=1}^{2} S_{(is)(2k)}^{(T)(2k)} p_{(is)(2k)}^{(T)} \right)$		
(5.77) $p_{i(2k)}^{(T)} = \sum_{s=1}^{2} S_{(is)(2k)}^{(T)(2k)} p_{(is)k}^{(T)}$		
Foreign demand for exports	G	i=1,. . .,g
(5.79) $x_{(id)}^{(E)} - f_{(Qi)}^{(E)} = -\varepsilon_{iie} \left(p_{(id)}^{(E)} + \phi - f_{(Pi)}^{(E)} \right), \quad i = 1, \cdots, g$		
Government demand	2g+1	i=1,. . .,g s=1,2
(5.81) $x_{(is)}^{(G)} = c_R + h_{(is)}^{(G)} + f_{(is)}^{(G)}$		
(5.82) $c_R = c - \text{cpi}$		

The basic values	3g+h	$j=1,\ldots,h$ $i=1,\ldots,g$ $s=1,2$ $r=1,\ldots g$
(5.84) $\sum_{r=1}^{g}\left(p_{(rd)}^{(0)}+x_{(rd)j}^{(0)}\right)S_{(rd)j}^{(0)}=\sum_{i=1}^{g}\sum_{s=1}^{2}\left(p_{(is)j}^{(\mathrm{ID})}+x_{(is)j}^{(\mathrm{ID})}\right)S_{(is)j}^{(\mathrm{IC})j}+\left(p_{(pf,L)j}+x_{(pf,L)j}\right)S_{(pf,L)j}^{(\mathrm{IC})j}$ $+\left(p_{(pf,K)j}+x(pf,K)j\right)S_{(pf,K)j}^{(\mathrm{IC})j}+(tp)_{j}S_{(tp)j}^{(\mathrm{IC})j}$		
(5.86) $p_{(pf,K)j}^{N}+x_{(pf,K)j}^{N}=\sum_{i=1}^{g}\sum_{s=1}^{2}\left(p_{(is)j}^{K}+x_{(is)j}^{K}\right)S_{(is)j}^{(K)j}$		
(5.88) $p_{(im)}^{(0)}=p_{(im)}^{(M)}+\phi+t_{(im)}^{(M)}$		
(5.90) $p_{(id)}^{(E)}+\phi=p_{(id)}^{(0)}+t_{(id)}^{(E)}$		
The purchasers' prices	2g(2h+q+2)	$j=1,\ldots,h$ $i=1,\ldots,g$ $s=1,2$ $k=1,\ldots q$
(5.96) $p_{(is)j}^{(\mathrm{ID})}=p_{(is)}^{(0)}+t_{(is)j}^{(\mathrm{ID})},\quad i=1,\cdots,g;s=d,m,\quad j=1,\cdots,h$		
(5.97) $p_{(is)j}^{(\mathrm{K})}=p_{(is)}^{(0)}+t_{(is)j}^{(K)},\quad i=1,\cdots,g;s=d,m,\quad j=1,\cdots,h$		
(5.98) $p_{(is)}^{(H)}=p_{(is)}^{(0)}+t_{(is)}^{(H)},\quad i=1,\cdots,g;s=d,m$		
(5.99) $p_{(is)k}^{(T)}=p_{(is)}^{(0)}+t_{(is)k}^{(T)},\quad i=1,\cdots,g;s=d,m$		
(5.100) $p_{(is)}^{(\mathrm{G})}=p_{(is)}^{(0)}+t_{(is)}^{(\mathrm{G})},\quad i=1,\cdots,g;s=d,m$		
Household income and consumption	3	$j=1,\ldots,h$
(5.103) $y^{H}=\sum_{j=1}^{h}\left(p_{(pf,L)j}+x_{(g+1,L)j}\right)S_{(pf,L)j}^{Y}+\sum_{j=1}^{h}\left(p_{(pf,K)j}+x_{(pf,K)j}\right)S_{(pf,K)j}^{Y}$		
(5.104) $c=f^{H}+\left(Y^{H}/\left(Y^{H}-\mathrm{CPF}\right)\right)y^{H}-\left(\mathrm{CPF}/\left(Y^{H}-\mathrm{CPF}\right)\right)cpf-\left(T_{Y}^{H}/\left(1-T_{Y}^{H}\right)\right)t_{Y}^{H}$		
(5.105) $\varDelta B^{H}=Y^{H}-C^{H}$		

(continued)

Table 5.1 (continued)

Identifier Equation	No. of equations	Subscript range
Government income	2	$j=1,\ldots,h$ $i=1,\ldots,g$ $s=1,2$ $k=1,\ldots q$
(5.107) $y^G = \sum_{i=1}^{g} t_{(im)}^M S_{(TM,i)}^G + \sum_{i=1}^{g} \left(p_{(im)}^M + \phi + x_{(im)}^M\right) S_{(tM,i)}^G + \sum_{i=1}^{g} t_{(im)}^E S_{(TE,i)}^G + \sum_{i=1}^{g} \left(p_{(id)}^{(0)} + x_{(im)}^E\right) S_{(tE,i)}^G$ $+\sum_{j=1}^{h}\sum_{i=1}^{g}\sum_{s=1}^{2} t_{(is)j}^{ID} S_{T(ID),(is)j}^G + \sum_{j=1}^{h}\sum_{i=1}^{g}\sum_{s=1}^{2} (p_{(is)}^{(0)} + x_{(is)j}^{ID}) S_{t(ID),(is)j}^G + \sum_{j=1}^{h}\sum_{i=1}^{g}\sum_{s=1}^{2} t_{(is)j}^K S_{TK,(is)j}^G$ $+\sum_{j=1}^{h}\sum_{i=1}^{g}\sum_{s=1}^{2} (p_{(is)}^{(0)} + x_{(is)j}^K) S_{tK,(is)j}^G + \sum_{i=1}^{g}\sum_{s=1}^{2} t_{(is)}^G S_{(TG,is)}^G + \sum_{i=1}^{g}\sum_{s=1}^{2} \left(p_{(is)}^{(0)} + x_{(is)}^G\right) S_{(tG,is)}^G$ $+\sum_{k=1}^{q}\sum_{i=1}^{g}\sum_{s=1}^{2} t_{(is)k}^T S_{(TT,is)k}^G + \sum_{k=1}^{q}\sum_{i=1}^{g}\sum_{s=1}^{2} \left(p_{(is)k}^{(0)} + x_{(is)k}^T\right) S_{(tT,is)k}^G + \sum_{i=1}^{g}\sum_{s=1}^{2} t_{(is)}^H S_{(TH,is)}^G$ $+\sum_{i=1}^{g}\sum_{s=1}^{2} \left(p_{(is)}^{(0)} + x_{(is)}^H\right) S_{(tH,is)}^G + t_Y^H S_{(tH,Ycpf)}^G + y^H S_{(tH,Y)}^G - cpf^H S_{(tH,CPF)}^G + \sum_{j=1}^{h} (tp)_j S_{(tp)j}^G$		
(5.108) $\Delta B^G = Y^G - \sum P_i^G X_i^G$		
Investment	4h+3	$j=1,\ldots,h$
(5.117) $r_j(0) = \left(p_{(pf,K)j} - p_{(pf,K)j}^N\right)$		
(5.118) $-\delta_j\left(x_{(pf,K)j}^{(1)} - x_{(pf,K)j}\right) + r_j(0) = r_j(1) = r(1)$		
(5.119) $x_{(pf,K)j}^{(1)} = x_{(pf,K)j}\left(1 - S_{(N)j}^{(1)j}\right) + x_{(pf,K)j}^{N} S_{(N)j}^{(1)j}$		
(5.120) $v = \sum_{j\in J} \left(p_{(pf,K)j}^N + x_{(pf,K)j}^N\right) S_j^V$		
(5.121) $v_j = i_R S_j^V + f_j^V$		

Equation	Number	Indices
(5.122) $v_R = v - \text{kpi}$		
(5.123) $V = \Delta B^H + \Delta B^G + \Delta B^T$		
Imports, exports, and balance of trade	g+3	$j=1,\ldots,h$
(5.128) $x^{(M)}_{(rm)} = \sum_{j=1}^{h} x^{(\text{ID})}_{(rm)} S^{M(rm)}_{(\text{ID})j} + \sum_{j=1}^{h} x^{(K)}_{(rm)} S^{M(rm)}_{(K)j} + x^{(H)}_{(rm)} S^{M(rm)}_{(H)} + \sum_{k=1}^{q} x^{(T)}_{(rm)k} S^{M(rm)}_{(T)k} + x^{(G)}_{(rm)} S^{M(rm)}_{(G)}$		$r=1,\ldots,g$ $k=1,\ldots q$
(5.129) $m = \sum_{r=1}^{g} (p^{(M)}_{(rm)} + x^{(M)}_{(rm)}) S^{M}_{(rm)}$		
(5.130) $e = \sum_{r=1}^{g} (p^{(E)}_{(rd)} + x^{(E)}_{(rd)}) S^{E}_{(rd)}$		
(5.131) $100\Delta B^T / GDP = Ee - Mm - (E - M)gdp$		
Price indices, wage indexation, and GDP price deflator	3	$J=1,\ldots h$
(5.135) $\text{cpi} = \sum_{i=1}^{g} \sum_{s=1}^{2} S^{(H)}_{(is)} p^{(H)}_{(is)}$		$i=1,\ldots,g$ $s=1,2$
(5.136) $\text{kpi} = \sum_{j \in J} S^{(K)}_{j} p^{N}_{(pf,K)j}$		
(5.137) $\text{wi} = \sum_{j \in J} S^{L}_{j} p_{(pf,L)j}$		
(5.139) $p_{(pf,L,o)j} = \overline{\varpi} \times cpi + f_{(pf,L)} + f_{(pf,L)j} + f_{(pf,L,o)j}$	nh	$j=1,\ldots,h$ $o=1,\ldots n$

(continued)

Table 5.1 (continued)

Identifier Equation	No. of equations	Subscript range
(5.141) $\mathrm{gdpi} = \sum_{j=1}^{g}\sum_{o=1}^{N}\left(p_{(pf,L,o)j} + x_{(pf,L,o)j}\right)S^{\mathrm{GDPI}}_{(pf,L,o)j} + \sum_{j=1}^{g}\left(p_{(pf,K)j} + x_{(pf,K)j}\right)S^{\mathrm{GDPI}}_{(pf,K)j} + \sum_{i=1}^{g} t^{M}_{(im)}S^{\mathrm{GDPI}}_{(TM,i)} + \sum_{i=1}^{g}\left(p^{M}_{(im)} + \phi + x^{M}_{(im)}\right)S^{\mathrm{GDPI}}_{(tM,i)} + \sum_{i=1}^{g} t^{E}_{(id)}S^{\mathrm{GDPI}}_{(TE,i)} + \sum_{i=1}^{g}\left(p^{(0)}_{(id)} + x^{E}_{(id)}\right)S^{\mathrm{GDPI}}_{(tE,i)} + \sum_{i=1}^{g}\sum_{s=1}^{2} t^{H}_{(is)}S^{\mathrm{GDPI}}_{(TH,is)} + \sum_{i=1}^{g}\sum_{s=1}^{2}\left(p^{(0)}_{(is)} + x^{H}_{(is)}\right)S^{\mathrm{GDPI}}_{(tH,is)} + \sum_{k=1}^{q}\sum_{i=1}^{g}\sum_{s=1}^{2} t^{T}_{(is)k}S^{\mathrm{GDPI}}_{(TT,is)k} + \sum_{k=1}^{q}\sum_{i=1}^{g}\sum_{s=1}^{2}\left(p^{(0)}_{(is)} + x^{T}_{(is)k}\right)S^{\mathrm{GDPI}}_{(tT,is)k} + \sum_{i=1}^{g}\sum_{s=1}^{2} t^{G}_{(is)}S^{\mathrm{GDPI}}_{(TG,is)} + \sum_{i=1}^{g}\sum_{s=1}^{2}\left(p^{(0)}_{(is)} + x^{G}_{(is)}\right)S^{\mathrm{GDPI}}_{(tG,is)} + \sum_{j=1}^{h}\sum_{i=1}^{g}\sum_{s=1}^{2} t^{\mathrm{ID}}_{(is)j}S^{\mathrm{GDPI}}_{T(\mathrm{ID}),(is)j} + \sum_{j=1}^{h}\sum_{i=1}^{g}\sum_{s=1}^{2}(p^{(0)}_{(is)} + x^{\mathrm{ID}}_{(is)j})S^{\mathrm{GDPI}}_{T(\mathrm{ID}),(is)j} + \sum_{j=1}^{h}\sum_{i=1}^{g}\sum_{s=1}^{2} t^{K}_{(is)j}S^{\mathrm{GDPI}}_{TK,(is)j} + \sum_{j=1}^{h}\sum_{i=1}^{g}\sum_{s=1}^{2}(p^{(0)}_{(is)} + x^{K}_{(is)j})S^{\mathrm{GDPI}}_{tK,(is)j} + \sum_{j=1}^{h}(tp)_{j}S^{\mathrm{GDPI}}_{(TP)j}$	2	$j=1,\ldots,h$ $i=1,\ldots,g$ $s=1,2$ $o=1,\ldots n$ $k=1,\ldots q$
(5.143) $\mathrm{gdpe} = \sum_{i=1}^{g}\sum_{s=1}^{2}\left(p^{H}_{(is)} + x^{H}_{(is)}\right)S^{\mathrm{GDPE}}_{H,is} + \sum_{k=1}^{q}\sum_{i=1}^{g}\sum_{s=1}^{2}\left(p^{T}_{(is)k} + x^{T}_{(is)k}\right)S^{\mathrm{GDPE}}_{Tk,is} + \sum_{i=1}^{g}\sum_{s=1}^{2}\sum_{j=1}^{h}\left(p^{K}_{(is)j} + x^{K}_{(is)j}\right)S^{\mathrm{GDPE}}_{K,(is)j} + \sum_{i=1}^{g}\sum_{s=1}^{2}\left(p^{G}_{(is)} + x^{G}_{(is)}\right)S^{\mathrm{GDPE}}_{G,is} + \sum_{i=1}^{g}\left(p^{E}_{(id)} + x^{E}_{(id)} + \phi\right)S^{\mathrm{GDPE}}_{E,id} - \sum_{i=1}^{g}(p^{M}_{(im)} + x^{M}_{(im)} + \phi)S^{\mathrm{GDPE}}_{M,im}$		

(5.144) $\text{rgdpe} = \sum_{i=1}^{g}\sum_{s=1}^{2}\left(x_{(is)}^{H}\right)S_{H,is}^{\text{GDPE}} + \sum_{k=1}^{q}\sum_{i=1}^{g}\sum_{s=1}^{2}\left(x_{(is)k}^{T}\right)S_{Tk,is}^{\text{GDPE}} + \sum_{i=1}^{g}\sum_{s=1}^{2}\sum_{j=1}^{h}\left(x_{(is)j}^{K}\right)S_{K,(is)j}^{\text{GDPE}}$ $+\sum_{i=1}^{g}\sum_{s=1}^{2}\left(x_{(is)}^{G}\right)S_{G,is}^{\text{GDPE}} + \sum_{i=1}^{g}\left(x_{(id)}^{E}\right)S_{E,id}^{\text{GDPE}} - \sum_{i=1}^{g}\left(x_{(im)}^{M}\right)S_{M,im}^{\text{GDPE}}$	1	j=1,…,h i=1,…,g s=1,2 k=1,…q
(5.145) $\text{pgdpe} = \sum_{i=1}^{g}\sum_{s=1}^{2}p_{(is)}^{H}S_{H,is}^{\text{GDPE}} + \sum_{k=1}^{q}\sum_{i=1}^{g}\sum_{s=1}^{2}p_{(is)k}^{T}S_{Tk,is}^{\text{GDPE}} + \sum_{i=1}^{g}\sum_{s=1}^{2}\sum_{j=1}^{h}p_{(is)j}^{K}S_{K,(is)j}^{\text{GDPE}}$ $+\sum_{i=1}^{g}\sum_{s=1}^{2}p_{(is)}^{G}S_{G,is}^{\text{GDPE}} + \sum_{i=1}^{g}\left(p_{(id)}^{E}+\phi\right)S_{E,id}^{\text{GDPE}} - \sum_{i=1}^{g}\left(p_{(im)}^{M}+\phi\right)S_{M,im}^{\text{GDPE}}$	1	j=1,…,h i=1,…,g s=1,2 k=1,…q
Market clearing equations		
(5.148) $x_{(rd)}^{(0)} = \sum_{j=1}^{h}x_{(rd)j}^{(ID)}S_{(ID)(rd)j}^{(0)rd} + \sum_{j=1}^{h}x_{(rd)j}^{(K)}S_{(K)(rd)j}^{(0)rd} + x_{(rd)}^{(H)}S_{(H)(rd)}^{(0)rd} + \sum_{k=1}^{q}x_{(rd)k}^{(T)}S_{(T)(rd)k}^{(0)rd} + x_{(rd)}^{(G)}S_{(G)(rd)}^{(0)rd}$ $+x_{(rd)}^{(E)}S_{(E)(rd)}^{(0)rd}$	2g	j=1,…,h r=1,…,g k=1,…q
(5.149) $x_{(rd)}^{(0)} = \sum_{j=1}^{h}x_{(rd)j}^{(0)}S_{(0)(rd)j}^{(0)rd}$		
(5.152) $l = \sum_{j=1}^{h}x_{(pf,L)j}S_{(pf,L)j}^{L} \quad j = 1,\cdots,h$	2	j=1,…,h
(5.153) $k = \sum_{j=1}^{h}k_jS_{(pf,K)j}^{K} \quad j = 1,\cdots,h$		

Total number of equations: 13gh+10gq+2nh+25g+11h+22. Given g=35, h=35, q=21, n=8 in the model, the total number of equations is 25,117.

Source: Authors

Table 5.2 Variables in the model

Variable	Definition	No.
Commodity demand and supply (all, i, COM) (all, s, SRC) (all, j, IND)		
$x^{ID}_{(is)j}$	Intermediate basic demands of industry *j* for good (is)	2gh
$x^{K}_{(is)j}$	Investment basic demands of industry *j* for good (is)	2gh
$x^{H}_{(is)}$	Household basic demands for good (*is*)	2g
$x^{T}_{(is)}$	Tourists basic demands for good (*is*)	2g
$x^{G}_{(is)}$	Government basic demands for good (*is*)	2g
x^{ID}_{ij}	Intermediate basic demands of industry *j* for good (*is*)	gh
x^{K}_{ij}	Investment basic demands of industry *j* for good (*is*)	2g
x^{H}_{i}	Household basic demands for good (*is*)	g
x^{T}_{ik}	Tourists basic demands for good (*is*)	qg
x^{G}_{i}	Government basic demands for good (*is*)	g
$x^{E}_{(id)}$	Export basic demand for good (*id*)	g
$x^{M}_{(im)}$	Import of good (*im*)	g
$x^{(0)}_{(id)j}$	Output of good (*id*) in industry *j*	gh
Powers of commodity taxes (all, i, COM) (all, s, SRC) (all, j, IND)		
$t^{ID}_{(is)j}$	Power of tax on intermediate demand for (*is*) in industry *j*	2gh
$t^{K}_{(is)j}$	Power of tax on investment demand for (*is*) in industry *j*	2gh
$t^{H}_{(is)}$	Power of tax on household demand for (*is*)	2g
$t^{T}_{(is)k}$	Power of tax on tourists demand for (*is*)	2qg
$t^{G}_{(is)}$	Power of tax on government demand for (*is*)	2g
$t^{E}_{(id)}$	Power of tax on exports (*id*)	g
$t^{M}_{(im)}$	Power of import tariff on good (*im*)	g
Prices system (all, i, COM) (all, s, SRC) (all, j, IND)		
$p^{(0)}_{(is)}$	Basic price of good (*is*)	2g
$p^{M}_{(im)}$	c.i.f. import prices in foreign currency	g
$p^{E}_{(id)}$	f.o.b. export prices in foreign currency	2g
$p^{ID}_{(is)j}$	Purchasers' price regarding intermediate demand for good (*is*)	2gh
$p^{K}_{(is)j}$	Purchasers' price regarding investors' demand for good (*is*)	2gh
$p^{H}_{(is)}$	Purchasers' price regarding households demand for good (*is*)	2g
$p^{T}_{(is)k}$	Purchasers' price regarding tourists demand for good (*is*)	2qg
$p^{G}_{(is)}$	Purchasers' price regarding government demand for good (*is*)	2g

(*continued*)

Table 5.2 (continued)

Variable	Definition	No.
p_{ij}^{ID}	Purchasers' price regarding intermediate demand for good (*is*)	2gh
p_{ij}^{K}	Purchasers' price regarding investors' demand for good (*is*)	2gh
p_{i}^{H}	Purchasers' price regarding households demand for good (*is*)	g
p_{ik}^{T}	Purchasers' price regarding tourists demand for good (*is*)	qg
p_{i}^{G}	Purchasers' price regarding government demand for good (*is*)	g
Usage of labour and capital (all, i, COM) (all, s, SRC) (all, j, IND)		
$x_{(pf,L,o)j}$	Employment of occupation o in industry *j*	nh
$p_{(pf,L,o)j}$	Wage of occupation *o* in industry *j*	nh
$x_{(pf,L)j}$	Employment in industry *j*	h
$p_{(pf,L)j}$	Wage in industry *j*	h
$x_{(pf,K)j}$	Capital stock in industry *j*	h
$p_{(pf,K)j}$	Rental price in industry *j*	h
Investment variables		
$r_j(0)$	Current rate of return on capital in industry *j*	h
$r_j(1)$	Expected rate of return on capital in industry *j*	h
$r(1)$	Expected rate of return on capital in economy	1
$x_{(pf,K)j}^{(1)}$	Expected capital stocks in industry *j*	h
$x_{(pf,K)j}^{N}$	Physical capital investment (new capital) in industry *j*	h
$p_{(pf,K)j}^{N}$	Value of a unit physical capital in industry *j*	h
v_j	Value of private investment in industry *j*	h
v	Aggregate private investment in economy	1
v_R	Aggregate real private investment in economy	1
kpi	Aggregate investment price index	1
Scalar or macro variables and other		
c	Nominal total household consumption	1
c_R	Real household consumption	1
q	Number of households in economy	1
$\bar{u}$	Average utility per household	1
y^H	Total household income	1
t_y^H	The income tax rate on households	1
ΔB^T	Balance of trade/GDP	1
ΔB^H	Household account balance	1
ΔB^G	Internal balance	1
CPI	Consumer price index	1
l	Aggregate employment: wage bill weights	1
ϕ	Exchange rate (S$ per foreign currency)	1
m	Foreign currency value of imports	1
e	Foreign currency value of exports	1

(*continued*)

Table 5.2 (continued)

Variable	Definition	No.
gdpi	Nominal GDP from income side	1
gdpe	Nominal GDP from expenditure side	1
rgdpe	Real GDP	1
pgdpe	GDP price deflator	1
realwage	Real wage	1
$f^{E}_{(pi)}$	Price shift parameter in export demand	g
$f^{E}_{(Qi)}$	Quantity parameter shift in export demand	g
$f^{G}_{(is)}$	Government demand shift	2g
f^{K}_{j}	Investment shifter in industry *j*	1
$h^{G}_{(is)}$	Ratio of government demand to real household consumption	2g
$f^{G}_{(is)}$	Government demand shifter	2g
$f_{(pl,L,o)j}$	Wage shifter by occupation and by industry	nh
$f_{(pl,L)j}$	Wage shifter by industry	h
$f_{(pl,L)}$	Overall wage shifter	1
f^{H}	Ratio of household consumption to household disposable income	1
a^{ID}_{ij}	Augmenting technical change in industry *j* to produce good *i*	gh
a^{K}_{ij}	Augmenting technical change in industry j in capital formation	gh
$a^{T}_{i(2k)}$	Preferences of tourists from market *k* on tourism services	qgh
δ_j	Risk aversion (weight on two-period capital ratio in industry *j*)	h
	Wage-CPI indexation	1
v_j	Investment level in industry *j*	h
z_j	Activity level of industry *j*	h

Total number of variables: qgh+20gh+6qg+3nh+37g+14h+26, where g=35, h=35, q=21, n=8.

Or: 21*35*35+20*35*35+6*21*35+3*8*35+37*35+14*35+26=57,286

Source: Authors

Table 5.3 Parameters and shares in the model

Elasticities or Shares		
$\sigma_{ij}^{(\mathrm{ID})}$	Armington elasticity for production in industry *j*	gh
$\sigma_{ij}^{(K)}$	Armington elasticity for capital formation in industry *j*	gh
$\sigma_{i}^{(H)}$	Armington elasticity for household consumption	g
$\sigma_{i(1k)}^{(T)}$	Armington elasticity for tourism shopping demand from generating market *k*	qg
$\sigma_{i(2k)}^{(T)}$	Armington elasticity for tourism service demand from generating market *k*	qg
$\sigma_{k}^{(T)}$	Elasticity of substitution for tourism demand from generating market *k*	m
$\sigma_{(pf,L)j}$	Elasticity of substitution among labour groups in industry *j*	h
$\sigma_{(pf)j}$	Elasticity of substitution between primary factors in industry *j*	h
$\sigma_{j}^{(0)}$	CET elasticity in industry *j*	h
$\varepsilon_{i,e}$	Expenditure elasticity	g
ε_{iie}	Own-price elasticity of exports	g
Shares in demand functions		
$S_{(is)j}^{(ID)}$	Share of (*is*) in total cost of intermediate input in industry *j*	2gh
$S_{(is)j}^{(K)}$	Share of (*is*) in total investors' demand in industry *j*	2gh
$S_{(is)}^{(H)i}$	Share of (*is*) in household demand for *i*	2g
$S_{i}^{(H)}$	Share of (*i*) in total household demand	g
β_i	Marginal budget share for LES	g
$S_{(v,k)}^{(T)}$	Share of tourism shopping and tourism service in tourism demand from generating market *k*	2q
$S_{i(1k)}^{(T)(1k)}$	Share of good (*i*) in total tourism shopping demand from generating market *k*	qg
$S_{(is),(1k)}^{(T)i(1k)}$	Share of good (*is*) in tourism shopping demand for i from generating market *k*	2qg
$S_{(is),(2k)}^{(T)(2k)}$	Share of good (*is*) in tourism service demand for i from generating market *k*	2qg
$S_{(pf,v)j}^{(pf)j}$	Share of *v* (*L* or *K*) in total cost of primary factors	2h
$S_{(pf,L,o)j}^{(pf,L)j}$	Share of occupational labour in total labour in industry *j*	nh
Shares in basic value, output supply, household income, and government income		
$S_{(rd)j}^{(0)}$	Share of sales of good (*rd*) in the total output in industry *j*	gh
$S_{(is)j}^{IC}$	Share of cost of input (*is*) in total cost in industry *j*	2gh
$S_{(pf,v)j}^{IC}$	Share of cost of labour or capital in total cost in industry *j*	2h

(*continued*)

Table 5.3 (continued)

Elasticities or Shares		
$S^{IC}_{(TP)j}$	Share of tax on production in total cost in industry *j*	h
$S^{Y}_{(pf,L)j}$	Share of labour income in total household income	h
$S^{Y}_{(pf,K)j}$	Share of capital income in total household income	h
$S^{G}_{(tM,i)}$	Share of tariff on import (*i*) in government income	g
$S^{G}_{(TM,i)}$	Ratio of tariff included value of import (*i*) to government revenue	g
$S^{G}_{(tE,i)}$	Share of tariff on export (*i*) in government income	g
$S^{G}_{(TE,i)}$	Ratio of export tax included value of export (*i*) to government revenue	g
$S^{G}_{t(ID),is}$	Share of sales tax on intermediate good (*i*) in government income	2g
$S^{G}_{T(ID),is}$	Ratio of tax included value of intermediate good (*i*) to government revenue	2g
$S^{G}_{(tH,is)}$	Share of sales tax on household demand for good (*i*) in government income	2g
$S^{G}_{(TH,is)}$	Ratio of tax included value of good (*i*) purchased by household to government revenue	2g
$S^{G}_{(tTk,is)}$	Share of sales tax on tourists demand for good (*i*) in government income	2qg
$S^{G}_{(TTk,is)}$	Ratio of tax included value of good (*i*) purchased by tourists to government revenue	2qg
$S^{G}_{(tG,is)}$	Share of sales tax on government demand for good (*i*) in government income	2g
$S^{G}_{(TG,is)}$	Ratio of tax included value of good (*i*) purchased by government to government revenue	2g
$S^{G}_{(tK,is)}$	Share of sales tax on investor demand for good (*i*) in government income	2g
$S^{G}_{(TK,is)}$	Ratio of tax included value of good (*i*) purchased by investors to government revenue	2g
$S^{G}_{(TP,j)}$	Share of production tax on industry *j* in government income	h
$S^{G}_{(tY)}$	Share of household income tax in government income	1
S^{K}_{j}	Share of investment in industry *j* in total investment in economy	h
S^{L}_{j}	Share of employment in industry *j* in total labour supply	h
Shares in market clearing equations		
$S^{(0)rd}_{(ID)j}$	Share of intermediate demand for (*rd*) in industry *j* in total output of (*rd*)	gh
$S^{(0)rd}_{(K)j}$	Share of investors' demand for (*rd*) in industry *j* in total output of (*rd*)	gh

(continued)

Table 5.3 (continued)

Elasticities or Shares		
$S^{(0)rd}_{(H)}$	Share of household demand for (*rd*) in total output of (*rd*)	g
$S^{(0)rd}_{(Tk)}$	Share in total output of (*rd*) of tourism demand from generating market *k*	qg
$S^{(0)rd}_{(G)}$	Share of government demand for (*rd*) in total output of (*rd*)	g
$S^{(0)rd}_{E}$	Share of export demand for (*rd*) in total output of (*rd*)	g
$S^{(0)rd}_{(0)j}$	Share of output of (*rd*) in industry *j* in total output of (*rd*) in economy	gh
$S^{M(rm)}_{(ID)j}$	Share of intermediate demand for (*rm*) in industry *j* in total import of (*rm*)	gh
$S^{M(rm)}_{(K)j}$	Share of investment demand for (*rm*) in industry *j* in total import of (*rm*)	gh
$S^{M(rm)}_{(H)}$	Share of household demand for (*rm*) in industry *j* in total import of (*rm*)	g
$S^{M(rm)}_{(Tk)}$	Share of tourists demand from generating market for (*rm*) in industry *j* in total import of (*rm*)	qg
$S^{M(rm)}_{(G)}$	Share of government demand for (*rm*) in industry *j* in total import of (*rm*)	g
Shares in the export and import receipts, shares in GDP, and weights in GDP price deflator		
$S^{M}_{(rm)}$	Shares of imports (*rm*) in total import receipts	g
$S^{E}_{(rd)}$	Shares of export (*rd*) in total export receipts	g
$S^{GDPE}_{(is)H}$	Shares of household demand for (*is*) in GDP	2g
$S^{GDPE}_{(is)Tk}$	Shares of tourists demand from generating market k for (*is*) in GDP	qg
$S^{GDPE}_{(is)j,K}$	Shares of investors demand for (*is*) in GDP	2gh
$S^{GDPE}_{(is)G}$	Shares of government demand for (*is*) in GDP	2g
$S^{GDPE}_{(id)E}$	Shares of export demand for (*is*) in GDP	g
$S^{GDPE}_{(im)M}$	Shares of import (*im*) in GDP	g
$S^{GDPI}_{(tM,i)}$	Share of tariff on import (*i*) in nominal GDP	g
$S^{GDPI}_{(TM,i)}$	Ratio of tariff included value of import (*i*) to nominal GDP	g
$S^{GDPI}_{(tE,i)}$	Share of tariff on export (*i*) in nominal GDP	g
$S^{GDPI}_{(TE,i)}$	Ratio of export tax included value of export (*i*) to nominal GDP	g
$S^{GDPI}_{t(ID),(is)j}$	Share of sales tax on intermediate good (*i*) of industry *j* in nominal GDP	2gh
$S^{GDPI}_{t(ID),(is)j}$	Ratio of tax included value of intermediate good (*i*) of industry *j* to nominal GDP	2gh

(*continued*)

Table 5.3 (continued)

Elasticities or Shares		
$S^{GDPI}_{(tH,is)}$	Share of sales tax on household demand for good (*i*) in nominal GDP	2g
$S^{GDPI}_{(TH,is)}$	Ratio of tax included value of good (*i*) purchased by household to nominal GDP	2g
$S^{GDPI}_{(tTk,is)}$	Share of sales tax on tourists demand from generating market *k* for good (*i*) in nominal GDP	2qg
$S^{GDPI}_{(TTk,is)}$	Ratio of tax included value of good (*i*) purchased by tourists from generating market *k* to nominal GDP	2qg
$S^{GDPI}_{(tG,is)}$	Share of sales tax on government demand for good (*i*) in nominal GDP	2g
$S^{GDPI}_{(TG,is)}$	Ratio of tax included value of good (*i*) purchased by government to nominal GDP	2g
$S^{GDPI}_{tK,(is)j}$	Share of sales tax on investor demand of industry *j* for good (*i*) in nominal GDP	2gh
$S^{GDPI}_{TK,(is)j}$	Ratio of tax included value of good (*i*) purchased by investors of industry *j* to nominal GDP	2gh
$S^{GDPI}_{(TP,j)}$	Share of production tax on industry *j* in nominal GDP	h

Source: Authors

References

Armington, P. S. (1969). A Theory of Demand for Products Distinguished by Place of Production. *IMF Staff Papers, 16*, 159–178.

Horridge, M. (2000). *ORANI-G: A General Equilibrium Model of the Australian Economy*. Centre of Policy Studies/IMPACT Centre Working Papers op-93, Monash University.

STB (Singapore Tourism Board). (2005). *Singapore Sets Out to Triple Tourism Receipts To S$30 Billion by 2015*. https://app.stb.gov.sg/asp/new/new03a.asp?id=2483

6
Preparing Database for a Tourism CGE Model

The chapter is structured as follows: Section 6.1 generally describes the data requirement of the model while Sect. 6.2 addresses data availability and sources. In Sect. 6.3, we check the required data account by account so as to validate the feasibility of the model. In some model accounts, the treatment of the relevant data will be discussed in detail. Since the various behavioural parameters used throughout the model are vital to the functions and thus the simulation results, they are discussed specifically in Sect. 6.4.

6.1 Data Requirements

Based on the theoretical structure of the CGE model displayed in the previous chapter, the data required by the model are I–O data, coefficients, and parameters (such as various elasticities and shares). Among them, the I–O data is the major part of database.

S. Meng, M. Siriwardana, *Assessing the Economic Impact of Tourism*,
DOI 10.1007/978-3-319-40328-1_6

6.1.1 I–O Data

The I–O data needed in our model are displayed in an absorption matrix shown in Tables 6.1, 6.2, and 6.3.

Table 6.1 is a schematic representation of the absorption matrix for our model, which is a variation of the standard database structure used in the ORANI-type models. Each row heading indicates different inputs (or costs) for various industries. The column headings show different agents involved in the economy, which includes I producers, I investors, H household groups, T tourism demands, one aggregate foreign demand, one government demand, and the changes in inventory. According to the number of commodities, sources, occupation types, and capital type, the first two columns of the table show the cost of each industry result from buying C*S kinds of commodities, paying C*S taxes, and employing O types of labour and 1 type capital.

Table 6.1 requires considerable data. For example, the vector V1BAS, V2BAS, V1TAX, and V2TAX each consists C*S*I data. 2005 Singapore I–O tables have 136 kinds of commodities and industries. Considering that each commodity can be obtained locally or imported from overseas, each of the four vectors will contain 136*2*136 = 36,992 data entries. In order to reduce the model size and emphasize the purpose of this study, we will aggregate relevant commodities and industries according to the characteristics of Singaporean economy and tourism industry.

Since some industries produce more than one commodity (and one commodity may be produced by more than one industry), we need a Make matrix (see Table 6.2) to describe this information. Moreover, since import duties are assumed to be levied according to the commodity types instead of the categories of users, we need a tariff vector (shown in Table 6.3).

6.1.2 Other Data

Besides the I–O data displayed above, economic data from various sources are also necessary. These data can be put into two categories. One is the data affecting the balance in the household account, investment account,

Table 6.1 Absorption matrix

Sales by commodity	Purchases by Industry	Producers ←I→	Investors ←I→	Households ←H→	Government ←1→	Exports ←1→	Tourism ←T→	Change in Inventories ←1→
Basic Folws	↑ C*S ↓	V1BAS	V2BAS	V3BAS	V4BAS	V5BAS	V6BAS	V7BAS
Product taxes	↑ C*S ↓	V1TAX	V2TAX	V3TAX	V4TAX	V5TAX	V6TAX	V7TAX
Production taxes	↑ 1 ↓	V1PTX	S = Source of commodity (i.e. domestic or imported) C = Number of commodities I = Number of industries					
Labour	↑ O ↓	V1LAB	O = Number of occupation types H = Number of households T = Number of tourism-generating markets					
Capital	↑ 1 ↓	V1CAP						

Source: Authors

Table 6.2 Make matrix

		Commodities
Sales by industry	Sales by commodities	←C→
Industries	↑ I ↓	

Source: Authors

Table 6.3 Tariff vector

		Import duty
		←1→
Imported commodities	↑ C ↓	

Source: Authors

and government account. These include base year data on income tax revenue and income tax rate, central provident funds (CPF) contribution and the average CPF contribution rate, along with social benefit transfer. The other category is the parameter data for functions in the model. The major part of parameters are behavioural parameters, for example, substitution elasticities for CES functions, elasticities for tourism demand and exports demand, household expenditure elasticities, and the Frisch parameter (to determine household subsistence consumption).

6.2 Data Availability and Sources

To obtain the data needed for this study, the authors have searched relevant databases, literature, and websites, and visited relevant government organizations in Singapore. However, some parameter values could not be found, so they were assigned on the base of economic theory or on previous studies. Available data and sources are briefly displayed in this section. We start with the major source of data—the 2005 Singapore I–O tables published by Department of Statistics (DOS 2010).

6.2.1 Singaporean I–O Tables

The DOS in Singapore has published several sets of I–O tables and the recent one has a base year of 2005. There are 23 tables in this set of I–O tables, but the most important ones for our model are the basic tables, namely, the Absorption matrix, the Make matrix, and the Import matrix. The structures of these three matrices are shown in Tables 6.4, 6.5, and 6.6.

These three tables provide most of the information needed about commodity flows, private and government expenditure, investment, inventory, export, labour, and capital contributions, along with import duties and other taxes. Considering the framework of Table 6.1, however, we find the following information is either unsatisfactory or may even be missing.

First, there is no information on tourism expenditure, which is crucial to our study. We need to find the detailed data on tourism demand and tax paid by tourists to fill in two C*S*21 matrices, V6BAS, and V6TAX in Table 6.1.

Second, the information on investment is highly aggregated both in Tables 6.4 and 6.6. There is only one investor column in the Singapore I–O table, but we need a C*S*I investment matrix according to Table 6.1. Since the data on investment by industry can be found nowhere, we have to obtain capital stock by industry and distribute the investment accordingly.

Third, in Table 6.4 there are aggregate data on import duties for each sector, but we need import duty data by each good and service according to Table 6.3. To achieve this data requirement, we need to obtain the tariff rate on each commodity and thus build a C*I tariff matrix.

Fourth, the information on product taxes in Table 6.4 is registered by each economic agent. We need to disaggregate the product tax data to detailed commodity level, so that we can fill in six product tax matrices in Table 6.1: V1TAX through to V7TAX.

Fifth, there is only one labour group in Table 6.4. According to Table 6.1, the wage information on each occupation type is required.

Table 6.4 Commodity analyses of purchases from domestic production, 2005 (Absorption matrix)

	Purchases by Industry									
	Industry 1 to Industry 136	Total intermediate output	Purchases by final demand sector	Private consumption expenditure	Government consumption expenditure	Gross fixed capital formation	Change in stocks	Exports of goods and services	Total final output	Total output
Sales by commodity	1 136	137		138	139	140	141	142	143	144
Commodity 1 To Commodity 136										
sub-total (row 1–row 136)										
138 Imports of goods and services										
139 Import duties										
140 Other taxes on products										
141 Taxes on Production										
142 Compensation of employees										
143 Gross operating surplus										
value added at basic values										
Total input										

Source: DOS (2010)

Table 6.5 Commodity analysis of domestic output, 2005 (Make matrix)

Sales by industry	Sales by commodity	Industry 1 to Industry 136 1 136	Total domestic output 137
Commodity 1 To Commodity 136			
Total Commodity output			

Source: DOS (2010)

To expand the labour income to different occupation groups, an occupation by industry wage bill data is needed.

Finally, there is an extra commodity type in row 137 in Table 6.6—other goods and services, which is not consistent with other tables. This inconsistency may be eliminated during data aggregation.

6.2.2 Other Sources

To obtain other data, the following sources (and methods) have been used:

STB Tourism Surveys Vital information on tourism expenditure is provided by STB tourism surveys. The yearly STB tourism survey reveals information on tourism arrivals, disaggregated tourism expenditure, and the tourism shopping pattern.

Other Government Agents To obtain other economic, welfare and tourism data, we had to approach various government agents. For example, detailed government tax income and social transfer from government budget estimation by the Ministry of Finance of Singapore (2009), the tariff revenue and rates published by the Singapore Customs (2009), the employment and wage distribution information from the Ministry of Manpower, the effects of tourism policies from the STB, and the CPF data from Singapore CPF board.

GTAP Database Version 6.0 There are a considerable number of behavioural parameters in the model, such as household expenditure

Table 6.6 Commodity analysis of retained imports, 2005 (Import matrix)

Imports by commodity	Purchases by industry	Industry 1 to Industry 152	Total intermediate supply	Purchases by final demand sector	Private consumption expenditure	Government consumption expenditure	Gross fixed capital formation	Change in stocks	Total final demand	Total Supply
		1 136	137		138	139	140	141	142	143
Commodity 1 To Commodity 136										
137 Other goods and services										
Imports of goods and services										

Source: DOS (2010)

elasticities, export demand elasticities, transformation elasticities, and various substitution elasticities. The GTAP database version 6.0 contains most of these parameters for Singapore.

Other Literature Some other parameters had to be found in earlier empirical papers, such as the tourism demand elasticity, and the substitution elasticity for occupation groups.

Author's Calculation and Calibration There are a large number of shares required to be calculated based on the various sources noted, while a number of coefficients needs to be calibrated using baseline data.

6.3 Model Accounts

After the brief introduction of data requirements and sources, it is necessary to discuss the database in detail given that so many data are involved. Since the parameters will be discussed in the next section, this section mainly discusses the baseline data for various accounts in the model and the way to convert the I–O data and tourism expenditure data into the model database.

6.3.1 Production Account

The production account concerns the production side of the economy. To specify and calibrate the production functions, the I–O data in the base year are extremely important. The I–O data are readily available in the Singapore I–O tables 2005. However, these data must be retreated and adjusted before they are ready for use in our model. First, it is necessary to update to our base year 2006 because the most recent set of Singapore I–O tables is based on the year 2005. Second, 2005 Singapore I–O tables contain 136 industries and commodities, so aggregation procedures are needed in order to reduce the simulation cost and emphasize the purpose of this study.

Updating the I–O Tables The RAS method is utilized to update the 2005 Singapore I–O tables. The basic assumption of the RAS method is that the Leontief coefficients do not change during this period. However, to know the advantages and disadvantages of the RAS method and to make sure that it is suitable for this study, we need to explain briefly the procedure and reasoning of this method. For more details about the RAS method, see O'Connor and Henry (1975) and Parikh (1979).

The RAS method requires data on inter-industry sales by industry and by commodity. Assume a_{ij} is the Leontief coefficient for industry i to produce commodity j, $X_j(0)$ stands for the total output of commodity j in base year 0, U_i (0) stands for the total sales of industry i in year 0, and V_j (0) stands for the total inter-industry purchases of commodity j in year 0. The I–O data in base year 0 should satisfy the following equation systems:

$$\begin{array}{l} a_{11}X_1(0) + a_{12}X_2(0) + \cdots + a_{1j}X_j(0) + \cdots + a_{1n}X_n(0) = U_1(0) \\ a_{21}X_1(0) + a_{22}X_2(0) + \cdots + a_{2j}X_j(0) + \cdots + a_{2n}X_n(0) = U_2(0) \\ \vdots \\ a_{i1}X_1(0) + a_{i2}X_2(0) + \cdots + a_{ij}X_j(0) + \cdots + a_{in}X_n(0) = U_i(0) \\ \vdots \\ a_{n1}X_1(0) + a_{n2}X_2(0) + \cdots + a_{nj}X_j(0) + \cdots + a_{nn}X_n(0) = U_n(0) \end{array} \quad (6.1)$$

and

$$\begin{array}{l} a_{11}X_1(0) + a_{21}X_1(0) + \cdots + a_{i1}X_1(0) + \cdots + a_{n1}X_1(0) = V_1(0) \\ a_{12}X_2(0) + a_{22}X_2(0) + \cdots + a_{i2}X_2(0) + \cdots + a_{n2}X_2(0) = V_2(0) \\ \vdots \\ a_{1j}X_j(0) + a_{2j}X_j(0) + \cdots + a_{ij}X_j(0) + \cdots + a_{nj}X_j(0) = V_j(0) \\ \vdots \\ a_{1n}X_n(0) + a_{2n}X_n(0) + \cdots + a_{in}X_n(0) + \cdots + a_{nn}X_n(0) = V_n(0) \end{array} \quad (6.2)$$

In year 1, U_i (0) and V_j (0) become U_i (1) and V_j (1), respectively, so we need to find the $X_j(1)$ which satisfy $\sum_{j=1}^{n} a_{ij}X_j(1) = U_i(1)$ and $\sum_{i=1}^{n} a_{ij}X_j(1) = V_j(1)$.

Multiplying equation system (6.1) with $\frac{U_i(1)}{U_i(0)}$, we have $\sum_{j=1}^{n} a_{ij} \frac{U_i(1)}{U_i(0)} X_j(0) = U_i(1)$. Since $\frac{U_i(1)}{U_i(0)} X_j(0)$ satisfies the total sales by industry, we can say $\frac{U_i(1)}{U_i(0)} X_j(0)$ is one step closer to $X_j(1)$. However, we reluctantly find that total intermediate use of commodity j is not necessarily equal to $V_j(1)$, or $\sum_{i=1}^{n} a_{ij} \frac{U_i(1)}{U_i(0)} X_j(0) = {}_1Vj \neq V_j(1)$. Multiplying equation system (6.2) by $\frac{V_j(1)}{{}_1Vj} \frac{U_i(1)}{U_i(0)}$, we find $\frac{V_j(1)}{{}_1Vj} \frac{U_i(1)}{U_i(0)} X_j(0)$ becomes more closer to $X_j(1)$, since $\sum_{i=1}^{n} a_{ij} \frac{V_j(1)}{{}_1Vj} \frac{U_i(1)}{U_i(0)} X_j(0) = V_j(1)$. However, we find $\sum_{j=1}^{n} a_{ij} \frac{V_j(1)}{{}_1Vj} \frac{U_i(1)}{U_i(0)} X_j(0) = {}_1Ui \neq U_i(1)$.

To satisfy the total inter-industry sales by industry in year 1, we multiply the equation system (6.1) with $\frac{U_i(1)}{{}_1Ui} \left(\frac{V_j(1)}{{}_1Vj} \frac{U_i(1)}{U_i(0)} \right)$, and $\frac{U_i(1)}{{}_1Ui} \frac{V_j(1)}{{}_1Vj} \frac{U_i(1)}{U_i(0)} X_j(0)$ should be increasingly closer to $X_j(1)$.

The iterative process can be performed k times until the ${}_kU_i(0)$ and ${}_kV_j(0)$ converge to $U_i(1)$ and $V_j(1)$, respectively.

From this procedure, it is clear that, since the RAS method updates the table mechanically according to the ratios in the original table, it can keep the features of the original table to a maximum. However, this mechanical procedure provides no explanation for the changes to form the new table. Since this study updates the I–O table from 2005 to 2006, the change in I–O ratios in 2005 can be regarded as very small, so the RAS method is suitable for this study.

The specific updating steps are as follows: first, we obtain from the Singapore yearbook (DOS 2007) the detailed 2006 GDP from the income side (payments to capital and labour and taxes) and the expenditure side (spending by various final demands); second, according to the ratios in I–O tables 2005, disaggregate the total tax revenue by intermediate and final demand and by the type of tax; third, deduct the product tax from total intermediate demand and each final demand to obtain the basic value; fourth, use the ratio in I–O 2005 to distribute the industry totals (intermediate demand, labour, capital, production tax, import duties) to each industry; fifth, deriving the Make matrix using the inputs ratio in I–O 2005 and the 2006 total inputs (including intermediate demand, labour, capital, production tax, import duties) for each industry; sixth, use the total intermediate inputs for each industry and the ratio in I–O 2005 to derive the intermediate input demand matrix; seventh, subtracting the total intermediate demand for each commodity from the total output of each commodity in the updated make matrix, we obtain the total final demand for each commodity; eighth, using the total final demand for each commodity derived from step 7, the total commodity consumed by each final demand obtained in step 3, and RAS method, we can derive the final demand matrix. Ninth and finally, using the total value of imports and tax by each intermediate demand (industry) and final demands, and the ratio in 2005 I–O tables, we can update the imports matrix and tax matrix.

Aggregating I–O Tables Considering the features of the Singapore economy, the contribution of different sectors to tourism and the purpose of our study, we aggregate the 136 sectors/commodities into 35 sectors/commodities. The mapping for this aggregation is shown in the Table 6.7. With this mapping, the aggregation can be done automatically by the Viewhar program in the GEMPACK software.

6.3.2 Household Account

This account will address the data related to household consumption. Household consumption largely depends on household disposable income, which is largely affected by the gross household income. Since we use the linear expenditure system (LES) for household consumption in our model, we also need the data on household subsistence and supernumerary consumption.

We start with household subsistence consumption. Although the DOS of Singapore estimated S$1040 per month for a family of four as an average basic household expenditure (Yap 2003), many public agencies adopted a guideline of around S$1500 as the indicator of the need for

Table 6.7 Mapping from I–O 2005 to aggregate I–O tables

Sectors/commodities in this study	I/C No. in I–O 2005
1. Agriculture	001–005
2. Food manufacturing	006–012
3. Drink and tobacco	013–014
4. Clothing	015–017
5. Wood and print	018–021
6. Manufacturing (oil)	022
7. Manufacturing (non-oil, non-metal)	023–037
8. Manufacturing (metal)	038–045
9. Electronics	046–053
10. Electrical	054–064
11. Transport engineering	065–069
12. Precise engineering	070–072, 074
13. Other manufacturing	073, 075–076
14. Utilities	077–079
15. Construction	080–081
16. Wholesale trade	082–083
17. Retailer trade	084–085
18. Food and beverage services	086
19. Accommodation services	087
20. Land transport	088, 095
21. Water transport	089–091
22. Air transport	092–094
23. Storage and related services	096–098
24. Sightseeing	099
25. Communications	100
26. Insurance	101–102
27. Bank and financial	103–105
28. Real estate	106
29. Legal and accounting	107–108
30. Information technology	109–110
31. Other business services	111–124
32. Education	125
33. Health services	126–127
34. Recreation services	128–130
35. Non-profit and other	131–136, 137[a]

Source: Authors
[a]I/C No 137 only appears in import matrix

social assistance (Leong 2008). We adopted the S$1500 for a family of four (or S$375 per capita) as the average household subsistence expenditure for two reasons. One is that the estimation by the DOS is four years earlier than 2006. With the expansion of the economy and the inflation in this period, the number therefore should be higher. The other reason is that the average size of households in Singapore has a declining trend. The average household size in 1998 ranged from 4.0-person for the second quintile group to 3.4-person for the top quintile group, and the average household size declined to 3.8 and 3.1 for corresponding household groups in 2003. With the smaller size of households, the cost of living per capita will increase.

Then, we think about the gross household income. Households obtain income by selling primary factors of production (i.e. capital and labour) or from remittances and transfer from overseas. Compared with the returns on primary factors, the income from overseas is relatively small, so we omit it in our study. Since we assume zero economic profit in our model, there is no net income for the corporate sector—all company income goes to capital returns as owned by households. As such, the household income has a broader meaning in our model than in a general situation: it includes both household income and company income, namely the compensation of employees and the gross operating surplus in the 2005 I–O tables.

Third, we consider household disposable income. Household disposable income is generally derived from gross household income by the subtracting of taxes and fees paid to government and adding in transfers from the government. Income tax, property tax, rental fee, and school and institution fees are imposed on Singaporean households. Income taxes are the bulk of total charges on household.

As in other countries, the income tax rate in Singapore is complex. Non-resident individuals (staying in Singapore less than 183 days in a calendar year) and resident individuals are subject to different taxation systems. While the former is taxed at a flat rate of 15% of total income, the latter is taxed through an accumulated taxation system: with a $20,000 income tax-free threshold, the interval tax rate starts from 4% to the highest, 22%. For the simplification of the study, we use the value of total household income and total income tax from the Ministry of Finance (2009) to determine the overall income tax rate.

According to the CPF rules, CPF is compulsory for all Singapore households so it must also be excluded from gross household income when we calculate the disposable household income. The CPF contribution rates vary depending on the age of the employee and the level of wage rate. According to the CPF board (2007), an employee aged 50 and below and earning more than \$1500 per month has to contribute to CPF 20% of his/her wage and the employer has to pay to CPF 14.5% of the payroll. The CPF board also allows limited voluntary contributions. Due to the complexity of the CGF policy, it is impossible to calculate an average contribution rate. However, we can obtain the total CPF fund contributions from the CPF board and that is \$16547.1 million for 2006. Together with the total household income, we can therefore calculate the average CPF contribution rate.

6.3.3 Tourism Account

The purpose of this study is to gauge the economic impact of tourism, so the data in the tourism account are crucial. Before we obtain these important data, we need to have a clear definition of tourism-related concepts, such as tourism, tourists, tourism expenditure, tourism products, and tourism industry.

Tourism has a long history and the word 'tourism' is used frequently in the literature and daily life. However, people have different interpretations of 'tourism' and 'tourists'. Conventionally, tourism has been viewed as a travel activity for the purpose of leisure and recreation. But in modern times, people travel from one place to another for many reasons, such as business, conferences, education, healthcare, shopping, visiting friends and family, adventure, and experience. Some people may plan travel for multiple purposes. So the traditional concept of tourism has had to evolve over time. The UNWTO defines tourists as people who 'travel to and stay in places outside their usual environment for not more than one consecutive year for leisure, business and other purposes not related to the exercise of an activity remunerated from within the place visited'. This definition incorporates the wide variety and multipurpose nature of modern tourism activity and it will be adopted for this study.

Tourism expenditure also has different interpretations. It may refer to all the money tourists spent during the journey or including the amount they prepaid before they start travelling (e.g. pre-booking for accommodation and sightseeing tours). It may just refer to the travelling costs or the spending related to the main purpose of travel such as shopping spending, education costs, and health treatment payments. Since this study concerns the contribution of inbound tourism spending to the Singapore economy, tourism expenditure in this study includes any spending by tourists and received by economic agents of/in Singapore.

Tourism products and the tourism industry are related concepts. In this study, tourism products include any commodity purchased by tourists. Because of the wide variation of, and change in, tourists' preference, tourism products are a very complex amalgam of goods and services. The definition of the tourism industry varies. As stated in Sect. 4.1, we define the tourism industry as a demand-side concept. From the point of view of the supply side, the tourism industry in this study includes any sectors producing tourism products. For most sectors, tourism demand consists of only a part of the final demand for their output, so they only partly belong to the tourism industry. According to the share of the tourism demand in the total sectoral output, this study classifies the sectors as core tourism sectors, extended tourism sectors or tourism-related sectors.

With the clarified concept about tourism, we can now consider creating tourism final demands in the I–O tables. The following is the method and reasoning to add tourism expenditure as a final demand.

For Singapore, as a city state, domestic tourism is assumed negligible, so we need only to consider inbound tourism. Since inbound tourism receipts are recorded in the Singapore national account system as part of exports, they should be extracted from the export demand in the I–O tables. However, the situation becomes more complicated when it comes to the detailed tourism spending. From the point of view of Singapore, tourism shopping plays a similar role to exports—tourists buy products in Singapore and take them home. As such, it is suitable to subtract inbound tourism shopping expenditure from the export column in the Absorption matrix. On the other hand, tourists consume all tourism services (e.g. F&B and accommodation) in Singapore, just like locals. So tourism services expenditure is suitable to be extracted from household consumption.[1] With both

[1] The other reason for this approach is that, in Singapore I–O tables, there is no exportation for non-shopping goods and services.

Table 6.8 Breakdown of major tourism expenditure items

Expenditure items	Commodity number in aggregate I–O tables	Spending (million $)
Shopping	17	3687
Accommodation	19	2239
Food and beverage	18	1052
Medical/healthcare	33	763
Local transport	20	477
Sightseeing/entertainment	24	124
Others	35	77
Total		8421

Source: Singapore Tourism Board (2001)

tourism shopping and services expenditure being extracted from relevant columns in the I–O tables, we can form a new column heading 'tourism expenditure' in the absorption matrix and the total final demand for each commodity remains the same.

It is clear that detailed tourism expenditure data are crucial to the creation of the 'tourism' final demand. These data for the study are provided by the Singapore tourism survey. The 2006 STB survey breaks down tourism expenditure by major items. Mapping the major expenditure items into commodities in Table 6.7, we have Table 6.8.

From Table 6.8, it is evident that tourism shopping expenditure is the single largest expenditure item—it occupies nearly half of the total expenditure. The STB survey further breaks down this part to different shopping items. Mapping each shopping item to commodity in aggregate I–O tables, we have Table 6.9.

Based on Table 6.9 and the total shopping expenditure in Table 6.8, we can calculate the shopping expenditure on each commodity. By doing so, however, there will be nothing left for the retailing sector. This clearly is not true as all tourism shopping goods are channelled by retailers. As the Singapore I–O tables treat trade sectors as service sectors, a proper method to overcome this problem should be to extract a certain amount of value from each item in Table 6.9 as services provided by the retailer sector. However, for this study, it has been decided to simply add some value for retailing sector proportional to the total shopping expenditure. This decision is made due to two considerations.

Table 6.9 Shopping items purchased as percentage of total shopping expenditure

Shopping items	Commodity No.	Spending (%)
Fashion and accessories	4	32
Cameras, video cameras	9	7
Computers, hard- and software	9	5
Audiovisual equipment	9	3
Handheld electronic devices	9	3
Toy or electronic games sets	9	2
Home appliances	10	*
Other electronic/electrical goods	10	4
Jewellery	12	11
Watches and clocks	12	3
Cosmetics and wellness products	7	10
Edibles	2	6
Alcohol, tobacco, and cigarettes	3	4
Gifts	5	6
Antiques, arts, and collector's items	5	1
Stationary, books, or magazines	5	1
Sports and recreational equipment	5	*
Spectacles and other optical goods	5	*
Other items	5	1

Source: Singapore Tourism Board (2001)
*Indicates the proportion is less than 0.05

One is that the numbers in Tables 6.8 and 6.9 are from the original tourism survey. It is undesirable to distort the survey data by proportional extraction. The other consideration is that the STB tourism survey has not included the expenditure by all tourists. The value in Singapore tourism receipts is much bigger than the survey results. The difference is expenditure from transit passengers, foreign air/sea crew, and foreign students. According to the definition of tourism by the UNWTO, the expenditure of transit passengers and foreign students (provided that they do not stay for more than one consecutive year) should be part of the tourism expenditure. If we use solely the survey data, the modelling results will be biased downwards. So adding some value to the tourism survey data will reduce this bias. Since shopping is obviously a significant part of spending by transit passengers and foreign students, adding some value for a retailing sector is suitable. In practice, around 25% margin is added on retail goods, so we assign to the retailing sector a value of one quarter of the total tourism shopping expenditure.

Besides the total tourism spending on goods and services, the STB survey also provides the expenditure by seven regions and further by 21 countries. The breakdown of the tourism expenditure at seven-region level is shown in Table 6.10.

This breakdown is useful to shed light on the influence of different tourism-generating markets, so we also include them in our modelling. According to the ratios of the total tourism expenditure by region (and country), the added spending of the retailing sector is disaggregated to region (and country) levels. Consequently, 21 tourism demands from 21 tourism-generating markets are added to the I–O tables.

6.3.4 Sectoral Employment

To disaggregate the labour input in the Singapore I–O tables to different occupations, we need the wage bill data both by industry and by occupation group. It takes us a few steps to obtain the occupational wage bill for each industry.

First, we found the industrial employment data from the Ministry of Manpower. Since the industry classification is not the same as in our model, we map the industrial employment data with the industrial classification in our model, as shown in Table 6.11.

In Table 6.11, we split the number of employees equally where there is more than one sector number in one row; and aggregate the number of employees where different rows share the same sector number.

To obtain the number of occupational employees in each industry, we have to rely on the data on employed residents aged 15 and over, shown in Table 6.12. Since Table 6.12 only includes the number of employed residents (the majority of the labour force), the sectoral total is not equal to the one in Table 6.11. However, we can use this table to obtain the occupational share of labour inputs in each industry, according to which we can disaggregate the data in Table 6.11 into employment both by industry and by occupation group. Since the last column in Table 6.12 consists mainly of agricultural workers whose wage rates are closer to the workers in the second last column, we merge the last two columns in Table 6.12. Since the classification of industry is not the same as the

Table 6.10 Tourism expenditure by source region

Expenditure items	Americas	Southeast Asia	North Asia	South Asia	Europe	Oceania	Africa
Shopping	141.9	1287.80	1060.80	488.8	407.7	249.2	51
Accommodation	208.8	611.4	589.40	246	354.8	205.6	23.3
Food and beverage	83.3	351.1	266.10	114.8	144.2	81.7	10.8
Medical/Healthcare	32.7	168.1	112.00	65.2	59	33.7	6.6
Local transport	8.7	26.2	37.90	13.2	25.6	11.4	1.2
Sightseeing/entertainment	0.7	661.8	30.60	67.5	0.3	0.1	2.3
Others	3.1	60.3	11.60	0.6	1.3	0.4	0.1
Total	479.2	3166.80	2108.60	996	992.8	582	95.4

Source: Singapore Tourism Board (2001)

Table 6.11 Employment by industry, 2006 (as at December 31)

Industry	Sector number	Employees (thousands)
Food, beverages and tobacco	2,3	30.1
Paper products and printing	5	26.8
Petroleum, chemical and pharmaceutical products	6-8	33.3
Rubber and plastic products	7	17.7
Fabricated metal products	8	29.2
Machinery and equipment	10	70.0
Electrical products	10	10.5
Electronic products	9	111.1
Medical and precision instruments	12	15.2
Transport equipment	11	122.3
Other manufacturing	4,13	51.3
Construction	15	255.5
Wholesale trade	16	219.1
Retail trade	17	145.9
Land transport and supporting services	20	69.2
Water transport and supporting services	21	38.2
Air transport and supporting services	22	28.5
Other transport and storage services	23	43.1
Hotels	19	26.3
Restaurants	18	119.5
Broadcasting and publishing	30	13.9
Telecommunications	25	17.7
IT and other information services	30	41.5
Financial institutions	27	104.4
Insurance	26	22.8
Real estate and leasing services	28	52.9
Legal, accounting and management services	29	68.1
Architectural and engineering services	31	33.9
Other professional services	31	26.3
Administrative and support services	34	113.2
Education and public administration	32	172.3
Health and social services	33	68.4
Other community, social, and personal services[a]	35	281.3
Other services[b]	1, 14	16.4

Source: Administrative Records and Labour Force Survey, Manpower Research & Statistics Department, Ministry of Manpower, Republic of Singapore

Notes

1. Data are compiled primarily from administrative records, with the self-employed component estimated from the Labour Force Survey
2. Data may not add up to total due to rounding
3. Industries were classified based on Singapore Standard Industrial Classification 2005

[a]Includes extraterritorial organizations and bodies

[b]Includes agriculture, fishing, quarrying, utilities, and sewerage and waste management

Table 6.12 Employed residents aged 15 and over by industry and occupation (thousands), June 2006

Industry (SSIC 2005)	Total	Managers, working proprietors and senior officials	Professionals	Technicians and associate professionals	Clerical workers	Service workers, shop and market sales workers	Production craftsmen and related workers	Plant & machine operators and assemblers	Cleaners, labourers and related workers	Others[b]
Total	1796.7	268.9	256.2	319.8	251.6	215.7	95.0	173.3	149.3	66.9
Manufacturing	301.7	46.9	52.2	55.1	31.8	3.1	38.3	64.6	9.5	–
Construction	95.0	20.1	11.0	9.5	9.9	0.6	30.1	6.4	7.4	–
Services	1377.5	198.8	190.4	248.9	207.1	211.1	25.5	100.3	129.7	65.7
Wholesale and retail trade	301.1	79.8	16.2	34.7	48.7	88.5	6.4	16.2	10.6	0.1
Transport and storage	174.0	16.1	6.0	20.4	31.3	11.3	2.3	73.0	13.6	–
Hotels and restaurants	128.8	11.4	0.9	3.3	9.6	51.2	1.2	2.2	49.0	–
Information and communications	74.8	16.0	31.3	14.5	9.6	0.9	1.0	0.7	0.7	–
Financial and insurance services	106.3	20.1	21.7	34.8	27.7	0.4	0.1	0.5	1.0	–
Real estate, renting and leasing activities	39.9	5.8	2.4	16.8	7.6	1.1	1.6	0.5	4.0	–
Professional, scientific and technical services	99.0	19.1	34.4	23.8	17.3	0.8	1.3	1.2	1.2	–
Administrative and support services	78.4	8.3	2.4	6.0	10.6	20.9	0.8	1.9	27.6	–
Public administration and education services	223.3	8.5	56.7	53.3	19.2	12.4	0.5	1.5	5.8	65.5
Health and social services	70.8	3.5	12.2	30.6	14.7	3.5	0.4	0.5	5.3	–

Other community, social and personal services	81.0	10.2	6.2	10.8	10.7	20.0	9.8	2.0	11.1	0.1
Others[a]	22.5	3.0	2.6	6.3	2.8	0.9	1.2	2.0	2.6	1.2

Source: MOM (2007a), Comprehensive Labour Force Survey, Manpower Research and Statistics Department, Ministry of Manpower, Republic of Singapore

Notes

1. Occupations were classified based on Singapore Standard Occupational Classification 2005 and industries were classified based on Singapore Standard Industrial Classification 2005
2. –: Nil or negligible

[a]Includes agriculture, fishing, mining and quarrying, utilities and activities not adequately defined

[b]Includes agricultural and fishery workers and workers not classifiable by occupation

aggregate industry in our study, we applied aggregation or disaggregation where it is necessary.

In order to obtain the wage bill by industry and by occupation, one more thing needed is the occupational wage rate for each industry. Fortunately, this information is provided by the Singapore labour force survey (see Table 6.13). Multiplying data in Table 6.13 with the corresponding employee numbers by industry and by occupation, we have the detailed wage bill by industry and by occupation. However, the aggregation of the wage bill for each industry is not necessarily equal to the compensation of employees for each industry in the Singapore I–O table because this wage bill is based on the survey data instead of the real disaggregation. So the last step is to amplify or reduce the wage bill so that the industry total matches the compensation of employees for each industry in the I–O tables.

6.3.5 Investment Matrices

The model also requires the information on investment allocation—the detailed information on investment by both commodity and industry, namely an investment matrix. However, this information is not available for Singapore. In spite of that, from the Singapore I–O table, we can find the total investment purchases by commodity. In the absence of more detailed information, we disaggregate the investment purchases according to the ratio of capital stocks among each industry.

The capital stock in each industry is provided by the DOS in Singapore. Mapping it with our study, we have Table 6.14.

In Table 6.14, we split assets evenly where more than one sector numbers in a row and add up assets where a sector number appears in more than one row. From Table 6.14, we can calculate the sectoral share of total assets. Using this share, we can distribute the investment by commodity to each industry. As such, we have obtained an investment matrix by commodity and by industry.

Table 6.13 Monthly gross wage of major occupation groups by industry, June 2006

	Managers ($)	Professionals ($)	Technicians and associate professionals ($)	Clerical workers ($)	Service workers and shop and market sales workers ($)	Production craftsmen and related workers ($)	Plant and machine operators and assemblers ($)	Cleaners, labourers and related workers ($)
All industries	7588	4596	3310	1994	2114	2346	1962	1166
Manufacturing	7141	4153	3243	1976	1996	2541	1885	1191
Food, beverages, and tobacco	5067	3476	2370	1734	1577	1441	1541	1171
Paper products and printing	6195	3477	2580	1788	2412	1917	1814	1346
Petroleum, chemical, and pharmaceutical products	8524	4998	4005	2452	2620	3481	2780	1545
Rubber and plastic products	6487	3227	2865	1840	1519	2197	1434	1211
Fabricated metal products	6397	3190	2628	1701	1534	2303	1717	1213
Machinery and equipment	7257	3791	2969	1989	–	2614	2405	1386
Electrical products	7284	3770	2961	1976	s	2783	1572	1787
Electronic products	8075	4084	2931	2179	2744	2392	1702	1538
Medical and precision instruments	7218	4099	2801	2070	s	2286	1932	1411
Transport equipment	6104	4929	4155	1828	2061	2705	2653	840
Construction	5496	3237	2646	1331	1100	2177	1975	896
Services	7882	4937	3360	2029	2116	2063	2122	1178
Wholesale and retail trade	7004	4351	3136	1828	1844	1932	1772	1450
Wholesale trade	7455	4371	3129	1980	2084	2027	1815	1579
Retail trade	4595	4032	3186	1446	1691	1580	1415	1109

(continued)

Table 6.13 (continued)

	Managers ($)	Professionals ($)	Technicians and associate professionals ($)	Clerical workers ($)	Service workers and shop and market sales workers ($)	Production craftsmen and related workers ($)	Plant and machine operators and assemblers ($)	Cleaners, labourers and related workers ($)
Transport and storage	7162	5085	5182	2291	3103	2449	2299	1819
Land transport and supporting services	5317	3446	2415	1731	s	2018	1902	1311
Water transport and supporting services	7443	5352	2841	2033	2010	1967	2392	1078
Air transport and supporting services	7678	4735	7849	2508	3118	2561	1997	2163
Hotels and restaurants	3971	3322	2374	1549	1691	1705	1490	1188
Hotels	4288	3282	2406	1611	2001	1730	1617	1349
Restaurants	3723	3419	2309	1422	1523	1386	1412	1002
Information and communications	8699	4417	2912	1885	1502	1947	1268	1155
Broadcasting and publishing	6317	3986	2880	1964	s	s	s	984
Telecommunications	9626	4308	2898	1855	s	s	s	s
IT and other information services	9328	4599	3011	1921	–	2381	1107	1327
Financial services	9682	5343	3898	2143	1219	2145	2440	1430
Financial institutions	9893	5545	4022	2165	1220	2164	2488	1422
Insurance	7440	4017	2929	1986	s	s	2147	1480
Real estate and leasing services	6504	3753	2538	1821	1446	1833	1902	747
Professional services	8870	4492	3086	2104	1461	2604	2166	1282
	9539	4457	2978	2151	1464	2170	1681	1367

Legal, accounting, and management services								
Architectural and engineering services	8432	4604	3186	2056	–	3159	2772	1169
Other professional services	7834	4368	3098	1783	s	1995	1541	1282
Administrative and support services	5398	3489	2514	1725	1640	2144	1676	700
Education, health, and social services	7258	5508	2367	1769	1395	1968	2254	1166
Health services	7887	3085	2763	1823	1910	s	1606	1225
Social and community services	3657	2583	1674	1486	1044	s	1282	1025
Arts, entertainment, recreation, and other services	5186	3548	–	1839	1867	2019	1881	–

Source: MOM (2007b), Occupational Wage Survey, Manpower Research & Statistics Department, Ministry of Manpower, Republic of Singapore

Notes

1. Data pertain to full-time resident employees in private sector establishments each with at least 25 employees
2. Monthly gross wage refers to the sum of the basic wage, overtime payments, commissions, allowances, and other regular cash payments. It is before deduction of employee CPF contributions and personal income tax and excludes employer CPF contributions, bonuses, stock options, other lump sum payments and payments in kind.
3. Mean wage refers to the sum of wages of all employees in a particular group divided by the group size
4. Occupations were classified based on Singapore Standard Occupational Classification 2005 and industries were classified based on Singapore Standard Industrial Classification 2005
5. s: Data have been suppressed because (a) the number covered was too small or (b) the coverage achieved is not deemed to be representative
6. –: Nil or negligible

Table 6.14 Sectoral capital stock in Singapore ($ Million)

Industry	Sector number	Total assets
Food, beverages and tobacco	2, 3	6760
Paper products and printing	4, 5	4447
Petroleum and petroleum products	6	24,254
Chemical and chemical products	7, 8	20,714
Pharmaceutical and biological products	7	49,641
Rubber and plastic products	7	47,76
Fabricated metal products	8	9942
Machinery and equipment, electrical machinery and apparatus	10	24,737
Electronic products and components	9	80,183
Instrumentation, photographic, and optical goods	12	3983
Transport equipment	11	19,877
Other manufacturing	13	7134
Construction	15	53,097
Wholesale trade	16	276,693
Retail trade	17	15,365
Hotel and restaurants	18, 19	13,446
Water transport and supporting services	21	72,774
Land and air transport and supporting services	20, 22	34,045
Warehousing, post, and courier services	23	13,578
Information and communications	25, 30	60,239
Banks	27	1,477,672
Investment holding	27	729,846
Other financial services	27	92,453
Insurance services	26	114,910
Real estate and leasing services	28	159,271
Professional services	30, 31	64,052
Other services	1, 14, 24, 32–35	34,510

Source: www.singstat.gov.sg/pubn/business/scs2006.pdf

6.3.6 Tax Matrices

Direct taxes are already addressed in 'household account', so we will only consider indirect tax flows here. There are numerous indirect taxes in Singapore, but according to the tax revenue raised in the government budget, the most important ones are the goods and service tax (GST), motor vehicle taxes, stamp duties, customs and excise taxes, betting taxes, assets taxes, and other taxes. The Singapore I–O table 2005 puts them into three categories: import duty, other taxes on products (GST makes up the majority), and taxes on production. We follow this classification in this study. Since taxes on production are included in the 'value added' as part of 'basic value', we only need to think about the other two categories.

Although import duties and sales tax (since the GST is the main part of other taxes on production, we call it sales taxes for convenience) are taxes on commodity, the I–O tables have summed them up for each industry and for each final demand. Thus, we only have aggregate import duty and sales tax for each industry. To derive the commodity flows at purchasers' prices, we need the import duty matrix and sales tax matrix corresponding to the commodity flows. This task is accomplished by solving for tax rates. The way of deriving tax rates is shown as follows.

Since the Singapore government imposes the same GST and tariff rates to all economic agents except itself (there is no tax on government purchases), it is reasonable to assume that the product tax rates is for all industries. Assume a_j stands for the tax rate (tariff rate or sales tax rate) for commodity X_j and X_{ij} stands for the amount of intermediate inputs X_j at the basic value purchased by industry *i*. The total taxes paid by industry *i* (T_i) should be equal to the sum of tax paid for purchasing each commodity, namely, $T_i = \sum_{j=1}^{n} a_j X_{ij}$. For an economy with *n* industries and *n* commodities, we have *n* equations to solve for *n* tax rates. When tax rates are known, we can obtain the tax flows simply through multiplying the commodity basic value flows by the corresponding tax rates. Thus, we can have two tax matrices: the import duty matrix and the sales tax matrix.

By principle, these tax rates should be applicable to final demands because the tax rates are assumed the same for all economic agents. However, when we apply them to final demands such as investment demand and household demand, the total value of taxes calculated did not agree with the total in the I–O tables. This is not surprising given that the product tax in the I–O tables is a bundle of numerous kinds of indirect taxes. To be consistent with the I–O tables, we scale up or down the tax flow for final demand to match the totals in the I–O tables.

6.4 Behavioural Parameters

The behavioural parameters describe the economic agents' responses to changing economic conditions. In this study, the behavioural parameters mainly consist of the Armington elasticities, the factor substitution elasticities, the product transformation elasticities, the consumer demand elasticities, and the export demand elasticities. Many previous CGE modelling studies on the Singapore economy use the GTAP database as the source of parameters, and it is especially true for literature on Singapore international trade (e.g. Park 2000; Sudsawasd and Mongsawad 2007; Chong and Hur 2007), but some researchers use their own judgement, based on the previous econometric estimations (e.g. Siriwardana 1997, 2000; Siriwardana and Schulze 2000). The selection of behavioural parameters in this study will be largely based on the GTAP database version 6.0. However, adjustment will be made based on the previous econometric estimations and based on the CGE modelling practices on the Singapore economy.

6.4.1 Input Substitution Elasticities

The input substitution elasticities in this study include the Armington elasticities and the factor substitution elasticities. Armington elasticities are also called source substitution elasticities because they concern the substitution between imports and domestic goods. Armington (1969) considered the similarity between imported and domestically produced goods. He assumed that imports and domestic goods were different from each other and therefore not perfectly substitutable. We adopt this assumption in this study. A high value of Armington elasticity means a high degree of substitution between imported and domestic goods. The Armington elasticities in GTAP 6 database are based on the recent econometric work by Hertel et al. (2004). Since no econometric estimation on these parameters for Singapore is available, we adopt these values (Table 6.15) and map them into our study.

Factor substitution elasticities measure the substitutability between primary factors (labour and capital in our study). The GTAP 6 database

Table 6.15 The source and factor substitution elasticities for the model

GTAP Commodities	Commodity No.	Armington elasticity	Factor substitution elasticity
Crops	1	3.25	0.24
Coal	1	3.05	0.20
Oil	1	5.20	0.20
Gas	1	17.20	0.20
Minerals n.e.c.	1	0.90	0.20
Bovine meat prods	1	3.85	1.12
Meat products	2	4.40	1.12
Sugar	2	2.70	1.12
Food products	2	2.00	1.12
Beverages and tobacco products	3	1.15	1.12
Textiles	4	3.75	1.26
Wearing apparel	4	3.70	1.26
Leather products	4	4.05	1.26
Wood products	5	3.40	1.26
Paper products, publishing	5	2.95	1.26
Petroleum, coal products	6	2.10	1.26
Chemical, rubber, plastic products	7	3.30	1.26
Mineral products	8	2.90	1.26
Ferrous metals	8	2.95	1.26
Metals n.e.c.	8	4.20	1.26
Metal products	8	3.75	1.26
Motor vehicles and parts	11	2.80	1.26
Transport equipment n.e.c.	11	4.30	1.26
Electronic equipment	9	4.40	1.26
Machinery and equipment n.e.c.	12, 13	4.05	1.26
Manufactures n.e.c.	13	3.75	1.26
Electricity	10	2.80	1.26
Gas manufacture, distribution	14	2.80	1.26
Water	14	2.80	1.26
Construction	15	1.90	1.00
Trade	16,17	1.90	1.68
Transport n.e.c.	20, 23	1.90	1.68
Water transport	21	1.90	1.68
Air transport	22	1.90	1.68
Communication	25, 30	1.90	1.26

(continued)

Table 6.15 (continued)

GTAP Commodities	Commodity No.	Armington elasticity	Factor substitution elasticity
Financial services n.e.c.	27	1.90	1.26
Insurance	26	1.90	1.26
Business services n.e.c.	28, 29, 31	1.90	1.26
Recreational and other services	18, 19, 24, 34	1.90	1.26
Public admin, defence, education	32, 33, 35	1.90	1.26
Dwellings	35	1.90	1.26

Source: based on elasticities from Dimaranan (2006)

also provides the factor elasticity in producing each commodity (see Table 6.15). Tan (1996) estimated unitary factor elasticity for the construction sector in Singapore, but it is different from that in the GTAP 6 database. We use this value for construction and adopt other values in the GTAP 6 database.

Considering the primary factor substitution, we also need elasticities of substitution between different labour types because we have eight occupation groups in our model. However, we could not find them either in the GTAP database or in other literature, so we follow the practice of Siriwardana and Schulze (2000) to assign the value of 0.5 for every industry.

6.4.2 Products Transformation and Export Demand Elasticities

The products transformation elasticities gauge the flexibility of industries to change their output mix according to the changed market preferences. There is no econometric estimation on them for Singapore nor are they in the GTAP 6 database. However, the estimates of constant ratio of elasticity of transformation, homothetic (CRETH) transformation parameters in the ORANI model for the Australian economy have the value between 0.06 and 4.55 and most of the estimates have the values around 0.3–0.5 or around 1.3–1.6. We adopt 0.4 for the agricultural sector in Singapore and 1.5 for the other sectors.

The export demand elasticities describe the change in foreign demand for Singaporean exports when the prices of exported goods changes. We cannot find the estimated export demand elasticity for Singapore in the GTAP 6 database or in other literature, so a judgement needs be made. Since Singapore is a small economy and thus a price taker in the world markets (except for some manufacturing goods), it is believed that the foreign demand elasticity for most of Singaporean exports is quite large. Following the practice of Siriwardana and Schulze (2000), we assign the value of −20.0 for most of the non-manufactured exports for Singapore. For manufactured goods, because of the huge capacity of Singapore manufacturing production in oil products, non-metal chemical products and electronic goods, we assign −5.5 for the correspondent sectors (e.g. sector 6, 7, and 9) and −10.0 for the other manufacturing sectors (e.g. sector 8, 10, 11, 12, and 13).

6.4.3 Tourism Demand and Tourism Substitution Elasticities

Tourism demand elasticity, or own-price elasticity of tourism demand, depicts the change in tourists' demand for a commodity in response to the change in its price. Tourism demand elasticity is well studied, but it is a very complex subject. There is a variety of definitions of tourism price, and the bundle of tourism goods differs from country to country and changes over time. The estimated elasticities vary considerably. Witt and Witt (1995) did a review of empirical research on tourism demand modelling. In 14 models listed by them, the elasticity estimates range from −0.04 to −4.3 if travel cost is used as a tourism price index; they range from −0.05 to −1.5 for destination cost; from 0.6 to 2.3 for exchange rate. De Mello et al. (1999) estimated the elasticity of UK demand for Spain tourism to be −1.93.

Gunadhi and Boey (1986) estimated the demand elasticity of tourism in Singapore. According to their estimation, if the shopping prices are chosen as the price index, the Australian demand for tourism in Singapore is −1.12, but the Japan demand for tourism in Singapore is −2.99. If the hotel rate is used as a benchmark, the world demand for tourism in

Singapore is −0.92. According to these studies, a value of −1.5 is suitable for the demand elasticity for tourism in Singapore. However, these estimations were done decades ago. With the worldwide increase in income and popularity of tourism in the recent 20 years, the tourism demand elasticity tends to increase.[2] In this study, we follow Blake et al. (2008) and assign a value of −2 as the tourism demand elasticity for Singapore.

Since we use a CES function to depict the demand for composite tourism shopping and non-shopping services, the substitution elasticity between tourism shopping and non-shopping services is required. There is no literature on this issue either. Since these two types of products have totally different functions and, as stated earlier, the demand for non-shopping tourism services is quite rigid, it is believed the substitution effect between them is quite small. So we assign it a value of 0.3.

6.4.4 Frisch Parameter and Household Expenditure Elasticities

We use the LES to describe household consumption, so household expenditure elasticities and the Frisch parameter are the key parameters required.

The calculation of the Frisch parameter is based on the average household subsistence expenditure described in the household account, the total household consumption, and the number of households in Singapore in 2006. Compared with household numbers, the population data are more accurate and easier to obtain, therefore, we use the subsistence consumption per capita of \$375 described in the household account. The number of total residents in Singapore is 3.608 million (DOS 2007), so household subsistence consumption is \$375*3.608 = \$1353.000 million. Given total household consumption \$87121.600 million in the I–O tables, the Frisch parameter is −87121.600/(87121.600 − 1353.000) = −1.016.

[2] This is confirmed by other estimations on tourism demand elasticities. For example, Syriopoulos and Sinclair (1993) estimated a value of −1.11 for own-price elasticity of tourism demand in Spain, but a later study by De Mello et al. (1999), in which Sinclair was also involved, estimated a value of −1.93 for the same elasticity for Spain.

Table 6.16 Singaporean household expenditure elasticities

Commodity categories	Commodity number	Household expenditure elasticity
Grains, other crops	1	0.18
Meat, dairy, fish	2	0.58
Other food, beverages, tobacco	3	0.60
Textiles, apparel, footwear	4,5	0.78
Utilities, housing	14,15	1.05
Wholesale/retail trade	16–19	1.10
Manufactures, electronics	6–13	0.86
Transport communication	20–25, 30	0.95
Financial and business services	26–29, 31	1.19
Housing, education, health, public services	32–35	1.16

Source: Based on elasticities from Dimaranan (2006)

When income changes, the household expenditure elasticity measures the change in household consumption on a commodity. These elasticities are provided in Dimaranan (2006), which are specifically estimated for GTAP countries including Singapore, so we adopt these values in our study. The elasticities for each kind of good and its mapping are presented in the Table 6.16.

Theoretically, the share weighted average expenditure elasticity should be equal to 1 (Engel aggregation). However, the elasticities listed in Table 6.16 are unlikely to satisfy the Engel aggregation for two reasons. One is that the elasticities are estimated a few years earlier than 2006. They may have changed or the shares of different commodities in consumption may have changed. In either case, the share weighted average elasticity may not be unity. The other reason is that, since the commodities are highly aggregated in Table 6.16, we have to disaggregate them. Even if the elasticities in Table 6.16 do satisfy the Engel aggregation, it may be destroyed during the disaggregation.

However, the Engel aggregation must be satisfied in a CGE model in order to obtain consistent simulation results. Moreover, there is an internal checking of the Engel aggregation in the model. If the elasticities cannot satisfy the condition, the model cannot pass the assertion command and will stop running. So we need to adjust the original elasticities. This adjustment involves two steps: (1) We use the expenditure shares and corresponding elasticities to calculate the average Engel elasticity (most likely it is not equal to one). (2) We then divide the original elasticity by the average Engel elasticity calculated in step 1 to obtain the standardized elasticity. Since the elasticities are scaled up or down according to the average Engel elasticity, the weighted average of standardized elasticities should be able to satisfy the Engel aggregation.

References

Armington, P. S. (1969). A Theory of Demand for Products Distinguished by Place of Production. *IMF Staff Papers, 16*, 159–178.

Blake, A. Arbache, J. Sinclair, M. and Teles, V. (2008). Tourism and Poverty Relief. *Annals of Tourism Research, 35*(1): 107–126.

Chong, S., & Hur, J. (2007). *Overlapping Free Trade Agreements of Singapore-USA-Japan: A Computational Analysis*. SCALE Working Paper Series, No. 2007/11.

CPF (Central Provident Fund) board. (2007). *CPF Contributions: CPF Contribution Rate Booklets from 1 January 2006 to 30 June 2007*. http://mycpf.cpf.gov.sg/Employers/Gen-Info/cpf-Contri/CPF+Contribution+Rate+Booklets+%28From+1+Jan+2006%29.htm

De Mello, M., Pack, A., & Sinclair, T. (1999). *UK Demand for Tourism in its Southern Neighbours*. TTRI Discussion Paper 99/2. Christel De Haan Tourism and Travel Research Institute, University of Nottingham.

Dimaranan, B. 2006. *The GTAP 6 Data Base*. Center for Global Trade Analysis, Purdue University.

DOS (Department of Statistics, Singapore). 2007. *Singapore Year Book*, various issues. Ministry of Trade & Industry, Singapore.

DOS (Department of Statistics, Singapore). (2010). *Singapore Input-Output Tables 2005*. Singapore: Ministry of Trade & Industry.

Gunadhi, H., & Boey, C. (1986). Demand Elasticities of Tourism in Singapore. *Tourism Management, 7*(4), 239–253.

Hertel, T., Hummels, D., Ivanic, M., & Keeney, R. (2004). *How Confident Can We Be in CGE-Based Assessments of Free Trade Agreements?* GTAP Working Paper No.26, Center for Global Trade Analysis, West Lafayette, Indiana, USA.

Leong, K. (2008). Overview of Singapore's Business Services Sector. In *Economic Survey of Singapore*. Singapore: Ministry of Trade and Industry.

Ministry of Finance of Singapore. (2009). *Total Estimated Receipts for FY2009 by Object Class*. http://www.mof.gov.sg/budget_2009/revenue.../Revenue_Estimates.pdf

MOM (Ministry of Manpower of Singapore). (2007a). *Labour Force Survey of Singapore*. http://www.singstat.gov.sg/stats/themes/economy/ess/aesa24.pdf.

MOM (Ministry of Manpower of Singapore). (2007b). *Wage Earnings Report*. http://www.mom.gov.sg/Documents/statistics-publications/wages-earnings/report2007/ 2007Wages_table 7.xls.

O'Connor, R., & Henry, E. (1975). *Input-output Analysis and Its Applications*, Griffin's Statistical Monogrphs, No. 36. London: Chareles Griffin's.

Parikh, A. (1979). Forecasts of Input-Output Matrices Using the R.A.S. Method. *The Review of Economics and Statistics, 61*(3), 477–481.

Park, I. 2000. Trade Liberalization and Long-run Economic Growth-A CGE Model Analysis of AFTA. *Korea Review of International Studies, 3*(1): 107–130.

Singapore Customs. (2009). *List of Dutiable Goods*. http://www.customs.gov.sg/leftNav/trad/val/List+of+Dutiable+Goods.htm

Siriwardana, M. (1997). Exchange Rate Policy and Market Power: A General Equilibrium Analysis for Singapore. *ASEAN Economic Bulletin, 14*(1), 57–79.

Siriwardana, M. (2000). A General Equilibrium Explanation of the Growth in Singapore's Exports: A Paradoxical Outcome? *Journal of the Asia Pacific Economy, 5*(3), 303–335.

Siriwardana, M., & Schulze, D. (2000). Singapore and the Asian Economic Crisis: An Assessment of Policy Responses. *ASEAN Economic Bulletin, 17*(3), 233–256.

STB (Singapore Tourism Board). (2001–2007). *Annual Report on Tourism Statistics*, Various Issues.

Sudsawasd, S., & Mongsawad, P. (2007). Go with the Gang, ASEAN! *ASEAN Economic Bulletin, 24*(3), 339–356.

Syriopoulos, T., & Sinclair, T. (1993). An Econometric Study of Tourism Demand: The AIDS Model of US and European Tourism in Mediterranean Countries. *Applied Economics, 25*, 1541–1552.

Tan, W. (1996). The Elasticity of Capital-Labour Substitution in Singapore Construction. *Construction Management and Economics, 14*(6), 537–542.

Witt, S., & Witt, C. (1995). Forecasting Tourism Demand: A Review of Empirical Research. *International Journal of Forecasting, 11*, 3447–3475.

Yap, M. (2003). Poverty Monitoring and Alleviation in Singapore. In K. L. Tang & C. K. Wong (Eds.), *Poverty Monitoring and Alleviation in East Asia*. Nova Science: New York.

7

Model Implementation and Testing

These aspects are discussed in three sections. Section 7.1 concerns the robustness in model implementation and discusses the procedures and tests to be conducted prior to any scenario simulation. Using Singaporean tourism CGE model as an example, Sect. 7.2 demonstrates how to set an appropriate simulation closure and illustrates how to design suitable simulation scenarios. Section 7.3 explains the necessity to perform sensitivity tests after simulations in order to gauge the sensitivity of modelling results. Based on the example modelling results, the section also shows how to conduct and report sensitivity tests.

7.1 The Integrity of Model Implementation

The rigorousness of model implementation generally results from the great care by the modeller at every modelling step—data preparation, model construction, computer programming, simulation consideration, and results analysis. However, the internal checking in the model of the consistency of I–O tables, the built-in checking in GEMPACK software,

S. Meng, M. Siriwardana, *Assessing the Economic Impact of Tourism*,
DOI 10.1007/978-3-319-40328-1_7

and the model validity tests provide a basic guarantee to the consistency and integrity of the modelling results.

7.1.1 The Accuracy and Consistency of Data

Accurate and reliable data are the foundation of robust modelling results. The main data used in this study are published by the Singapore government, for example, the I–O data and the tourism survey data. Besides the rigorous government publishing procedure, the internal consistency in these data is also an indicator of the quality of the data. For example, in the I–O tables, the output of each commodity in the Make matrix should be equal to the total used by all demands in the Absorption matrix; the output of each industry in the Make matrix should equal the total input of each industry in the Absorption matrix; and the total income in the economy (the total of the third quadrant of the Absorption matrix) should be identical to the total expenditure of the economy (the total of the second quadrant of the Absorption matrix).

This accounting identity checking is built into the ORANI-type models. There is an 'assertion' command in GEMPACK. If the accounting identity checking is not satisfied, for example, the difference between the summary of each commodity output and that of each commodity used by the economy is greater than a small number (e.g. 0.001), the assertion is invalid, and then the program will stop. In fact, the computer checking is so restrictive that the original data are most unlikely to satisfy the assertion command due to the rounding error in the process of summation. For the programme to continue running, one has to check and eliminate the rounding error before loading the data into the computer file (har file).

The model can also check the consistency of parameters. As has been explained in Chap. 6, the parameter data are obtained from previous studies or selected by the modeller. Some of them are also subject to the assertion command, for example, the weighted average of Engel elasticity (household expenditure elasticity) should sum up to one. The suitability of other parameters is also subject to sensitivity tests. These will be conducted at the end of this chapter.

7.1.2 The Rigorous Simulation Procedure in GEMPACK

GEMPACK is a suite of software designed for general and partial equilibrium models. GEMPACK version 10 includes a number of software such as WINGEM, RUNGEM, VIEWSOL, VIEWHAR, ANALYSGEM, TABMATE, BUILDGP, and THE CHARTER. The core function of GEMPACK is to provide accurate solutions for an economic model (performed by WINGEM or RUNGEM), but it also contains useful tools that can transform algebraic representation of an economic model to computable codes (TABLO), arrange databases (VIEWHAR), display simulation results (VIEWSOL or GEMPIE), and assist simulation results analyse (THE CHARTER or ANALYSGEM).

To ensure the validity and accuracy of modelling results, a rigorous simulation procedure is developed in GEMPACK. The simulation procedure is slightly different depending on the different programs in GEMPACK. We introduce the procedure of TABLO-generated programs (which is used for our model simulation), but also mention the difference when using GEMSIM. There are mainly four steps for a model simulation, shown in Fig. 7.1.

Step 1 creates the TABLO input file and runs TABLO. To let the GEMPACK software simulate the model, the equation system of the model has to be transformed into a text file with extension TAB, which must satisfy the syntax and semantic requirements. The TABLO mate program can check for the syntax and semantic errors. It can also check the validity and consistency of the sets, variables, coefficients, and other name duplications in the model. The run-TABLO program also can detect any errors in the TABLO input file. If there is any error in the TABLO input file, run-TABLO will fail. If there is no error in the TAB file, the run-TABLO program will generate a FORTRAN program based on the TABLO input file—the TABLO-generated program.

In step 2, a FORTRAN compiler will compile and link the FORTRAN code in the TABLO-generated program and produce an executable file—the executable image of the TABLO-generated program. If step 1 succeeds, step 2 normally will proceed without an error.

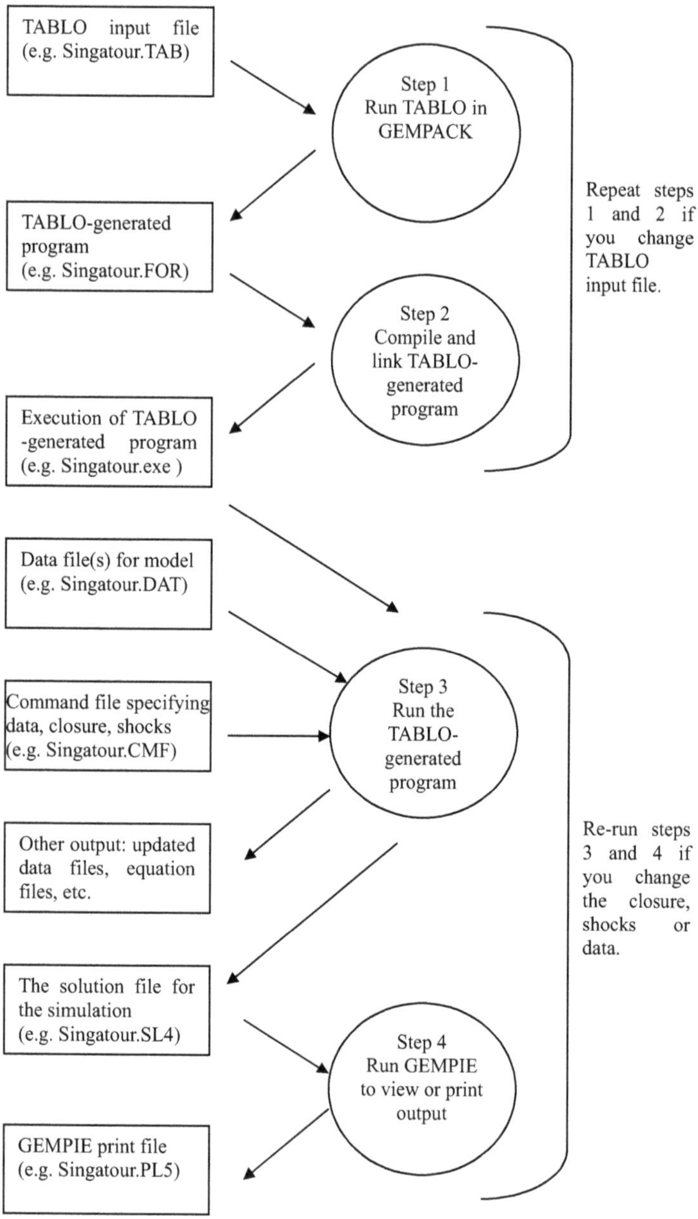

Fig. 7.1 Steps in carrying out a simulation in GEMPACK

With the executable file, command file, and the data files, step 3 is to conduct a simulation, and the simulation results are recorded in output files (such as the solution file, the updated data file, summary file, etc.). In this step, the programme will check the consistency between the data file and TABLO file, for example, the set name, set size, coefficient name, and argument type. Any inconsistency will lead to the programme failing with a log file indicating the types of inconsistency.

The setting of exogenous or endogenous variables (model closure) and specification of shocks comprise the main part of the command file. Since the model is a system of equations and variables, we can pair the equations and the variables for solution, which are assumed endogenous. All variables unmatched by equations are left exogenous. The exogenous variables can be an instrument for imposing shocks. In step 3, the software will check the validity of closure and shocks. If there are any problems in the TABLO file which affect the validity of closure or shocks, the programme will stop with an error message such as 'error in Bach model', invalid variable, or structural singular matrix. Simulation proceeds only if no errors are found.

In step 4, the users can use the GEMPIE, viewSOL, or AnalyseGE to view and/or print the simulation results. Take viewSOL as an example. The percentage change or nominal change of the variables will be displayed. If there are abnormal results such as the changed sign of some variables (or more than 100% decrease in variables), the system will issue a warning. The summary file contains the coefficients that can be used to diagnose any problems in the simulation.

For GEMSIM, step 2 is omitted—step 1 will generate GEMSIM Auxiliary files. Then step 3 will directly run the GEMSIM Auxiliary file combined with the data files and command file to produce the simulation results.

7.1.3 Model Validity Tests

Besides the error detection in the simulation procedure, GEMPACK also provides some validity tests to detect other errors in the model. The major tests include the price homogeneity test, the real homogeneity test, and the GDP test.

Price homogeneity test: Price homogeneity is an axiom of neoclassical economic theory, which claims that economic agents respond to changes of relative prices instead of a change in the price level. As such, a uniform increase in all prices will not affect any real variables, namely there is no money illusion in the model.

To perform the test, we can use the exchange rate or the consumer price index as the numeraire. For example, if we set all exogenous variables to zero (no change) except for the CPI, all endogenous nominal variables should change by the same proportion as that of the CPI, while all real variables will have zero change. If this is not the case, there must be some computational problems in the model.

Real homogeneity test: The real homogeneity test is a test of constant returns to scale, which is assumed in most CGE models including the present model. Constant returns to scale imply that if all inputs into production double, all outputs will double. So if we shock all real exogenous variables by 1%, all endogenous real variables should move in the same direction by 1%, and all nominal variables should be unchanged. If not, there must be some problems in the model.

GDP test: the GDP test is based on the fact that the GDP can be calculated either from the expenditure side or from the income side. The GDP from the expenditure side is made up of household consumption, investment, government expenditure, and the trade balance, while from the income side it consists of tax payments and total payments to factors of production. In the TABLO code, we write formulae to calculate the GDP from both sides, so we can check if the results are identical.

Besides the above simulation procedure and tests, other methods can also be adopted to ensure the correctness of simulation results. For example, the updated database should be balanced (satisfying the accounting identity), and signs in updated database should be correct. The model for this study has passed all the above tests and other possible debugging strategies.

7.2 Simulation Design

Simulation design involves simulation environment and scenario design. The economic environment for simulation concerns the different closures used for the short run and for the long run, and their implications to modelling results. Scenario design is largely related to the central research question. Both the background information collected in Chap. 3 and the review of previous studies on CGE modelling on tourism are important to form modelling scenarios.

7.2.1 Economic Environment for Simulation

The basic economic environment for modelling is selected according to the reality of Singapore, for example, competitive markets, a price taker in the world market, and flexible exchange rate regime. The other considerations about the economic environment involve a time frame because the effects of the tourism demand in the short run may differ from that in the long run. We start with the long-run economic environment.

In the long run, capital can move between industries to achieve an economy-wide rate of return. In the meantime, the real wage rate is flexible while the total employment is fixed. Moreover, Singapore must maintain its internal or external balance in the long run, so the government budget and trade balance are set as exogenous. The environment for long-run simulation is shown in Fig. 7.2.

Figure 7.2 shows that the exogenous rate of return on capital predominantly affects the capital stock while the effective employment also influences it through factor substitution effects. On the other hand, the real wage rate is determined by the level of effective employment (labour shortage can bid up the real wage rate), but it is also affected by the rate of return on capital through the factor-price frontier. Given the exogenous effective employment and the determined capital stock, real GDP and investment are endogenously settled, and real private consumption is determined by the level of household disposable income. While the level of imports is subject to Armington substitution effects, the levels of tourism spending and exports are driven by prices of domestic goods. Trade balance is exogenous, and it puts a constraint on endogenous exports and imports. Tax rates affect all

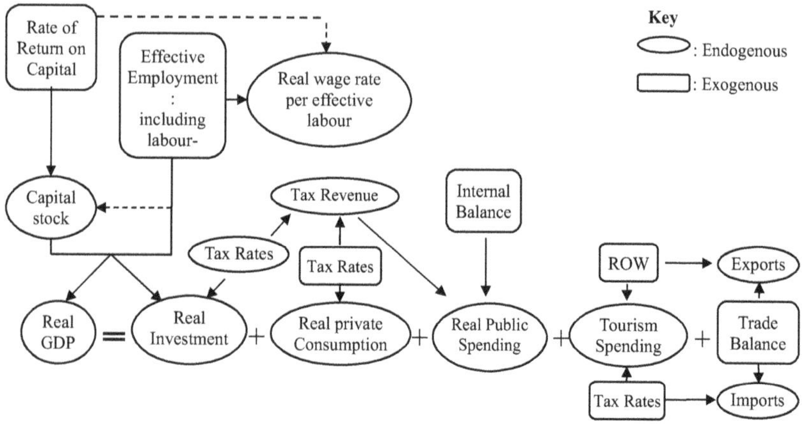

Fig. 7.2 Macroeconomic closure in the long run

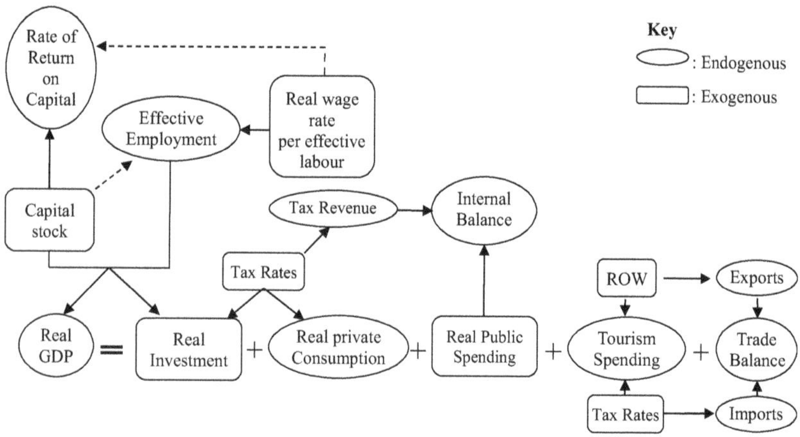

Fig. 7.3 Macroeconomic closure in the short run

demands except those of government and exporters. Government spending (real public consumption) is assumed to follow household consumption. The difference between tax revenue and government spending determines the internal balance, which is set as exogenous and influences tax revenue (through change in tax rate on investment) and government spending.

Macroeconomic closure in the short run is different in a number of ways, as shown in Fig. 7.3. In the labour market, the real wage rate is assumed fixed due to real wage rigidity (this will give the simulation some Keynesian flavour), and it determines the level of employment (higher real wages induce more labour supply). In the capital market, the total capital stock is assumed fixed and so is the real investment by industry. This imposes capital immobility between industries in the short run. Different levels of capital stock in different industries, together with the level of the real wage rate, determine the rate of return on capital for each industry. Government spending is assumed fixed in the short run. Since Singapore is a modern open economy, it is reasonable to assume that, in the short run, it is not subject to either an internal or external balance constraint—the Singapore government can borrow money from households or from foreigners. Thus, the government budget and trade balance can be set as endogenous. However, this assumption must be treated with caution. The deterioration of internal or external balance must be to a controllable extent; otherwise, the economy will either enter a super inflation cycle or become insolvent, as shown by many debt crises in Europe and in Latin America in recent decades.

7.2.2 Simulation Plans

To assess the impact of inbound tourism in detail, it is desirable to investigate the effects of tourism demand components and also put tourism demand in a different environment and under the influence of different tourism policies. Therefore, this study will investigate the impact of tourism demand in the following three aspects:

Effects of Various Tourism Demand Components A number of factors are considered in this simulation plan. First, we disaggregate tourism demand into two groups: tourism shopping demand and tourism service demand. The reasons for this disaggregation are: (1) tourism shopping spending behaviour greatly differs from non-shopping tourism spending and (2) tourism shopping is a very important part of total tourism demand. According to the STB tourism survey, the tourism shopping accounts for around half of total expenditure in recent years.

Second, we disaggregate tourism demand based on tourism generating markets. STB tourism survey data reveal the contribution of international tourism by seven regions, comprising 21 countries. We simulate the effects at country level but, due to the length constraint, we present the effects of tourism demands mainly by region.

Last, the recent STB tourism survey reveals that inbound tourism has increased by an average of 8% per year, so an 8% increase in total tourism demand, and in its different components, is suitable to be used as a shock to assess the economic impact.

Impact of Tourism Demand in a Special Economic Environment In normal economic times, tourism contributes positively to economic growth. However, the economic growth is not smooth. Negative mega economic events frequently occur in modern times, such as the Asian Financial Crisis, Bird flu, 9/11 event, Foot and Mouth disease, the global financial crisis, and the Europe debt crisis. In the case of negative mega events, tourism demand will decline significantly (e.g. tourism demand in Singapore contracted by around 13% during the Global Financial Crisis). The substantial decrease in tourism demand exerts a powerful contractive force on the economy, so it is desirable to find a way to overcome this negative effect.

In this study, we use the global financial crisis as an example to gauge the effects of negative mega events. Since STB estimated that the global financial crisis has caused about a 13% decrease in tourism expenditure in Singapore, a shock of 13% decrease in tourism demand is imposed on the model in the baseline case. Since the global financial crisis has a tremendous negative effect on final demand, four policy responses are considered: a decrease in the power of the GST, indiscriminate subsidy for all industries (decrease in the power of production tax), subsidy for tourism related industries (decrease in the power of production tax for tourism sectors), and a decrease in household income tax rates.

However, there is difficulty in simultaneously assessing the effect of the negative tourism demand shock on the economy and the effects of policy responses on tourism demand. To assess the effects of policy responses on tourism demand, the tourism demand should be endogenous. However, to mimic the effects of the global financial crisis, we need to impose a negative shock on tourism demand, so it should be exogenous. This dilemma is settled by shift variables: we set tourism demand endogenous and shock the quantity shift variable for tourism demand. This shock can be analogized as a change in household income in tourism generating countries. As such, we consider in the baseline case a shift of tourism demand which can generate a 13% decrease in tourism demand.

The sizes of policy responses are based on the tax rates in Singapore and the comparison between different policies. Since the tax rates in Singapore are relatively low (the average GST rate and income tax rate are 6% and 7%, respectively[1]), a small shock on tax rates is appropriate. This study considers a 0.5% decrease in the power of GST (for 6% GST rate, the power of tax would decrease by 1.06 − 0.0053 = 1.0547, so the GST rate becomes 5.47%, a decrease of 0.53%). The proper size of shocks on other tax rates (production tax rate and income tax rate) is chosen so that the total tax revenue loss can match that of 0.5% decrease in the power of GST.

Impact of Tourism Demand under Different Tourism Polices Realizing that tourism plays a very important role in Singaporean economy, the Singaporean government actively fosters tourism industry. For example, to encourage tourism shopping, the Singaporean government offers to return GST to tourists when they leave Singapore. It also provides tax reduction or subsidies to the tourism industry such as the tourism development assistance scheme (TDAS) and double tax deduction (DTD) scheme. The Singapore tourism board (STB) is also very active in developing business events (e.g. conferences, festivals, exhibitions, and sports and culture events). The "Be in Singapore" incentive scheme committed S$170 million to finance these events over the five years (2006–2010). Thanks to the effort of the STB, numerous business activities have been staged in Singapore, including hosting Formula One racing and building two casinos.

This effort of the Singaporean government should be effective in developing Singapore tourism and the economy, but the effectiveness of these policies has not been quantified. By simulating the impact of

---

[1] The income tax rate is lower than the 15 % flat income tax rate in Singapore because the income to corporate is attribute to households in the model and income tax rate on corporate income is lower.

tourism demand under each tourism policy, we can compare the effectiveness of each policy and provide a direction for future tourism policies.

Singapore tourism policies are embodied in the following shocks: reduction of the GST on tourism shopping (GST return on leaving policy), decrease in the power of production tax for tourism sectors (DTD scheme), and output increase in conventional tourism sectors (TDAS). An additional GST reduction shock is used on total tourism expenditure to test the effects of reducing the tax rate on both tourism shopping and tourism services.

Since we tend to test the effects of tourism policies in normal economic times, the baseline case is the tourism demand growth rate at normal economic times (8%) generated by a shock on the tourism quantity shifter. In GST deduction scenarios, 4% deductions in the tax rate are imposed on (1) tourism shopping expenditure and (2) total tourism expenditure. The size of the decrease in production tax rate for tourism sectors and the size of subsidy in tourism activity subsidy policy are chosen so that the total loss of tax revenue is the same as that of 4% GST reduction on total tourism expenditure. To mimic TDAS, an average 30% subsidy rate on tourism projects is assumed (there are four individual schemes in TDAS; the maximum subsidy rates are either 20% or 50%, so we use 30% as an average), so S$1 of government spending will generate S$1/0.30 = S$3.33 output (using the zero profit assumption). Once a tourism project (e.g. building of casinos) is established, it will last for a long period of time. If the project is assumed to last for a ten-year period, the output of this project should be magnified by 10 times. As such, a S$1 subsidy in the conventional tourism sector will induce S$1/0.30*10 = S$33.33 output.

In summary, we have the following three simulation plans to test the effects of tourism demand. Each simulation plan consists of a number of simulations.

(1) The Contribution of Tourism Spending Patterns and Tourism Generating Markets

Scenario 1: 8% increase in tourism shopping demand;
Scenario 2: 8% increase in tourism service demand;

Scenario 3: 8% increase in total tourism demand; and
Scenarios 4 to 10: 8% increase in tourism demand, from each of 7 tourism generating regions (or 21 tourism generating countries).

(2) The Impact of Tourism During a Negative Mega Event And Policy Responses

Scenario 1: 13% decrease in tourism demand induced by 16.552% decrease in tourism demand shifter (baseline case);
Scenario 2: baseline case plus a 0.5% decrease in the power of GST;
Scenario 3: baseline case plus a 0.786% decrease (in absolute term) in production tax rate for all industries;
Scenario 4: baseline case plus a 2.0124% decrease (in absolute term) in production tax rate for tourism industries; and
Scenario 5: baseline case plus a 3.03% decrease (in absolute term) in income tax rate.

(3) The Effectiveness of Current Singaporean Tourism Policies

Scenario 1: 8% increase in the total tourism demand induced by 9.08% increase in the tourism demand shifter (baseline case);
Scenario 2: baseline case plus a 4% deduction in the power of the GST on total tourism expenditure;
Scenario 3: baseline case plus a 4% deduction in the power of the GST on tourism shopping;
Scenario 4: baseline case plus a 0.138% reduction (in absolute term) in the production tax rate for tourism sectors; and
Scenario 5: baseline case plus S$81.282 million production tax relief as well as a total output increase of 81.282*33.33 = S$2709.408 million for each of four traditional tourism industries—food and beverage, accommodation, sightseeing, and recreation sectors.

7.3 Sensitivity Tests

In the implementation of the model, we have used a number of behaviour parameters. Some of them are based on estimations by econometricians, but some are assigned values based on economic knowledge and assumptions. So it is not valid to claim that all parameter values used in the model reflect reality. If some values are wrongly assigned and the simulation results are sensitive to these values, the modelling results will not be reliable. Besides, we use 100% indexation of money wage to CPI. This full indexation may not be the case in reality. Thus, the sensitivity test is necessary for the behavioural parameter values used in the model.

There are many behavioural parameters in the model, including the tourism demand elasticity, the export demand elasticity, the product transformation elasticity, and the substitution elasticities between imported and domestically produced intermediate inputs (Armington elasticity), between tourism shopping and tourism services, between occupation groups, and between labour and capital. We put these elasticities into three groups. They are: the demand elasticities (including tourism demand and export demand), the product transformation elasticities, and the substitution elasticities. We conduct sensitivity tests on these three groups as well as on wage indexation. At the end of this section, we introduce the systematic sensitivity analysis (SSA) provided by RunGEM; SSA can indicate the overall sensitivity of modelling results.

7.3.1 Testing Tourism and Export Demand Elasticities

In normal sensitivity tests, we double and halve the values which are used in the model application and compare the new simulation results with the baseline case. In this model application, however, we assume that the tourism demand and most exports are very elastic and have chosen relatively high values for them. Thus, in the tests for tourism and exports demand, we test downwards. That is to halve and quarter the value used in model application.

In testing the demand elasticity, it is desirable to check the results of tourism policies which may be sensitive to demand elasticity values. In the foregoing analysis, we find the policy of GST deduction on the tourism demand causes substantial change in our simulations. So it is important to reexamine the simulation results of the GST deduction policy with different tourism demand elasticities. Based on this consideration, we choose scenario 3 in the tourism policy simulation plan as the baseline case. The results of sensitivity tests are shown in Table 7.1.

A glance at Table 7.1 shows that the values used for the tourism demand elasticities in the previous simulation are moderately sensitive, while those for exports demand elasticities are only slightly sensitive. Since there are many indicators in Table 7.1, we select only some major ones to discuss. For the whole economy, the GDP price index, the exchange rate, the real GDP, the average real wage, and the contribution of BOT to real GDP are important indicators. Since tourism is the focus of our study, the tourism price index and real tourism expenditure require consideration. Moreover, since the total indirect tax revenue is the benchmark in deciding the size of shocks for simulations, it also needs our attention.

The sensitivity of the tourism demand elasticity values manifests itself in almost all indicators. Take the real GDP as an example. When the elasticity values are halved, the simulation results change by 12% from 0.057 to 0.050. The real tourism expenditure results also experience large change, from 12.099 in the baseline case down to 10.666 when the elasticity values are halved, and further down to 9.893 when the elasticity values are quartered. This indicates that the simulation results tend to be high when the tourism demand elasticity is a key element in simulations, for example, under the tourism GST deduction policies. However, even so, the results of sensitivity tests show that the general conclusions about the tourism GST deduction policies still hold: even if the tourism demand elasticity is quartered, the simulation results for the GST deduction policies are still much better than for the other two policies.

The exports demand elasticity values show different degrees of sensitivity according to different indicators. When the values are halved, the real GDP results change around 3% from 0.057 to 0.059, the real tourism expenditure results change less than 0.4% from 12.099 to 12.053, and the tourism price index results change around 0.5% from −1.507 to −1.500. Similar marginal change occurs to the total indirect tax revenue, and the contribution of BOT to real GDP. From all these indicators, the values

Table 7.1 Results of sensitivity tests for tourism and export demand elasticities

8 % increase in tourism demand and 4 % GST deduction on tourism shopping	(1) Baseline case	(2) Tourism demand elasticity (half)	(3) Tourism demand elasticity (quarter)	(4) Exports demand elasticity (half)	(5) Exports demand elasticity (quarter)
Indirect taxes*	−123.458	−136.289	−143.238	−120.49	−116.796
Production tax*	11.495	10.147	9.416	12.355	13.074
Tariff revenue*	−0.615	−0.542	−0.506	0.173	1.286
Tax on tourism shopping*	−201.653	−205.226	−207.139	−201.741	−201.832
Taxes on tourism service*	65.544	57.767	53.539	65.345	65.142
GDP price index	−0.08	−0.083	−0.085	−0.062	−0.039
Exchange rate (local currency/ $world)	−0.127	−0.112	−0.104	−0.14	−0.155
Real devaluation	−0.047	−0.029	−0.019	−0.078	−0.116
Terms of trade	0.018	0.016	0.015	0.026	0.038
Exports price (local currency)	−0.109	−0.096	−0.089	−0.114	−0.117
Tourism shopping price	−3.755	−3.784	−3.799	−3.748	−3.744
Tourism service price	0.986	0.881	0.823	0.994	1.002
Tourism price index	−1.507	−1.571	−1.606	−1.5	−1.493
Employment (wage bill weights)	0	0	0	0	0
Average real wage	0.074	0.065	0.061	0.096	0.121
Aggregate payments to capital	0.009	0.008	0.007	0.028	0.057
Aggregate payments to labour	0.074	0.065	0.061	0.096	0.121
Nominal GDP	−0.023	−0.033	−0.038	−0.004	0.022
Real GDP	0.057	0.05	0.046	0.059	0.061
Utility per household	0.077	0.068	0.064	0.119	0.174
Household nominal income	0.038	0.034	0.031	0.058	0.086
Real household consumption	0.042	0.037	0.034	0.064	0.094
Real tourism shopping expenditure	12.989	11.459	10.638	12.943	12.897

Real tourism service expenditure	11.132	9.808	9.088	11.087	11.041
Total real tourism expenditure	12.099	10.666	9.893	12.053	12.008
Value of imports plus duty	−0.155	−0.136	−0.126	−0.152	−0.147
Import volume	−0.028	−0.024	−0.023	−0.011	0.008
Nominal exports (local currency)	−0.372	−0.328	−0.304	−0.365	−0.355
Export volume	−0.263	−0.232	−0.215	−0.252	−0.239
Contribution of BOT to real GDP*	−0.575	−0.506	−0.47	−0.581	−0.591
BOT/GDP (Nominal)*	−0.006	−0.005	−0.005	−0.006	−0.005

Source: Authors

*denotes nominal value

for the export demand elasticity are only marginally sensitive. However, the changes in the GDP price index, the exchange rate, and the average real wages are much larger but still at moderate level. Overall, the simulation results are slightly sensitive to the value of the exports demand elasticities.

7.3.2 Testing Wage Indexation and Product Transformation Elasticities

Through our analysis, we learnt that the short-run effects generally display larger change than the long-run effects. To avoid bias, we use as the benchmark the 8% increase in the tourism demand in the short run. The results of tests are listed in Table 7.2.

The results of sensitivity tests show that the wage indexation rates are completely insensitive. These results stem from the simulation assumption. We assume a flexible exchange rate regime and a fixed CPI in model simulations. Since the CPI does not change, any indexation rate will not affect money wages and thus will not affect the simulation results.

The values for CET elasticities demonstrate minor sensitivity. The results on total indirect tax revenue, real GDP, real tourism expenditure, and contribution of BOT to real GDP are marginally sensitive. But the results on the GDP price index, the exchange rate, the tourism price index, and the aggregate employment are moderately sensitive. Overall, the CET elasticity values are mildly sensitive, so the modelling results based on them are reliable.

7.3.3 Testing Substitution Elasticities

To test the substitution elasticities, we use the same baseline case as testing the production transformation elasticity. Since the tests involve a number of substitution elasticities and the real GDP is a good indicator of testing results, we display in Fig. 7.4 the changes in real GDP of each test.

Figure 7.4 shows that the simulation results are marginally sensitive to the values we used in model applications for the Armington elasticity

Table 7.2 Results of sensitivity tests for supply and product transformation elasticities

8 % increase in tourism demand in the short run	(1) Baseline case	(2) Money wage indexation (80 %)	(3) Money wage indexation (50 %)	(4) CET function elasticity (half)	(5) CET function elasticity (double)
Indirect taxes*	99.533	99.533	99.533	98.846	100.42
Production tax*	9.684	9.684	9.684	10.576	8.539
Tariff revenue*	3.163	3.163	3.163	2.172	4.451
Tax on tourism shopping*	34.544	34.544	34.544	34.306	34.904
Taxes on tourism service*	46.338	46.338	46.338	46.189	46.554
GDP price index	0.015	0.015	0.015	0.016	0.013
Exchange rate (local currency/$world)	–0.084	–0.084	–0.084	–0.089	–0.078
Real devaluation	–0.099	–0.099	–0.099	–0.106	–0.09
Terms of trade	0.01	0.01	0.01	0.01	0.009
Exports price (local currency)	–0.075	–0.075	–0.075	–0.08	–0.068
Tourism shopping price	0.154	0.154	0.154	0.164	0.139
Tourism service price	0.692	0.692	0.692	0.744	0.61
Tourism price index	0.41	0.41	0.41	0.44	0.363
Employment (wage bill weights)	0.093	0.093	0.093	0.085	0.101
Average real wage	0	0	0	0	0
Aggregate payments to capital	0.031	0.031	0.031	0.034	0.027
Aggregate payments to labour	0.093	0.093	0.093	0.085	0.101
Nominal GDP	0.098	0.098	0.098	0.096	0.099
Real GDP	0.083	0.083	0.083	0.079	0.087
Utility per household	0.12	0.12	0.12	0.116	0.123

(continued)

Table 7.2 (continued)

8 % increase in tourism demand in the short run	(1) Baseline case	(2) Money wage indexation (80 %)	(3) Money wage indexation (50 %)	(4) CET function elasticity (half)	(5) CET function elasticity (double)
Household nominal income	0.059	0.059	0.059	0.057	0.06
Real household consumption	0.065	0.065	0.065	0.062	0.066
Real tourism shopping expenditure	8.096	8.096	8.096	8.029	8.198
Real tourism service expenditure	7.894	7.894	7.894	7.811	8.021
Total real tourism expenditure	8	8	8	7.925	8.114
Value of imports plus duty	−0.076	−0.076	−0.076	−0.085	−0.065
Import volume	0.008	0.008	0.008	0.005	0.013
Nominal exports (local currency)	−0.218	−0.218	−0.218	−0.226	−0.209
Export volume	−0.143	−0.143	−0.143	−0.146	−0.141
Contribution of BOT to real GDP*	−0.363	−0.363	−0.363	−0.361	−0.366
BOT/GDP (nominal)*	−0.004	−0.004	−0.004	−0.004	−0.004

Source: Authors

*denotes nominal value

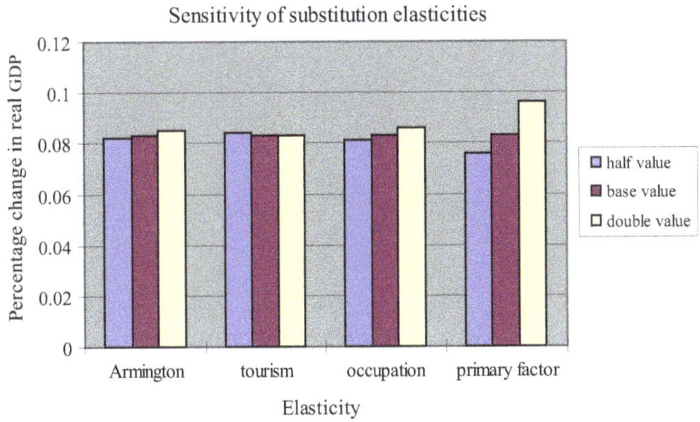

Fig. 7.4 Results of sensitivity tests for substitution elasticities

(between imported and locally produced intermediate inputs) and tourism elasticity (between tourism shopping and tourism services), are slightly sensitive to the value of occupation elasticity (between different occupation groups), and are moderately sensitive to values of primary factor elasticity (between capital and labour). The moderate sensitivity of primary factor elasticity value is a little worrying as it may vary the simulation results to a certain degree. However, the moderate-level sensitivity does not affect the general conclusions we obtained. Moreover, the values for the primary factor elasticity are obtained from the GTAP database, which are estimated by econometricians, and thus we should think they are close to reality. Nevertheless, we should bear in mind that, when the values for this elasticity are higher, the simulated economic growth could be higher.

7.3.4 Systematic Sensitivity Analysis

The systematic sensitivity analysis (SSA) is described by Arndt and Pearson (1998) and is based on the Gaussian quadrature method by Stroud (1957), Liu (1996), and De Vuyst and Preckel (1997). RUNGEM program provides a function for SSA. Click on the 'Tools' menu on the main interface of RUNGEM, there will be three options appearing: SSA with respect to parameters, SSA with respect to shocks, and help on SSA. The first option can test the sensitivity of all parameters, and the second option can test the sensitivity of all shocks. The program can generate the

Table 7.3 The results of systematic sensitivity tests

100 % increase in total tourism demand in the long run	Modelling results	Mean value	Standard deviation
Nominal GDP	0.879	0.885	0.02
Real GDP	0.535	0.536	0.002
Employment (wage bill weights)	0	0	0
Average real wage	0.854	0.861	0.034
Aggregate payments to capital	0.02	0.026	0.025
Aggregate payments to labour	0.854	0.861	0.034
GDP price index	0.342	0.348	0.019
Exchange rate (local currency/ $world)	−1.102	−1.105	0.016
Real devaluation	−1.439	−1.448	0.027
Terms of trade	0.16	0.163	0.007
Exports price (local currency)	−0.943	−0.944	0.013
Tourism shopping price	1.33	1.331	0.016
Tourism service price	6.504	6.515	0.152
Tourism price index	4.179	4.185	0.084
Utility per household	0.801	0.814	0.043
Household nominal income	0.394	0.4	0.021
Real household consumption	0.431	0.438	0.023
CPF funds*	3.351	3.367	0.002
Real tourism shopping expenditure	101.623	101.627	0.046
Real tourism service expenditure	98.718	98.716	0.036
Total real tourism expenditure	100	100	0.004
Value of imports plus duty	−1.409	−1.409	0.023
Import volume	−0.311	−0.307	0.02
Value of exports (local currency, f.o.b.)	−3.232	−3.231	0.022
Export volume	−2.311	−2.309	0.018
Contribution of BOT to real GDP*	−4.862	−4.865	0.011
BOT/GDP (nominal)*	−0.049	−0.049	0
Total indirect taxes*	1158.267	1159.259	3.932
Production tax*	101.016	101.208	1.736
Tariff revenue*	−2.118	−1.969	3.051
Tax on tourism shopping*	436.202	436.221	0.233
Taxes on tourism service*	603.067	603.183	1.689

*Nominal change: Singapore dollars (million)

Source: Based on author's simulation test results

mean value and standard deviation for each simulation conducted in RUNGEM.

We have used RUNGEM to perform an SSA for our Singapore tourism model. An independent, symmetric, triangular distribution of parameters is assumed, and the Stroud method is adopted with 50% variation in parameter values (e.g. the minimum and maximum values used are, respectively, 0.5 and 1.5 times of values used in the model). The tests are conducted for a baseline scenario that the total tourism demand increases by 100% in the long run. The macro results of SSA are listed in Table 7.3.

The mean values in Table 7.3 are very close to the modelling results. With the exception of the last panel, the differences are less than 0.1. Although the difference in the last panel can be as large as 1 (e.g. a difference of 0.992 for total indirect taxes), given the large mean value for the nominal variables, the difference as percentage change of mean value is very small. The largest difference in percentage form happens to tariff revenue: $(-1.969 + 2.118)/1.969*100\% = 7.6\%$. This is also an acceptable testing result.

The standard deviations for the first four panels are tiny: with the exception of 0.152 for tourism service price, all are less than 0.1. The standard deviation for the last panel seems relatively big (e.g. 3.932 for total indirect taxes), but given the large mean value, they are very small in percentage form. However, caution should be taken for the result of tariff revenue. With a small mean value of −1.969, it has a relatively large standard deviation of 3.051. By adding one standard deviation from the negative mean value, the change in tariff revenue becomes positive. This means that the estimated result for tariff revenue could increase or decrease as the parameter values in the model change. Thus, we can conclude that most simulation results are insensitive to the parameter values in the model, but tariff revenue is sensitive to the change of parameter values.

References

Arndt, C., & Pearson, K. R. (1998). Implementing Systematic Sensitivity Analysis Using GEMPACK. *GTAP Technical Paper,* 3, 45–50.

De Vuyst, E. A., & Preckel, P. V. (1997). Sensitivity analysis revisited: A quadrature-based approach. *Journal of Policy Modeling, 19*(2), 175–185.

Liu, S. (1996). *Gaussian Quadrature and its Applications.* Unpublished doctoral dissertation, Department of Agricultural Economics, Purdue University.

Stroud, A. H. (1957). Remarks on the disposition of points in numerical integration formulas. *Mathematical Tables and Other Aids to Computation, 11*, 257–261.

8

Interpretation of Results from a Tourism CGE Model

Using the modelling results from the Singapore tourism industry, this chapter demonstrates how to analyse the modelling results categorically and rigorously. The chapter consists of three sections. Section 8.1 analyses the impact of tourism demand by type (tourism shopping and tourism service) and by generating markets. Section 8.2 assesses the impact of a negative mega event like GFC and of policy responses. Section 8.3 gauges the effectiveness of Singaporean tourism policies.

8.1 The Impact of Disaggregated Tourism Demand[1]

In this section, we investigate the effects of tourism spending patterns as well as tourism-generating markets. The economic impact is discussed through three aspects: macroeconomic effects, sectoral effects, and

[1] Section 8.1 has been significantly revised from Journal of Travel & Tourism Marketing, 31:1071–1089, 2014, 'The Role of Inbound Tourism in the Singaporean Economy: A Computable General Equilibrium (CGE) Assessment' by Samuel Meng.

S. Meng, M. Siriwardana, *Assessing the Economic Impact of Tourism*,
DOI 10.1007/978-3-319-40328-1_8

employment effects. All simulation results are shown as percentage change, except variables with * in macroeconomic effects.

8.1.1 The Macroeconomic Effects

The macroeconomic effects in the short and long run are shown in Tables 8.1 and 8.2, respectively. We start with the short-run effects of an 8 % increase in total tourism demand, which are displayed in the third column in Table 8.1.

First, the overall effects are indicated by changes in the GDP and employment. The change in nominal GDP and employment (0.098 % and 0.094 %, respectively) shows that tourism alone generates nearly 0.1 % growth in the Singaporean economy and employment.[2] However, in terms of real GDP, the contribution is slightly lower (0.084 %). The smaller change in real GDP is explained by the increase in price level—although CPI is assumed unchanged in the model simulation (the incipient change in CPI is fully expressed by the change in the exchange rate), the GDP price index increases by 0.015 %. Employment follows the nominal GDP closely because the employment data in the model is wage-bill weighted.

Second, the changes in prices are not even. Understandably, the tourism price index increases by 0.417 % because of the increase in tourism demand. In disaggregating the tourism price index into tourism service price and tourism shopping price, it is interesting to find that the tourism service price increases by 0.707 % while tourism shopping price rises by only 0.154 %. The significantly larger increase in the tourism service price highlights the importance of tourism demand to the tourism services industry.

The exchange rate (local currency/foreign currency) decreases by 0.085 %, which indicates the implicit rise in price levels due to the

[2] Although 0.1 % seems a small number, the contribution of tourism is very significant due to the large base of GDP and employment. For example, Singapore's GDP was $243,169 million and employment 2733 thousand in 2007 (MIT 2008). Around 8 % growth in tourism demand in 2007 would have induced $243 million GDP growth and created 2733 new jobs. These are significant numbers for a city state economy.

Table 8.1 Macroeconomic effects of tourism components in the short run

Macros	(1) 8 % increase in tourism shopping demand	(2) 8 % increase in tourism service demand	(3) 8 % increase in total tourism demand	(4) 8 % increase in tourism demand (America)	(5) 8 % increase in tourism demand (S.E. Asia)	(6) 8 % increase in tourism demand (N. Asia)	(7) 8 % increase in tourism demand (S. Asia)	(8) 8 % increase in tourism demand (Europe)	(9) 8 % increase in tourism demand (Oceania)	(10) 8 % increase in tourism demand (Africa)
Total indirect taxes*	36.17	63.976	99.789	6.628	38.17	27.04	9.214	9.895	8.055	0.441
Production tax*	2.971	6.824	9.746	0.697	3.505	2.676	0.926	1.022	0.822	0.046
Tariff revenue*	−1.851	5.136	3.213	0.437	0.847	0.775	0.226	0.494	0.37	0.005
Tax on tourism shopping*	34.221	−0.084	34.482	1.423	12.34	11.036	3.98	2.821	2.653	0.194
Taxes on tourism service*	−0.021	47.076	46.515	3.722	18.709	11.257	3.76	4.995	3.808	0.168
GDP price index	0.006	0.009	0.015	0.001	0.005	0.005	0.001	0.002	0.001	0
Exchange rate (local currency/ $world)	−0.035	−0.05	−0.085	−0.006	−0.03	−0.024	−0.009	−0.008	−0.007	0
Real devaluation	−0.042	−0.058	−0.1	−0.007	−0.035	−0.029	−0.01	−0.01	−0.008	0
Terms of trade	0.005	0.004	0.01	0.001	0.004	0.003	0.001	0.001	0.001	0
Exports price (local currency)	−0.03	−0.045	−0.075	−0.005	−0.027	−0.021	−0.008	−0.007	−0.006	0
Tourism shopping price	0.172	−0.02	0.154	0.006	0.052	0.049	0.02	0.013	0.013	0.001
Tourism service price	−0.004	0.721	0.707	0.063	0.235	0.206	0.057	0.094	0.065	0.004
Tourism price index	0.09	0.339	0.417	0.033	0.139	0.124	0.037	0.052	0.038	0.002

(continued)

Table 8.1 (continued)

Macros	(1) 8 % increase in tourism shopping demand	(2) 8 % increase in tourism service demand	(3) 8 % increase in total tourism demand	(4) 8 % increase in tourism demand (America)	(5) 8 % increase in tourism demand (S.E. Asia)	(6) 8 % increase in tourism demand (N. Asia)	(7) 8 % increase in tourism demand (S. Asia)	(8) 8 % increase in tourism demand (Europe)	(9) 8 % increase in tourism demand (Oceania)	(10) 8 % increase in tourism demand (Africa)
Employment (wage bill weights)	0.009	0.085	0.094	0.006	0.045	0.02	0.005	0.009	0.006	0
Average real wage	0	0	0	0	0	0	0	0	0	0
Aggregate payments to capital	0.015	0.017	0.032	0.002	0.01	0.01	0.003	0.004	0.003	0
Aggregate payments to labour	0.009	0.085	0.094	0.006	0.045	0.02	0.005	0.009	0.006	0
Nominal GDP	0.027	0.071	0.098	0.006	0.04	0.025	0.008	0.01	0.008	0
Real GDP	0.021	0.063	0.083	0.005	0.035	0.021	0.006	0.008	0.006	0
Utility per household	0.025	0.097	0.121	0.008	0.052	0.03	0.008	0.012	0.009	0.001
Household nominal income	0.012	0.047	0.059	0.004	0.026	0.014	0.004	0.006	0.004	0
Real household consumption	0.013	0.052	0.065	0.004	0.028	0.016	0.004	0.007	0.005	0
Real tourism shopping expenditure	8	0	8.082	0.334	2.898	2.588	0.932	0.661	0.622	0.045

Real tourism service expenditure	0	8	7.911	0.63	3.244	1.888	0.644	0.836	0.644	0.027
Total real tourism expenditure	1.254	3.942	8	0.473	3.059	2.26	0.797	0.743	0.632	0.037
Value of imports plus duty	−0.025	−0.051	−0.076	−0.006	−0.026	−0.022	−0.008	−0.008	−0.007	0
Import volume	0.01	−0.002	0.008	0	0.004	0.002	0.001	0.001	0	0
Value of exports (local currency border)	−0.103	−0.115	−0.218	−0.014	−0.08	−0.063	−0.022	−0.021	−0.018	−0.001
Export volume	−0.073	−0.07	−0.144	−0.009	−0.053	−0.041	−0.015	−0.014	−0.012	−0.001
Contribution of BOT to real GDP*	−0.2	−0.163	−0.363	−0.021	−0.137	−0.104	−0.037	−0.034	−0.029	−0.002
BOT/GDP (Nominal)*	−0.002	−0.002	−0.004	0	−0.001	−0.001	0	0	0	0

Source: Authors

*Nominal change: Singapore dollars (million)

Table 8.2 Macroeconomic effects of tourism components in the long run

Macros	(1) 8 % increase in tourism shopping demand	(2) 8 % increase in tourism service demand	(3) 8 % increase in total tourism demand	(4) 8 % increase in tourism demand (America)	(5) 8 % increase in tourism demand (S.E. Asia)	(6) 8 % increase in tourism demand (N. Asia)	(7) 8 % increase in tourism demand (S. Asia)	(8) 8 % increase in tourism demand (Europe)	(9) 8 % increase in tourism demand (Oceania)	(10) 8 % increase in tourism demand (Africa)
Indirect taxes*	34.934	55.363	90.007	6.017	33.612	24.847	8.64	8.952	7.367	0.394
Production tax*	2.746	5.086	7.796	0.575	2.588	2.245	0.814	0.835	0.686	0.037
Tariff revenue*	−2.256	2.199	−0.107	0.23	−0.705	0.035	0.033	0.176	0.137	−0.011
Tax on tourism shopping*	34.222	−0.073	34.502	1.424	12.35	11.04	3.981	2.823	2.654	0.194
Taxes on tourism service*	−0.012	47.156	46.592	3.727	18.743	11.272	3.764	5.001	3.813	0.168
GDP price index	0.007	0.015	0.022	0.001	0.008	0.006	0.002	0.002	0.002	0
Exchange rate (local currency/ $world)	−0.035	−0.05	−0.085	−0.006	−0.031	−0.024	−0.009	−0.008	−0.007	0
Real devaluation	−0.042	−0.065	−0.107	−0.007	−0.039	−0.03	−0.01	−0.011	−0.009	−0.001
Terms of trade	0.005	0.006	0.012	0.001	0.005	0.003	0.001	0.001	0.001	0
Exports price (local currency)	−0.03	−0.044	−0.073	−0.005	−0.026	−0.021	−0.008	−0.007	−0.006	0
Tourism shopping price	0.172	−0.017	0.156	0.006	0.054	0.05	0.02	0.014	0.013	0.001
Tourism service price	−0.002	0.735	0.723	0.063	0.242	0.209	0.057	0.096	0.066	0.004
Tourism price index	0.09	0.347	0.426	0.034	0.143	0.126	0.038	0.053	0.038	0.002
Employment (wage bill weights)	0	0	0	0	0	0	0	0	0	0
Average real wage	0.005	0.047	0.052	0.003	0.025	0.011	0.003	0.005	0.004	0
Aggregate payments to capital	0.012	−0.007	0.005	0	−0.003	0.004	0.001	0.001	0.001	0

Aggregate payments to labour	0.005	0.047	0.052	0.003	0.025	0.011	0.003	0.005	0.004	0
Nominal GDP	0.024	0.04	0.064	0.004	0.024	0.018	0.006	0.007	0.005	0
Real GDP	0.017	0.025	0.042	0.003	0.016	0.012	0.004	0.004	0.003	0
Utility per household	0.018	0.034	0.053	0.003	0.02	0.015	0.004	0.006	0.004	0
Household nominal income	0.009	0.017	0.026	0.002	0.01	0.007	0.002	0.003	0.002	0
Real household consumption	0.01	0.019	0.028	0.002	0.011	0.008	0.002	0.003	0.002	0
Real tourism shopping expenditure	8	0	8.083	0.334	2.898	2.589	0.932	0.661	0.622	0.045
Real tourism service expenditure	0	8	7.909	0.63	3.243	1.887	0.643	0.835	0.644	0.027
Total real tourism expenditure	1.262	4.031	8	0.473	3.059	2.26	0.797	0.743	0.632	0.037
Value of imports plus duty	−0.029	−0.078	−0.106	−0.007	−0.04	−0.029	−0.01	−0.011	−0.009	0
Import volume	0.007	−0.028	−0.021	−0.002	−0.009	−0.005	−0.001	−0.002	−0.002	0
Value of exports (local currency border)	−0.106	−0.143	−0.249	−0.016	−0.094	−0.069	−0.024	−0.024	−0.02	−0.001
Export volume	−0.077	−0.1	−0.176	−0.011	−0.068	−0.049	−0.016	−0.017	−0.014	−0.001
Contribution of BOT to real GDP*	−0.201	−0.178	−0.379	−0.022	−0.145	−0.107	−0.037	−0.035	−0.03	−0.002
BOT/GDP (Nominal)*	−0.002	−0.002	−0.004	0	−0.001	−0.001	0	0	0	0

Source: Authors

*Nominal change: Singapore dollars (million)

increase in tourism demand. With the 0.015 % increase in the GDP price index and 0.085 % appreciation of Singapore currency, the Singapore dollar is overall inflated by 0.015 + 0.085 = 0.100 % (−0.100 % real devaluation). Given the unchanged world price, the appreciation of the Singapore dollar makes imports cheaper to Singaporeans. In the meantime, it discourages export demand and the decreased export demand leads to a decrease in export prices denominated in local currency. Since the decrease in the price of exports is less than that of imports, Singapore's terms of trade improves by 0.01 %.

Third, the contribution of different factors to real GDP varies. On the income side, capital income (payment to capital) increases by 0.032 % while labour income (payment to labour) increases nearly three times more (0.094 %). The remarkably larger increase in labour income is explained by the fact that the tourism industry is labour intensive. On the expenditure side, the decrease in exports and increase in imports have negative effects on real GDP, which lead to the decrease of both the contribution of balance of trade (BOT) to real GDP and the ratio of BOT to nominal GDP. The positive growth of GDP mainly comes from two final demands: tourism demand and household demand. The 8 % increase in tourism demand is imposed exogenously. Interestingly, this positive tourism demand shock induces a 0.065 % increase in real household consumption. This result can be explained as follows: the increase in tourism demand stimulates production of tourism goods. The expansion of production increases capital and labour income and thus household income by 0.059 %. Under the Keynesian consumption function, household consumption will increase.

Last, the increase in tourism demand can bring considerable tax revenue for the Singaporean government. Total GST tax on tourism shopping and tourism service increases by $80.997 million. Thanks to the increase in other tax revenue (e.g. production tax increases by $9.746 million and the tariff by $3.213 million), the total indirect tax induced by the positive tourism demand shock reaches $99.789 million. The increase in production tax is, understandably, the result of the expansion in the production of tourism goods. The significant increase in tariff revenue comes as a surprise because Singapore is a country with tariffs on only a few kinds of commodities. However, this unexpected result can be explained by the specific tariff policy of the Singapore government and the spending behaviour of tourists. Although most items are tariff free in Singapore, there are very high tariff rates imposed on items such as liquors, tobacco, petroleum products, and motor vehicles. Consumption of these items by tourists is quite high (in the form of drinks, cigarettes, and transportation), so the large increase in tariff revenue is understandable.

The short-run effects of an 8 % increase in tourism shopping and in tourism services are shown in the first two columns of Table 8.1. The overall impression is that the increase in tourism services demand has a larger effect than the increase in tourism shopping demand, which indicates the importance of tourism services demand to the tourism industry. The bigger influence of the tourism services is manifested in many macro variables. The increase in GDP (both real and nominal) in column 2 is three times as much as that in column 1. Household nominal income, real consumption, and utility per household are about four times higher in column 2 than in column 1. Total tax revenue in column 2 is around twice as much as in column 1. In terms of employment, the difference is even bigger. Employment increases by 0.085 % in column 2 but only 0.009 % in column 1. The large difference in employment indicates that the tourism services industry is more labour-intensive than the tourism shopping industry. This employment result is also consistent with the fact that the increase in aggregate payments to capital in column 2 is only slightly higher than that in column 1 while the change in aggregate payments to labour is very different. (The change in aggregate payments to labour is the same as the change in employment since employment is wage weighted and the average real wage is assumed unchanged in the short run.)

However, there are some macro variables for which column 2 has a smaller number. Take the tourism shopping price and tax on tourism shopping as an example. While column 1 has significant positive numbers, column 2 has a small negative number. This can be explained by the nature of the shock and the substitution effects. Since we have imposed a positive shock on tourism shopping in scenario 1, the tourism-shopping-related items should have a bigger number in column 1. The negative number in column 2 can be explained by the substitution effect. As tourists spend more on tourism shopping, under limited budgets, their demand for tourism services will decrease. As a result, the tourism services price and related tax will drop. Since the substitution effect is limited (we assigned a small substitution elasticity value), the decrease is very small.

A similar situation appears for real exports. The negative real export values for both scenarios are expected, since the exchange rate decreases in both cases—the appreciation of the Singapore dollar makes exports more expensive to foreigners. However, the exchange rate decreases more in scenario 2, so the real exports should decrease more in column 2. The only explanation left is that tourism shopping and exporting are competing activities—the goods tourists bought may be part of exports otherwise, so the increase in tourism shopping will directly reduce exports more.

The short-run effects of different tourism-generating markets are shown in the last seven columns of Table 8.1. Two features can be gleaned from the simulation results. One is that the importance of tourism-generating markets differs greatly. Southeast Asia and North Asia are most important to Singapore, as shown by many indicators such as real and nominal GDP, employment, indirect tax revenue, and real household consumption. Due to the increase in tourism demand from Southeast Asia and North Asia, real GDP increases by 0.035 % and 0.021 %, accounting for more than 42 % and 25 % of the total contribution of all markets, respectively. For other markets, Americas, South Asia, Europe, and Oceania have a similar small contribution to Singapore's GDP, and the role of Africa is largely negligible. The other feature is that tourism shopping and tourism services have a different weight in different markets. For North Asia, South Asia, and Africa, tourism shopping contributes more than tourism services; for Southeast Asia, America, and Oceania, tourism services contributes more; for Oceania, their contributions are largely equal.

Table 8.2 displays the long-run effects, which have some similar features as the short–run effects. For example, the growth of the GDP, the decrease in exports, appreciation of Singapore dollar, the larger impact of the increase in the tourism services demand, and the important role of Southeast Asia and North Asia in all tourism generating markets. However, the long-run results are significantly different from the short run ones.

First of all, in the short run employment increases while wage is unchanged; in the long run employment is unchanged while wage increases. This difference stems directly from the simulation assumption: real wage is fixed in the short run and employment is fixed in the long run. While real wage is fixed, the increase in tourism demand will generate employment, so employment increases for all but the last columns in Table 8.1 (the tourism demand from Africa is so small that an 8 % change in it hardly affects employment). On the other hand, since total employment is fixed in the long run, the increased demand for labour induced by an increase in the tourism demand will bid up the real wage significantly. As a result, the real wage rises significantly for each column in Table 8.2, except the last column.

Second, the price level is significantly higher in the long run. For example, the change in the GDP price index is higher for most of the columns in Table 8.2 than those in Table 8.1. These results seem surprising. The factors can flow freely among sectors in the long run, so the market mechanism should reduce the overall production cost for the economy. As a result, the price level should be lower in the long run. However, other factors in model simulation cannot be overlooked: the total employment is fixed in the long run. Under this assumption, the increase in final demand will bid up the labour cost and thus cause cost-push inflation.

Finally and most importantly, the GDP increase is remarkably smaller in the long run than in the short run. In the face of an 8 % increase in total tourism demand, the nominal GDP in the long run increases by only 0.064 % while it increases by 0.098 % in the short run. Since the price increase in the long run simulation is larger, the difference between the long run and the short run real GDP is even bigger (0.042 % in the long run against 0.083 % in the short run). This difference can also be addressed by different closures in the long run and in the short run. Although the free capital movement in the long run will lead to a better allocation of resources and thus may increase GDP more, the fixed employment imposes a greater constraint on GDP growth.

8.1.2 The Sectoral Effects

Before analysing the sectoral effects, we need to find out which sectors belong to the tourism industry. Since the tourism industry is a demand-side concept, we classify sectors according to what percentage of sectoral output is consumed by tourists. If more than 90 % of the sectoral output is purchased by tourists, we regard the sector as a 'core tourism sector'; if 10–90 % of the sectoral output is purchased by tourists, we name it an 'extended tourism sector'; if only less than 10 % of the output is consumed by tourists, we call it a 'tourism-related sector'; if none of the output is directly purchased by tourists, we call it a 'non-tourism sector'. According to this classification, only accommodation and sightseeing sectors are core tourism sectors (marked with *** in the relevant Tables); six sectors (drink and tobacco, clothing, wood and print, food and beverage [F & B], local transport, and healthcare) are extended tourism sectors (marked with **); another six sectors (food manufacture, chemical, electronics, electrical, precision engineering, and recreation) are tourism-related sectors (marked *). All the above sectors are tourism sectors and the other sectors are non-tourism sectors. In addition, F & B, accommodation, sightseeing, and recreation are traditionally thought of as falling under the tourism sector; we also name them as conventional tourism sector (marked ^' in the tables).

There are many indicators for the sectoral effects, but output is the most important one. The sectoral output in the short run and in the long run is shown in Tables 8.3 and 8.4, respectively. We start with discussing the short-run effects of the total tourism demand (Column 3 in Table 8.3), tourism shopping demand and tourism service demand (Columns 1 and 2), and different generating markets (the last seven columns in Table 8.3). Afterwards, we address the long-run effects.

First, with an 8 % increase in the total tourism demand, tourism sectors largely experience output increases while most non-tourism sectors are suffering. This could be explained by resource reallocation. For example, labour moves from non-tourism sectors to tourism sectors in the face of an increasing tourism demand, and non-tourism sectors have to contract due to a shortage of workers. However, a close look delivers quite a complex

Table 8.3 Effects of tourism components on sectoral output in the short run

Output	(1) 8 % increase in tourism shopping demand	(2) 8 % increase in tourism service demand	(3) 8 % increase in total tourism demand	(4) 8 % increase in tourism demand (America)	(5) 8 % increase in tourism demand (S.E. Asia)	(6) 8 % increase in tourism demand (N. Asia)	(7) 8 % increase in tourism demand (S. Asia)	(8) 8 % increase in tourism demand (Europe)	(9) 8 % increase in tourism demand (Oceania)	(10) 8 % increase in tourism demand (Africa)
1. Accommodation***^	0.026	5.279	5.23	0.453	1.649	1.521	0.405	0.692	0.000	0.000
2. Sightseeing***^	−0.023	0.651	0.619	0.047	0.118	0.209	0.062	0.112	−0.006	−0.001
3. Drink and tobacco**	0.564	0.022	0.593	0.031	0.207	0.214	0.063	0.047	0.030	0.001
4. Clothing**	5.153	−0.023	5.184	0.277	1.845	1.451	0.662	0.436	0.458	0.029
5. Wood and print**	0.317	−0.045	0.276	0.005	0.072	0.079	0.053	0.036	0.030	0.001
6. Retailer**	1.089	−0.029	1.071	0.046	0.364	0.353	0.126	0.09	−0.001	0.000
7. Food and beverage**^	−0.043	1.074	1.019	0.126	0.225	0.282	0.131	0.13	−0.002	0.000
8. Local transport**	−0.004	0.396	0.387	0.029	0.138	0.1	0.044	0.041	−0.007	0.000
9. Healthcare**	−0.001	0.729	0.727	−0.001	0.732	0.003	−0.003	−0.003	−0.002	0.000
10. Food manufacture*	0.097	−0.037	0.062	0.003	0.015	0.062	−0.008	−0.004	−0.008	0.000
11. Chemical*	−0.006	−0.016	−0.022	−0.002	−0.007	−0.006	−0.002	−0.002	−0.013	−0.001
12. Electronics*	−0.005	−0.025	−0.029	−0.002	−0.011	−0.007	−0.003	−0.003	0.014	0.000
13. Electrical*	−0.028	−0.069	−0.097	−0.007	−0.034	−0.027	−0.011	−0.01	−0.023	−0.001
14. Precision engineering*	0.373	−0.134	0.244	−0.005	0.08	0.074	0.047	0.035	0.007	0.000
15. Recreation*^	−0.011	0.095	0.083	0.005	0.06	0.019	−0.002	0.001	−0.013	−0.001
16. Agriculture	−0.059	0.025	−0.035	0.002	−0.024	−0.008	−0.004	−0.001	−0.020	−0.001
17. Oil manufacture	−0.003	−0.004	−0.007	0	−0.003	−0.002	−0.001	−0.001	0.085	0.006
18. Metal	−0.03	−0.052	−0.081	−0.006	−0.029	−0.023	−0.008	−0.008	0.124	0.001
19. Transport engineering	−0.062	−0.09	−0.152	−0.01	−0.054	−0.043	−0.016	−0.015	0.473	0.031
20. Other manufacture	−0.133	−0.15	−0.283	−0.018	−0.103	−0.08	−0.03	−0.029	0.031	0.002
21. Utilities	0.01	0.064	0.073	0.006	0.024	0.021	0.006	0.009	−0.005	0.000
22. Construction	−0.109	−0.046	−0.155	−0.009	−0.052	−0.048	−0.018	−0.014	−0.011	−0.001
23. Wholesale	−0.126	−0.129	−0.255	−0.015	−0.096	−0.071	−0.027	−0.025	−0.010	−0.001
24. Water transport	−0.025	−0.033	−0.059	−0.004	−0.021	−0.017	−0.006	−0.006	0.067	0.004

(continued)

Table 8.3 (continued)

Output	(1) 8 % increase in tourism shopping demand	(2) 8 % increase in tourism service demand	(3) 8 % increase in total tourism demand	(4) 8 % increase in tourism demand (America)	(5) 8 % increase in tourism demand (S.E. Asia)	(6) 8 % increase in tourism demand (N. Asia)	(7) 8 % increase in tourism demand (S. Asia)	(8) 8 % increase in tourism demand (Europe)	(9) 8 % increase in tourism demand (Oceania)	(10) 8 % increase in tourism demand (Africa)
25. Air transport	−0.021	−0.104	−0.123	−0.01	−0.042	−0.035	−0.011	−0.014	−0.006	0.000
26. Storage and transport service	−0.053	−0.069	−0.122	−0.008	−0.044	−0.035	−0.012	−0.012	−0.003	0.000
27. Communication	−0.036	−0.032	−0.068	−0.004	−0.024	−0.02	−0.007	−0.007	−0.010	−0.001
28. Insurance	−0.015	−0.021	−0.036	−0.003	−0.012	−0.01	−0.004	−0.004	0.011	0.001
29. Banking and Finance	−0.047	−0.071	−0.118	−0.008	−0.042	−0.033	−0.012	−0.012	−0.008	0.000
30. Real estate	0.07	0.057	0.127	0.009	0.043	0.037	0.014	0.012	−0.015	−0.001
31. Legal and accounting service	−0.039	−0.05	−0.089	−0.006	−0.029	−0.026	−0.01	−0.009	−0.004	0.000
32. Information technology	−0.091	−0.093	−0.184	−0.012	−0.064	−0.053	−0.02	−0.019	−0.007	0.000
33. Other business service	−0.028	−0.017	−0.045	−0.003	−0.015	−0.013	−0.006	−0.004	−0.002	0.000
34. Education	−0.048	−0.034	−0.082	−0.005	−0.03	−0.023	−0.01	−0.008	0.000	0.000
35. Non-profit and other	0	0.044	0.044	0.003	0.018	0.011	0.003	0.005	0.003	0.000

Source: Authors

*** indicates core tourism sector

** indicates extended tourism sector

^ indicates conventional tourism sector

Table 8.4 Effects of tourism components on sectoral output in the long run

Output	(1) 8 % increase in tourism shopping demand	(2) 8 % increase in tourism service demand	(3) 8 % increase in total tourism demand	(4) 8 % increase in tourism demand (America)	(5) 8 % increase in tourism demand (S.E. Asia)	(6) 8 % increase in tourism demand (N. Asia)	(7) 8 % increase in tourism demand (S. Asia)	(8) 8 % increase in tourism demand (Europe)	(9) 8 % increase in tourism demand (Oceania)	(10) 8 % increase in tourism demand (Africa)
1. Accommodation***^	0.023	5.252	5.199	0.451	1.635	1.514	0.404	0.689	0.471	0.031
2. Sightseeing***^	−0.028	0.61	0.573	0.044	0.096	0.199	0.059	0.108	0.063	0.003
3. Drink and tobacco**	0.558	−0.023	0.543	0.028	0.184	0.203	0.061	0.042	0.026	0.001
4. Clothing**	5.149	−0.055	5.149	0.275	1.828	1.444	0.66	0.433	0.456	0.029
5. Wood and print**	0.313	−0.085	0.232	0.002	0.051	0.07	0.05	0.032	0.027	0.001
6. Retailer**	1.085	−0.065	1.031	0.043	0.345	0.344	0.124	0.087	0.082	0.006
7. Food and beverage**^	−0.047	1.036	0.977	0.124	0.205	0.273	0.129	0.126	0.121	0.001
8. Local transport**	−0.008	0.361	0.349	0.027	0.119	0.091	0.042	0.037	0.029	0.002
9. Healthcare**	−0.007	0.678	0.67	−0.004	0.704	−0.009	−0.007	−0.008	−0.006	0
10. Food manufacture*	0.091	−0.09	0.003	−0.001	−0.013	0.049	−0.011	−0.01	−0.01	−0.001
11. Chemical*	−0.007	−0.027	−0.034	−0.002	−0.013	−0.009	−0.003	−0.004	−0.003	0
12. Electronics*	−0.006	−0.041	−0.047	−0.003	−0.019	−0.011	−0.004	−0.005	−0.004	0
13. Electrical*	−0.033	−0.113	−0.146	−0.01	−0.057	−0.038	−0.014	−0.014	−0.011	0
14. Precision engineering*	0.368	−0.183	0.191	−0.009	0.055	0.062	0.044	0.03	0.01	0
15. Recreation*^	−0.016	0.052	0.036	0.002	0.037	0.009	−0.004	−0.003	−0.003	0
16. Agriculture	−0.063	−0.006	−0.069	0	−0.041	−0.015	−0.005	−0.004	−0.003	0
17. Oil manufacture	−0.004	−0.009	−0.013	−0.001	−0.005	−0.003	−0.001	−0.001	−0.001	0
18. Metal	−0.034	−0.088	−0.122	−0.008	−0.048	−0.031	−0.011	−0.012	−0.01	−0.001
19. Transport engineering	−0.07	−0.155	−0.224	−0.015	−0.089	−0.059	−0.02	−0.022	−0.018	−0.001
20. Other manufacture	−0.14	−0.207	−0.347	−0.022	−0.133	−0.094	−0.034	−0.035	−0.027	−0.001
21. Utilities	0.007	0.04	0.047	0.005	0.011	0.015	0.005	0.006	0.005	0
22. Construction	−0.12	−0.117	−0.237	−0.014	−0.089	−0.067	−0.023	−0.022	−0.019	−0.001
23. Wholesale	−0.132	−0.184	−0.315	−0.019	−0.125	−0.084	−0.03	−0.031	−0.024	−0.001
24. Water transport	−0.028	−0.059	−0.086	−0.006	−0.034	−0.023	−0.008	−0.008	−0.007	0

(continued)

Table 8.4 (continued)

Output	(1) 8 % increase in tourism shopping demand	(2) 8 % increase in tourism service demand	(3) 8 % increase in total tourism demand	(4) 8 % increase in tourism demand (America)	(5) 8 % increase in tourism demand (S.E. Asia)	(6) 8 % increase in tourism demand (N. Asia)	(7) 8 % increase in tourism demand (S. Asia)	(8) 8 % increase in tourism demand (Europe)	(9) 8 % increase in tourism demand (Oceania)	(10) 8 % increase in tourism demand (Africa)
25. Air transport	−0.028	−0.161	−0.188	−0.014	−0.073	−0.049	−0.015	−0.02	−0.015	−0.001
26. Storage and transport service	−0.06	−0.133	−0.192	−0.013	−0.078	−0.05	−0.016	−0.019	−0.015	−0.001
27. Communication	−0.038	−0.057	−0.095	−0.006	−0.037	−0.026	−0.009	−0.009	−0.008	0
28. Insurance	−0.017	−0.04	−0.056	−0.004	−0.022	−0.015	−0.005	−0.006	−0.005	0
29. Banking and Finance	−0.054	−0.13	−0.183	−0.012	−0.073	−0.048	−0.016	−0.018	−0.014	−0.001
30. Real estate	0.066	0.032	0.099	0.007	0.03	0.031	0.012	0.01	0.009	0
31. Legal and accounting service	−0.045	−0.102	−0.146	−0.01	−0.057	−0.038	−0.013	−0.015	−0.012	−0.001
32. Information technology	−0.097	−0.143	−0.239	−0.015	−0.091	−0.065	−0.023	−0.024	−0.019	−0.001
33. Other business service	−0.028	−0.046	−0.074	−0.005	−0.03	−0.019	−0.007	−0.007	−0.006	0
34. Education	−0.053	−0.083	−0.136	−0.008	−0.056	−0.035	−0.013	−0.013	−0.01	−0.001
35. Non-profit and other	−0.004	0.005	0.001	0.001	−0.003	0.002	0	0.001	0.001	0

Source: Authors

*** indicates core tourism sector

** indicates extended tourism sector

^ indicates conventional tourism sector

picture. In the core tourism industry, the accommodation sector experiences a 5.230 % increase in output, but the sightseeing sector grows only by 0.619 %. This difference may be explained by the different shares of accommodation and sightseeing in the total tourism expenditure: sightseeing only accounts for a very small part of the tourism expenditure while accommodation occupies a significant part. All extended tourism sectors experience growth, but the growth rates also differ. Some sectors grow almost as fast as a core tourism sector, for example, the clothing sector grows at 5.184 %, but some only grow slightly (e.g. the wood and print sector and local transport sector only grow at 0.276 % and 0.387 %). Nevertheless, most extended tourism sectors grow at 0.727 % to 1.071 %. When it comes to the tourism-related sectors, we find some sectors show marginal growth while others experience slight contraction. The divergence of sectors in this group is not surprising. In this boundary group, if tourism demand contributes significantly to sectoral output, the sector may experience growth; otherwise, it may contract. For non-tourism sectors, most experience decline, but three sectors demonstrate mild growth: real estate sector grows by 0.127 %, the utility sector by 0.073 %, and the non-profit sector by 0.044 %. The expansion of these three sectors might indicate they are indirectly related to tourism. For example, the real estate sector may be related to accommodation services and thus directly linked with tourism demand. Many tourism service sectors purchase the products from the utility sector. The contraction of other non-tourism sectors may be explained by labour movement among sectors.

Secondly, tourism shopping demand and tourism services demand affect sectors differently. We start with the tourism shopping demand. An 8 % increase in tourism shopping demand will lead to a significant expansion of tourism-shopping-related sectors, including food manufacture, drink and tobacco, clothing, wood and print, precision engineering, and retailer. Impressively, clothing sector experiences 5.153 % growth, which signals the importance of clothing in tourism shopping expenditure. Understandably, the retailer sector shows a 1.089 % growth—all tourism shopping items are channelled by the retailer sector. With three exceptions, the other sectors that are not directly related to tourism shopping are in contraction. The contraction of non-tourism sectors is easily understood through resource reallocation or substitution effects. The three exceptional sectors are utility, accommodation, and real estate, which enjoy positive growth. This may indicate that these sectors are indirectly related to tourism shopping.

Similarly, an 8 % increase in the tourism services demand stimulates the tourism service sectors at the expense of other sectors. The accommodation sector benefits most (5.279 % growth) followed by F & B (1.074 % growth). Other tourism service sectors (local transport, sightseeing, healthcare, and recreation) grow by 0.095 % to 0.729 %. For all the other sectors, most experience contraction with the exception of agriculture, drink and tobacco, utilities, real estate, and non-profit, which experience positive growth. As for tourism shopping, these effects can be explained through sectoral linkage, substitution effect, or crowding-out effect.

Thirdly, the effects of different tourism generating markets share some common features but also differ considerably. No matter from which generating market the increase in tourism demand comes, it tends to benefit sectors which indirectly relate to tourism including utility, real estate, and non-profit, at the expense of other sectors. The accommodation and clothing sectors always benefit most. The characteristics of individual markets are as follows: the increase in tourism demand from America tends to bring more benefits to the accommodation sector and the F & B sector. Among all the tourism-generating markets, Southeast Asia contributes most to the growth of clothing, accommodation, retailer, local transport, recreation, and healthcare sectors; tourists from this area seem to enjoy much of Singapore's shopping environment, recreation activities, and healthcare facilities. North Asia tourists contribute almost equally to the clothing and accommodation sectors; and these tourists are the biggest contributors to local transport and sightseeing sectors. The overall contribution of South Asia to the clothing sector much outweighs its contribution to the accommodation sector. The contribution of tourists from Europe and Oceania to Singapore is quite similar, but Europeans contribute slightly more on accommodation and sightseeing while Oceania tourists contribute to accommodation and clothing sectors more evenly. The contribution of Africa is very small, mainly to being the areas of accommodation, clothing, and sightseeing.

Finally, the long-run sectoral effects are less optimistic than the short-run effects. For example, the numbers in Table 8.4 are less positive or more negative than those in Table 8.3. Just as in the macroeconomic effects, this difference may be due to the fixed employment in the long run. However, it is worth noting that, while some numbers in Table 8.3 are positive, the corresponding numbers become negative in Table 8.4, for example, agriculture in column 2, food manufacturing in columns 4 and 5, and drink and tobacco in column 2. This change of sign indicates that some effects in the long run might differ remarkably from those in the short run.

8.1.3 Employment Effects

In this subsection, we discuss the effects of tourism components on employment. In our study, we think of eight occupational groups: managers, professionals, para-professionals, tradesmen, clerks, plant workers, and other labourers. The first four occupations are high skilled, while the rest are low skilled. The employment effects in the short run are shown in Table 8.5 while the effects in the long run are listed in Table 8.6. We start with the short-run effects.

The general feature of Table 8.5 is that low-skilled workers (e.g. clerks, plant workers, and other labourers) benefit most and the high-skilled workers benefit only slightly. Specifically, with an 8 % increase in the total tourism demand, the employment for other labourers occupation will increase by 1.307 % and, for clerks occupation, 0.897 %. Managers and salesmen occupations suffer from reduced employment opportunities. Other occupations show marginal improvements in employment.

In the comparison of the effects of the tourism shopping demand and the tourism services demand in the first two columns, an increase in the tourism services demand seems to have bigger positive effects on all occupations except managers, salesmen, and plant workers, which are negatively affected. These larger effects are consistent with the fact that

Table 8.5 Effects of tourism components on occupational employment in the short run

Employment	(1) 8 % increase in tourism shopping demand	(2) 8 % increase in tourism service demand	(3) 8 % increase in total tourism demand	(4) 8 % increase in tourism demand (America)	(5) 8 % increase in tourism demand (S.E. Asia)	(6) 8 % increase in tourism demand (N. Asia)	(7) 8 % increase in tourism demand (S. Asia)	(8) 8 % increase in tourism demand (Europe)	(9) 8 % increase in tourism demand (Oceania)	(10) 8 % increase in tourism demand (Africa)
Managers	0.002	−0.021	−0.019	−0.002	−0.009	−0.004	−0.003	−0.002	−0.001	0.000
Professionals	−0.005	0.010	0.006	−0.005	0.043	−0.015	−0.006	−0.006	−0.005	0.000
Para-Professionals	0.023	0.031	0.055	−0.002	0.060	−0.001	−0.001	−0.002	−0.001	0.000
Tradesmen	0.007	0.070	0.077	0.004	0.046	0.013	0.003	0.005	0.004	0.000
Clerks	0.056	0.851	0.897	0.082	0.262	0.261	0.079	0.114	0.086	0.005
Salesmen	0.008	−0.029	−0.020	−0.003	−.008	−0.006	−0.002	−0.001	−0.002	0.000
Plant workers	0.029	−0.009	0.020	0.000	0.003	0.006	0.005	0.002	0.001	0.000
Other labourers	0.000	1.325	1.307	0.119	0.409	0.365	0.112	0.165	0.122	0.006

Source: Authors

Table 8.6 Effects of tourism components on occupational employment in the long run

Employment	(1) 8 % increase in tourism shopping demand	(2) 8 % increase in tourism service demand	(3) 8 % increase in total tourism demand	(4) 8 % increase in tourism demand (America)	(5) 8 % increase in tourism demand (S.E. Asia)	(6) 8 % increase in tourism demand (N. Asia)	(7) 8 % increase in tourism demand (S. Asia)	(8) 8 % increase in tourism demand (Europe)	(9) 8 % increase in tourism demand (Oceania)	(10) 8 % increase in tourism demand (Africa)
Managers	−0.008	−0.109	−0.115	−0.008	−0.054	−0.025	−0.008	−0.011	−0.008	0.000
Professionals	−0.012	−0.051	−0.072	−0.010	0.006	−0.032	−0.011	−0.014	−0.011	−0.001
Para-Professionals	0.014	−0.055	−0.040	−0.008	0.015	−0.021	−0.006	−0.011	−0.008	0.000
Tradesmen	−0.002	−0.018	−0.020	−0.002	−0.001	−0.008	−0.002	−0.004	−0.003	0.000
Clerks	0.045	0.750	0.785	0.075	0.209	0.237	0.073	0.103	0.078	0.004
Salesmen	−0.003	−0.116	−0.117	−0.009	−0.054	−0.027	−0.007	−0.010	−0.009	0.000
Plant workers	0.018	−0.105	−0.086	−0.007	−0.047	−0.017	−0.001	−0.008	−0.006	0.000
Other labourers	−0.010	1.238	1.211	0.113	0.363	0.344	0.106	0.155	0.116	0.006

Source: Authors

an increase in the tourism services demand generates higher GDP growth, as we have shown in the macro results. Although the effects of the tourism shopping demand are much milder overall, it brings more benefit to managers, salesmen, and plant workers. Understandably, these occupations are more involved in tourism shopping than in tourism services.

Regarding the effects of different tourism-generating markets, it is apparent that the influence of Southeast Asia and North Asia dominates while Africa has the least effect. Plant workers benefit most from tourists from North Asia and South Asia because these groups of tourists are the biggest shoppers, bringing much benefit to the manufacturing industry where plant workers are found. Professionals and para-professionals benefit most from tourists from Southeast Asia, probably because tourists from this area use considerable amounts of healthcare services, which involve a number of highly trained staff.

The long-run effects are considerably different from the short run effects, shown in Table 8.6. Looking into column 3, we find that, in the short run, only managers and salesmen are worse off with the other occupational groups benefiting from the growth of tourism demand. When it comes to the long run, most of the occupational groups are worse off except 'clerks' and 'other labourers'. Even for these two lucky groups, the increase in employment is much smaller in the long run than in the short run. The less optimistic effects in the long run are explained by the fact that total employment can increase in response to increasing tourism demand in the short run, but it is fixed in the long run. Tourism sectors seem to be using more clerks and other labourers. As an increase in tourism demand pushes up the demand for clerks and other labourers, some people have to change occupations and join in the clerks and other labourers groups. However, some features in the short run are also presented in the long run, for example, tourism services demand has a bigger effect than tourism shopping demand; Southeast Asia and North Asia are the most important tourism-generating markets; and tourists from Southeast Asia bring most benefit to professionals and para-professionals.

8.2 The Impact of Negative Mega Events and Policy Responses[3]

This section will consider the short-run effects of a negative mega event and policy response. There are two reasons for only analysing the short-run effects. One is that, although the long-run effects are much milder than the short-run effects, previous analyses suggest that they have many similarities. Thus, many conclusions in the short run are equally applicable to the long run. The other reason is that, in the face of a negative mega event, the main concern is how to restore the economic growth as quickly as possible. So the short-run effects are more important. The simulated short-run effects are interpreted in terms of macroeconomic effect, tourism effect, sectoral effect, and employment effect.

8.2.1 The Macroeconomic Effects

Table 8.7 displays the projected macroeconomic effects of all policy simulation scenarios. All values are as percentage change, except for variables with * in the table.

A glance at Table 8.7 reveals that the income tax cuts policy has little effect on macro variables. This is somewhat surprising. The decrease in the income tax rate leads to the same amount of tax revenue loss as other policy options do. This means a substantially higher disposable income for the Singaporean household. Given unchanged consumer preferences, higher disposable income results in higher domestic consumption and thus will lead to a higher price level (demand-pull inflation). As such, many macro variables will be affected significantly. However, Singapore is a small country and its domestic consumption is very small compared with other final demands, so the influence of income tax reduction on price level is negligible. Consequently, its influence on other final

[3] Section 8.2 has been significantly revised from Tourism Analysis, 16(3):343–359, 2011, DOI: 10.3727/108354211X13110944387284, 'A Computable General Equilibrium Analysis of Potential Policy Responses to A Negative Tourism Demand Shock in Singapore' by Meng, X., Siriwardana, M. and Dollery, B. Thanks for the copyright permission from Cognizant Communication Corporation.

Table 8.7 Macroeconomic effects of a negative mega event and policy responses

Macros	(1) Baseline case 13 % decrease in tourism demand	(2) Baseline plus 1 % decrease in power of GST	(3) Baseline plus 0.79 % production tax cuts (all sectors)	(4) Baseline plus 2.01 % production tax cuts (tourism)	(5) Baseline plus 3.03 % income tax cuts
Indirect taxes*	−159.747	−5976.25	−5977.01	−5996.47	−159.49
Production tax*	−15.45	140.102	−6653.45	−6553.42	−15.433
Tariff revenue*	−4.8	347.778	307.015	241.612	−4.718
Tax on tourism shopping*	−55.918	−81.903	−58.917	−54.122	−55.92
Taxes on tourism service*	−74.754	−98.64	−79.096	−73.384	−74.756
GDP price index	−0.023	−0.779	−0.827	−0.74	−0.023
Exchange rate (local currency/ $world)	0.137	−0.299	−0.558	−0.463	0.136
Real devaluation	0.16	0.483	0.271	0.279	0.159
Terms of trade	−0.016	−0.195	−0.169	−0.199	−0.016
Exports price (local currency)	0.121	−0.494	−0.726	−0.662	0.121
Tourism shopping price	−0.256	−0.468	−0.695	−1.686	−0.256
Tourism service price	−1.215	−1.529	−1.834	−2.944	−1.216
Tourism price index	−0.713	−0.973	−1.238	−2.285	−0.713

Employment (wage bill weights)	−0.141	4.499	4.706	3.235	−0.142
Average real wage	0	0	0	0	0
Aggregate payments to capital	−0.049	4.773	4.675	4.677	−0.049
Aggregate payments to labour	−0.141	4.499	4.706	3.235	−0.142
Nominal GDP	−0.153	1.353	1.387	0.798	−0.153
Real GDP	−0.13	2.146	2.229	1.547	−0.13
Utility per household	−0.184	9.458	9.538	8.2	−0.181
Household nominal income	−0.09	4.65	4.689	4.031	−0.091
Real household consumption	−0.099	5.089	5.132	4.411	−0.097
Real tourism shopping expenditure	−13.143	−13.474	−13.472	−11.418	−13.144
Real tourism service expenditure	−12.84	−13.128	−13.102	−10.998	−12.841
Total real tourism expenditure	−13	−13.31	−13.297	−11.219	−13
Value of imports plus duty	0.125	2.297	1.771	2.068	0.125
Import volume	−0.012	2.603	2.34	2.541	−0.012

(continued)

Table 8.7 (continued)

Macros	(1) Baseline case 13 % decrease in tourism demand	(2) Baseline plus 1 % decrease in power of GST	(3) Baseline plus 0.79 % production tax cuts (all sectors)	(4) Baseline plus 2.01 % production tax cuts (tourism)	(5) Baseline plus 3.03 % income tax cuts
value of exports (local currency border)	0.355	1.704	1.255	1.37	0.354
Export volume	0.234	2.208	1.993	2.043	0.233
Contribution of BOT to real GDP*	0.588	−0.219	−0.163	−0.523	0.587
BOT/GDP(Nominal)*	0.006	−0.011	−0.011	−0.013	0.006

Source: Authors

*Nominal change: Singapore dollars (million)

demands (e.g. tourism and exports) and thus on the economy as a whole is negligible. Since the income tax cuts policy is almost ineffective, we will omit it in our discussion.

In the first place, Panel 1 discloses the tax revenue effects in the face of a 13 % negative shock to the tourism demand in Singapore, with and without policy responses. Without a policy response, the total indirect tax revenue decreases by 159.75 million dollars, the bulk of which comes from the decrease in tourism tax revenue. This is easily understood given the nature of the negative tourism shock. Although all three policies are designed to have the same amount of loss in indirect tax revenue, the behaviour of the tax revenue component is quite different under different policies. The GST deduction policy response leads to a decrease of almost 6 billion dollars in indirect tax revenue, but tariff revenue and production tax revenue actually increase by a small amount. It is noticeable that the tax revenue from tourism services decreases much more than that on tourism shopping. The 0.79 % indiscriminate production tax cuts results in a loss of 6.65 billion dollars of production tax income, but because of the increase in tariff and other tax revenue, the total loss of indirect tax revenue is similar to that under the GST policy. Compared with the indiscriminate subsidy policy, the 2.01 % production tax cuts to the tourism industry leads to a similar loss in production tax revenue, but a much smaller increase in tariff revenue.

Second, the effects on prices are shown in the second panel. At first glance it would appear that all prices except that real exchange rates are affected negatively under all scenarios (since positive real devaluation also means the decrease of domestic currency value) and that all policy responses tend to aggravate this negative effect. A close look reveals a more complex picture. Since CPI is unchanged under the flexible exchange assumption, the GDP price index (GDP deflator) acts as the indicator of the price level of the economy. In the baseline case, the GDP deflator decreases by 0.023 %, and it can be readily appreciated that this is due to the contraction of the final demand (i.e. the antithesis of demand-pull inflation). Accelerated deflation under the GST policy is explained by increased efficiency due to the decreased tax distortion to the economy (more specifically, a sales tax deduction will reduce the tax payment burden not only on consumers but also on producers). The production tax cuts policies decrease domestic prices by reducing the production costs. It is apparent that the prices faced by tourists drop more than the GDP deflator, which is readily explained by the negative shock in the tourism demand. By the same reasoning, it is not a surprise that the tourism-focused production tax cuts will lead to much bigger decreases in prices faced by tourists. The increase in the exchange rate (depreciation of the Singapore dollar) in the baseline case is explained by the decrease in the inbound tourism demand: fewer tourists visiting Singapore means lower demand for the Singapore dollar and thus a lower value of the Singapore dollar. The decrease in the exchange rate (appreciation of the Singapore dollar) under the three policy responses may stem from the decreased domestic price level: the lower local price attracts exports demand and thus the demand for Singapore dollars.

The immediate effects of drops in domestic prices are the devaluation of local currency and worsening of the terms of trade. The real devaluation is calculated as the sum of the decrease in the GDP deflator and the increase in the exchange rate. The large decrease in the GDP deflator outweighs the decrease in the exchange rate and thus commands a positive real devaluation in all scenarios. Under the assumption that the world prices do not change, a decrease in export price in local currency bigger than that of the exchange rate leads to a lower domestic/world price ratio, and therefore the terms of trade worsen.

Third, employment in the third panel is significantly and negatively affected by the negative tourism demand shock and all three policy responses seem very effective in improving employment. As a result of the negative tourism demand shock, the production of goods and services contracts and thus unemployment increases. The GST policy improves employment by about 4.5 %, which can be explained by the increase in final demand induced by a GST deduction. The production tax cuts policies stimulate employment through two channels: stimulating production through reduced production costs and stimulating final demand through lower prices. The simulation results show that the indiscriminate production tax cuts policy is the most effective for creating jobs and the tourism-focused production tax cuts policy improves employment least.

The effects on employment are confirmed by the change in the GDP. The indiscriminate production tax cuts policy performs best but the tourism production tax cuts policy performs worst, according to both the nominal and real GDP. The performance of the real GDP seems much better than that of the nominal GDP due to the deflation in all scenarios.

Fourth, household demand and tourism demand are listed in the second last panel. The real tourism expenditure decreases by 13 % in the baseline case, which is designed by the modeller. Interestingly, this negative shock is relieved only by the tourism-focused subsidy policy. The other two policies actually cause a deterioration of the situation. The reasons will be given in the next subsection.

Household income, consumption, and utility level all drop in the baseline case. The reasoning may be that the decrease in the tourism demand leads to a contraction of the economy. As output and employment shrink, household income decreases and so does household consumption. Under all policy responses, household consumption improves greatly. The indiscriminate production tax cuts policy performs best, the GST deduction policy follows very closely, and the tourism production tax cuts policy has the least but still very significant effect. The reason for the effectiveness of these policy responses is straightforward: all policy responses stimulate production and provide more jobs and thus more income for households.

Finally, international trade improves under all policy options, as shown in the last panel in Table 8.7. In a baseline case, imports decrease due to the depreciation of the Singapore dollar (imports become dearer to Singaporeans). Since the prices of imports are based on world prices and the world price level is assumed unchanged in the model, the differences between changes in real imports and in nominal imports are changes in the exchange rate. All three policies reverse the decrease in imports. The GST policy encourages importation most, followed by the tourism-focused production tax cuts policy. The performance of exports under the impact of the negative tourism demand shock is significantly positive. This effect may result from the increase in the exchange rate in the face of a negative tourism demand shock: the depreciation of the Singapore dollar makes domestic prices relatively lower than world prices and thus stimulates exports. Under all policy responses, real and nominal exports increase significantly. However, since imports increase much faster than exports under all policies, the contribution of the BOT to GDP decreases.

Table 8.8 Tourism effects of a negative mega event and policy responses

Tourism demand	(1) Baseline case 13 % decrease in tourism demand	(2) Baseline plus 1 % decrease in power of GST	(3) Baseline plus 0.79 % production tax cuts (all sectors)	(4) Baseline plus 2.01 % production tax cuts (tourism)	(5) Baseline plus 3.03 % income tax cuts
Shopping (nominal)	−13.371	−13.888	−14.088	−12.942	−13.372
Service (nominal)	−13.924	−14.488	−14.733	−13.669	−13.925
Canada (nominal)	−13.283	−13.795	−14.017	−12.99	−13.284
USA (nominal)	−13.444	−14.019	−14.227	−13.092	−13.444
Indonesia (nominal)	−13.944	−14.415	−14.635	−13.483	−13.945
Malaysia (nominal)	−13.555	−14.097	−14.323	−13.262	−13.555
Philippines (nominal)	−13.337	−13.877	−14.1	−12.987	−13.338
Thailand (nominal)	−13.172	−13.678	−13.895	−12.876	−13.172
China (nominal)	−13.795	−14.378	−14.609	−13.511	−13.795
Taiwan (nominal)	−13.31	−13.818	−14.038	−12.949	−13.311
Hong Kong (nominal)	−13.133	−13.621	−13.833	−12.756	−13.134
Japan (nominal)	−13.683	−14.285	−14.505	−13.434	−13.683
South Korea (nominal)	−13.48	−14.052	−14.274	−13.296	−13.481
India (nominal)	−13.71	−14.3	−14.531	−13.404	−13.71
France (nominal)	−13.072	−13.553	−13.769	−12.724	−13.072
	−13.121	−13.588	−13.801	−12.728	−13.122

Germany (nominal)					
Italy (nominal)	−13.179	−13.678	−13.9	−12.868	−13.179
Netherlands (nominal)	−13.144	−13.636	−13.846	−12.773	−13.145
Switzerland (nominal)	−13.109	−13.577	−13.79	−12.684	−13.109
UK (nominal)	−13.702	−14.305	−14.525	−13.342	−13.703
Australia (nominal)	−13.6	−14.177	−14.397	−13.278	−13.601
New Zealand (nominal)	−13.257	−13.748	−13.973	−12.93	−13.258
South Africa (nominal)	−13.49	−14.018	−14.246	−13.235	−13.49
World (nominal)	−13.635	−14.174	−14.396	−13.289	−13.635
Shopping (real)	−13.143	−13.474	−13.472	−11.418	−13.144
Service (real)	−12.84	−13.128	−13.102	−10.998	−12.841
Canada (real)	−12.291	−12.544	−12.53	−10.609	−12.291
USA (real)	−12.615	−12.997	−12.956	−10.819	−12.615
Indonesia (real)	−13.621	−13.795	−13.781	−11.615	−13.622
Malaysia (real)	−12.839	−13.155	−13.149	−11.164	−12.839
Philippines (real)	−12.4	−12.71	−12.699	−10.603	−12.4
Thailand (real)	−12.066	−12.308	−12.282	−10.376	−12.067
China (real)	−13.322	−13.721	−13.727	−11.673	−13.322
Taiwan (real)	−12.346	−12.591	−12.572	−10.526	−12.346
Hong Kong (real)	−11.988	−12.191	−12.156	−10.131	−11.988
Japan (real)	−13.096	−13.534	−13.517	−11.515	−13.096
	−12.689	−13.063	−13.05	−11.234	−12.689

(continued)

Table 8.8 (continued)

Tourism demand	(1) Baseline case 13 % decrease in tourism demand	(2) Baseline plus 1 % decrease in power of GST	(3) Baseline plus 0.79 % production tax cuts (all sectors)	(4) Baseline plus 2.01 % production tax cuts (tourism)	(5) Baseline plus 3.03 % income tax cuts
South Korea (real)					
India (real)	−13.151	−13.564	−13.569	−11.456	−13.151
France (real)	−11.864	−12.053	−12.025	−10.066	−11.864
Germany (real)	−11.964	−12.124	−12.091	−10.072	−11.964
Italy (real)	−12.08	−12.307	−12.292	−10.36	−12.081
Netherlands (real)	−12.011	−12.222	−12.182	−10.164	−12.011
Switzerland (real)	−11.938	−12.102	−12.068	−9.982	−11.938
UK (real)	−13.135	−13.575	−13.557	−11.328	−13.136
Australia (real)	−12.93	−13.316	−13.299	−11.197	−12.93
New Zealand (real)	−12.238	−12.45	−12.44	−10.486	−12.239
South Africa (real)	−12.708	−12.995	−12.993	−11.11	−12.708
World (real)	−13	−13.31	−13.297	−11.219	−13

Source: Authors

8.2.2 The Tourism Effects

The effects of a 13 % decrease in the tourism demand and four proposed responses on nominal and real tourism demand by tourism-generating countries are tabulated in Table 8.8.

A noteworthy feature of Table 8.8 is that, of all policy responses, only production tax cuts for the tourism sector effectively improves the tourism demand; the first two policies, GST deduction and indiscriminate production tax cuts, decrease the tourism demand further; the income tax cut has little impact on the tourism demand. This feature can be explained by price mechanisms. The first two policies will lead to the decrease in the purchasing price faced by all consumers. As the prices faced by tourists decrease, their demand for tourism products should increase. However, since the first two policies indiscriminately affect the prices of all products in the economy, the decrease in the tourism price index is small. As the decrease in the tourism price is smaller than the appreciation of the Singapore dollar, the actual price faced by inbound tourists (price denominated in foreign currency) is actually higher. For example, compared with the baseline case, the GST deduction policy leads to a further decrease in the tourism price index by $-0.973 - (-0.713) = -0.260$ % (the negative sign means the decrease), but the exchange rate differs by $-0.299 - 0.137 = -0.436$ % (Singapore dollar is appreciated), so the price of tourism goods denominated in foreign currency has actually increased by 0.436–0.260 = 0.176 %. Given a downward-sloped tourism demand function, an increase in tourism price will lead to a decrease in tourism demand.

However, if the production tax cut is focused on the tourism sectors, as shown in the third policy, it is quite a different story. This policy generates a much bigger price decrease for tourism products. As the decrease in the domestic price of tourism goods is larger than the degree of appreciation of the Singapore dollar, the price faced by foreign tourists is lower. Using tourism prices in Table 8.7, we can easily calculate the following: the tourism price index changes by $-2.285 - (-0.713) = -1.572$ %; the exchange rate changes by $-0.463 - 0.137 = -0.600$ %; so the tourism price index denominated in foreign currency changes by

Table 8.9 Effects on sectoral output of a negative mega event and policy responses

Output	(1) Baseline case 13 % decrease in tourism demand	(2) Baseline plus 1 % decrease in power of GST	(3) Baseline plus 0.79 % production tax cuts (all sectors)	(4) Baseline plus 2.01 % production tax cuts (tourism)	(5) Baseline plus 3.03 % income tax cuts
1. Accommodation***^	−8.281	−7.21	−7.165	−6.117	−8.281
2. Sightseeing***^	−0.987	1.284	1.317	0.039	−0.988
3. Drink and tobacco**	−0.943	0.294	0.439	0.058	−0.944
4. Clothing**	−8.291	−4.929	−5.227	2.473	−8.291
5. Wood and print**	−0.446	1.408	1.514	4.856	−0.446
6. Retailer**	−1.741	0.974	1.241	1.382	−1.74
7. Food and beverage**^	−1.665	0.97	1.091	0.772	−1.664
8. Local transport**	−0.607	1.631	1.741	2.558	−0.607
9. Healthcare**	−1.232	1.141	1.285	0.893	−1.233
10. Food manufacture*	−0.098	5.72	5.479	16.645	−0.099
11. Chemical*	0.035	1.037	0.938	2.624	0.035
12. Electronics*	0.047	2.116	1.834	4.96	0.046
13. Electrical*	0.156	4.12	3.686	10.6	0.156
14. Precision engineering*	−0.394	0.625	0.736	0.166	−0.395
15. Recreation*^	−0.134	2.48	2.634	2.424	−0.134
16. Agriculture	0.057	0.798	1.029	0.453	0.057
17. Oil manufacture	0.012	1.567	1.279	−0.002	0.012
18. Metal	0.132	2.864	2.894	0.049	0.131
19. Transport engineering	0.246	3.992	4.17	−0.584	0.245
20. Other manufacture	0.46	2.153	2.667	0.23	0.459
21. Utilities	−0.115	1.721	1.879	1.425	−0.115

22. Construction	0.258	6.2	6.954	1.99	0.258
23. Wholesale	0.415	1.517	1.659	−0.08	0.415
24. Water transport	0.095	2.207	2.011	−0.201	0.095
25. Air transport	0.205	5.247	4.858	0.231	0.205
26. Storage and transport service	0.198	1.674	1.781	−0.595	0.198
27. Communication	0.11	0.884	0.932	−0.073	0.11
28. Insurance	0.057	0.657	0.675	−0.137	0.057
29. Banking and Finance	0.191	1.744	2.194	−0.506	0.191
30. Real estate	−0.205	1.362	1.444	1.009	−0.205
31. Legal and accounting service	0.146	1.718	1.985	0.687	0.145
32. Information technology	0.299	2.224	2.377	0.908	0.299
33. Other business service	0.074	1.831	2.1	1.129	0.074
34. Education	0.138	3.407	3.569	2.35	0.138
35. Non-profit and other	−0.066	3.469	3.739	2.782	−0.065

Source: Authors
*** indicates core tourism sector
** indicates extended tourism sector
^ indicates conventional tourism sector

$-1.572 - (-0.600) = -0.972$ % (negative sign indicates a decrease). A decrease in the tourism price denominated in foreign currency will stimulate the inbound tourism demand.

A decrease in income tax should affect tourism demand negatively. As stated earlier, since Singapore is a small country, the effect of income tax cuts on its domestic consumption and thus on price level is very little. As a result, its influence on tourism demand is negligible.

The second feature of Table 8.8 is that the real change in tourism demand is smaller than the corresponding nominal tourism demand. This feature results from the price change after a negative mega event. A negative event depresses the tourism demand. The decrease in the final demand will lead to a decrease in the price level, other things being equal. The nominal change includes both real change and price change, so the nominal value in Table 8.8 is bigger (more negative) than the real value. It is of interest to notice the behaviour of the tourism shopping demand and the tourism services demand. According to nominal value, the tourism service demand drops more than that of the tourism shopping demand, but this conclusion reverses in terms of real value. The different conclusions indicate that the price of tourism services must drop much more than that of tourism shopping, which is confirmed in the changes in tourism prices in Table 8.7.

Finally, the change in the tourism demand for each region is different. The decrease in the tourism demand from each country is generated by the tourism demand quantity shifter (left shift of tourism demand curve). When the same amount of tourism demand shift is imposed on different tourism-generating markets simultaneously, as we did in this study, the countries contributing more to Singapore tourism (e.g. Indonesia, China, and India) have larger changes in the tourism demand. The reasoning is as follows: a tourism demand shift in countries with a larger market share will cause larger changes in the tourism prices. This price change will adversely affect the tourism demand from other countries. For example, a decrease in the tourism demand from a large tourism-generating market like Indonesia would reduce the tourism prices significantly and the reduced tourism prices may have a significant positive effect on the tourism demand from other countries. But the price effect of a tourism demand shift in a small tourism source country is very little. Thus, this

Table 8.10 Effects on sectoral profitability of a negative mega event and policy responses

Gross rate of return on capital	(1) Baseline case 13 % decrease in tourism demand	(2) Baseline plus 1 % decrease in power of GST	(3) Baseline plus 0.79 % production tax cuts (all sectors)	(4) Baseline plus 2.01 % production tax cuts (tourism)	(5) Baseline plus 3.03 % income tax cuts
1. Accommodation***^	−9.079	−7.468	−7.378	−6.591	−9.079
2. Sightseeing***^	−1.043	1.72	1.798	0.112	−1.043
3. Drink and tobacco**	−2.327	1.138	1.538	0.215	−2.328
4. Clothing**	−8.638	−4.708	−4.976	2.635	−8.639
5. Wood and print**	−0.647	2.33	2.519	6.663	−0.647
6. Retailer**	−2.097	1.568	1.929	1.699	−2.097
7. Food and beverage**^	−1.551	1.296	1.451	0.769	−1.551
8. Local transport**	−1.155	3.411	3.657	4.751	−1.155
9. Healthcare**	−1.277	1.562	1.752	0.965	−1.276
10. Food manufacture*	−0.186	8.706	8.401	24.491	−0.186
11. Chemical*	0.116	5.22	4.799	12.383	0.115
12. Electronics*	0.104	7.32	6.435	16.499	0.104
13. Electrical*	0.172	6.166	5.604	14.903	0.171
14. Precision engineering*	−0.958	1.876	2.181	0.458	−0.959
15. Recreation*^	−0.298	5.131	5.471	4.665	−0.297
16. Agriculture	0.371	6.397	8.241	3.417	0.369
17. Oil manufacture	0.056	14.502	11.887	0.053	0.056
18. Metal	0.148	4.65	4.742	0.145	0.148
19. Transport engineering	0.248	5.197	5.457	−0.624	0.247
20. Other manufacture	0.484	2.909	3.548	0.338	0.484
21. Utilities	−0.636	9.472	10.372	7.518	−0.635
22. Construction	0.297	8.743	9.812	2.722	0.298

(continued)

Table 8.10 (continued)

Gross rate of return on capital	(1) Baseline case 13 % decrease in tourism demand	(2) Baseline plus 1 % decrease in power of GST	(3) Baseline plus 0.79 % production tax cuts (all sectors)	(4) Baseline plus 2.01 % production tax cuts (tourism)	(5) Baseline plus 3.03 % income tax cuts
23. Wholesale	0.561	2.642	2.894	−0.044	0.561
24. Water transport	0.176	5.59	5.177	−0.396	0.176
25. Air transport	0.22	7.199	6.745	0.371	0.22
26. Storage and transport service	0.241	2.844	3.046	−0.786	0.24
27. Communication	0.259	2.869	3.049	−0.13	0.258
28. Insurance	0.146	2.626	2.73	−0.383	0.146
29. Banking and Finance	0.245	3.077	3.812	−0.694	0.245
30. Real estate	−1.144	7.888	8.395	5.565	−1.142
31. Legal and accounting service	0.11	2.259	2.589	0.806	0.11
32. Information technology	0.276	2.817	3.027	1.048	0.276
33. Other business service	0.026	2.188	2.493	1.161	0.026
34. Education	0.175	5.912	6.221	3.844	0.176
35. Non-profit and other	−0.184	7.802	8.431	5.966	−0.182

Source: Authors

*** indicates core tourism sector

** indicates extended tourism sector

^ indicates conventional tourism sector

price effect works towards improving the tourism demand from small tourism-generating markets. However, this pattern is correct only in theory. In reality, the changes in tourism demand depend on a variety of factors in tourism source countries and thus vary in different ways.

8.2.3 The Sectoral Effects

We discuss the output and the profitability for each sector in this section. The sectoral output is displayed in Table 8.9.

The results are interpreted in the order of each scenario as we see again in Table 8.9. Since the income tax policy is almost ineffective, we omit it from our discussion.

With respect to scenario 1, it is clear that the tourism-related sectors (i.e. the first 15 sectors in Table 8.9) are generally more greatly affected than the other sectors. These results are explained by the source of shock. However, the specific effects on sectors, both within and outside the tourism industry, are different. In the tourism industry, accommodation, clothing, retailer, and the F & B are affected most. Their outputs fell by 8.281 %, 8.291 %, 1.741 %, and 1.665 % respectively. The sightseeing, drink and tobacco, healthcare, wood and print, and local transport sectors are affected adversely and moderately, whereas the other sectors are affected negatively but only slightly. For example, the output in the recreation sector decreases by only 0.134 %. Most non-tourism sectors showed slight positive growth in output. For instance, the wholesale and other manufacture sectors increased output by 0.415 % and 0.460 %, respectively. This may suggest that these sectors are tourism-competing industries. The exceptions are the utilities, non-profit, and real estate sectors, which are affected negatively and mildly. These results may suggest that these three sectors are indirectly linked to the tourism sector.

Under scenario 2, some sectors show a significant increase in output. The food manufacture and sightseeing sectors in the tourism industry, for example, expand production by 5.72 % and 1.28 %, respectively, but many tourism sectors only increase their output mildly. In the non-tourism industry, the construction sector increases its output by as much as 6.20 %. Other sectors, such as the oil manufacture, electronics,

Table 8.11 Effects on sectoral employment of a negative mega event and policy responses

Employment	(1) Baseline case 13 % decrease in tourism demand	(2) Baseline plus 1 % decrease in power of GST	(3) Baseline plus 0.79 % production tax cuts (all sectors)	(4) Baseline plus 2.01 % production tax cuts (tourism)	(5) Baseline plus 3.03 % income tax cuts
1. Accommodation***^	−14.785	−12.904	−12.825	−10.973	−14.785
2. Sightseeing***^	−1.256	1.637	1.678	0.05	−1.256
3. Drink and tobacco**	−2.554	0.803	1.2	0.159	−2.555
4. Clothing**	−10.727	−6.401	−6.785	3.236	−10.728
5. Wood and print**	−0.758	2.404	2.587	8.356	−0.758
6. Retailer**	−3.429	1.931	2.463	2.744	−3.428
7. Food and beverage**^	−2.52	1.473	1.658	1.172	−2.52
8. Local transport**	−1.86	5.052	5.394	7.959	−1.859
9. Healthcare**	−1.55	1.438	1.62	1.125	−1.55
10. Food manufacture*	−0.157	9.287	8.891	27.64	−0.158
11. Chemical*	0.203	6.059	5.467	15.701	0.202
12. Electronics*	0.188	8.729	7.544	21.034	0.188
13. Electrical*	0.273	7.26	6.489	18.961	0.273
14. Precision engineering*	−1.15	1.832	2.16	0.486	−1.151
15. Recreation*^	−0.318	5.946	6.32	5.811	−0.318
16. Agriculture	0.114	1.602	2.073	0.906	0.113
17. Oil manufacture	0.128	17.941	14.51	−0.024	0.128
18. Metal	0.243	5.337	5.395	0.091	0.243
19. Transport engineering	0.369	6.031	6.302	−0.876	0.368
20. Other manufacture	0.668	3.135	3.885	0.334	0.667
21. Utilities	−0.745	11.476	12.566	9.45	−0.743
22. Construction	0.342	8.295	9.314	2.648	0.343

23. Wholesale	1.021	3.745	4.097	−0.195	1.019
24. Water transport	0.372	8.783	7.994	−0.785	0.371
25. Air transport	0.446	11.565	10.697	0.502	0.445
26. Storage and transport service	0.361	3.054	3.251	−1.079	0.36
27. Communication	0.383	3.084	3.255	−0.255	0.382
28. Insurance	0.241	2.778	2.853	−0.573	0.241
29. Banking and Finance	0.366	3.348	4.218	−0.964	0.365
30. Real estate	−1.383	9.452	10.039	6.956	−1.381
31. Legal and accounting service	0.196	2.315	2.675	0.925	0.195
32. Information technology	0.405	3.02	3.227	1.23	0.404
33. Other business service	0.09	2.226	2.554	1.372	0.09
34. Education	0.277	6.937	7.271	4.768	0.279
35. Non-profit and other	−0.176	9.343	10.085	7.467	−0.173

Source: Authors

*** indicates core tourism sector

** indicates extended tourism sector

^ indicates conventional tourism sector

other manufacture, storage service, and finance, also expand their output significantly. These different growth rates may be explained by the volume of output in each sector. Due to the ad valorem nature of the GST, the sectors with a high volume of output would benefit more from the GST deduction. Although most sectors show positive growth, the accommodation and clothing sectors are still in contraction.

The output in scenario 3 tells a similar but variant story. As in scenario 2, accommodation and clothing are still in deep recession while construction enjoys the highest growth. However, for each sector the change in output in scenario 3 is different from that in scenario 2, although the difference between two scenarios is very small. Since the GST is based on the volume of products and the production tax is based on production activity, the similar results in scenarios 2 and 3 indicate that there is a high correlation between the amount of output and the level of production activity. This is obviously consistent with intuition.

Scenario 4 provides a substantial improvement in all tourism sectors except accommodation. The food manufacture sector shows the biggest gain, increasing its output by 16.65 %. It is followed by the electrical sector with an increase of 10.60 %. Most tourism sectors expand their output in the range 0.89–4.96 %. However, sightseeing, drink and tobacco, and F & B show only marginal growth and the accommodation sector experiences a 6.12 % decrease in output. The sluggishness of the accommodation sector manifests itself in the vitality of the tourism demand. Although no subsidies are paid to the non-tourism sectors, some of them experience significant growth; noticeably, utility grows by 1.43 %, construction by 1.99 %, real estate by 1.01 %, education by 2.35 %, and non-profit by 2.78 %. This indicates the linkage between the tourism industry and these industries. However, some sectors like oil manufacture, banking and finance, and wholesale experience a slight contraction, which confirms the fact that they appear to compete with the tourism industry.

The sectoral profitability or the gross rate of return on capital illustrates the performance of sectors from another perspective, shown in Table 8.10.

From Tables 8.9 and 8.10, we find that the behaviour of the gross rate of return on capital largely follows that of output. However, a few features are worth noting.

Firstly, not all changes in the return to capital are in the same direction as that of the correspondent output. For example, in the oil manufacture sector under scenario 4, return on capital improves slightly while its output decreases marginally. This may be explained by the behaviour of firms under recessionary conditions: reducing output to keep profit positive.

Secondly, the changes in the rate of return on capital are higher than the change in output in most cases, but a few sectors exhibit the opposite under certain circumstances. These results may stem from firms' profit-maximizing behaviour. The aim of a firm is to maximize profit rather than output, so the change in rate of return tends to be bigger than the change in output. However, in some adverse situations such as tough competition in a recession, firms may change this strategy. For example, the baseline case in the F & B sector and in the production tax cut case in the wholesale sector, output is reduced more to avoid large losses. However, the shortcomings of a static model may lead to these results. Since the capital stock is assumed unchanged in our model, the change of the tourism demand may cause a large change in the capital rental price and thus exaggerate the change of returns on capital.

Thirdly, under the three policies, the difference of the changes in the rate of return on capital and in output is substantial for some sectors. Noticeably, they are the electronics and the non-profit sectors in scenarios 2, 3, and 4, agriculture, oil manufacture, utility in scenarios 2 and 3, real estate in scenarios 2 and 4, and food manufacture, chemical, and electrical in scenario 4. Take for example the oil manufacture sector in scenario 2, its rate of return on capital is 14.50 % (in Table 8.10) but its output only grows at 1.57 % (in Table 8.9). The remarkable difference indicates that, during a recession, the government's effort to restore economic growth is likely to be taken advantage by firms. To let the policy work more efficiently, auxiliary measures should also be made to improve the performance of these policies.

8.2.4 The Employment Effects

Since the aggregate employment has been discussed in the macro analysis, we only consider the change in employment by sector and by occupation. The effects on sectoral employment are shown in Table 8.11.

Table 8.12 Occupational employment effects of a negative mega event and policy responses

Employment	(1) Baseline case 13 % decrease in tourism demand	(2) Baseline plus 1 % decrease in power of GST	(3) Baseline plus 0.79 % production tax cuts (all sectors)	(4) Baseline plus 2.01 % production tax cuts (tourism)	(5) Baseline plus 3.03 % income tax cuts
Managers	0.04	4.387	4.636	3.058	0.039
Professionals	−0.01	3.939	4.169	3.259	−0.01
Para-Professionals	−0.088	4.617	4.839	3.217	−0.088
Tradesmen	−0.117	4.553	4.78	2.772	−0.118
Clerks	−1.391	3.038	3.318	0.897	−1.391
Salesmen	0.041	7.099	7.3	6.985	0.041
Plant workers	−0.021	6.745	6.477	4.932	−0.022
Other labourers	−2.038	3.63	3.831	2.475	−2.038

Source: Authors

Since employment is closely related to output, we refer to both Tables 8.9 and 8.11 in our discussion. Comparing Table 8.11 with Table 8.9, it is evident that the changes in employment and output always move in the same direction, with no exception. This is not surprising. The change in output results from changes in labour, capital, and technology. In the short-run closure, we assume that there is no technological change and that capital is immobile between sectors. Since the change in capital input is very limited, the increase (decrease) in output largely relies on the increase (decrease) in labour inputs. Thus output and employment should move in the same direction.

It is also noticeable that the change in employment is generally greater than that in output, but the degree of difference varies in different sectors. The greater change in employment is explained by the constant returns to scale (CRS) assumption in the model. Based on the CRS assumption, the same percentage change of capital, employment, and technology level should give rise to the same percentage change in output. However, since the technology level is not changed, and capital input is barely changed under our simulation assumptions, the change of labour input has to be greater.

Finally, Table 8.11 describes the different effects on employment of the different policy options. The GST policy significantly improves employment in the manufacturing sectors. For example, there is a 17.94 % increase in oil manufacture, 9.29 % in food manufacture, 8.73 % in electronics, and 7.26 % in electrical. Many services sectors also benefit a great deal; an 11.48 % increase in the utility sector, 8.78 % in water transport, and 11.57 % in the air transport sector. The indiscriminate production tax cuts policy affects employment in a similar way to the GST policy but, generally speaking, it improves employment more mildly than the GST policy. The tourism production tax cuts policy makes a decisive and positive difference to employment in the tourism sectors: a 27.64 % increase in food manufacture, 8.36 % in wood and print, 5.81 % in recreation, and 7.96 % in local transport. Some non-tourism sectors also exhibit significant improvements (6.96 % in real estate, 9.45 % in utility, 7.47 % in non-profit, and 4.77 % in education). However, even with this tourism-focused policy, the accommodation sector is still in deep

Table 8.13 Macroeconomic effects of Singapore tourism policies in the long run

Macros	(1) Baseline case 8 % increase in total tourism demand[#]	(2) Baseline plus 4 % decrease in power of GST tourism demand	(3) Baseline plus 4 % decrease in power of GST tourism shopping	(4) Baseline plus 0.14 % production tax cuts for tourism industry	(5) Baseline plus $81.3 million tourism activity subsidy
Indirect taxes*	89.801	−325.129	−123.458	−325.128	−206.033
Production tax*	7.744	15.416	11.495	−429.983	−318.504
Tariff revenue*	−0.14	−0.285	−0.615	6.74	10.364
Tax on tourism shopping*	34.568	−194.4	−201.653	34.608	39.113
Taxes on tourism service*	46.412	−148.338	65.544	46.497	47.123
GDP price index	0.022	−0.174	−0.08	−0.011	0.02
Exchange rate (local currency/ $world)	−0.085	−0.169	−0.127	−0.125	−0.075
Real devaluation	−0.107	0.005	−0.047	−0.114	−0.096
Terms of trade	0.012	0.024	0.018	0.005	0.017
Exports price (local currency)	−0.073	−0.145	−0.109	−0.12	−0.058
Tourism shopping price	0.157	−3.702	−3.755	0.061	0.229
Tourism service price	0.707	−2.677	0.986	0.62	−0.571
Tourism price index	0.419	−3.214	−1.507	0.327	−0.152

Employment (wage bill weights)	0	0	0	0	0
Average real wage	0.052	0.105	0.074	0.181	0.253
Aggregate payments to capital	0.004	0.008	0.009	0.251	0.149
Aggregate payments to labour	0.052	0.105	0.074	0.181	0.253
Nominal GDP	0.064	−0.104	−0.023	0.044	0.078
Real GDP	0.042	0.07	0.057	0.055	0.057
Utility per household	0.052	0.105	0.077	0.447	0.398
household nominal income	0.026	0.052	0.038	0.22	0.196
Real household consumption	0.028	0.056	0.042	0.24	0.214
Real tourism shopping expenditure	8.099	16.09	12.989	8.21	9.106
Real tourism service expenditure	7.892	15.668	11.132	8	9.393
Total real tourism expenditure	8	15.889	12.099	8.11	9.242
Value of imports plus duty	−0.105	−0.21	−0.155	−0.051	−0.102
Import volume	−0.02	−0.041	−0.028	0.074	−0.027
Nominal exports (local currency)	−0.249	−0.495	−0.372	−0.25	−0.297

(continued)

Table 8.13 (continued)

Macros	(1) Baseline case 8 % increase in total tourism demand[#]	(2) Baseline plus 4 % decrease in power of GST tourism demand	(3) Baseline plus 4 % decrease in power of GST tourism shopping	(4) Baseline plus 0.14 % production tax cuts for tourism industry	(5) Baseline plus $81.3 million tourism activity subsidy
Export volume	−0.176	−0.35	−0.263	−0.131	−0.239
Contribution of BOT to real GDP*	−0.379	−0.755	−0.575	−0.474	−0.515
BOT/GDP(Nominal)*	−0.004	−0.007	−0.006	−0.005	−0.005

Source: Authors

*Nominal change: Singapore dollars (million)

#Due to indirect shock, the baseline results slightly differ from those in the third column of Table 8.2

Table 8.14 Tourism effects of Singapore tourism policies in the long run

Tourism demand	(1) Baseline case 8 % increase in total tourism demand	(2) Baseline plus 4 % decrease in power of GST tourism demand	(3) Baseline plus 4 % decrease in power of GST tourism shopping	(4) Baseline plus 0.14 % production tax cuts for tourism industry	(5) Baseline plus $81.3 million tourism activity subsidy
Shopping (nominal)	8.266	11.897	8.83	8.275	9.353
Service (nominal)	8.645	12.646	12.209	8.661	8.778
Canada (nominal)	8.208	11.782	10.108	8.211	9.12
USA (nominal)	8.316	11.994	9.442	8.327	9.331
Indonesia (nominal)	8.656	12.668	10.537	8.673	8.903
Malaysia (nominal)	8.392	12.146	10.549	8.4	9.028
Philippines (nominal)	8.245	11.854	10.121	8.257	9.144
Thailand (nominal)	8.133	11.633	9.699	8.133	9.161
China (nominal)	8.557	12.471	11.29	8.572	9.016
Taiwan (nominal)	8.226	11.817	10.051	8.236	9.151
Hong Kong (nominal)	8.106	11.582	9.544	8.113	9.247
Japan (nominal)	8.48	12.32	10.605	8.49	9.149
South Korea (nominal)	8.343	12.049	10.622	8.342	9.086
India (nominal)	8.498	12.353	10.891	8.513	9.046

(continued)

Table 8.14 (continued)

Tourism demand	(1) Baseline case 8 % increase in total tourism demand	(2) Baseline plus 4 % decrease in power of GST tourism demand	(3) Baseline plus 4 % decrease in power of GST tourism shopping	(4) Baseline plus 0.14 % production tax cuts for tourism industry	(5) Baseline plus $81.3 million tourism activity subsidy
France (nominal)	8.066	11.502	9.478	8.069	9.229
Germany (nominal)	8.098	11.566	9.553	8.106	9.315
Italy (nominal)	8.137	11.643	9.814	8.14	9.122
Netherlands (nominal)	8.114	11.597	9.427	8.121	9.339
Switzerland (nominal)	8.09	11.549	9.523	8.101	9.303
UK (nominal)	8.492	12.343	10.306	8.512	9.233
Australia (nominal)	8.423	12.205	10.316	8.436	9.185
New Zealand (nominal)	8.191	11.748	10.164	8.197	9.112
South Africa (nominal)	8.349	12.06	10.817	8.353	9.042
Total (nominal)	8.447	12.254	10.442	8.459	9.079
Shopping (real)	8.099	16.09	12.989	8.21	9.106
Service (real)	7.892	15.668	11.132	8	9.393
Canada (real)	7.525	14.922	11.425	7.617	9.325
USA (real)	7.74	15.356	10.084	7.847	9.748
Indonesia (real)	8.418	16.742	12.294	8.536	8.891
Malaysia (real)	7.892	15.667	12.317	7.992	9.142
Philippines (real)	7.599	15.07	11.452	7.707	9.373
Thailand (real)	7.375	14.618	10.6	7.461	9.408
China (real)	8.22	16.336	13.822	8.336	9.117

Taiwan (real)	7.561	14.994	11.31	7.665	9.387
Hong Kong (real)	7.323	14.512	10.288	7.421	9.581
Japan (real)	8.068	16.026	12.43	8.172	9.383
South Korea (real)	7.794	15.468	12.466	7.877	9.258
India (real)	8.102	16.094	13.012	8.218	9.177
France (real)	7.242	14.349	10.156	7.333	9.543
Germany (real)	7.307	14.48	10.306	7.407	9.716
Italy (real)	7.385	14.637	10.832	7.473	9.328
Netherlands (real)	7.339	14.544	10.052	7.436	9.764
Switzerland (real)	7.291	14.446	10.245	7.396	9.692
UK (real)	8.091	16.072	11.825	8.215	9.551
Australia (real)	7.953	15.79	11.844	8.064	9.455
New Zealand (real)	7.491	14.852	11.538	7.587	9.31
South Africa (real)	7.805	15.491	12.861	7.899	9.169
Total (real)	8	15.889	12.099	8.11	9.242

Source: Authors

Table 8.15 Effects on sectoral output of Singapore tourism policies in the long run

Output	(1) Baseline case 8 % increase in total tourism demand#	(2) Baseline plus 4 % decrease in power of GST tourism demand	(3) Baseline plus 4 % decrease in power of GST tourism shopping	(4) Baseline plus 0.14 % production tax cuts for tourism industry	(5) Baseline plus $81.3 million tourism activity subsidy
1. Accommodation***^	5.071	10.071	7.155	5.125	7.841
2. Sightseeing***^	0.564	1.119	0.8	0.527	1.087
3. Drink and tobacco**	0.53	1.051	0.846	0.479	0.674
4. Clothing**	5.159	10.307	8.29	5.72	5.75
5. Wood and print**	0.232	0.461	0.391	0.481	0.161
6. Retailer**	1.031	2.046	1.666	1.141	1.196
7. Food and beverage**^	0.984	1.953	1.39	1.046	1.001
8. Local transport**	0.345	0.691	0.491	0.463	0.425
9. Healthcare**	0.706	1.403	0.978	0.713	0.779
10. Food manufacture*	0.003	0.005	0.027	0.937	−0.059
11. Chemical*	−0.034	−0.068	−0.05	0.114	−0.077
12. Electronics*	−0.047	−0.094	−0.068	0.243	−0.1
13. Electrical*	−0.145	−0.291	−0.212	0.421	−0.283
14. Precision engineering*	0.192	0.38	0.344	0.102	0.224
15. Recreation*^	0.038	0.074	0.05	0.097	0.513
16. Agriculture	−0.07	−0.14	−0.11	−0.127	−0.087
17. Oil manufacture	−0.013	−0.025	−0.019	−0.027	−0.029
18. Metal	−0.121	−0.243	−0.178	−0.228	−0.246
19. Transport engineering	−0.223	−0.446	−0.329	−0.454	−0.433
20. Other manufacture	−0.346	−0.689	−0.516	−0.522	−0.382
21. Utilities	0.046	0.091	0.066	0.087	0.079

22. Construction	−0.236	−0.47	−0.357	−0.386	−0.422
23. Wholesale	−0.315	−0.628	−0.471	−0.493	−0.34
24. Water transport	−0.086	−0.172	−0.127	−0.174	−0.149
25. Air transport	−0.186	−0.369	−0.267	−0.347	0.088
26. Storage and transport service	−0.192	−0.383	−0.283	−0.418	−0.337
27. Communication	−0.095	−0.19	−0.142	−0.172	−0.146
28. Insurance	−0.056	−0.112	−0.083	−0.121	−0.102
29. Banking and Finance	−0.183	−0.366	−0.269	−0.39	−0.374
30. Real estate	0.099	0.196	0.153	0.095	0.075
31. Legal and accounting service	−0.146	−0.291	−0.215	−0.243	−0.2
32. Information technology	−0.238	−0.476	−0.356	−0.328	−0.256
33. Other business service	−0.074	−0.148	−0.111	−0.022	−0.015
34. Education	−0.136	−0.271	−0.203	−0.115	−0.112
35. Non-profit and other	0.001	0.001	0	0.09	0.063

Source: Authors

#Due to indirect shock, the baseline results slightly differ from those in the third column of Table 8.4

*** indicates core tourism sector

** indicates extended tourism sector

^ indicates conventional tourism sector

Table 8.16 Effects on sectoral profitability of Singapore tourism policies in the long run

Gross rate of return on capital	(1) Baseline case 8 % increase in total tourism demand	(2) Baseline plus 4 % decrease in power of GST tourism demand	(3) Baseline plus 4 % decrease in power of GST tourism shopping	(4) Baseline plus 0.14 % production tax cuts for tourism industry	(5) Baseline plus $81.3 million tourism activity subsidy
1. Accommodation***^	5.542	10.963	7.808	5.754	8.687
2. Sightseeing***^	0.652	1.296	0.926	0.762	1.355
3. Drink and tobacco**	1.376	2.736	2.184	1.4	1.902
4. Clothing**	5.426	10.842	8.705	6.161	6.219
5. Wood and print**	0.395	0.788	0.645	0.88	0.472
6. Retailer**	1.295	2.572	2.079	1.574	1.664
7. Food and beverage**^	0.969	1.926	1.372	1.174	1.159
8. Local transport**	0.713	1.429	1.016	1.078	1.033
9. Healthcare**	0.787	1.568	1.095	0.943	1.034
10. Food manufacture*	0.086	0.17	0.156	1.575	0.169
11. Chemical*	−0.074	−0.147	−0.109	0.75	−0.095
12. Electronics*	−0.069	−0.138	−0.1	1.012	−0.065
13. Electrical*	−0.12	−0.239	−0.177	0.813	−0.139
14. Precision engineering*	0.526	1.047	0.917	0.465	0.776
15. Recreation*^	0.152	0.303	0.212	0.411	1.223
16. Agriculture	−0.424	−0.847	−0.68	−0.69	−0.379
17. Oil manufacture	−0.027	−0.054	−0.043	−0.002	0.008
18. Metal	−0.097	−0.193	−0.145	−0.106	−0.107
19. Transport engineering	−0.185	−0.368	−0.275	−0.313	−0.262
20. Other manufacture	−0.318	−0.631	−0.478	−0.373	−0.187
21. Utilities	0.318	0.632	0.459	0.678	0.659

22. Construction	−0.232	−0.46	−0.356	−0.284	−0.307
23. Wholesale	−0.38	−0.755	−0.572	−0.493	−0.243
24. Water transport	−0.12	−0.238	−0.18	−0.178	−0.094
25. Air transport	−0.159	−0.314	−0.229	−0.22	0.369
26. Storage and transport service	−0.195	−0.389	−0.291	−0.374	−0.233
27. Communication	−0.18	−0.359	−0.273	−0.245	−0.147
28. Insurance	−0.106	−0.21	−0.158	−0.173	−0.086
29. Banking and Finance	−0.196	−0.391	−0.291	−0.363	−0.313
30. Real estate	0.614	1.22	0.94	0.742	0.659
31. Legal and accounting service	−0.074	−0.147	−0.112	−0.031	0.041
32. Information technology	−0.175	−0.348	−0.266	−0.124	−0.022
33. Other business service	0.01	0.021	0.01	0.208	0.24
34. Education	−0.136	−0.27	−0.207	0.044	0.074
35. Non-profit and other	0.083	0.167	0.118	0.418	0.387

Source: Authors
*** indicates core tourism sector
** indicates extended tourism sector
^ indicates conventional tourism sector

Table 8.17 Effects on sectoral employment of Singapore tourism policies in the long run

Employment	(1) Baseline case 8 % increase in total tourism demand	(2) Baseline plus 4 % decrease in power of GST tourism demand	(3) Baseline plus 4 % decrease in power of GST tourism shopping	(4) Baseline plus 0.14 % production tax cuts for tourism industry	(5) Baseline plus $81.3 million tourism activity subsidy
1. Accommodation***^	9.308	18.659	13.184	9.408	14.467
2. Sightseeing***^	0.719	1.426	1.019	0.672	1.386
3. Drink and tobacco**	1.45	2.881	2.315	1.31	1.843
4. Clothing**	6.768	13.586	10.908	7.507	7.548
5. Wood and print**	0.396	0.785	0.665	0.819	0.274
6. Retailer**	2.045	4.067	3.31	2.264	2.373
7. Food and beverage**^	1.495	2.971	2.113	1.59	1.521
8. Local transport**	1.062	2.129	1.512	1.427	1.308
9. Healthcare**	0.89	1.769	1.232	0.898	0.981
10. Food manufacture*	0.005	0.007	0.043	1.506	−0.095
11. Chemical*	−0.195	−0.391	−0.285	0.656	−0.44
12. Electronics*	−0.189	−0.38	−0.273	0.986	−0.402
13. Electrical*	−0.253	−0.507	−0.37	0.735	−0.494
14. Precision engineering*	0.561	1.112	1.008	0.298	0.656
15. Recreation*^	0.089	0.175	0.12	0.23	1.219
16. Agriculture	−0.138	−0.277	−0.218	−0.252	−0.173
17. Oil manufacture	−0.137	−0.274	−0.202	−0.29	−0.31
18. Metal	−0.224	−0.448	−0.329	−0.421	−0.454
19. Transport engineering	−0.335	−0.669	−0.494	−0.681	−0.649
20. Other manufacture	−0.502	−0.999	−0.749	−0.756	−0.554
21. Utilities	0.298	0.589	0.43	0.565	0.509

22. Construction	−0.313	−0.623	−0.473	−0.512	−0.56
23. Wholesale	−0.773	−1.538	−1.154	−1.207	−0.833
24. Water transport	−0.337	−0.674	−0.498	−0.681	−0.584
25. Air transport	−0.403	−0.8	−0.58	−0.752	0.192
26. Storage and transport service	−0.348	−−0.696	−0.513	−0.758	−0.612
27. Communication	−0.329	−0.657	−0.491	−0.595	−0.505
28. Insurance	−0.235	−0.471	−0.347	−0.505	−0.428
29. Banking and Finance	−0.349	−0.698	−0.514	−0.744	−0.713
30. Real estate	0.672	1.331	1.037	0.646	0.509
31. Legal and accounting service	−0.196	−0.391	−0.289	−0.327	−0.268
32. Information technology	−0.323	−0.644	−0.482	−0.443	−0.347
33. Other business service	−0.09	−0.18	−0.134	−0.027	−0.018
34. Education	−0.274	−0.546	−0.408	−0.232	−0.226
35. Non-profit and other	0.002	0.004	0.001	0.238	0.167

Source: Authors
*** indicates core tourism sector
** indicates extended tourism sector
^ indicates conventional tourism sector

Table 8.18 Occupational employment effects of Singapore tourism policies in the long run

Employment	(1) Baseline case 8 % increase in total tourism demand[#]	(2) Baseline plus 4 % decrease in power of GST tourism demand	(3) Baseline plus 4 % decrease in power of GST tourism shopping	(4) Baseline plus 0.14 % production tax cuts for tourism industry	(5) Baseline plus $81.3 million tourism activity subsidy
Managers	−0.115	−0.23	−0.164	−0.144	−0.156
Professionals	−0.068	−0.138	−0.101	−0.025	−0.109
Para-Professionals	−0.036	−0.073	−0.05	−0.045	−0.083
Tradesmen	−0.019	−0.039	−0.028	−0.06	−0.026
Clerks	0.77	1.541	1.101	0.652	1.206
Salesmen	−0.117	−0.234	−0.166	0.072	−0.247
Plant workers	−0.086	−0.17	−0.116	−0.026	−0.145
Other labourers	1.191	2.382	1.685	1.249	1.812

Source: Authors

#Due to indirect shock, the baseline results slightly differ from those in the third column of Table 8.6

contraction and the sightseeing sector and the drink and tobacco sector experience only very slight improvements.

Employment by occupation reveals another facet of the labour market, as shown in Table 8.12.

We start with the general features of Table 8.12. Looking into the table by scenario, we find that, in the baseline case, most occupations suffer from a negative tourism demand shock but 'managers' and 'salesmen' occupations benefit from it (they may benefit from the increase in exports in the face of a negative tourism demand shock); Scenarios 2, 3, and 4 manifest that all three policy responses have effectively improved the employment for all occupation groups. The indiscriminate production tax cuts policy is the most effective and the tourism-focused production tax cuts policy the least. This conclusion is consistent with the one obtained from the analysis of sectoral output and sectoral employment. The income tax cuts policy seems not effective at all, so we disregard it. Looking into the table by occupation group, it is apparent that the 'other labourers' and 'clerks' are worst affected by the negative tourism demand shock and these occupations are least improved in all three policy responses. On the contrary, although 'salesmen' and 'plant workers' are only marginally affected by the shock (positively for 'salesmen' and negatively for 'plant workers'), they are the biggest beneficiaries under the three policy responses. According to the best results for each occupation, 'plant workers' would prefer the GST policy, and all other occupations would prefer the indiscriminate production tax cuts policy.

8.3 The Effectiveness of Singaporean Tourism Policies*[4]

To assess the effectiveness of Singapore tourism policies, we use the simulated long-run effects. There are two reasons to justify this choice. One is that, in normal economic times, the purpose of a policy is to

[4] A simplified version of this section was published in Tourism Management, 34:25–36, 2013. 'A CGE Assessment of Singapore's Tourism Policies' by Meng, X., Siriwardana, M. and Pham, T. Thanks for the copyright permission from Elsevier.

achieve sustainable economic growth, so a good policy cares more about the long-run effects. The other reason is that Singapore has a long history of labour shortages, so a good policy for Singapore should take this into account. The labour constraint is better captured in the long-run simulation assumption, and therefore a long-run simulation is more suitable for Singapore policy simulation. The effectiveness of selected Singapore tourism policies are analysed in terms of the macroeconomic effect, tourism effect, sectoral effect, and the employment effect.

8.3.1 The Macroeconomic Effects

The macroeconomic effects of Singapore tourism policies are displayed in Table 8.13. Before analysing the simulation results, we must explain why the results of the baseline case are slightly different from that in column 3 in Table 8.2, which has the same size of shock (8 % increase in the total tourism demand). The difference is caused by the way the shock is imposed. In Table 8.2, we directly imposed a shock of 8 % increase in tourism demand since we only care about the effects of change in tourism demand. Besides the economic effects of tourism demand, we need to consider in this section the effects of the tourism policy on tourism demand, so the tourism demand cannot be exogenous and thus could not act as a shock. The solution is to impose a shock of 9.08 % quantity shift of the tourism demand for each of the tourism-generating markets, which results in an 8 % increase in tourism demand. As a result, the baseline results appearing in Tables 8.13, 8.14, 8.15, 8.16, 8.17, and 8.18 in this section slightly differ from those in the third column of Tables 8.2, 8.4, and 8.6.

The simulation results are to be interpreted in the order of tax revenue, price indexes, real wages and GDP, household and tourism demand, and international trade.

The first panel of Table 8.13 shows the effects on tax revenue. The total indirect tax revenue losses in Columns 2 and 4 are almost the same because we choose the size of the production tax cuts policy to match the tax revenue loss caused by the GST deduction on the total tourism demand. The indirect tax revenue loss in column 3 is much smaller than that in Column 2. This is not surprising because we impose a 4 % GST deduction only on tourism shopping in Column 3 instead of on the total tourism demand in Column 2. The production taxes in Columns 2 and 3 are both increased compared with the baseline case. This can be explained as follows. In both cases, the GST deduction on tourism goods leads to lower prices for tourists and thus stimulates tourism demand. The increased final demand induces industry to produce more. As output increases, production tax rises.

It is of interest to note that, in the last column, although we impose $ 81.282 million production tax relief for each of the four conventional tourism sectors to match the total indirect tax revenue loss of $325.129 million in column 2, the total loss of production tax revenue is $318.504 million, slightly less than the total production tax cuts 81.282*4 = $325.129 million. Apparently this is because of the increase in production tax revenue from other sectors. Because the production tax reduction in four sectors leads to an output expansion of sectors related to them, the increase in output will raise the amount of product tax revenue. As a result, the total loss of indirect tax revenue in the last column is only two-thirds of that in Column 2.

The second panel in Table 8.13 shows the effect on prices. Since the CPI is assumed unchanged when we adopt the flexible exchange rate regime, the GDP price index is used to indicate the price level of the economy. The increase in the GDP deflator in column 1 is readily explained by demand-pull inflation due to the increase in the tourism demand. The decrease in the GDP deflator under the first three policies is explained by the decreased tax distortion to the economy and the reduced production cost, which is detailed in the previous section. In the last column, the GDP price index is only marginally higher than that in Column 1. This may indicate that the price effect of reduced cost due to production tax cuts on conventional tourism industry is largely cancelled out by the price effect of the increased tourism demand due to increased tourism activities.

The exchange rate decreases in all scenarios, which indicates that the Singapore dollar has appreciated. A more expensive Singapore dollar is explained by the increased tourism demand in all cases: increased inbound tourism demand leads to increased demand for Singapore dollars, which will bid up the price of the Singapore dollar. The difference between the decrease in the GDP deflator and the decrease in the exchange rate constitutes the real devaluation.

The appreciation of the Singapore dollar leads to the decrease of foreign demand for Singapore exports. As a result, the local-currency prices of exports decreases. Since the world price is assumed unchanged, the prices of imports denominated in local currency decrease proportionally as the Singapore dollar appreciates. Since the prices of imports decrease more than that of exports in all scenarios, the terms of trade (the ratio of export price to import price) improve.

The third panel in Table 8.13 lists the effects on the GDP and its income side components. In the baseline case, a positive tourism demand shock stimulates production. As the production in the economy expands, real GDP increases. Under four policy influences, tourism demand (as well as household demand, as we will see shortly) increases further. As a result, the total output of the economy increases further, and so does the real GDP. The percentage change in the nominal GDP is the sum of the percentage change in the GDP deflator and the percentage change in the real GDP, so it is negative in Column 2 due to the large price drop in scenario 2.

The increase in the real GDP in all scenarios could not be reflected in aggregate employment in the long-run simulation (total employment is fixed), but it explains the significant increase in real wages in all cases. Since the fixed amount of labour produces higher volume output, the marginal product of labour rises. The increased labour productivity commands higher real wages. Since the nominal wage is fully indexed into CPI and the CPI is assumed unchanged, the change in real wage is the same as the change in nominal wage. Thus, we see the change in aggregate payments to labour is exactly the same as the change in real wages. Comparing the aggregate payments to labour and aggregate payments to capital, we find that, in most cases, the increase in payment to labour is much higher than that to capital. This is consistent with the fact that tourism goods and services involve more labour than capital. The only exception is in Scenario 4, in which the payment to capital increases more than the payment to labour. This may be explained as follows: because some sectors in the tourism industry only produce less than 10 % of the tourism goods, the production tax cuts on them may benefit non-tourism production more. Unlike tourism goods, non-tourism goods involve more capital than labour and this leads to higher payment to capital.

The fourth panel in Table 8.13 displays the results of two important final demands: household consumption and tourism expenditure. Both household consumption and tourism expenditure increase significantly from the baseline case. This may indicate the effectiveness of all policies. Since tourism spending will be discussed in detail in the next subsection, we only consider household demand here. The significant increase in household income and consumption can be attributed to expansion of production. It is interesting to notice that the increase in utility per household is much higher than household consumption. Household utility is measured by luxury consumption. According to LES consumption function, the household subsistence consumption does not change, given the unchanged number of households and tastes. Since total household consumption is largely contributed by luxury consumption which has a much smaller base, the percentage change in luxury consumption (or household utility) is much higher than that of total consumption.

The last panel in Table 8.13 shows the effects of different policies on international trade. With a decrease in the exchange rate (appreciation of Singapore dollars) under all policy responses, it is reasonable to see real exports decrease. Nominal exports decrease more due to the decreases in the prices of exports. All nominal imports decrease which may be explained by the lower import price denominated in local currency due to the decrease in exchange rates. Surprisingly, real imports decrease for all cases except Column 4.

The decrease in real imports is counter-intuitive. The determinants of real imports are largely household income (or GDP for the economy) and the price of imports denominated in local currency. The former has increased for all cases and thus the demand for imported goods should rise. Consequently, real imports should increase. On the other hand, while the world price is unchanged, the appreciation of the Singapore dollar makes imported goods cheaper to Singaporeans. In this reasoning, the volume of imports should also increase. This intriguing result of a decrease in real imports should be comprehended in the light of the nature of policies. Because the policies are designed to increase tourism demand, given the fixed aggregate employment in the long run, labour inputs will shift to produce tourism products. Since most tourism products are locally produced using local inputs, the policies will encourage local production instead of importation. As a result, the demand for imports, and thus the real imports, decreases. The only exception is in the second last column, where we see a positive change in real imports. This may be due to the broadly defined tourism industry and thus unfocused tourism policy.

Since exports decrease more than imports in all cases, in both real and nominal terms, the BOT deteriorates. As a result, the contribution of BOT to real GDP decreases in all cases, as does the ratio of BOT to nominal GDP. However, compared with the baseline case, the BOT improves in all cases except in Scenario 4, in which the increased real imports deteriorate the BOT even further.

8.3.2 The Tourism Effects

The effects of simulated tourism policies on tourism demand are shown in Table 8.14.

A number of features can be gleaned from Table 8.14. First, all policies look effective but to a differing degree. From both the real and nominal total tourism demand, we can conclude that the GST deduction on tourism demand is most effective, followed by the GST deduction on tourism shopping and the subsidy on tourism activity. The production tax cuts for the tourism industry is least effective. However, these results should be interpreted with care. Although the tourism GST deduction policies look much more effective than the other two, the figures are subject to the value of tourism demand elasticity. If a smaller demand elasticity is used, the increase in the tourism demand induced by the tourism GST deduction policy may be much smaller. We do find this is true in our sensitivity tests. However, even when we change the value of the tourism demand elasticity from −2 to −0.5, the increase in tourism demand under the tourism GST reduction policies is still much higher than the other two policies. Caution is also needed in interpreting the results of the tourism activity subsidy policy. The output–subsidy ratio is the key to this policy. If the amount of output induced by subsidy is smaller, the effectiveness of this policy may be reduced.

Second, the increase in the tourism demand from different source countries differs under all scenarios. In our simulation, each source country faces the same tourism demand quantity shift (a right shift of the tourism demand curve), so the country with the higher share will be affected more significantly. The reasoning has been explained earlier. However, this pattern is not necessarily the case in reality.

Finally, all nominal values are bigger than the corresponding real values. This suggests a price increase for each tourism component. Combining the similar finding from Table 8.7, we can conclude that, for tourism demand, the nominal value is always subject to a larger change than its correspondent real value: as the tourism demand increases, it will inflate the tourism price, so the nominal value will increase more; when the tourism demand decreases, it will depress the tourism price, so the nominal value will decrease more.

8.3.3 The Sectoral Effects

The sectoral effects are represented by the changes in sectoral output and in profitability under the different policies. We start with the sectoral output, shown in Table 8.15.

From Table 8.15, it is immediately noticeable that the accommodation sector and clothing sector are leading sectors under all scenarios. In the baseline case, they expand at an outstanding rate of around 5 %. Four policies increase their growth rate even further. Under the policy of GST deduction on the total tourism demand, the accommodation sector and clothing sector enjoy double-digit growth. Even under the production tax deduction policy, the least wanted policy for them, their growth rates are over 5 %, which is still a significant increase compared with the baseline case. The extraordinary performance of these two sectors demonstrates the effectiveness of the proposed tourism policies on the one hand and, on the other hand, indicates the high contribution of these two sectors to the tourism demand.

For other core and extended tourism sectors (with two or three *'s), most demonstrate significant growth. This is further evidence of the effectiveness of proposed policies. In comparing the effects of different policies, it is apparent that the GST deduction policies have a much stronger influence. The exceptions in the core and extended tourism sectors are the wood and print sector and also the local transport sector, all of which only experience mild growth. This may be due to their low share in tourism expenditure. We should also notice that some policies have negative effects on certain tourism sectors. For example, under the production tax cuts policy, the growth rate for the sightseeing sector and the drink and tobacco sector is less than that in the baseline case. The same happens to the wood and print sector under the tourism activity subsidy policy. This may be explained by the crowding-out effect under the proposed policies.

Tourism-related sectors (with one *) are slightly affected, either positively or negatively, by tourism demand and tourism policy. The precision engineering sector has the best performance. It experiences 0.192 % increase in baseline case and enjoys significant improvement under all polices except the production tax cuts policy, under which its growth is smaller than in the baseline case. Chemical, electrical, and electronics undergo mild contraction in the baseline case and the contraction becomes more severe under two GST deduction policies and the tourism activity subsidy policy. However, under the production tax cut policy, they enjoy positive growth. Food manufacture has only a small growth in the baseline case and has improved marginally under the two GST deduction policies. It has improved its performance significantly under the production tax cut policy but experiences contraction under the tourism activity subsidy policy. The recreation sector has mild but improved growth under the first three policies. Understandably, its performance improved significantly because of the heavy subsidy it gets under this last policy. The mild and mixed performance of the tourism-related sectors is underpinned by their loose link with the tourism demand.

Most non-tourism sectors experience mild contraction in the baseline case and all policies have magnified this contraction. These results can be explained by the input movement in the long run: as labour and capital flow from these sectors to the tourism sectors, the contraction in the non-tourism sector is inevitable. The exceptions are the utility sector, the real estate sector, and the non-profit sector, which experience only marginal or slight positive growth. As stated in the macroeconomic effects analysis, this may signal their indirect link with tourism demand.

It is also interesting to notice that, under the tourism activity subsidy policy, the air transport sector reverses the trend of contraction and enjoys slight growth. The surprising growth of the air transport sector is explained by the fact that the sightseeing and recreation sectors use a significant amount of air transport services. When the sightseeing and recreation sectors are heavily subsidized and expand output greatly under the tourism activity subsidy policy, they lift the air transport sector out of contraction.

Another indicator for sectoral performance is profitability, or more precisely, the gross rate of return on capital, which is listed in Table 8.16.

The features of Table 8.16 can be summarized as follows.

First, the changes in the rate of return on capital are bigger than the changes in output in some cases while it is the opposite in other cases. It is worth noting that, when the change in the rate of return is positive, it tends to be larger than the change in output; when it is negative, it seems smaller than the change in output. This is consistent with the firms' profit-maximizing behaviour: when firms' sales grow (final demand is resilient), firms are more interested in increasing the rate of return; when final demand is weak, firms are keen to rein in output to avoid a loss. However, as we stated earlier, this could also stem from shortcomings of a static model.

Second, the change in output and the change in rate of return go in different directions in some cases. Notable examples include food manufacture, oil manufacture, legal and accounting service in scenario 5, other business service in scenarios 1, 2, 4, and 5, and education in scenarios 4 and 5. Interestingly enough, in all these cases, the change in output is negative but the change in rate of return is a small positive number. This may be explained by the firms' cautious behaviour: when the rate of return stagnates, firms try to reduce output to avoid a potential loss.

Lastly, the tourism GST deduction policies are the most effective, followed by tourism activity subsidy policy. Under the tourism GST deduction policies, the rate of return for core and extended tourism sectors increases to a greatest degree but, at the same time, the rate of return for the non-tourism sectors deteriorates mostly. The GST reduction on the total tourism demand is more effective than the GST reduction on tourism shopping. This is reasonable because the government loses much more tax revenue in the GST reduction on the total tourism demand. Although the tourism activity subsidy policy has less positive influence on the tourism sectors, its negative effect is also much milder and affects only a few non-tourism sectors. Production tax cuts for the tourism sectors are the least effective policy overall, but this policy has positive effects on all tourism sectors. The manufacturing sectors such as chemical, electronics, and electrical benefit greatly from this policy: they reverse the contraction in the baseline case and enjoy significant growth.

8.3.4 The Employment Effects

The simulated sectoral employment is shown in Table 8.17.

From Table 8.17, the sectoral employment effects of tourism policies can be summarized as follows:

First, with a few exceptions, employment in both core and extended tourism sectors improve significantly under all policy options. The exceptions are the sightseeing sector and the drink and tobacco sector under production tax cuts policy, and the wood and print sector under the tourism activity subsidy policy. Tourism GST deduction policies are extraordinarily effective for the accommodation and the clothing sectors, largely due to their high contribution to the tourism demand. However, these big increases in employment are subject to the sensitivity of the tourism demand elasticity. The employment in the accommodation sector is quite responsive to heavy subsidy in the tourism activity subsidy policy but, with the same amount of subsidy, the employment in the sightseeing, F & B, and recreation sectors, does not improve substantially.

Second, the performance of the tourism-related sectors is mixed. The employment in the precision engineering sector improves significantly under all policies except production tax cuts. The recreation sector improves slightly in all policies. The food manufacture sector benefits marginally under the tourism GST deduction policy and greatly under production tax cuts, but it suffers mildly from the tourism activity subsidy policy. Tourism-related manufacture sectors (e.g. chemical, electronics, and electrical) significantly benefit from the production tax cuts policy but are worse off under the other policies.

Third, most non-tourism sectors suffer mildly under all policy options. A few exceptions are the utility sector in all scenarios, air transport in scenario 5, real estate in scenarios 2 and 3, the other business services sector and the education sector in scenarios 4 and 5, and the non-profit sector in scenarios 2, 4 and 5. These results can be explained by inter-sectoral linkages with the tourism industry and/or the crowding-out effect.

Occupational employment is displayed in Table 8.18. The results can be briefly interpreted as follows: clerks and other labourers are the only occupations which enjoy a positive increase in employment and benefit from all policy options; other occupations experience a decrease in employment in the baseline case and are worse off under all policy options except the production tax cuts policy. Managers and salesmen suffer most under most policy options but, thanks to the production tax cuts policy, the employment for the salesmen group experiences positive growth; for professionals and plant worker groups, employment growth is negative but demonstrates improvement compared with the baseline case. The positive effects on 'clerks' and 'other labourers' are consistent with the fact that the tourism industry employs more unskilled workers. The negative effects for other occupation groups in most scenarios manifest the fixed aggregate employment in the long run and the substitution effect among occupation groups.

References

MTI (Ministry of Trade and Industry). (2008). *Economic Survey of Singapore*, Singapore.

Meng, X. (2014). The Role of Inbound Tourism in the Singaporean Economy: A CGE Assessment. *Journal of Travel and Tourism Marketing.*, *31*(8), 1071–1089.

Meng, X., Siriwardana, M., & Dollery, B. (2011). A Computable General Equilibrium Analysis of Potential Policy Responses to a Negative Tourism Demand Shock in Singapore. *Tourism Analysis, 16*(3), 343–359.
Meng, X., Siriwardana, M., & Pham, T. (2013). A CGE Assessment of Singapore's Tourism Policies. *Tourism Management, 34*, 25–36.

9

Frontiers of Tourism CGE Modelling

9.1 Modelling Tourism in a Richer Environment

Due to the significant linkage between tourism and the rest of the economy, tourism demand can be affected by and can have influence on many events and policies. Current tourism CGE modelling is centred on tourism demand. Although some events and policies are also modelled by some researchers, most policies or events are directly related to tourism demand, for example, FMD, the Olympic games, tourism policies, and transportation policies. The topics of tourism CGE modelling can be extended widely to include policies and events not directly related to tourism, for example, the introduction of a carbon price, a change in the income tax rate, the start or subsidence of a mining boom, the Fukushima nuclear meltdown, and the change in Japanese energy policy. A few researchers have extended the use of tourism CGE models on these fronts.

S. Meng, M. Siriwardana, *Assessing the Economic Impact of Tourism*,
DOI 10.1007/978-3-319-40328-1_9

9.2 Modelling Tourism with a Multi-Regional CGE Model

Most tourism CGE models are single-country single-region models, which are useful for an economy of a particular nation. However, this type of model is unable to reveal the impact of tourism on local economies. In reality, the local economies of popular tourism destinations rely heavily on tourism, so research in this area is much needed. Multi-regional CGE models are very common in other areas such as environmental studies and research into energy markets. There is no problem in applying multi-regional models to tourism studies, but the problem becomes the availability of detailed tourism data at the region level. Given the data issue, a top-down approach may be employed for a multi-regional model, but caution must be taken because the regional results from a top-down model may be only indicative. Eventually, tourism surveys have to be conducted at regional levels to support a bottom-up multiregional tourism CGE model.

9.3 Modelling Tourism with a Global Context

The drawback of a single-country model is that it is unable to take into account the feedback effect from the rest of the world. Given the essential inter-country linkage of international tourism, the explanatory power of a single-country CGE model is limited. So far there is no global tourism CGE model. This is largely due to the unavailability of detailed tourism demand data for all countries in the world. One way to gauge the multi-country effects is to link a single-country model with a multi-country model. This link approach can overcome the shortcoming that the world outside is assumed unchanged in a single-country model and is especially suitable for analysing the effects of mega events.

However, the link approach involves multiple simulations, that is, through repeatedly feeding the simulation results of two models into each other until the simulation results converge. This approach is not only inefficient but also potentially problematic: the results from both models may not converge because of the different mechanisms in the two models. The other way to gauge the multi-country effects is to embed a single-country model into a multi-country model. This approach can provide consistent and more efficient simulation results, but it requires more computer power and needs skilfully designed model structure to integrate the two models.

9.4 Modelling Tourism Using a Dynamic CGE Model

The other direction tourism CGE modelling can take is to upgrade the static model to a dynamic model. A dynamic model will not only overcome the problem of overstating the effects of a perturbation, but also incorporate more information in the model and result in many important results related to investment decisions, which can in turn provide more valuable information. Moreover, recursive dynamic CGE models can provide year-on-year forecasting and are therefore very popular in CGE modelling, but it seems that this type of models have seldom been used for tourism studies. A dynamic CGE model will be a very promising tool for tourism research.

Index

S. Meng, M. Siriwardana, *Assessing the Economic Impact of Tourism*,
DOI 10.1007/978-3-319-40328-1

www.ingramcontent.com/pod-product-compliance
Lightning Source LLC
Chambersburg PA
CBHW040823150926
51501CB00010B/197
* 9 7 8 3 3 1 9 4 0 3 2 7 4 *